D1265679

THE SURVIVAL OF THE JEWS IN FRANCE

COMPARATIVE POLITICS
AND INTERNATIONAL STUDIES SERIES

Series editors, Christophe Jaffrelot and Alain Dieckhoff
Series managing editor, Miriam Perier

The series consists of original manuscripts and translations of note-worthy manuscripts and publications in the social sciences emanating from the foremost French researchers.

The focus of the series is the transformation of politics and society by transnational and domestic factors—globalisation, migration and religion. States are more permeable to external influence than ever before and this phenomenon is accelerating processes of social and political change the world over. In seeking to understand and interpret these transformations, this series gives priority to social trends from below as much as to the interventions of state and nonstate actors.

JACQUES SEMELIN

The Survival of the Jews
in France

1940–44

Translated by
CYNTHIA SCHOCH and NATASHA LEHRER

OXFORD
UNIVERSITY PRESS

Oxford University Press is a department of the
University of Oxford. It furthers the University's objective
of excellence in research, scholarship, and education
by publishing worldwide.

Oxford   New York
Auckland   Cape Town   Dar es Salaam   Hong Kong   Karachi
Kuala Lumpur   Madrid   Melbourne   Mexico City   Nairobi
New Delhi   Shanghai   Taipei   Toronto

With offices in
Argentina   Austria   Brazil   Chile   Czech Republic   France   Greece
Guatemala   Hungary   Italy   Japan   Poland   Portugal   Singapore
South Korea   Switzerland   Thailand   Turkey   Ukraine   Vietnam

Oxford is a registered trade mark of Oxford University Press
in the UK and certain other countries.

Published in the United States of America by
Oxford University Press
198 Madison Avenue, New York, NY 10016

Copyright © Jacques Semelin 2018

Library of Congress Cataloging-in-Publication Data is available
acques Semelin.
The Survival of the Jews in France: 1940–44.
ISBN: 9780190939298

Printed in the United Kingdom on acid-free paper
by Bell and Bain Ltd, Glasgow

In memory of Simone Veil, who deeply encouraged my research,
and Stanley Hoffmann, who strongly supported it.

For Serge Klarsfeld, whose life and work have been a constant inspiration.

CONTENTS

ACKNOWLEDGMENTS

This work was made possible thanks to the support of the Foundation for the Memory of the Shoah, which enabled Clotilde Meyer to abridge the original text, published in 2013 with the title *Persécutions et entraides dans la France occupée* (Seuil-Les Arènes, 904pp). Clotilde Meyer used her intelligence, tact, and skill to do the impossible: drastically reduce the length of a text, while preserving the central narrative thread. Working with the author, she completed an exceptional job of cutting and stitching, using her talent to condense the work. I owe her my profound thanks.

My deep gratitude also goes to Michael Dwyer, the publisher at Hurst, for believing in this new book, the third of my works to be released by his publishing house.

I am extremely grateful to Miriam Perier, editorial manager of publications at CERI Sciences Po, not only for her dynamism in putting together applications for the various grants to finance the translation, but also for her cheerful coordination with the publisher.

I furthermore warmly thank Cynthia Schoch and Natasha Lehrer for their exceptional work as translators of this book, the subject of which is so sensitive. I was very confident of this achievement since Cynthia had already done a wonderful job translating my earlier book *Purify and Destroy* (2007).

And I do not want to forget Lara Weisweiller-Wu, managing editor for this manuscript at Hurst, who has been very responsive and efficient in overseeing the whole process to bring this book to fruition.

The English translation received funding from the Centre National du Livre, the Foundation for the Memory of the Shoah, the Fondation

ACKNOWLEDGMENTS

du Judaïsme Français and the Direction de la Mémoire et des Archives (Ministère des Armées), to which I also owe my thanks.

The preparation of this abridged version was an occasion to rework some of my ideas, taking into account various responses to the original edition. I owe a debt of gratitude to my colleague Laurent Joly for the time that he took to read my work, in particular the introduction and the conclusion, which were entirely rewritten.

During the years I spent researching the book, I benefited from the advice of several historians and specialists of the period, with whom I corresponded regarding various issues. I must particularly thank Claire Andrieu, Patrick Cabanel, Bernard Delpal, Jean-Marc Dreyfus, Laurent Douzou, Jeannine Levana Frenk, Philippe Joutard, Serge Klarsfeld, Michel Laffitte, Philippe Landau, Lucien Lazare, and Annette Wieviorka.

At the Centre de Documentation Juive Contemporaine in Paris, Karen Taïeb went out of her way to help me consult files and testimonies (in particular the 967 and the Latour archives).

I could not have been welcomed with more generosity at the multimedia center at the Shoah Memorial in Paris. My thanks to all those who were particularly helpful when it came to exploring the "hidden children" archives.

Philippe Allouche (Foundation for the Memory of the Shoah) and Dominique Missika from the National Audiovisual Institute helped me obtain the transcripts of a number of interviews undertaken between 2005 and 2006 as part of the FMS-INA series.

In July 2009, I visited the US Holocaust Museum in Washington, DC to consult a number of different archives dealing with France.

In Jerusalem, Jeannine Levana Frenk was enormously generous with her time and knowledge, and made a number of files dating from between 2000 and 2005 of nominees for the title "Righteous of France" available to me.

At Sciences Po Paris, Martine Jouneau of the CNRS (*Centre national de la recherche scientifique*) provided vital help in collecting and verifying data relating to synagogues and religious locales from before 1940, as well as data about Jews during the Occupation. Her meticulous work in the Consistory archives and the National Archives made it possible to put together the previously unpublished maps that appear in Chapter 1. The maps were drawn by Dorian Ryser, also from Sciences Po, to whom I also owe thanks.

ACKNOWLEDGMENTS

I also benefited from the assistance of doctoral students from EHESS and Sciences Po, whose help when it came to consulting archives, articles, and books has been invaluable: thank you to Laura Hobson Faure, Samuel Ghiles-Meilhac, Lisa Vapné, and Arnaud Siad.

I owe an immense debt to Maureen Attali, a teaching fellow in history, my research assistant from May 2010 to February 2012. Whether it was collating and presenting testimonies, researching in the archives, editing chapters, or putting together the bibliography, her services were absolutely irreplaceable. Her deep interest in the topic meant that she frequently raised pertinent issues that stimulated new ideas and helped with the process of writing. Without her precious help this book would simply not be what it is.

LIST OF ACRONYMS AND ABBREVIATIONS

AIP	Association des Israélites Pratiquants [Union of Orthodox French Jews]
CAR	Comité d'assistance aux réfugiés [Committee for Aiding Refugees]
CDC	Caisse des Dépôts et Consignations [Deposits and Consignments Fund]
CDJC	Centre de documentation juive contemporaine [Contemporary Jewish Documentation Center]
CIMADE or Cimade	Comité inter-mouvements auprès des évacués [Joint Committee of Evacuee Support Groups]
CGQJ	Commissariat général aux questions juives [General Commission for Jewish Affairs]
EI or EIF	Éclaireurs israélites [de France] [Jewish Scouts Organization]
FFL	Forces françaises libres [Free French Forces]
FTP	Francs-tireurs et partisans [armed resistance organization]
GTE	Groupement de travailleurs étrangers [Foreign Workers Group—a foreign internee labor unit]
JEC	Jeunesse étudiante chrétienne [Christian Student Youth movement]
JOC	Jeunesse ouvrière chrétienne [Christian Worker Youth movement]
Joint	American Jewish Joint Distribution Committee

LIST OF ACRONYMS AND ABBREVIATIONS

MBF	Militärbefehlshaber in Frankreich [German military command in France]
MJS	Mouvement de la jeunesse sioniste [Young Zionist Movement]
MNCR	Mouvement national contre le racisme [National Anti-Racism Movement]
MOI	Main-d'œuvre immigrée [Immigrant Workers Union]
OJC	Organisation juive de combat [Jewish Combat Organization]
ORT	Organisation reconstruction travail [Professional Training and Reorientation Organization]
OSE	Œuvre de secours aux enfants [Children's Welfare Organization]
SEC	Section d'Enquête et de Contrôle [Section for Investigation and Control, part of the CGQJ]
SSAE	Service social d'aide aux émigrants [Social Service for Aid to Emigrants]
STO	Service du travail obligatoire [German forced labor program]
UGIF	Union générale des Israélites de France [General Union of French Jews]
WIZO or SF-WIZO	Women's International Zionist Organization [French Section]
YMCA	Young Men's Christian Association

LIST OF MAPS

AUTHOR'S NOTE

It was in 1984, as a young history PhD student, that I entered the Centre de documentation juive contemporaine in Paris for the first time. In 1985, in a little Latin Quarter movie theater, I was probably among the first to see the film *Shoah*. That same year, I visited Auschwitz. The genocide of European Jews has haunted me ever since. The doctoral dissertation I was writing at the time focused on methods of civil resistance in Nazi Europe. But I knew that someday I would work on the Holocaust and other forms of mass violence.

This new book both follows on from my previous research and revisits it. The reader will not find in it yet another study of the "Final Solution," or of modes of civil resistance and rescue studied elsewhere. The argument here is different: my aim is to describe how the Jews who were persecuted in France managed—or did not manage—to elude their persecutors, through individual and/or family micro-tactics of survival. This is the product of a years-long historical investigation, and with it I hope to make a fundamental contribution to a long-neglected question: how and why did three-quarters of the Jews in France—in other words, approximately 240,000 people out of the 320,000 Jews living in France in 1940, according to figures established by Serge Klarsfeld—escape death?[1]

French presidents since Jacques Chirac in 1995 to Emmanuel Macron in 2017 have all emphasized the dark side of French history characterized by the Vichy regime's role in deporting Jews, but also the "light" emanating from the Righteous who rescued three-quarters of the Jews in France.[2] Those who are familiar with my work know that

AUTHOR'S NOTE

I have always been uncompromising toward the anti-Semitic, xenophobic policies of the French government that collaborated with the Nazi occupier. On the other hand, to claim that three-quarters of the Jews in France survived thanks to the Righteous alone, however admirable their actions were, is unacceptable from an historian's point of view. A range of factors must be considered to explain why so many Jews in France escaped deportation.

In this regard, the book's title perfectly describes its argument. The aim is not to maintain that three-quarters of the Jews were "saved" in France, but rather that they survived, which is not the same thing. For while survival includes intentional acts of rescue and self-rescue, with the active or passive complicity of non-Jewish French citizens, it also depends on general factors, structural or contextual in nature. These relate to the Nazis' political and strategic objectives in Europe; the existence of a so-called Free Zone in France; the evolution of public opinion at the time of roundups; protest from eminent Church officials; the creation of the Italian Zone; the development of the Resistance; failures and shortcomings of the repressive machinery; and the evolution of the international context and the military front.

The present volume is the abridged, revised and updated version of *Persécutions et entraides dans la France occupée* (Le Seuil/Les Arènes, 2013, 904 pp.). Major cuts were made and many passages summarized, without altering the general line of argument. Some testimonies were, unfortunately, deleted or drastically condensed. But the most significant among them have been kept. Two sections were removed[3] and the final chapter on civil resistance and rescue was cut. Readers of French, of course, might find it useful to refer to the 2013 edition.

This book provides new information and has specific advantages. As a shortened version, it will hopefully reach a broader public. New bibliographical references have been added, and the new text opens up international comparisons, primarily with two other occupied countries in Western Europe: Belgium and the Netherlands.

My analyses also take into account the historiographic debate raised by the first edition. The introduction and the conclusion in particular were entirely rewritten to integrate remarks, suggestions and criticisms made of the original work. Having devoted most of my life as a researcher to the study of genocide and civil resistance, I am proud and honored to present this book to an English-speaking audience.

PREFACE

Serge Klarsfeld[*]

There is one particularly indispensable category of works of history: books that fill unacceptable historical gaps and enable a broad public to understand the how and the why of facts and events that until that point have remained inexplicable or unexplained.

Jacques Semelin's volume belongs to the category of books that are immediately adopted as standard reference works and which are both so useful and so utilized that they seem always to have been in print.

The role that the French played in protecting Jews in France during the German occupation and under Vichy has been recognized since 1983, when in *Vichy-Auschwitz* I highlighted the pressure exerted on the Vichy government by the French population of the Free Zone, as well as by the Church, to end the mass roundups of foreign Jews in areas that were not under German authority, from where Jewish families who had been arrested were being sent by Vichy to the Occupied Zone and Drancy concentration camp, then to be deported by the Germans. I concluded my work with a paragraph that I was sure would go down in history, since it summed up the truth of a situation which historians did not appear to want to acknowledge:

> The Jews of France will always remember that, even though the Vichy regime had led to a moral collapse and brought shame upon itself by its

*Historian and Lawyer. Founder and President of the Sons and Daughters of Jewish Deportees in France.

well-organized contribution to the loss of a quarter of the Jewish population of this country, the three-quarters who survived largely owed
their lives to the genuine compassion of the French and to their active
support as soon as they realized that once Jewish families fell into the
hands of the Germans they were doomed to death.

At the time, people preferred to highlight the stereotype of the
Frenchman who was at best cowardly or indifferent, at worst an active
informer. My book made clear that in the summer of 1942 it was
French hostility to the anti-Jewish laws that led to the French refusal
to cooperate with the German plan to fill fifty trains provided to the
Gestapo by the Reich Transport Ministry between 15 September and
31 October 1942: a trainload a day of a thousand Jews. The Gestapo
was forced to abandon the large-scale program for lack of Vichy support, itself a result of pressure exerted on the regime by the French
public, despite obstacles.

I also drew attention to the fact that at the end of the summer of
1943 "the war against the Jews that was being waged by the Gestapo
practically on their own" had precisely the opposite effect to what was
intended, of triggering:

> a sweeping movement of solidarity towards the Jews. This active support
> was evident not only among the general population but also sometimes
> even in government and among the police. Meanwhile, Jewish organiza-
> tions were reacting energetically, bravely and selflessly coming to the aid
> of vast numbers of Jews who were suffering. In these conditions even Jews
> of little means, mostly impoverished foreign Jews, were able to hide from
> the Gestapo because they found themselves among people who were
> sympathetic to them and ready to help them escape their executioners.

All this was fact; it was still necessary to explain precisely what was
behind the multiple facets of this active support. To achieve this objective would require undertaking an immense open-ended project to
research, analyze, and synthesize a vast number of documents and
testimonies. That book, which I would have loved to have written, has
been written by Jacques Semelin. It is a remarkable achievement and a
milestone, which since it was first published has established itself as a
must-read. Basically, someone had to explain how it was that in France,
where a massive administrative and police net had descended upon the
Jews, three-quarters of the Jews managed to escape arrest.

PREFACE

In his book, Semelin chooses to follow his witnesses on their journey through a France divided until November 1942 between the so-called "Free" Zone, where Vichy exercised its power, and the Occupied Zone, where the French authorities were under the yoke of the Germans. The police exercised tight control over the Jews in both zones, with the brief exception of the nine months when the Italians occupied eight administrative departments in the southeast of the country and, owing to the benevolence of both the Italian military and its diplomats, protected the Jews there. After the Italian capitulation of September 1943, the whole country came under German occupation, as the German military situation deteriorated and their murderous rage against the Jews intensified. In 1942, foreign Jews and their French-born children became the targets of the French police who, following orders from the Vichy government, carried out in both zones the dirty work that the Germans, for want of sufficient police officers, either did not want or were unable to carry out themselves. The mass roundup of 16 July 1942 in the Occupied Zone led to the deportation of 15,000 Jews; the mass roundup of August 1942 in the Free Zone led to the deportation of 10,000 Jews. In total, 41,951 Jews were deported in 1942. The pace slowed in 1943, when there were 17,069 deportations. During the first seven months of 1944, the Germans, who by then were carrying out mass arrests with the active collusion of the French, deported 16,025 Jews. It is obvious from these figures that the turning point for the Jews was when the French population made clear to the Vichy leadership at the end of August 1942 that they were hostile to the deportations.

This is the background against which the Jews' struggle for their survival must be set, which is crucial to understanding that their condition in France was not comparable to the condition of the Jews in Poland, Ukraine, or Belarus. Up until summer 1943, French Jews could not be arrested unless they were caught in contravention of anti-Jewish legislation, and the Paris police prefecture did not carry out any mass roundups of French Jews. At the liberation of Paris there were still around 30,000 Jews living there and wearing the yellow star, with children who continued to go to school, although they knew that the police might at any moment arrest them either because someone informed on them or at because the Gestapo demanded it.

PREFACE

Every Jew in France was in the grip of the fear that they might be arrested at any moment, in any place, for any reason whatsoever, whether they had taken refuge in a village, a small town or a major city. In October 1940 and in July 1941, 90 per cent of Jews were forced to register in the Occupied Zone and then in the Free Zone: they were on file with the police and subject to surveillance. Many foreign Jews left their homes to escape the roundups and found refuge in the French countryside. How did Jews, both those who obeyed the law and those who took the risk of flouting it, manage to get by? To find out, Semelin meticulously combed through thousands of testimonies and where possible cross-checked them against documents that confirmed or provided additional information about their experiences, often recalled by witnesses who were unaware of all the different elements that had had an impact on their fate. Foreign Jews were the hardest hit; older Jews were the most vulnerable because it was harder for them to react and to leave their homes, as well as because many of them were needy or destitute. Children were also very vulnerable, but in France both families and Jewish organizations made a huge effort to protect them and many among the non-Jewish French population also came to their aid, even though anti-Semitic prejudices were widespread. Some 11,400 Jews under the age of 18 were deported, but at least 59,000 survived, either with their families, or having been placed in care by their parents or by a Jewish organization with a non-Jewish foster family, or in a religious or secular school. Some managed to escape to Switzerland or Spain. The Nazi pressure on Vichy to set up a central Jewish organization, the UGIF (General Union of Israelites of France), was a tactical error, because the UGIF leadership, behind its official façade, made it possible for many poverty-stricken Jews to survive through the subsidies, both official and illegal, that the organization received, which they then expertly redistributed to tens of thousands of Jews who, without this financial aid, would have found themselves on the street where they would no doubt have been picked up by the police. Semelin also shows that while magistrates complied with the political powers that be, never challenging the anti-Jewish laws, there were some who took into consideration the problems of Jews who were taken to court and helped them to avoid the punishment provided by law.

Semelin has meticulously researched the strategies used by Jews to earn what was needed to survive in spite of the spoliation and

Aryanization of which they were victims, how they tried to circumvent the law, hold on to their jobs, find odd jobs or work in farming, use the black market, and receive state benefits for refugees and the homeless. Semelin's perseverance enables the reader better to understand how Jews managed to disappear into the French population, making themselves invisible and avoiding checks and denunciations, getting hold of false identity papers, and generally adapting to rural life. How many Jewish children were introduced to the countryside because of their experiences, often happy, sometimes disappointing, of living with farmers who fostered them, and for whom they worked? How many of them pretended to be Catholic and became believers, praying for the safety of their parents from whom they had been separated for a long time without any news? How many doggedly continued their education, some, even during the worst period of the persecution, managing to pass highly competitive examinations, but then failing to avoid deportation?

For the Jews of France, this period was a decisive moment in its relationship with the wider French population, who are shown to have been human and supportive. There is little evidence of denunciations of Jews after the roundups began, despite narratives intended to blacken the reputation of the French at the time. There were an infinite number of small but vital gestures at key moments—at the time of a roundup, in a railway station or on a train; prejudices overcome by committed supporters of Marshal Pétain who nonetheless reached out to help Jews being persecuted by the French government; numberless gestures of sympathy. There were thousands of Righteous, who deserve the honor, and hundreds of thousands of "virtual" Righteous, who make up the majority of these French men and women educated and forged by the republican ideal or by Christian charity, by a schoolteacher or a local priest. As individuals, French people gave help to Jews, and they also helped collectively, through the networks that Semelin explores in detail, helping Jews to hide or smuggling them across the border to Switzerland or Spain.

Semelin's book is filled with a wealth of examples that shed light on both this tragedy and this rescue. He shows the character—exceptional in Europe—of this civil resistance, when, in an era of respect for authority, the duty of disobedience imposed itself upon so many citizens and even upon many low-level functionaries (there were many more secretaries in municipal government than prefects who broke ranks). Armed resistance participated in the liberation of France; civil resistance participated in the rescue of three-quarters of its Jews, by putting pressure on Vichy, by actively helping Jews, and by its opposition to the murderous drive of the Gestapo.

It is important that Jacques Semelin's book has been translated into many different languages since it draws attention to the courage of French citizens and their respect for the individual; it also emphasizes the ingenious capacity of the Jews to survive within a human environment that, despite prevailing anti-Semitism, proved itself to be compassionate when confronted with the threats and suffering to which the Jews were subjected.

An altogether remarkable and indispensable book for all those with an interest in France and the Shoah.

INTRODUCTION

THE ENIGMA OF THE 75 PER CENT

In some countries, the French have the reputation of being anti-Semitic. This goes back to the Dreyfus Affair and even more to the role played by the Vichy government in the persecution and deportation of Jews during the Nazi period. In all, 80,000 Jews in France were victims of the genocide, or 25 per cent of the Jewish population. 75 per cent of the Jews in France survived, a fact that Serge Klarsfeld, renowned for his tireless campaign to preserve the memory of the Shoah, has constantly reiterated. Yet this high survival rate, on which historians concur, appears to be little known and recognized. It is not mentioned by the United States Holocaust Memorial Museum in Washington or by Yad Vashem in Jerusalem.

A new development, however, was signaled in a speech given on 8 December 2014 by Stuart Eizenstat, former special representative for Holocaust issues under President Obama, in which he declared that, "France had by far the highest percentage of Jews saved of any country under Nazi occupation. 75 per cent of French Jews were saved."[1] Could this unprecedented diplomatic statement be the sign of a palpable change in the perception of France with respect to the "Final Solution"?

Any sense of satisfaction at these figures would, it goes without saying, be misplaced. Statistics cannot eclipse the painful memory of all those whose lives ended at Auschwitz. Vichy's participation in the deportation of Jews will forever remain a dark stain on the history of France. But in the field of research into the genocide of the Jews, there is an unsettling fact to be explored: how was it that, first under an anti-Semitic French government, and then once the country was entirely occupied by the Germans, as of November 1942, an overwhelming majority of Jews, about 220,000 people, were still alive in France at the end of the war?

For nearly thirty years now, I have been trying to understand the stark differences in the number of Jews who were killed depending on the country.[2] While the Nazi intention was to destroy the "Jewish race" everywhere, they had to adapt their strategy to local realities, and found themselves confronted by a multiplicity of hindrances. Substantial disparities exist between Poland, most of whose Jews were killed, and Bulgaria, where the majority survived, at least within the "Old Kingdom";[3] between Norway (50 per cent of the Jews killed) and Denmark (5 per cent); and between the Netherlands (75 per cent) and Belgium (45 per cent). A multitude of variables must be taken into account to explain these differences: the structure of the relationship between the occupiers and the occupied, the intensity of local anti-Semitism, the size and geographical distribution of the Jewish population, the chronology of persecution and the perception of the danger it represented. The question is how to conduct an analysis that focuses on the specificities of France.

Some international comparisons with other countries have been done, though not all of them as rigorous as might be hoped. While all comparisons are theoretically possible, some are more pertinent than others. In this instance, the French case needs to be considered within the overall context of the very different Nazi policies in Eastern and Western Europe. In Poland and in the USSR, regarded by the Germans as territories to be colonized, the occupying forces displayed extreme brutality. In Western Europe, on the other hand, Berlin showed relative restraint, seeking instead to derive the greatest possible economic and industrial benefit from the countries under occupation. That aim inevitably had an effect on the handling of the "Jewish question." It makes sense therefore to consider the case of France alongside comparable countries, in this case Belgium and the Netherlands, as Pim Griffioen and Ron Zeller do in their remarkable research.[4] As Griffioen and Zeller make clear, such a comparative framework is all the more justified as the three countries were occupied during the same period

(May–June 1940) and the "Final Solution" was initiated at the same time (June 1942). While a comparison with Italy has a certain logic, the parallel is less persuasive, as Italy was the Reich's principal ally in Europe until August 1943, which gave it some autonomy. But ultimately the percentage of Italian Jews who were killed (21 per cent) is comparable to that in France.[5]

There has been little research focusing on the reasons why so many Jews survived in France, compared to the large body of work devoted to the history of their persecution and deportation, of which the seminal work is Michael Marrus's and Robert Paxton's *Vichy France and the Jews*. Marrus and Paxton devote a mere two paragraphs to the question of the 75 per cent survival rate,[6] which amounts to saying that they virtually ignore it. In the revised and augmented French edition published in 2015, twenty years after the book first came out, the authors devote a few pages to the question without in any way modifying their original thesis.[7] While we must take into account the key insight of their analysis, namely the Vichy government's wholehearted collaboration with Nazi Germany, a new historiographical turn is required that considers in a more balanced fashion both the fact that 25 per cent of Jews were killed and the fact that 75 per cent of Jews in France survived. The pioneering work by Susan Zuccotti, a former student of Robert Paxton, must be acknowledged in this regard for its emphasis on the importance of this statistical aspect.[8] Wolfgang Seibel, for his part, stresses the moral authority of the Catholic Church and its influence on Vichy,[9] a suggestion already advanced by Serge Klarsfeld. Further references can be found in the bibliography.

Pursuing this tentative and relatively new vein of research, the present work suggests a somewhat different but complementary approach, not through international comparisons or the history of the negotiations between Vichy and the Germans (already the subject of intensive research), but rather focusing on how Jews themselves reacted to their persecution. Important work has already been conducted in this area, highlighting the development of a Jewish resistance that counters the cliché of Jewish passivity during the Holocaust.[10] These rescue and resistance operations, which other faith-based, primarily Christian, organizations also participated in, probably saved the lives of some ten thousand Jews in France, mainly children. However, this admirable resistance movement does not explain how more than 200,000 Jews survived. Nor do the actions of the 4,000 or so men and women recognized (as of 2017) as "Righteous Among the Nations," in spite of their importance in terms of French memory. Other avenues need to be explored.

The more I immersed myself in the subject, the more the following hypothesis became clear to me: persecuted Jews were forced to devise tactics for their own survival, once they became aware of the threat that was hanging over them. They became agents of their own survival. This is the principal thesis of this book, in line with Bob Moore's work.[11] While Moore mainly focuses on organized forms of rescue and "self-help" in Western Europe, my own research is a comparative study of everyday acts of micro-resistance performed by individuals in their attempts to at least partially escape the persecution. In order to ensure a detailed analysis, I have limited myself to an in-depth and chronological analysis of France, which nonetheless takes into account the international context.

The fruit of several years of research, the book is illustrated by the trajectories of French and foreign Jews, both individuals and families, following their paths from the pre-war period through the years of the Occupation. I have drawn on German and Vichy government documents and reports, personal diaries, published memoirs, and oral testimonies. The second, though not secondary, hypothesis is that the Jews discovered the existence in France of a supportive web of social relationships, even as there was a parallel social current of denunciation and anti-Semitism.[12] The maintenance of these social bonds between Jews and non-Jews was paramount when it came to thwarting a genocidal enterprise whose intention was to create an ever-widening gulf between the designated victims and the general population.[13] As historian Annie Kriegel (née Annie Becker, one of the witnesses whose accounts illustrate this book) has written, "The secret of the most effective survival strategies must be sought at the most basic level, in the nature of the interpersonal relationships between Jews and non-Jews in everyday life."[14]

In this respect, Renée Poznanski's important book, *Jews in France during World War II*, served as a starting point for my research. Originally published in France in 1994 and reissued with a new afterword in 2018,[15] this extensively documented work, which provides a remarkably detailed picture of the daily realities of Jewish persecution in France, has been immensely helpful to me. Yet as my own research progressed, often using the same documents as Poznanski, I began to realize that my colleague and I were not always drawing the same conclusions. Could it be my initial training as a psychologist that enabled me to interpret them differently and led me to seek out additional sources? There is no doubt that we both share a common foundation of knowledge about Nazi and Vichy anti-Semitism. But our analyses diverge when it comes to our interpretation of how the persecution was experienced by the victims themselves and our understanding of their relationships to wider French society.

Poznanski contends that the Jews were forced into a total uncoupling from French society and could rely on no one but each other to survive. In the afterword to the new French edition of her book, she again insists upon this "sense of isolation experienced by the Jews (...) and the parallel worlds of 'normal' society and that of the Jews."[16] This impression of two entirely separate worlds, indeed the case for the Jews imprisoned in Polish ghettos, makes no sense when discussing France. Otherwise, how do we explain that nearly 90 per cent of French Jews, 60 per cent of foreign Jews and 86 per cent of Jewish children (French and foreign alike) managed to survive the war?[17] While the persecution of Jews established a vast legal, economic, and physical gulf between Jews and non-Jews, at the same time personal bonds persisted in the form of marriages, friendships among young people, and so on. In a recent and original study, Daniel Lee points out that Jewish war widows and wives of prisoners of war continued to receive their war pensions up until the Liberation. Similarly, he shows how between 1940 and 1942, even as Vichy was enacting and carrying out its anti-Semitic legislation, it was subsidizing the *Eclaireurs israélites de France* (EIF) to encourage Jewish scouts to move to the countryside and work the land, an ideal that it shared with this movement.[18]

During the period of the deportations, there can be no doubt that victims felt wholesale abandonment. It was an utter tragedy for the deportees and their families, who remained forever devastated. There is also no doubt that the horrific scenes these deportations entailed gave rise to a surge of compassion and solidarity throughout the country. Witnesses have recounted how people reached out to help Jews to escape arrest. The assertion that during the worst years, between 1942 and 1944, Jews were totally isolated in France is therefore nothing short of excessive. As Simone Veil said in 2008, "Many French people—although far from all of them were awarded the Righteous medal—helped Jews and sheltered children. In rural villages, no-one was blind to the fact that the kids supposedly placed in care by the social services were Jewish—all the more as some of them spoke with a foreign accent. People looked the other way or simply didn't want to know."[19]

Simone Veil's words corroborate the results of my own research. Having sifted through a vast number of documents and testimonies, I eventually narrowed down the sources I used so as not to entangle the reader in an overly complex web of narratives. I sought instead to focus on a limited number of personal case histories to illustrate the extraordinary diversity of these individual experiences. While this "bottom-up" approach is a fertile one, as I hope this book will attest, it is not sufficient to account for the large-scale survival of Jews in France. A host of other factors must be brought into view and considered, which are summarized in the conclusion.

It is often believed that Jews were forced to live hidden in attics or apartments with secret rooms or annexes, like Anne Frank's family in Amsterdam. This cliché is not true of France. While a minority of Jews did go into hiding, most did not. They went out into the streets, not always wearing the yellow star, sometimes but not always carrying forged identity documents, and their children continued to go to school, sometimes but not always under a false name. It may seem hard to believe, but it is true. Today, many imagine that all the Jews in France had to hide in cellars during the war to have any chance of surviving. My hope is that they will read these pages and revise their opinion. For all that, this is not a rosy history of Jews in France. The occupying forces and Vichy made those they persecuted into social outcasts who were often reduced to living in extreme poverty. The danger of arrest hung over them to the very end. We must never forget those who were captured and deported, never to return. But as a complement to the countless works on the deportation and extermination of Jews, this book recounts in detail, I believe for the first time, the history and memory of the non-deportation of Jews in France.

1

IN SEARCH OF SAFETY

On 1 September 1939, Nazi Germany invaded Poland, marking the beginning of World War II. In response to this act of aggression, on 3 September France and Britain declared war on Germany, but they did not come to Poland's aid. The "phoney war" had begun. France had a population of 43 million, with a Jewish population of at least 300,000, most living in Paris and Alsace-Lorraine.[1] A few communities were living in the southwest (Bordeaux, Bayonne), the southeast (Provence) and the Mediterranean region (Avignon, Marseille). In spring 1940, France and the French experienced a bewildering cascade of tragedies in the space of a few weeks: military defeat, the ensuing exodus of several million people to the south, the formation of Marshal Pétain's collaborationist government in Vichy, and the division of the country into several zones. Four long years of suffering and death followed for a deeply demoralized population. When the Allied armies finally managed to oust the occupying forces from France in late 1944, the geographical distribution of the Jewish population had been totally altered. Many Jews had been forced to leave their homes; they fled mainly to the southern and central regions of France that were under the authority of Marshal Pétain, unless they went into exile in a neutral or allied country.

As of summer 1940, the Vichy government put in place anti-Semitic policies, the legal provisions of which partially duplicated the measures taken by the occupying forces in the Northern Zone. Many accounts suggest, however, that living conditions for both Jews and non-Jews in the so-called Free Zone were not as difficult as in the Occupied Zone. The wave of departures that began in 1940 gathered momentum in 1941 and increased considerably in summer 1942 after it became mandatory to wear the yellow star in the Northern Zone, and even more after the mass arrests of foreign Jews in Paris on 16 and 17 July 1942 in what is known as the "Vel' d'Hiv' roundup." These were not random arrests but were made on the basis of police files identifying the people to be captured as Jews. To escape persecution, people fled in increasing numbers to the Mediterranean coast, the Rhône-Alpes region, Vichy and the Allier administrative department in central France, Toulouse and the southwest, as well as to the mountain regions of the Cévennes and the Massif Central. At least there, in the zone governed by Vichy, Jews were not obliged to wear the yellow star, and it was somewhat easier to find food. Still, people had to reach Vichy France, which meant taking the risk of crossing the demarcation line that separated the two zones and was guarded by German and French soldiers, an operation that was never certain to be successful.

Even once they did reach the Free Zone, Jews were still not safe, as the Vichy government itself made arrests in late August 1942, hauling in so-called stateless and foreign Jews from Germany, Poland, Austria and Czechoslovakia. The situation of the Jews further worsened a few weeks later: on 11 November, the Wehrmacht invaded the rest of France in response to the Allied landing in North Africa, further stepping up the pressure on Jews. Nevertheless, most of them stayed in southern and central France. Where else could they go? Some tried to make it to Switzerland or Spain, not always successfully. The majority had no other choice than to move farther afield, seeking refuge in places that were ever more remote where there was less risk of running into a German patrol.

Comparing where Jews were living in France prior to 1939 and then in 1944 suggests that their geographic dispersal may explain their high survival rate. It is as though two contradictory forces were at work during the four years of occupation: on the one hand there were the combined German and French state apparatuses which sought to identify, keep track of, round up and arrest individuals defined as Jews; on the other hand, the Jews were able to respond to ever more coercive, brutal measures of repression by finding ways to escape, fleeing to more and more remote places. This population dispersal was neither wanted nor ordered. The different migratory flows were triggered by the pressure of events, at different moments, unsystematically, usually with no planning or preparation. But various organizations—mainly Jewish and Christian—did their best to help and even hasten these departures by aiding and encouraging families and individuals hoping to flee, and finding them temporary accommodation and hiding places.

Throughout Europe, for instance in Poland or the Netherlands, the method developed by the Nazis involved forcing Jews into enclosed areas for future deportation. In France, however, this process did not happen. France had no ghettos for the Nazis to subsequently "clear out" by deporting the Jews who had been walled up there. There were a number of internment camps in France for those who were perceived as suspects or enemies of the regime: foreigners (Spanish, German, and Austrian refugees), Jews, Gypsies, resistance fighters, and other political prisoners.[2] During the 1942 deportations, these internment camps served as "human pools" the French authorities drew from in order to fulfill the Nazi quotas of Jews to be deported: mainly from the Gurs camp, the Rivesaltes camp, and the Camp des Milles in the Southern Zone, and Drancy in the Northern Zone. In time, the camp in Drancy became the main holding center for Jews rounded up in France prior to deportation to Auschwitz. But the system was partly thwarted precisely by the wave of dispersal of the Jewish population, which was a major *de facto* obstacle to the arrest-concentration-deportation process. Both the German and French authorities soon noted this evolution.

The mobility of the Jewish population in this period is a remarkable phenomenon that has not yet been the topic of sufficient study in terms of duration and chronological modulations. The spontaneous dispersal of the Jewish population was certainly a factor in their survival. The fact that the railway network was considerably more extensive than it is today, with regular bus connections to extend its reach to smaller towns and villages, facilitated their successive moves. It is necessary to evaluate these migratory flows, which were both voluntary and forced, in both numerical and geographical terms. Is it possible to draw up maps of France to show where Jews were living in 1941, 1942, and 1943? This first chapter sets out to do just that, using the itineraries of various individuals, whether prominent or unknown, whose trajectories are fairly representative of the different profiles and experience that emerged during the years of occupation.

Two other factors should be kept in mind, however, that balance out this approach. First, the migratory flows of Jews are only one aspect of a broader phenomenon, which was the massive population exodus that took place during this period. Between 1940 and 1944 an estimated one in three people in France, Jewish and non-Jewish, left their homes.[3]

The other essential point is that not all those who suffered persecution for being Jewish were equally mobile. Confronted by the same set of circumstances, individuals reacted differently depending on their character and personal history, their familiarity with the country and their private resources. Another essential differentiating factor was whether they were French or foreign. There were at least 40,000 Jews living in Paris in the summer of 1944. Some wore the yellow star, in some cases with complete impunity.[4] This is not the smallest paradox of the situation in France, which has been almost entirely neglected by historians of the war.

French Israélites and Jewish Émigrés

To understand the evolution of these migratory flows, it is necessary to explain the differences between "French Jews" and "foreign Jews" in terms of their backgrounds and their fates. These differences are immediately obvious when one examines the figures tallied by Serge Klarsfeld. "We estimate that 330,000 Jews were living in France at the end of 1940," he writes.

> Some 190,000 to 200,000 of them were French Jews and between 130,000 and 140,000 were foreign Jews. The number of Jews deported was 75,721, or about 76,000. Around 3,000 Jews died in France in internment camps—especially in the free zone—without having been deported. The number of Jews summarily executed or shot because they were Jewish was about 1,000. The total number of victims of the "Final Solution" in France is in the neighborhood of 80,000. We can therefore categorically affirm that 25 per cent of the Jews in France were victims of the "Final Solution" and that 75 per cent of them escaped the genocide. As for the proportion of French Jews and foreign Jews among these 80,000 victims, we have good reason to believe, on the basis of the list of the nationalities of people imprisoned in Drancy and the tallies we

have made in our book *Le Mémorial de la déportation des Juifs de France* for convoys other than those that left from Drancy, that there were about 24,500 French Jews and 56,500 foreign Jews (i.e. of various nationalities, or stateless, or of "indeterminate" nationality).[5]

These figures demonstrate that the survival rates of French Jews and foreign Jews were very different. The survival rate for French Jews can be estimated at between 87 per cent and 88 per cent, whereas for foreign Jews it was between 56 per cent and 60 per cent. What explains such a significant difference?

One answer is to be found in the life histories of individuals before the war. A French Jew who had been fully assimilated into the republican national fabric for one or more generations would have had very little in common with a foreign Jew who had recently immigrated to France who spoke little or no French. Their ways of thinking and behaving would have been extremely different; foreign Jewish families were more vulnerable to persecution than French Jews right from the start.[6]

In addition, each category grouped together people with very different experiences. The "French Jew" category designates mainly those of "French of the Israelite faith" ["*Français de confession israélite*"], so called since the emancipation of the Jews in 1789 during the French Revolution. The category of "French Jew" also included foreign Jews naturalized in the 1920s and 1930s, as well as the children of Jewish immigrants who were born in France and had either acquired French citizenship during the same period on reaching their majority, or who were French by birth, whether or not their parents had been naturalized. Within the category of "foreign Jews," a distinction has to be made depending on their country of origin. They came from Russia, Poland, Turkey, Greece, Germany, Morocco, Austria, and so on; they did not all speak the same language or practice the same customs and traditions, nor did they necessarily have the same relationship to their Jewish identity. In short, the term "Jew" refers to very different human, historical, political, cultural, and religious realities.

Citizens in their own right

The fact of being French was of primary significance in terms of someone's trajectory both before and during the war. Nationality, more than any ethno-religious affiliation, determined how rooted they were in society. The labels "French Jew" and "foreign Jew," which are often used today, can be misleading when looking back at the context of the time. To label as "*Juifs français*" those who had long been an integral part of the nation is an anachronism, as it implies that they placed their Jewish identity above their commitment to the French republic and that their citizenship was basically secondary. In fact, they considered themselves first as belonging to the national community of France and only second-arily—and then not always—did they define themselves by their Jewish heritage and religious practice. In the period in question they were commonly described, by others and by themselves, as French *Israélites*.

It is useful here to review the history of the integration of Jews into the French Republic since their emancipation by the Constituent Assembly on 27 September 1791. For the first time in the West, Jews were granted full political citizenship with the attendant civil and political rights that such recognition by a modern state implied, includ-ing the right to practice their own religion. In 1807, Napoleon I con-vened the Grand Sanhedrin (assembly of Jewish representatives), which resulted in the establishment of the *Consistoire Central des Israélites de l'Empire*, the official institution for French Jewry that would henceforth be seen as the official representative body for all the *Israélites* of France.

The emancipation of the Jews in the nation of the rights of man soon prompted the first wave of Jewish immigration to France, especially Paris. These immigrants were Sephardim from the Netherlands and the future Belgium, as well as from Bordeaux and Provence.[7] In 1815, in reaction to mounting anti-Semitism in eastern France, Ashkenazim of German origin, from the left bank of the Rhine[8] and in larger numbers from Alsace and Lorraine, began arriving in Paris. They came to find work and to do business, but also because it seemed to them that anti-Semitism could not possibly flourish in the cosmopolitan atmosphere of the capital. The largest wave of immigration of Jews from Alsace and Lorraine took place after 1871, after the two provinces were annexed by Germany. The sentimental ties connecting them to France and the fear that under German rule they would lose their rights as citizens prompted thousands to flee to Paris and its outskirts. By the end of the nineteenth century, the Jewish population in France is estimated to have been 71,000; it rose to 150,000 in 1918, after Alsace-Moselle was returned to France.[9]

In the space of a few generations, the political and social emancipation of the Jews in France had contributed significantly to their social integration and economic ascent, which went hand in hand with their urbanization. They tended to leave the countryside to settle in cities, usually, but not always, Paris. In Alsace, many Jews settled in Strasbourg, Colmar, and Mulhouse.

This was the case for the Becker family. Annie was born in 1926 and Jean-Jacques was born in 1928.[10] The family had been living in Paris for two generations, but its roots were in Alsace-Moselle. Their great-grandparents had moved to the capital after the region was annexed by Germany in 1871, while other members of the family stayed in Alsace. Annie and Jean-Jacques had an older brother, Henri, and a younger sister, Françoise. Their father was a sales representative for the Le Jouet firm in Paris. In 1939 the family was living in an apartment in the République neighborhood of Paris.[11]

The Dreyfus family, on the other hand (no relation to the family of Captain Alfred Dreyfus), had remained in Alsace. The father, Gaston Dreyfus, was born in 1897 in the village of Marmoutier (Bas-Rhin). After apprenticing as a leather merchant in Strasbourg, he found work in Tuttlingen, Wurttemberg. Gaston had fought in the First World War in the German Army as part of the occupation force in Romania, while his father Joseph had been drafted into the air force. In 1932, Gaston married Jeanne Kahn, born in Sarreguemines in 1909. They had two children: Gérard, born in 1933, and Huguette, born in 1938. At the outbreak of war the family was living in a recently built apartment building in a modern section of Strasbourg, near the Parc de l'Orangerie, together with Annie, Huguette's nursemaid.[12]

Another significant consequence of the emancipation of French Jews was that they were fervently patriotic and loyal to the French Republic. The political storm stirred up by the Dreyfus Affair may have shaken their convictions, but the outcome of the crisis in favor of the falsely accused army captain, whose name was finally cleared on 12 July 1906, strengthened their confidence in the protective mantle of the state.[13] They offered irrefutable proof of their attachment to the nation's values during the First World War when they fought and often died for their country. Countless declarations of gratitude and a deep sense of belonging were made by these French *Israélites*, often drawing attention to the price their own families had paid in the defense of France. Historian Marc Bloch's statement, in his fine book *Strange Defeat*, written in 1940 and first published in 1946, is one of the most moving.[14]

As these French *Israélites* subscribed to the secular religion of patriotism, their integration into French culture generally led to their abandoning the religious practice of Judaism. Some ran Jewish organizations, such as the *Éclaireurs Israélites de France* (EIF—the Jewish Scouts of France), founded in 1923 on the model of the Protestant *Éclaireurs Unionistes* and the Catholic *Scouts de France*. But these assimilated Jews rarely if ever went to synagogue, and tended not to become members of the Jewish institutions that were supposed to represent them. In Paris, affiliation with the Central Consistory is estimated to have been one in four.[15] On the other hand, smaller, older communities such as those in Strasbourg, Belfort, and Bordeaux, had higher rates of membership. Despite a generally low level of frequentation, the map of synagogues and religious organizations registered with the Consistory gives an indication of the French Jewish presence in the country prior to 1940.

This map is all the more valuable because under the Third Republic it was prohibited to take a census along "ethnic" lines. While the map does not illustrate the geography of Jewish religious practice in France (thousands of Jewish immigrants, unsympathetic to French Judaism, set up their own synagogues), it nevertheless has the advantage of showing the regions and cities of France where synagogues were already located in 1937. It is not merely by chance, then, that the names of the cities mentioned here often recur in accounts of Jews on the run during the Occupation; synagogues served as important meeting points and information centers, particularly since neither the Vichy government nor the Germans shut them down, even if their activities were curbed.[16]

France, land of asylum

There were several waves of Jewish immigration to France from the late nineteenth century until the beginning of the Second World War. Jewish immigrants from Russia and Eastern Europe as well as the Balkans and North Africa had started arriving prior to 1914 and increasingly during the 1920s and 1930s. The causes of these successive migrations are diverse. The primary cause was economic: they were

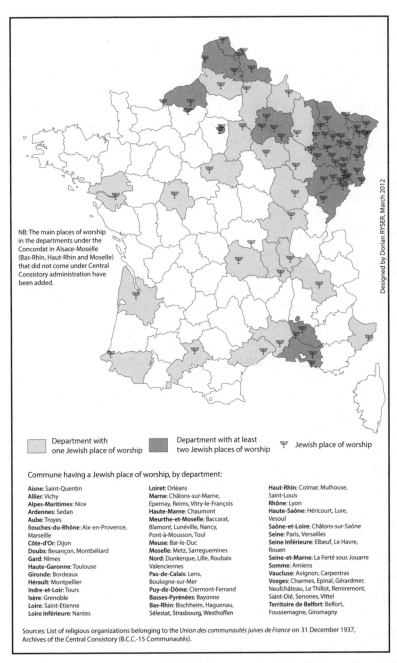

NB: The main places of worship in the departments under the Concordat in Alsace-Moselle (Bas-Rhin, Haut-Rhin and Moselle) that did not come under Central Consistory administration have been added.

Designed by Dorian RYSER, March 2012

Department with one Jewish place of worship

Department with at least two Jewish places of worship

Jewish place of worship

Commune having a Jewish place of worship, by department:

Aisne: Saint-Quentin
Allier: Vichy
Alpes-Maritimes: Nice
Ardennes: Sedan
Aube: Troyes
Bouches-du-Rhône: Aix-en-Provence, Marseille
Côte-d'Or: Dijon
Doubs: Besançon, Montbéliard
Gard: Nîmes
Haute-Garonne: Toulouse
Gironde: Bordeaux
Hérault: Montpellier
Indre-et-Loir: Tours
Isère: Grenoble
Loire: Saint-Etienne
Loire Inférieure: Nantes

Loiret: Orléans
Marne: Châlons-sur-Marne, Epernay, Reims, Vitry-le-François
Haute-Marne: Chaumont
Meurthe-et-Moselle: Baccarat, Blamont, Lunéville, Nancy, Pont-à-Mousson, Toul
Meuse: Bar-le-Duc
Moselle: Metz, Sarreguemines
Nord: Dunkerque, Lille, Roubaix Valenciennes
Pas-de-Calais: Lens, Boulogne-sur-Mer
Puy-de-Dôme: Clermont-Ferrand
Basses-Pyrénées: Bayonne
Bas-Rhin: Bischheim, Haguenau, Sélestat, Strasbourg, Westhoffen

Haut-Rhin: Colmar, Mulhouse, Saint-Louis
Rhône: Lyon
Haute-Saône: Héricourt, Lure, Vesoul
Saône-et-Loire: Châlons-sur-Saône
Seine: Paris, Versailles
Seine Inférieure: Elbeuf, Le Havre, Rouen
Seine-et-Marne: La Ferté sous Jouarre
Somme: Amiens
Vaucluse: Avignon, Carpentras
Vosges: Charmes, Epinal, Gérardmer, Neufchâteau, Le Thillot, Remiremont, Saint-Dié, Senones, Vittel
Territoire de Belfort: Belfort, Foussemagne, Giromagny

Sources: List of religious organizations belonging to the *Union des communautés juives de France* on 31 December 1937, Archives of the Central Consistory (B.C.C.-15 Communautés).

Map 1: Location of Jewish Places of Worship, 1937

fleeing poverty. Rising anti-Semitism in a number of countries also played a role. Lastly, there were more political factors: in Russia, for example, there were pogroms in the wake of the murder of Tsar Alexander II in 1881, followed by the failed 1905 Revolution and the Bolshevik takeover in 1917. Some attempted to make their way to France because they knew Jews there had been emancipated. At the beginning of the nineteenth century a Yiddish proverb expressed the appeal of the land of the 1789 Revolution and the Declaration of the Rights of Man and the Citizen: "*men ist azoy wie Gott in Frankreich*"— "Happy as God in France." The figures for Jewish immigration from the late nineteenth century up to 1914 vary considerably from one source to another. According to Nancy Green, the immigrants numbered no more than 35,000.[17]

Sophie, Annette Krajcer's mother, a native of Rovno in the Russian Empire (today in Ukraine) arrived in France with her whole family in 1903, when she was only a few months old. She spoke French perfectly, and continued her studies up to the school certificate. Her parents and her two sisters, Berthe and Fanny, easily obtained naturalization in 1925, as their father had enlisted in the French Army as a volunteer and fought in World War I. Nevertheless, despite numerous applications, Sophie herself was not granted citizenship. She had married a Polish Jew, Simon Krajcer, in 1924, who out of pacifist conviction refused to sign up for military service. Sophie and her husband thus remained of "indeterminate" nationality, although their two daughters, Lea and Annette, were declared French at birth in accordance with the law. The Krajcers owned a clothes shop on rue Saint-Antoine and lived on rue de Sévigné in the 4th arrondissement.

Albert Grunberg, born in 1898 in Galatz (Romania), arrived in France with his older brother Sami in 1912. Albert, who was then 14 years old, had lost his mother at the age of 7 and was raised by Sami. The two of them volunteered for the army during World War I. After the war, Albert took night classes and became a hairdresser's assistant in Montreuil-sur-Seine. Not long after, he met Marie-Marguerite Durand, a young French woman from the Auvergne region. They married in 1919 and, in accordance with the law, Marie-Marguerite took her husband's nationality. However, their two children, Robert and Roger, born in 1919 and 1926 respectively, were French. In 1934, the

Grunbergs bought a hairdressing salon located at 8 rue des Écoles in the 5th arrondissement, which they managed together. The family lived on the same street at number 14.[18]

After the First World War, immigrant workers arrived in France in droves. Whereas the United States had decided to set immigration quotas in 1924, France continued to welcome immigrants with open arms: almost 3 million foreigners settled in the country between 1919 and 1939. The French government encouraged immigration at the time to make up for the serious deficit in the male population as a result of the Great War. The need to revitalize the country was answered with a liberal policy of mass naturalization established through the nationality law of 10 August 1927. From 1926 to 1936, the number of naturalized citizens more than doubled, from 248,727 to 516,647.[19]

Although France had opened up to foreigners for primarily economic and demographic reasons, the situation in Europe had spawned large numbers of candidates for immigration. The new nation-states created after 1918 (Poland, Romania, Hungary, Turkey) proved quite intolerant towards their own minorities (for example Jews and Armenians). In Italy, Mussolini's accession to power and the establishment of a fascist regime triggered a wave of emigration to France. But whether in Italy, Poland or the Baltic states, apart from persecution and repression, poverty was the main reason that induced people to leave. In 1931 France was home to 2.9 million immigrants, or 7 per cent of its population. At the time it had the largest immigrant population in the world.[20]

The number of Jews who came to live in France, however, remained low, some tens of thousands of people in all. Some settled in Alsace, others in the north, but most went to Paris, settling mainly in the 11th, 18th, and 20th arrondissements.[21] They found coreligionists there, from the same cities or towns they were from and speaking the same language. Some of them shared a history of political activism as communists, socialists, or Bundists.[22] Admiring of France, they fully intended to obey the laws of their host country and wanted to give their children a French education.[23] In total, 70,000 Russian, Polish, Romanian, Lithuanian, Latvian, and Hungarian Jews are estimated to have settled in Paris between 1920 and 1939.[24]

Joseph Minc was born in Brest-Litovsk in 1908 into a Jewish family that spoke only Hebrew and Yiddish. He had two younger sisters,

Frouma (born in 1910) and Bella (born in 1914). During the First World War, the family spent time in Biala Podlaska and then returned to Brest-Litovsk, which was later incorporated into Poland. After the war, Joseph, who had become Polish together with the rest of his family, considered becoming a rabbi. But he was soon attracted to communism and turned his back on religion. He began to study to become a dental prosthetist. Following a friend's advice, he came to Bordeaux in 1931, where he continued his studies while working in a dental laboratory. He learned French, which he spoke with a Bordeaux accent, by reading the communist newspaper *L'Humanité*, with the help of his laboratory comrades. His fiancée, Lisa, joined him in the autumn of 1937, and the couple moved to Paris where Joseph and a friend opened their own laboratory. A few months later, Lisa got her residence permit. Joseph and Lisa married in May 1938 and their daughter Betty was born on 1 August.[25]

Léon Poliakov, born in 1910, came from a family of well-to-do Russian émigrés who arrived in France in the early 1920s to escape the Bolshevik revolution. After a transitional stay in Germany, where "the economic situation was favorable to those who had foreign currency," the family moved to Paris in 1924. His father owned an advertising agency and dealt primarily with publishers of foreign language newspapers. The Poliakovs settled in Auteuil, in the 16th arrondissement, and Léon went to school at the Lycée Janson-de-Sailly. In 1933 his father started a newspaper intended for a German émigré readership, called *Pariser Tageblatt*, which led to his financial ruin. After his baccalaureate Léon began studying law while working for his father. And after his father died in October 1939, Léon found a salaried job "for a company benefit scheme." When his mother died in February 1940, legally speaking, he belonged to the category of stateless persons.

Not all Jews who immigrated to France at that time were fleeing poverty and anti-Semitism. Some of them were world travelers who decided to settle in the country they liked best.

This was the case for Stanley Hoffmann's mother, a Viennese Austrian who was very drawn to France, which she had visited in her youth. Her relationship with Stanley's father, an American lawyer, was short-lived. In 1928, shortly after Stanley's birth, she decided to move with her son to Nice, a city she had fond memories of since she had visited it as a child. Born Jewish, she converted to Protestantism and had her son baptized. In 1936, the Hoffmanns left the French Riviera for Neuilly-sur-Seine, west of Paris, where Stanley was sent to school at the Lycée Pasteur. He was not happy in this new environment; although he had always felt perfectly French, here the other pupils treated him as a foreigner. After the Anschluss, Stanley's uncles joined them in Neuilly with their families. His mother was intensely hostile towards Nazism and refused to take on German nationality. As a result, she and her son were considered stateless, for despite becoming socially integrated in France, she never attempted to become naturalized.[26]

Serge Klarsfeld's parents met in Paris in the 1920s. They had not come to the French capital because of persecution or a desire for economic betterment: Klarsfeld's Romanian father was from a wealthy background, and his Russian mother was born to an equally well-off family. They were drawn to the cosmopolitan and intellectual atmosphere of the French capital, at the time a beacon for all young people from Eastern Europe. They married in 1929 and had two children; Georgette-Mireille, born in France in 1931, and Serge, born in 1935 in Romania, where his mother was spending the holidays with her in-laws. The family was not religious and the parents had little interest in politics or the condition of the Jews. According to Serge, they applied unsuccessfully for French nationality in 1937. Consequently, of the four members of the family, only the daughter held French citizenship prior to the war.[27]

Studies on these waves of Ashkenazi Jewish immigration have neglected the parallel influx of Jews from the Balkans. The so-called Levantine Jews from the Ottoman Empire (Crete, Salonica, Anatolia, and Bulgaria) also came to France during and following national revolts that took place in their respective countries at the end of the nineteenth century and the beginning of the twentieth century. An estimated 15,000 Levantine Jews arrive in France during the interwar period. They usually arrived in Marseille, from where some traveled up to Paris. In the case of Salonica, these factors were heightened by the appalling fire of 1917, which destroyed much of the Jewish quarter and prompted a major wave of emigration from the city.

Vidal Nahum, father of the well-known French sociologist Edgar Morin, was a native of Salonica: he was born in 1894 to a family with origins in Livorno. After attending the Franco-German school in the city, he was employed by the branch of a bank managed by one of his brothers-in-law. During the First World War, as a result of confusion over their military status (the Italian army considered them to be Italian citizens who should have been enlisted in the Italian army), Vidal and his brother Henri were not called up but instead sent to prison in Marseille in January 1916. Released in May, Vidal obtained a residence permit and stated his nationality as "Salonican." Vidal and Henri settled in Marseille, where their parents and younger sister Mathilde joined them. The father resumed his trade as an agent and went into business with his two sons. In 1918, Vidal Nahum went to Paris to open a subsidiary. After his father's death in 1920, he set up shop in the garment district of Paris on rue d'Aboukir, selling hosiery wholesale. He soon married Luna Mosseri Beressi, the daughter of acquaintances in Salonica. Edgar was born on 8 July 1921 at 10 rue Mayran in the 4th arrondissement of Paris. He was therefore French by birth. Vidal, registered as a Levantine Jew, obtained Greek nationality in 1925. He was finally naturalized French in 1931.[28]

Another little-known migration is that of Moroccan Jews who arrived in the 1910s. Recruited by the French army during the First World War, some of them remained in mainland France after 1918, thus escaping repatriation. Others joined them in the 1920s and 1930s, fleeing wretched living conditions. These Moroccan Jews managed to be hired as manual workers in the Rhône-Poulenc pharmaceutical plants and Saint-Gobain petrochemical plants, mainly in Saint-Fons, in the outskirts of Lyon.[29] This population numbered no more than 400 people prior to 1940.

Among immigrants from North Africa were Jews from Algeria, who had been granted French citizenship under the Crémieux decree of 24 October 1870.[30] While some Algerian Jews, fearing the French presence, left to settle in Morocco or Tunisia, a large number of families from these two bordering countries went the opposite route, increasing the ranks of the Jewish population in cities such as Oran in the west and Constantine in the east. In the 1920s, and then following the Constantine pogrom of 1934, some of these Algerian Jews came to France, motivated above all by economic reasons.

Simon and Guy, born in 1934 and 1937 respectively, were Joseph and Dinah Benayoun's two youngest sons. Their father, born in Algeria in 1890, fought and was injured in the First World War fighting in a Zouave regiment. After the war he began farming, only to see his farm ruined by drought and the locust plague in 1933–1934. In 1937 he decided to leave and seek work in France, leaving his wife and their six children in Oran. On arriving in Paris, Joseph immediately found work, first as a sleeping car attendant at the Gare de Lyon, then as a salesman for a jeweler in the République district. In early 1938, his family joined him and they moved into a small apartment on rue Popincourt in the 11th arrondissement, a neighborhood popular with Greek and Turkish immigrants. They were practically the only French Algerians but it did not take them long to fit in. They were very religious, and attended synagogue every week at the rue Popincourt synagogue, where the service was conducted in the Turkish tradition.

French Algerian Jews mainly lived in the center of Paris, between rue de Rivoli and the River Seine, running cafés and restaurants that served Algerian Jewish fare. Singers often performed in these convivial venues. Rue de Rivoli was a virtual border at the time, with North Africa on one side and Central Europe on the other.[31]

The 1929 stock market crash in the United States, followed by a sharp rise in unemployment in Europe during the 1930s, as well as the development of xenophobic and anti-Semitic propaganda and destabilized democracies further contributed to an increase in the number of migrants into France from neighboring countries that were in the throes of dictatorship and war.

1933: Adolf Hitler in power

On 30 January 1933, Hitler came to power in Germany, a political event that spelled danger for freedom and for peace. The first to realize this were Germans, both Jews and political adversaries of Nazism, who directly bore the brunt of repressive measures and persecution that were immediately put in place by the new regime. They left their homes, often in haste, seeking refuge in the nearest country, France. In summer 1933, at the height of this initial crisis, France had already absorbed some 25,000 of these 60,000 German émigrés, putting it at the top of host countries.

The Hanau family, from Saarland, fled the Nazi regime. In 1914, the father had fought in the German army. They lived in Gerolstein

(Rhineland-Palatinate), where the parents owned a wholesale food business. The couple had two children: Edith, born in 1920, and Edgar, born in 1925. After Hitler's rise to power, the Hanaus wanted to immigrate to France. In 1936, the whole family arrived in Bouzonville (Moselle), where the father opened a confectionery shop while Edith worked in a fabric store. The parents spoke no French. However, as one of the father's grandmothers was from Lorraine, and therefore a French citizen, a provision in the Treaty of Versailles concerning the inhabitants of Alsace-Moselle entitled the family to be accorded French nationality by court decision (Tribunal of Thionville). The Hanaus were therefore considered French from birth rather than Germans who had been naturalized. They were soon accepted by the city's Jewish community, where the father became an officiant.[32]

Alfred Grosser's family was also among these new immigrants. Alfred's father, the head physician at the Frankfurt children's hospital and professor of medicine at the city's university, became a victim of anti-Semitic measures and was forced to give up both positions. The Grossers decided to leave Germany: because the father already spoke French, they chose France. Shortly after arriving, on 6 February 1934, he died of a heart attack. His wife, now a widow with two children, Alfred and Margerete, did not consider returning to Germany. With the help of friends and her husband's former assistant, Thérèse, who, although not Jewish, had followed them into exile, she transformed the house her husband had bought in Saint-Germain-en-Laye with the idea of converting it into a sanatorium and a children's home. Alfred adapted well to the local school, where he learned to speak French, before entering the *lycée*. He joined the Protestant scouts (*Éclaireurs Unionistes*), and soon felt perfectly French. He was naturalized in 1937 at the same time as his mother and sister. His maternal grandmother joined them in France in 1938. Resolute pacifists despite the happenings in Germany, Alfred and his mother wept with joy on learning of the Munich Agreement.[33]

A second wave of immigrants from Eastern European arrived in France in the wake of the political maneuvers and military operations undertaken by the Nazi regime in 1938 and 1939: the *Anschluss* (the annexation of Austria), *Kristallnacht*, which took place on 9 November 1938, and the invasion of Czechoslovakia in March 1939. Thousands of people from these countries began to make their way towards France.

The Friedländers came from Czechoslovakia. Part of the family, which belonged to the Prague bourgeoisie, came from Sudetenland, and thus saw itself as German. They did not practice Judaism at all. Yet, after Germany occupied Czechoslovakia in March 1939, the family felt threatened and wanted to leave. Saul, born in 1932, whose first name was then Pavel, was not aware at the time that his parents wanted to flee because they were Jewish. The Friedländers arrived in Paris but did not intend to remain in France; they began the application process first to emigrate to Palestine, then to Canada, but in both cases their applications were refused. The family moved into a furnished apartment. They had lost everything. To make a living, the mother began training to be a beautician while the father learned a variety of trades, first taking a course in electrical mechanics and then going to Auvergne to learn cheese-making.[34]

The Kanners, German citizens of Polish origin, fled Germany just before war was declared. The parents, Mia and Sal, had three daughters, Ruth, Eva and Léa. The family had been living in Halle (Saxony-Anhalt), where Sal ran a clothing store. When Hitler came to power, pressure mounted on the Kanners, who were trying calmly to organize their departure for Palestine. In 1938, their situation worsened: Mia's father-in-law was sent to Poland, the shop was vandalized on Kristallnacht, and her husband was interned at Buchenwald. Mia realized she had to try to get her family out of Germany as quickly as possible, whatever the destination. She managed to obtain a French visa for Sal, who was finally released from the camp and escorted to the French border. With the help of a cousin, Mia managed to have a million francs deposited into an account in her name to give the authorities the impression she was rich, so that she and her daughters would be granted French visas. In July 1939 she was reunited in Paris with her husband and two of her sisters who were already living in the capital. The Kanners had to leave most of their belongings behind when they left; the few possessions they were allowed to take with them had been shipped to Palestine, and the family awaited a visa to emigrate there.[35]

The year 1939 would see a much larger wave of immigration, this time in the south of France, prompted by the Spanish Civil War that broke out in 1936 between General Franco's troops and the Republican forces. Thousands of Spaniards had already fled across the Pyrenees in

1937; by late 1938 they numbered between 40,000 and 45,000. The defeat of the Republicans in January and February 1939 precipitated an unprecedented exodus of nearly half a million people over the border into France. In a state of utter confusion, the government set up internment camps in Saint Cyprien, in the Pyrénées-Orientales department, and Gurs, in the Pyrénées-Atlantiques department, to accommodate the fighters. Civilians were sent to regional reception centers. This twofold immigration, from Eastern and from Southern Europe, the causes of which were so different, meant that on the eve of the Second World War France was host to the largest number of asylum seekers of any country in the world. But fear was intensifying within the country, surrounded as it was by the three fascist or totalitarian regimes now in place in Italy, Germany and Spain: fear of war was as great as fear of foreigners, perceived as scheming enemies within, traitors to the Nation.

Anti-Semitism and Xenophobia

How did the successive French governments of the 1930s deal with these waves of refugees? Several historians have put forth the idea that French policy towards immigrants grew progressively harsher over the years, prefiguring Vichy policies.[36] However, Vicki Caron, in her remarkable study, shows that such an approach is far too linear.[37] True, the conservative governments of Pierre-Etienne Flandin and Pierre Laval (1934 and 1935), aware that they had the support of a segment of public opinion, enacted measures to limit conditions of residence and labor for foreigners in France and to combat illegal immigration. When Léon Blum became head of the government in 1936, he tried to halt this repressive and protectionist trend. Blum's Popular Front sought to implement a policy of peaceful regulation and integration of foreigners. But in 1938, the fear of a "deluge" of refugees triggered by events in Germany and Central Europe induced Édouard Daladier's government to embark once again on a policy hostile to foreigners. It issued decree-laws restricting the admission of foreign nationals, distinguishing between desirable and undesirable immigrants (2 May 1938) and restricting their right to work and engage in business activities (12 November 1938). Border controls were also tightened. German Jews trying to enter France after Kristallnacht were turned back. In a context of appeasement of Berlin at all costs, concretized by the Munich Agreement (29–30 September 1938), Jewish refugees were seen as troublemakers. Anti-Semitic incidents increased in both Paris and Alsace.[38] Together with their supposed communist allies, Jews were allegedly seeking to draw France into war against Germany simply to satisfy their thirst for revenge. Many felt that France in any case already had too many foreigners on its soil, which is why, when the Evian Conference was convened at the initiative of United States President Roosevelt (6–15 July 1938), a French foreign ministry official expressed satisfaction at the fact that not one of the thirty-two countries gathered to address the refugee problem set a quota for taking in refugees.[39] In fact, none of the countries present wanted to admit Jewish refugees, except perhaps the tiny Dominican Republic.[40]

The climate of intolerance and rejection of foreigners had been disseminated for many years in France in certain parts of society that were openly xenophobic and anti-Semitic, whose ideas were particularly widespread in the newspaper and publishing industries. This led in the late nineteenth century to a "severe bout of anti-Semitism that manifested itself in the dual form of a doctrine that inspired many theoretical texts, and a social practice expressed in demonstrations, marches and physical attacks."[41] The popular success of polemicist Edouard Drumont, author of *La France Juive* (1886) and founder in 1892 of the newspaper *La Libre Parole*, the unleashing of passions during the Dreyfus Affair, and the malicious writings of Urbain Gohier (the first person to translate the *Protocols of the Elders of Zion* into French) are all examples of the ferocious anti-Semitism that permeated parts of French society at the turn of the twentieth century.

It is not surprising that during the 1930s, in a climate of increasing fear and intolerance, this ideological current of hatred persisted and continued to be openly expressed. In 1933 the writer Léon Daudet, one of the leaders of *Action Française*, the far right movement led by Charles Maurras, asserted that German refugees formed a pool of potential traitors. These "Semitic emigrants" were so eager to "return to grace in the eyes of the German authorities" that they would not hesitate to "place themselves at the command of the latter in the event of war and invasion."[42] Such remarks yoked foreigners, viewed as potential traitors, to inassimilable Jews. Louis-Ferdinand Céline, whose literary talent was universally acclaimed at the time, penned words of sheer poison in 1938 in his *L'École des cadavres*: "The Jews, who are Afro-Asiatic hybrids, quarter or half nigger, half Near Easterner, are unbridled fornicators who have no place in this country. They should fuck off."[43] There was a segment of the right-wing bourgeoisie and nationalist Catholics who expounded similar ideas, without resorting to such vitriolic invective.

Even though xenophobic ideas were also gaining ground among the middle classes and in some professional milieus, it is not possible to conclude that the French public was overwhelmingly anti-Semitic, or that anti-refugee sentiment prevailed during the 1930s. A significant part of the population remained favorable to the refugee cause.[44] The second part of Ralph Schor's important book on the anti-Semitism of the 1930s, *"La défense des Juifs et les cheminements de la raison"* ("The defense of Jews and the ways of reason"), with the two chapters entitled *"Unité et division du front philosémite"* ("Unity and division of the pro-Semitic front") and *"Les formes de l'action philosémite"* ("Forms of pro-Semitic action"), though too rarely cited, is essential reading in order to understand how events unfolded during the Occupation.

The issue of the acceptance or rejection by French *Israélites* of the different waves of Jewish immigrants has sparked heated controversy. A number of historians and journalists, some children of deported Eastern European Jews themselves, have claimed that the French Jews betrayed the Jewish refugees in the 1930s. The most serious indictment comes from historian Maurice Rajsfus, a Polish Jew who was picked up, along with his parents, by the French police during the notorious "Vélodrome d'Hiver" roundup of foreign Jews on 16 and 17 July 1942. His parents were deported and murdered.[45] He has accused French Jews not only of failing to offer support to Jewish immigrants when they arrived in France, but of actively collaborating with the government when it sought to clamp down on this immigration.

This opinion appears partially justified,[46] but overall Rajsfus's judgment is too harsh. Leaders of the French Jewish community did indeed fear that the influx of Jewish immigrants would exacerbate anti-Semitism in France and thereby jeopardize their own position in society. But that does not mean they stood by passively in the face of the flood of refugees arriving from Central Europe, particularly since these immigrants, unlike those who had arrived in France in the 1920s, were met with a closed job market and increasingly restrictive rules on residence and work permits. Against this new background, several committees were set up in France to come to the aid of German refugees, among them the *Comité National de Secours aux Refugiés Allemands Victimes de l'Anti-Sémitisme* (National Committee for Aiding German Refugee Victims of Anti-Semitism), headed by Baron Robert de Rothschild, the *Comité pour la Défense des Droits des Israélites en Europe Centrale et Occidentale* (Committee for the Defense of the Rights of Jews from Central and Western Europe), and, a little later, the *Comité d'Assistance aux Réfugiés* (CAR—Committee for Aiding Refugees), founded in July 1936 and headed by Raymond-Raoul Lambert, a close friend of Robert de Rothschild[47] and editor-in-chief of *Univers israélite* (Jewish World), a weekly newspaper that served as the mouthpiece of the Paris Central Consistory.[48]

Although the CAR basically took over from the *Comité de Secours* (Aid Committee), which was criticized for its overly philanthropic and apolitical position, it instituted one important innovation, the establishment of vocational training in rural and manual activities for immigrants, in particular through the *Organisation Reconstruction Travail* (ORT-Professional Training and Reorientation Organization), founded in 1921, which offered various training programs in craftsmanship and technical skills. Refugees were sent to the provinces, usually to the countryside, to take up jobs as manual workers and artisans. The French Jewish "notables" certainly deserve criticism for their "political apathy," as Catherine Nicault rightly points out, a mind-set that enabled them to "carry out the expulsion orders issued in 1938 without qualm, which afterwards gave rise to justified unease." She nevertheless concludes that "the French Jewish community had no inkling of the tragedies to come, but with the material and psychological capacities it had at its disposal, it demonstrated a sense of solidarity, rather more than some other very affluent communities."[49]

The Descent into War and State Control over Civilian Populations

As soon as war was declared between France and Germany on 3 September 1939, the governments of these countries set about organizing the movement of their respective civilian populations, well before actual fighting broke out. This kind of state control over civilian populations was nothing new; indeed, it had already expanded significantly during the "Great War" of 1914–1918. During the Second World War it took on unprecedented proportions, whether it was a question of conscripting citizens into the army, or protecting them, transferring them or exploiting them—or interning them, deporting them, and, at its most extreme, systematically killing them. The example of France is highly revealing of this evolution.

The war began with a general mobilization order and the immediate conscription of young men into the country's armed forces. Mobilization took place on an even greater scale than in 1914: nearly 5 million men between the ages of 20 and 45 were recruited from metropolitan France and the colonial empire,[50] 3 million of them enlisted in fighting units. A few months later, the crushing defeat of the French army in May–June 1940 delivered 1.6 million of these men to Germany. Once soldiers, they were now prisoners of war, valuable human booty for the Third Reich. Berlin swiftly transferred them to within German borders, interning most of them in *Stalags* and *Oflags*. Aside from those who managed to escape or who were granted release or returned to France in a prisoner exchange agreement, these men would remain in Germany for the entire duration of the war.

At the same time, the French government felt a duty to protect its most vulnerable citizens. Fearing an enemy air attack on Paris, thousands of women, children and the elderly were evacuated. They were sent to Brittany, Anjou or the Limousin region, where the conditions in which they were received were sometimes less than satisfactory. Parisians also left of their own accord for the provinces, usually to stay with family. Some would later return to Paris. People living near the Belgian, German or Italian borders were also evacuated from their homes for fear that they would be caught up in the fighting. In the east, for instance, Strasbourg was virtually emptied of its inhabitants in record time.[51] These precautionary measures were drawn up in the late 1930s, somewhat reluctantly, by military officials: any of these scenarios would mean that the French armed forces had been unable to withstand enemy pressure, a hypothesis deemed most unlikely, such was the faith in the impregnability of the Maginot Line.

During this period of the "phoney war," it was clear that although the government was acting as a protector for some people, it was simulta-

neously suspicious of and hostile towards those of whom it was suspected that they might become allies of the enemy. The great fear in
1939 was of a "fifth column" of foreign conspirators from the east who
were plotting the country's defeat. The government thus sought to
increase the efficiency with which it controlled and restricted the
movements of these people. With this in mind it embarked on a policy
of interning refugees from Central Europe, who were declared "for-
eigner-enemies." Despite the serious lack of manpower on the domestic front, the government made it harder than ever for foreigners to be
employed, with the aim of allaying people's fears that foreigners were
going to take the jobs left vacant by men who had been enlisted into
the army. Pressure in favor of more liberal policies towards refugees
nevertheless continued to mount. The government set up screening
committees, whose task was to examine the case files of all internees
to determine who was a Nazi sympathizer and who was loyal to the
Allied cause. Officials also convinced themselves that refugees could be
enlisted in the military. Some of them—Polish and Czechoslovakian
nationals—were allowed to leave to join their national armies. Others,
depending on their age and health, had the choice of either joining the
Foreign Legion or volunteering for the French armed forces.

Despite the general mobilization, the disaster none had foreseen
came to pass: in the space of a few weeks, France was defeated militarily and once again invaded by its old enemy. This triggered the movement of an incredible flood of people, an endless, chaotic stream of
distraught men and women in absolute panic, who took to the road by
the thousands, on foot, in handcarts or by car, fleeing the horror and
heading as far south as possible. As Hanna Diamond has observed, "At
a time when refugees are a sadly familiar sight, it is difficult now to
imagine how unprecedented this kind of population displacement was
in 1940."[52] In the scheme of French history, there is a before and an
after May–June 1940, so traumatic was the impact of the defeat and
the exodus during these terrible months.

Marc Bloch was an officer and an eyewitness to the tragedy. *Strange
Defeat*, which he wrote almost as it was happening, is an acute and
penetrating analysis of the causes of the disaster.[53] Literature provides
a more vivid description of the hardships experienced by civilians than
the historian's analysis. In *Suite Française*, Irène Némirovsky captures

the atmosphere of fear and despair that gripped the terrified population overnight. She writes of the refugees, "There were just too many of them. Too many weary, pale faces, dripping with sweat, too many wailing children, too many trembling lips asking, 'Do you know where we could get a room? A bed? ... Would you tell us where we could find a restaurant, please, Madame?' It prevented the townspeople from being charitable. There was nothing human left in this miserable mob; they were like a herd of frightened animals."[54] At the heart of this magnificent novel is the moral collapse of a people, the "strange sadness that had nothing human about it any more, for it lacked both courage and hope."[55]

Only Marshal Pétain's proposal for an armistice managed to halt this stupefying collective flight. Hitler agreed to the request, and the armistice was signed on 22 June 1940, but at enormous political, financial, economic, and human cost. Berlin carved up the French territory to suit its strategic interests; the country was effectively dismembered. France was now divided into several zones of administration. The departments of the Nord and Pas de Calais were placed under the German military command in Brussels. The areas in the north and northeast, intended for German settlers, were declared "Forbidden Zones." The Occupied Zone, by far the largest, was administered by the German military command installed in Paris, called the *Militärbefehlshaber*, or MBF. The so-called Free Zone and all the territories of the colonial empire came under the authority of the French government, which had relocated to Vichy. By late July 1940, two frontiers ran through metropolitan France: the demarcation line between the Southern Zone and the Northern Zone, and the *Nordost Linie*, running from the Somme to the Swiss border, the so-called black line. This dismemberment was unprecedented in the history of France: the gradual territorial consolidation that had taken place from the baptism of Clovis in 496 up to the annexation of Savoy and the Duchy of Nice 1860—in other words over a period of fourteen centuries—was brutally destroyed by the conditions of this surrender.

The administrative and territorial division of France would play a significant role in the fate of the population, making travel and thus flight difficult and risky. For the Jews, as will be seen, the status of the area in which they were living would largely decide their opportunities to escape arrest. Of course they did not know this yet.

Let us return to the political consequences of France's defeat and the subsequent formation of the government, headed by Marshal Pétain. The new leader suggested a policy of "collaboration" with the occupying forces, but he intended to use the new situation as an opportunity to set the country on a moral path, based on a program he called the National Revolution. The policy of the new rump state was a strategy of excluding those elements of the population deemed undesirable and dangerous, who were held responsible for the catastrophic defeat—primarily foreigners, Jews and Freemasons. As Robert Paxton has shown, the policy of the new government did not evolve solely as a result of the very real pressure exerted by the occupying forces, but was also born of independent initiatives taken by the new authorities in Vichy who, while hewing to Berlin's demands, sought to preserve a degree of national autonomy.[56] But the imposing presence of the German powers in France, which plundered the country's economic and industrial wealth and pillaged its financial resources, not to mention its works of art, considerably reduced the already extremely limited room for maneuver of a government ruling over a France that had already been bled dry.

One of the first laws passed by the Vichy government, on 22 July 1940, made it possible to strip naturalized citizens of their French citizenship. This reflected a desire to purify society, drawing on the rhetoric of building a new France that would be purged of its corrupt elements.[57] This was the same spirit as Marshal Pétain's policies seeking to exclude Jews from public life. In a move that had no precedent in French history, in the autumn of 1940 the government announced the existence of a "Jewish race" with the publication of a number of laws, the most significant of which was the *Statut des Juifs* of 3 October 1940. The text of the *Statut des Juifs* represented a legal and civic rupture with the "republican pact," the most fundamental tenet of the post-revolutionary French state, which guarantees equality for every citizen, regardless of their religion. The institution of state anti-Semitism in French law essentialized the ethno-religious nature of a Jewish identity, which Vichy's legal texts would always struggle to define, all the more so as Vichy's definition of who was a Jew was not based on the same premise as that of the German occupying forces, which always referred to the Jewish "religion" rather than "race."

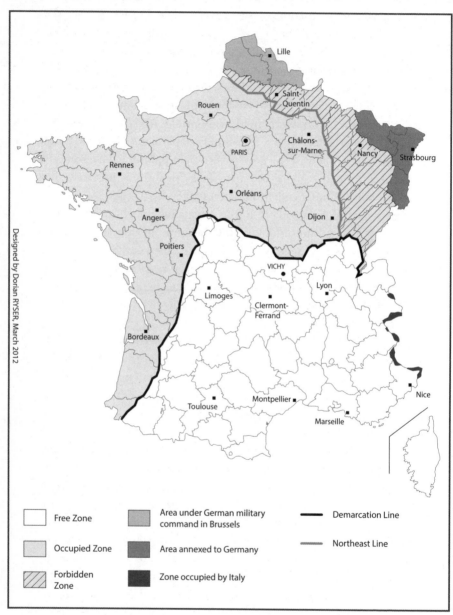

Legend:

- Free Zone
- Occupied Zone
- Forbidden Zone
- Area under German military command in Brussels
- Area annexed to Germany
- Zone occupied by Italy
- Demarcation Line
- Northeast Line

Map 2: French territory following the armistice of June 1940

Vichy did not treat people who held French citizenship and those who did not in the same way. A specific law, enacted the day after the *Statut des Juifs*, on 4 October 1940, pertained to foreigners. By virtue of this law, "foreign nationals of the Jewish race" were considered suspect and could therefore be arrested and interned in special camps or placed under house arrest by decision of the prefect. By contrast, the law of 3 October 1940, the principal aim of which was to diminish "Jewish influence" on society, provided for a different treatment for French Jewish citizens, who could not be arrested simply for being Jewish. Its purpose was to strip Jews of their positions of responsibility and more generally to turn them into social outcasts. From this moment on, French citizens of the "Jewish race" were victims of legal and administrative provisions that effectively excluded them from a number of jobs and professions including in the legal, educational, medical fields. Theoretically, the only exceptions to these new discriminatory measures were veterans of the 1914–1918 war. In autumn 1940, however, the process of stigmatization and economic and social ostracism was only just beginning. In the eighteen months that followed, a string of legal measures taken by both the German and French authorities contributed to making conditions for Jews in France, both French and foreign, increasingly harsh. Then, in 1942, the process of mass deportation and the systematic attempt to destroy the Jews began. In this infernal logic of destruction of the so-called "Jewish race," French Jews as well as foreign Jews were increasingly imperiled.

How did dozens of thousands of Jews manage at least partially to escape the infernal machinery of persecution in France? In 1939 and 1940 they were caught up in different waves of forced population displacement where the fact of their Jewishness did not play an important role. But once state anti-Semitism was introduced, the different migrations of the Jews evolved spontaneously in reaction to the different stages of persecution and the political geography of Occupied France. This spontaneous, multidirectional, haphazard dispersal was the first response in the attempt to evade the threat.

Evacuated and Expelled from Alsace-Lorraine and Baden-Palatinate

The evacuation of the inhabitants of the border areas of Alsace-Lorraine was planned with the aim of shielding the civilian population in the event of a German attack. The appellation "Alsace-Lorraine" does not refer to a geographic locality but rather to a historic reality, which includes the three departments of Bas-Rhin, Haut-Rhin, and Moselle, annexed by the German Reich in 1871. Following the order to evacuate on 3 September 1939, an estimated 630,000 people were forced to leave their homes, including the 193,000 inhabitants of Strasbourg, of whom 3,500 remained to ensure minimal public services.[58] The plan to disperse the population was drawn up by the Interior Ministry and its conditions were detailed in a circular dated 1 July 1938, "L'instruction générale sur les mouvements et transports de sauvegarde" (General guidelines on migrations and rescue transports). Each border department from which part of the population was evacuated was connected with host departments. The implementation of these measures was impressive. Departures took place in often unbelievable circumstances. In a matter of days, entire towns were emptied of their inhabitants. Strasbourg was bleak and deserted.[59] Several thousand French and foreign Jews were caught up in this flood of escapees. Some left without waiting for the official evacuation order. Having arrived in eastern France in the 1930s, they foresaw the danger and decided of their own accord to leave the region.

Alsatians and Mosellans were thus the first victims of a conflict that was not yet full-blown war. They were obliged to leave their homes, which they did with a sense of resignation; forced by the government and the army, they had no choice but to comply without protest. They knew it was for their safety and their own good. Most were evacuated by train, in conditions that were difficult, even degrading. As there were not enough passenger carriages, they were transported in cattle cars. The journey to the southwest, which could take between one and three days, was grueling, especially for the elderly. For young people, on the other hand, it was more of an adventure, a new experience that they approached with interest and curiosity.

Occasionally positive accounts[60] should not obscure the considerable difficulties many people had in adapting to a new and unfamiliar region. Evacuees often had problems adjusting to their new lives. Many found themselves living in rural areas in very rudimentary conditions. As the evacuees did not always speak French, the local inhabitants sometimes called them "Boches" and nicknamed them "ja-jas." This forced population transfer engendered substantial culture shock for both the new-comers and those who saw them arrive: practicing religious Alsatian Jews found themselves transplanted in a matter of days to the south-west, to areas that were often radical-socialist or communist.

The authorities allowed those who were able the opportunity to choose their destination, which also included towns in their home department or neighboring departments that had not been evacuated. In such cases, evacuees often filled the vacuum left by men who had been drafted or families who had chosen of their own accord to move to less exposed areas. People who owned a car (a means of travel that was still rare at the time) often headed into the Vosges mountains, while others went to Vichy, in the Allier, or much farther, to the Gers or Lot-et-Garonne.

Gérard Dreyfus recounts the Dreyfus family's odyssey after leaving Strasbourg:

> We left in my father's Citroën Traction Avant. We were all packed in tight. We also brought along our nanny, Annie. We'd taken with us to Contrexéville as much linen and dishes as we could [...] We figured that in three months the glorious French army would crush the German army and we'd soon be home [...] After that we went to Limoges, where we first stayed in a centrally located hotel near the train station that smelled awful [...]. After that, we rented a very nice little house. [...] Out front, there was a little garden with roses, and in the back, a big yard with fruit trees, including an immense cherry tree. We stayed there with my mother, my grandmother, and Uncle Paul.

Gérard's father was unable to leave with them. He had been requisitioned at the tannery where he worked in Halluin, not far from the Belgian border, to make shoe leather for the French army. After the Germans invaded Belgium, he managed to leave just in time to try to reach his family in Limoges.

In May 1940, in the wake of the German invasion of the Netherlands and Belgium, the French military authorities decided to expand the evacuation area. A month later, on 14 June, when the Wehrmacht entered Paris and defeat was inevitable, the authorities ordered all men aged between 18 and 55 to head south under their own steam. The mad rush had begun, with those who were able set off for central and southern France joining the flood of refugees.

After they invaded the territories of Alsace, Lorraine, and Moselle, the Germans immediately began to expel those who were considered "undesirables" according to Nazi ideology. Expulsion measures were prepared in secret for several categories of person. In addition to Jews, the list included "non-Alsatian/Moselle senior officials, Alsatians and Lorrainers accused of being Francophiles [...], deserters from the German army between 1914 and 1918, civil servants, journalists and magistrates who had criticized or prosecuted members of the autonomist movement during the interwar period, newspaper and radio journalists who were paid to disseminate French propaganda, veterans of the International Brigades during the Spanish Civil War, Roma, "Gypsies," people of foreign races (Africans, Asians, Australians), common criminals," and lastly, "beggars, vagabonds, pimps" and other "antisocial elements."[61] The aim could not have been clearer: to set in motion the ethnic and political "purification" of the territory conquered in order to Germanize it and annex it to the Third Reich.

Many accounts attest to the particularly harsh treatment these "undesirables" were subjected to, even before they were expelled. Jews were from the start targets of this German brutality.

Beginning in July 1940, the Germans expelled a total of 17,783 Jews to the Free Zone. On 22 April 1941, the last remaining 3,255 Jews were expelled.[62] This did not, however, seal their fate: some were interned and deported; others managed to survive in the Free Zone or made their way to Switzerland. Considerable research would be required to reconstruct the itineraries of all those who fled, whether they lost their lives or managed to survive despite everything.[63]

The measures that the German forces took immediately upon occupying Alsace-Lorraine indicate that Nazi policy towards the Jews at the time was to get rid of them by expelling them from the Reich. To this end, on 23 October 1940, Berlin began the evacuation to the Free Zone of 6,300 Jews from Baden and 1,150 from the Palatinate.

Among the Jews expelled was the Mayer family, who were living in the village of Hoffenheim (Baden region). The father, Karl, was born in 1894 in Frankfurt. His family had moved to Hoffenheim when he was a child. After fighting in the German army during the First World War and receiving the Iron Cross, Karl became a cattle merchant and was also a cantor in the village synagogue. In 1927 he married Mathilde

Wertheimer, from Neidenstein, a neighboring village. The couple had two boys: Manfred, nicknamed Fred, born in 1929, and Heinz, born in 1932. After Hitler came to power, the Mayers' life grew increasingly difficult: their children were taunted by their schoolmates, their neighbors abused them, the father got into fights with local Nazis. In August 1938 their identity cards were stamped with a J. The following year, Karl lost his job. To feed his family, he had to resort to mending roads for a pittance. Fred and Heinz had to leave the local school and attend a Jewish school located some 20 km from their home. After Kristallnacht, the father was interned at Dachau for a month while his wife and children were taken in by a relative. On 22 October 1940, the Gestapo arrested the seventeen Jews who lived in Hoffenheim, including the Mayers. They were transferred to France and interned at the Gurs transit camp where they found relatives who lived in a neighboring village.[64]

At the same time, Germany compelled defeated France to pledge the return of all those who had been evacuated and enlisted since 1939, except, of course, those who were considered "undesirable." This requirement was formally imposed by article 16 of the Armistice Agreement. All through summer and autumn 1940, about 500,000 people who had retreated to either the Southern or the Occupied Zones agreed to return to their homes in this newly annexed territory. As this return was not mandatory, evacuees who wanted to go back to their homes had to request a certificate of repatriation from the town hall in the municipality where they were living. The return of these refugees, evacuees, and demobilized people was declared officially terminated on 30 October 1940. Nonetheless, a German document estimated there were 180,000 Alsatians and Lorrainers still living "outside" the territory. Indeed, out of a population of 180,000 prior to evacuation, only 130,000 inhabitants were still in Strasbourg in October 1940. For instance, in autumn 1940 there were still 22,800 Alsatians in Dordogne. Among them, of course, were Jews, for whom there was no question of returning to their homes.

From the Fear of Bombardments to the Panic of Exodus

The declaration of war on 3 September prompted the first departures from Paris, whether organized or spontaneous. The population was made ready for war and what to do in the event of air raids: gas masks were handed out to civilians, safety messages were communicated through the press, and schoolroom evacuation exercises were held.

After war was declared, thousands of Parisian children were evacuated to the provinces. More than 38,000 schoolchildren left, mostly for Auvergne, Burgundy, Limousin, and parts of western France.[65] The fathers having been either called up or volunteered to fight, their children were now packed off to French towns or villages. This was the case for the Benayouns. Simon and Guy remember:

> After war was declared, our father, although he was disabled and head of a large household, volunteered for the army, and was assigned to the cartridge factory in Vincennes. He would say, "By defending my country, I'm defending my family." We were sent to the country, to Sury-en-Vaux (Cher), with our mother and brothers and sisters. We were given the top floor of a house; another family was living on the ground floor. We all went to school. We stayed in the village until June 1940, when our mother decided to return to Paris.[66]

Children were not always kept away for such a long time. As war had not yet broken out and the dreaded aerial bombardments had not materialized, children were often brought back to Paris.

Serge Klarsfeld remembers being given a gas mask at school during this period. "We went to Conches, in Normandy, for a month or two, but then we came home." His father decided to enlist in the army and joined up to the 22nd regiment of foreign volunteers.[67]

Although they were not obliged to, some parents decided to leave Paris and its surrounding areas with their children or to send them away.

This was the case for Stanley Hoffmann and his mother: "When… war began we left for Nice, in order to escape from bombs that never fell. After three months back in my old *lycée*… we moved north again to Neuilly—since the phoney war seemed to entail no risks."[68]

In Paris, Joseph and Lisa Minc reacted in a similar manner to protect their very young daughter. They had married on 20 May 1938 and had a little girl named Betty:

> After war was declared, in September 1939, fearing bombardments, I sent Lisa and Betty to the country to stay with a dentist friend, Doctor Frankel, who lived near Mont-de-Marsan, in Saint-Sever (Landes). Meanwhile in a single special session I received my degree in dental surgery and then volunteered for the military. In late February 1940, I

was posted as a battalion dentist to the second division of the Polish army, which was stationed in Parthenay (Deux-Sèvres). Many Polish officers were anti-Semitic, but since they were happy with my services, they saw me as a "good Jew" and I had a fine relationship with them.[69]

This obsession with bombardments comes through in a number of accounts. It prompted some people to leave the capital of their own accord. That, of course, implied being able to leave, in other words, knowing where to go and having the means to live elsewhere. It was mostly French Jews who had family or friends in the provinces who left unbidden in this way.

The story of Arlette and Elie Scali is a case in point. Arlette, née Hirsh-Lévy, was part of Parisian Jewish high society. After a failed first marriage, she remarried in 1939. Her second husband, Elie Scali, owned and managed a tobacco and leather sales company. Arlette often visited Graulhet, a small town in the Tarn department where her husband owned a tannery. She often accompanied him there and had got to know the area. When war was declared, Scali made the decision to move there. "With war on the horizon, we didn't stay in Paris," she wrote in her memoirs. "We had lived through the war of 1914, when I was a child, and the still visible shrapnel damage from 'Big Bertha' on Boulevard Saint-Germain was fresh in our minds."[70] The young couple, now expecting a child, gave up their comfortable apartment in Neuilly-sur-Seine for a house equipped with only the basics. Arlette gave birth to a boy, named Philippe-David. Her husband, whose factory had been requisitioned, joined them for the circumcision ceremony. In May 1940, the whole Scali household arrived in Graulhet.[71]

The Lindons' story is similar to that of the Scalis. Denis Lindon's father, a Parisian lawyer, was also mayor of Etretat, a small seaside resort in Normandy. His wife came from a family of bankers from Alsace, the Baurs. They lived in the 16th arrondissement of Paris. In addition to Denis, the Lindons had three other children: Jérôme, Laurent and Hélène. Denis's grandfather, Alfred Lindenbaum, was a British Jew who had come to live in France in the first decade of the 1900s. He had married Fernande Citroën, and the couple had five sons, including Raymond, Denis's father. The Lindenbaums had taken the precaution of changing their name to Lindon, since at the time it was not ideal to have a name that sounded both German and Jewish. In 1939, Raymond Lindon, not yet 40 and a reserve officer, was called up as soon as the war broke out. His wife, meanwhile, afraid that the capital would be bombed, left for Etretat with their four children.[72]

For others, the question of leaving Paris did not arise, as they were already in the countryside when war was declared and decided it was wiser to remain where they were. The government moreover advised those who could to remain where they were vacationing.

Such was the situation of the Becker family, who every year spent the three summer months in Cayeux-sur-Mer (Somme), from 1 July to 1 October. But because of the war, they ended up staying for a year. Jean-Jacques Becker recalls that a mixed secondary school was opened in some requisitioned buildings and teachers were recruited locally. He recalls it as an idyllic time: "Decades later, the students of the Cayeux *lycée* reminisced wistfully about the happiest school year of their lives." As there were not enough primary school teachers, Jean-Jacques' mother was able to realize her desire to teach. According to Jean-Jacques, "the war did not take up a huge part of our lives," since "nothing happened." "For us children, we weren't in the least concerned about the outcome of the war. We had complete faith that our country, which had won the Great War not so long ago, was invincible. And in the meantime, we were delighted with our school year at the seaside."[73]

Francine Weiller and her sister Nicole had an experience similar to the Becker family. These two young girls from an Alsatian Jewish family spent their summer holidays in Saint-Malo. Their father, a lawyer in Strasbourg, had remarried in 1933 after his wife died. The girls, then aged 14 and 17, were there with their stepmother. Francine recalls that:

> It was impossible for us to get back to Strasbourg, as the evacuation of the city had been ordered. My father went to Saverne (Alsace) where the court had been transferred temporarily and got permission to go to our Strasbourg apartment. Since he did not take the conflict seriously, he just tidied up a bit and took a few things with him: he was convinced it would be over within a few months [...]. My stepmother, my sister Nicole, and I stayed in Saint-Malo until 1942. Nicole and I were enrolled in secondary school, which took both boys and girls given the circumstances, but then the following year we went to a girls' school that had just opened.[74]

The German attack on 10 May 1940 forced several hundred thousand civilians of other countries onto the roads of France. The first to leave their homes were the Dutch, Belgians and Luxembourgers, who hoped to find protection behind the Franco-British defense lines. The French were also panic-stricken. Some 2 million people were soon fleeing the departments of the Nord and Pas-de-Calais. The largest contingent, around 250,000, headed for Brittany.[75] The general rush southward was even more noteworthy since the migration was partially set in motion by the fleeing local elites, elected officials such as mayors, and industrialists. Those who remained behind felt abandoned. From 23 May to 5 June, military operations took place north of the Somme, temporarily halting the flood of departures. Some people even turned back, believing that the front was stabilizing.

The Markscheid family was among the first to flee as part of this exodus. They had come from Belgium. They were Polish Jews, originally from Galicia (now in Poland and Ukraine). Meir Markscheid was an erudite man who spoke ten languages and who, in addition to his job as an accountant, had served as a rabbi in his native Galicia. In the early 1920s, he became engaged to one of his young cousins, Taube. They immigrated to Belgium in 1927 and in 1928 respectively, and married in December 1929. Meir was working as head of publicity for the Liège World's Fair, before becoming, in 1932, the Belgian sales representative for the German firm Kraemer, which manufactured meat-processing machines. The Markscheids settled in Brussels, and then, as their business expanded, moved to Anderlecht in 1936. They had two children: Fanny, born in 1930, and Léa, born in 1936.

"In the late 1930s [...] my parents were well on their way to be fully integrated in their adoptive country," Léa wrote in her memoirs. But the German invasion wrecked everything. The family decided to leave as soon as they could:

> On 13 May 1940, we set off very early in the morning, having piled all we could into the car [...]. Our initial destination was Normandy, and from there, England, where my father hoped to be able to join a resistance movement while we waited to continue our journey and emigrate to the United States where we had relatives. [...] We headed towards the French border, the only one that could still be crossed, along with tens of thousands of terror-stricken civilians. [...] We carried all of our savings hidden on our persons. My parents were used to challenges and uncertainty and knew how to survive. My mother hadn't forgotten her escape with her own parents during World War I."
> After many hitches and scares they reached Dunkirk, but the last boat

for England had left, so they decided to head to southern France in the hope of reaching Portugal.[76]

Millions of civilians on the roads

The German offensive of 5 June unleashed another tidal wave of refugees, even more overwhelming than the first. The rapid advance of the *panzers*, backed up with air support, was spectacular. Civilians soon recognized the gravity of the situation: overcome by a collective sense of panic, several million fled southward by any means possible.

The incredible deluge of people grew as the government itself, headed by Paul Reynaud, fled the capital. Almost 2 million Parisians left, amid utter chaos. Hundreds of overcrowded trains left the city between 8 and 13 June, choking the southbound lines. Swarms of people were trying to cross the Loire, as a persistent rumor held that the river was France's ultimate line of defense. Some refugees perished in aerial bombardments or hails of bullets from Stuka bombers as they attempted to get across. At the same time, streams of refugees converged in Lyon on their way south or to the Massif Central. After Italy entered the war on 10 June, another swell of refugees began to move towards the center of the country and the Pyrenees. In all, approximately 8 million people found themselves on the roads during those terrible weeks of May and June 1940.[77]

A journalist from Paris, Léon Werth, a French Jew and veteran of the Great War, was part of this immense caravan of people fleeing the capital to escape the Germans. A native of the Vosges, he had planned to go to his house in Saint-Amour (Jura). On 11 June, he left Paris with his wife Suzanne and their maid Andrée. Werth kept a diary of this extraordinary journey in which he described the unbelievable chaos of the stream of refugees in which he was caught up, frequently brought to a halt and targeted by dive-bombers. Along the way, the Werths were sometimes given shelter by farmers, but they also spent many nights in the open. In their car they drove past dazed and filthy French soldiers. Once, having run out of gas, they camped out near a farm where the mistress of the house, Madame Soutreux, willingly housed German soldiers, even going so far as to offer them champagne. With the help of a German soldier, Léon Werth managed to get hold of some petrol and the group was able to continue on its way to the Jura. As they neared their final destination, they were overcome by an intoxicating sense of freedom: "We were no more than 60 km from home. We were in the Free Zone [...]. We were free! Free and in France! The words made us giddy. The land was no longer covered with Germans; the land was no longer covered with defeat. We could go where we pleased. An hour later, we arrived. We had left Paris on 11 June. It was 13 July. I found my son and the peace of familiar fields, land and sky."They had arrived at their destination, thirty-three days after leaving Paris.[78]

No place to go: the case of Jewish immigrants

Among the hordes of panic-stricken civilians were not only French Jews like Léon Werth, but immigrant Jews as well. They had left the capital in smaller numbers, since they had nowhere to go. They had few if any options of somewhere to stay in the countryside, and so they tended to head for cities or towns. Arriving somewhere more or less by accident, they would stay for a while in a furnished room, boarding house or small hotel. But competition was fierce; towns and cities were so overcrowded with refugees that they sometimes had to sleep in the street. Some tried their luck by heading out to the countryside and finding a village to stay in. Their different trajectories are infinitely diverse.

The Markscheid family, for instance, made its way as best they could southward in the hope of crossing into Spain. When they eventually reached Toulouse, they were not allowed to continue. They had to register with the "Foreigner Police," as Léa recalled in her memoir, and have their visa renewed every six months. So much for their plan to go to Portugal and from there to the United States. The Markscheids did not know a soul in Toulouse. The city was overflowing with refugees, so they looked for lodgings in the environs. They ended up finding shelter in Larra, a few kilometers from Toulouse, with a farming couple, the Duffauts, who agreed to give them lodgings in exchange for help on the farm.

The story of Sal and Mia Kanner, who arrived in Montmorency, 13 km north of Paris, is very different. When war was declared, Sal, the father, was interned as a German citizen in a camp in Maisons-Laffitte. Mia found herself alone with her three daughters. The wife of the mayor of Montmorency, who was herself Jewish, suggested that she place them in the care of the Œuvre de Secours aux Enfants (OSE, the Children's Welfare Organization), which ran a center in the town in the Villa Helvetia. Mia was at first very reluctant, but as she had no way of providing for them, she eventually agreed to this solution. The OSE found her a job as a cook and secured a visa for her as a foreign resident that entitled her to work. It is clear that from the very beginning of the war that the assistance the family received from this Jewish charity was of decisive importance. After of the attack of May 1940, the Montmorency care center was evacuated on 5 June to the department of Haute-Vienne, where the OSE rented premises near the Château de Montintin. But Mia discovered that her papers would not permit her to follow her daughters there. And so this foreign woman, separated from her three daughters and her husband, found herself itinerant and alone during the tumultuous period of France's catastrophic defeat. Although she had received a letter saying that the visas for Palestine her husband had applied for five years before were ready, she was told she had to go and pick them up in person—in London. She and three other OSE members who, foreigners like herself, could not leave for Montintin as none of them had the proper papers, took to the road and headed for Paris, merging into the flood of people joining the exodus. When she arrived in Paris, Mia went to the offices of the Zionist Organization, but found the building deserted. Her traveling companions meanwhile were unable to locate any of their friends in the capital. The four of them decided to board a southbound freight train without knowing its destination. When the train ran out of coal, the passengers found shelter in a village, whose name Mia could not remember. After two days, the little group decided to set out for Montintin on foot. After walking for five days, the group split, with two of them deciding to try to cross the Pyrenees into Spain and the other two, Mia and Hilda, who continued on to Montintin. Mia was finally reunited with her three overjoyed daughters, Ruth, Eva and Léa. Mia had walked so far that her feet were raw and her legs extremely painful, but all that mattered was that she had been reunited with her daughters. She returned to her job as cook at the children's home, where she single handedly prepared meals for over 100 people.[79]

The Becker family, who had remained in the department of the Somme, had no contact with any type of organized network. "In

Cayeux, we were theoretically far from the front, but panic had started to set in," writes Jean-Jacques Becker. "It was clear that the Germans were getting closer." One day, during a gym class, a cannon shot rang out. The teacher tried to reassure the pupils by saying it was merely an exercise, but it really was the Germans, who were now in Abbeville, 30 km away from Cayeux. At noon, his father arrived in his car and the whole family joined the exodus. The Beckers wanted to get at least as far as Saint-Brévin-les-Pins (Loire-Atlantique) where they knew they would be taken in by their former concierge, with whom they remained on good terms, who ran a hotel that she had invited them to visit. The journey proved to be long and arduous. They spent one night in a town called Les Andelys, and as the hotels were all full, Jean-Jacques and Henri slept in the car. When they at last reached their destination, the father found a house to rent and the three oldest went to school in Saint Nazaire. But when the Germans closed in on Nantes, "it didn't make sense to keep running. It was obvious that nothing would stop them. I lived through scenes that would forever leave their mark on me, the crushing defeat of the French army.[80] Jean-Jacques claims not to remember the episode his sister Annie Kriegel recounts in her memoirs, when their father supposedly wept when he heard about the defeat. "In a trembling voice, our father said, 'Children, France has been defeated' and then he added, 'and we are Jewish.'"[81]

The mother of the Lindon family also decided to leave Etretat with her children. Still without news of her husband, she took them to Brittany, "where relatives of ours lived," as Denis recalled. Then, as the Germans advanced, they went further, towards the Tarn, where friends had invited them to join them. "It was there, in Anglès, that we found my father, demobilized and fortunate enough not to have been taken prisoner."

Stanley Hoffmann's mother knew very few people in France. She wanted to leave Neuilly-sur-Seine as quickly as she could, but her son had to have an appendectomy on 10 May, the very day the Germans attacked. "On May 10, 1940, my unquiet world collapsed: the Germans invaded the Low Countries and France—and I had an emergency operation for appendicitis! Barely convalescent, I fled with my mother, and 10 million other people, just two days before the Germans entered Paris. It took three days—in someone else's car—to travel the 100 miles from Paris to Tours. We reached Bordeaux in time to hear Marshal Pétain's call for an armistice." The Hoffmanns finally ended up in Lamalou-les-Bains, a small spa town in Languedoc where they had spent a few days in summer 1939. Several thousand refugees from Belgium and northern France had gathered there.[82]

Other foreign Jews also went to spa towns, often the few places they knew in France. Some of them, like the Hoffmanns, had visited as tourists before the war, or had heard about them through friends, like the Friedländers, who left Paris shortly after war was declared and headed to Néris-les-Bains (Allier). Other Jewish families also went to Vichy, another famous spa town.

Turning around and going back

The end of military combat and the formation of the Vichy government helped to stem the tide of refugees and restore calm. But the new peace had the bitter taste of surrender. Hundreds of thousands of French soldiers had been made prisoners of war, while others were demobilized. From then on, the country had to go back to a semblance of normal life and somehow resume routine activities. Philippe Burrin calls this period, whose compromises took a heavy toll on a nation that was so proud of its values and its rank in the world, a time of "accommodation."[83]

Refugees who had joined the exodus manifested early signs of this desire to return to normalcy, setting out on the road home to get back to work. The French and German authorities encouraged them, but under certain conditions. "On 1 August 1940, instructions for planning their return were published in a booklet handed out to the French entitled *Lignes de démarcation et dispositions générales* (Demarcation Lines and General Arrangements); a map accompanied the text showing the checkpoints where refugees were to cross. Refugees were divided into several categories."[84] It stated that refugees could return to the Central Zone as well as the Paris area, while the Germans forbade any return beyond the Northeast Line. This new boundary, which was not anticipated by the armistice, separated the Occupied Zone from what was called the "Forbidden Zone." 250,000 refugees from the "Northern" and "Eastern" zones were thus stuck in the Free Zone and another 500,000 in the non-forbidden Occupied Zone.

Moreover, the Germans made it known that Jews who were in the so-called Free Zone were not authorized to return to the Occupied Zone, by virtue of an MBF ordinance dated 27 September 1940. This was a ban imposed specifically on Jews, making it clear that that Berlin did not yet have plans to implement the "Final Solution." Nazi Germany intended to chase the Jews out and in fact viewed the Free Zone as a "dumping ground" for all "undesirables." In a letter dated 10 February 1941 to General Stülpnagel, General Doyen called the Free Zone a "spillway."[85] This policy had dramatic consequences on Jews from Baden and Palatinate, such as the Mayer family from Hoffenheim, who were interned in Gurs, while 8,400 German Jews who had fled to Bordeaux were expelled on 8 August 1940 to the Free Zone.

Whether or not they were aware of the German prohibition, those who sensed danger did not rush back to their homes in the Occupied Zone.

Vidal Nahum was not among the throngs of the exodus. He was mobilized in March 1940 at the age of 46 and stationed with his brigade at a munitions factory in Bourges. In June 1940, the regiment was caught up in the retreat; his outfit scattered and he made his way to Toulouse. Many members of the Nahum family were in the city; one of his brothers had arrived there from Brussels. His brothers and sisters planned to settle there, but once he was demobilized, Vidal decided to return to Paris. Edgar Morin tells how his father asked several people whether the fact that he was Jewish put him at risk in the city, now occupied by the Reich. His captain said to him, "Nahum, don't worry. You are a French soldier. Go back home to Paris. It's not written on your face that you're Jewish. Go home calmly, don't worry, you go back with your head high." Vidal, having managed to secure a mission order from the Marseille chamber of commerce, left for Paris on 16 August 1940. He returned to his apartment and his store, while his son Edgar stayed on in Toulouse to continue his studies.[86]

Léon Poliakov was called up in September 1939. His unit was captured at Saint-Valéry-en-Caux. Poliakov, who spoke German, was sent to negotiate their surrender, which was granted with military honors. The prisoners were made to walk to Germany, averaging 30 km per day, and suffered terribly from hunger. Knowing German was a precious asset, Léon Poliakov notes, making it possible to communicate with the victors and to become part of the group of "prosperous" prisoners who ate far better than the others. Poliakov, who wanted to avoid leaving French territory, made plans for his escape. He volunteered to do the stocktaking of the supplies left behind by the British, under the command of *Oberzahlmeister* Rohr, who told him that from then on the French and Germans were going to live together as brothers. Rohr favored the smarter prisoners under his command, among them several Jews, who helped to siphon off supplies for him to send back to his family in Germany. It was an "unbelievable" situation, in which the prisoners found themselves fraternizing with their jailers. One German soldier even confessed to Poliakov his doubts that the Nazi regime would survive. When Rohr's unit received orders to go to Le Mans, the *Oberzahlmeister* invited the Jews either to remain with him, telling them that "you'll be better off than with the SS," or proposing to drop them off on the way in Paris, which is how Poliakov managed to get back to the capital.[87]

Joseph Minc joined a regiment of the Polish army in Deux-Sèvres, from where he was sent to Alsace as a stretcher-bearer. After the German attack, he was taken prisoner on 23 June 1940 in Montbéliard and interned in a camp in Belfort, where he declared himself to be Jewish. The inmates in the camp were mistreated and forced to collect mortar shells in the surrounding woods. Then:

> On 30 September 1940, in spite of the fact that I was Jewish, I was released on account of my qualifications—they were freeing certain categories of people, including people who worked in the medical service and, as a dental surgeon, I was one of them. I was given German papers certifying that I'd been released from the camp, which, for a while, protected me from arrest. I went back to Paris, where I was reunited with my wife and daughter, who had also returned. We lived near the Rex cinema in the 2nd arrondissement.

Some of those who found themselves in the Occupied Zone after the exodus preferred to return home. Moving from one place to another within the Occupied Zone made little difference, except that for some it meant they could go home.

The Beckers left the Nantes area in September 1940 to return to Paris. Jean-Jacques recalls: "No one was in the mood to laugh anymore. The future seemed dark. After being away for a year, what a change!

The Paris of our childhood had abruptly turned into 'German' Paris. All over the city Germans had put up signposts for their soldiers, and Nazi flags waved over public buildings."[88]

The Benayouns returned to Paris from Sury-en-Vaux in the summer of 1940. "The journey was long and tiring," Guy and Simon recalled. [...] We had grown and there were now too many of us to squeeze into our one-bedroom apartment on rue Popincourt, so our father rented another place on rue de la Roquette and we split up between the two apartments."

Those who had made it to the Free Zone usually stayed where they were, either because they did not have the means to leave, or because they had no desire to throw themselves into the jaws of the enemy. In any event, if they were identified as Jews, they were prohibited from entering the Occupied Zone. Accordingly, they tried to find somewhere to settle in Vichy France, where German uniforms were a rare sight and where one still had a semblance of freedom, as Léon Werth put it in his diary upon his arrival in Saint Amour. Whether this decision was taken freely or because they had no other choice, most of those whose biographies are interwoven here decided to remain in the Free Zone.

Mia Kanner was living at Montintin with her daughters where, in October 1940, her husband Sal arrived, after several very eventful months. Having been initially imprisoned in Maisons-Laffitte, he was then transferred to a camp in Bordeaux. Shortly before the German invasion the prisoners were released by their French guards. Sal made his way to Bayonne in the vain hope of leaving for England; he managed instead to get to Spain but, worried about his family, he decided to turn back. With no papers, he was interned at Gurs, where he found his sister-in-law Edith, who told him that that Hannah, another of Mia's sisters, and her husband Herman were living in Villeneuve-sur-Lot. Having assured the camp authorities that he had relatives he could go to, Sal was released. He and Edith went to Hannah's home, where he discovered that Mia and their daughters were at Montintin, and so he set out to join her.[89]

Meanwhile, the Markscheids remained in the Toulouse area. In autumn 1940 they left the farm in Larra for the small town of Grenade where they rented a house in the Bastide neighborhood.

The Hoffmanns decided to leave Lamalou for Nice, where they had lived before, while Alfred Grosser stayed in Saint-Raphaël with his sister and their mother, who had come to join them. The Lindons left for Aix-en-Provence while the Scalis saw no reason to leave Graulhet, near Albi.

This was how gathering points tended to form, especially in the southeast and the southwest regions of the Free Zone. In the south, the city of Marseille attracted those who hoped to leave France by boat while there was still time. In this "city of last hopes,"[90] a young American journalist and writer, Varian Fry, was entrusted with the mission of helping "great minds" in all intellectual domains escape to the United States.[91]

During this period, people clearly made different choices depending on their personal histories and the opportunities open to them. Among the biographies drawn on for this study, some, such as the Markscheids, wanted to leave but were unable to bring their plans to fruition. Some people were also torn by contradictory choices, like Sal Kanner who, after having managed to enter Spain decided to return to France, not wanting to abandon his wife and children. Sometimes even within the same family paths diverged and different choices were made.

From the Occupied Zone to the Free Zone

By winter 1940–1941, tens of thousands of Jews, both French and foreign, had relocated to the central, southwestern, and southeastern regions of the country. With some exceptions, the fact that they were Jewish generally passed unnoticed by the local people they encountered on the way. They were simply seen as refugees, unfortunates— victims of the war and thus of the Germans. Not always intentionally, some ended up in the Occupied Zone, while others found themselves in the Free Zone, separated by what was now called the "demarcation line." This division was of major importance until 11 November 1942, but at that time no one really knew what impact the artificial border would have on individual destinies, depending on whether a person was on the "right" or the "wrong" side, and whether they made it across the line without being captured.

The decision to leave Paris and yet remain in the Occupied Zone seems surprising today. This, however, was the choice made by the novelist Irène Némirovsky, who lived in Paris with her husband, Michel Epstein, and their two daughters, Denise and Elisabeth. After war was declared, the children were sent to stay with their nanny's mother in Issy-L'Évêque, a small village in the Morvan, where Irène and Michel joined them after the fall of France. The village ended up within the Occupied Zone, but things might have been different: the demarcation line was very close by. However, Irène and Michel seem to have had no plans to cross it. The family moved into a large house in the center of the village. Michel often served as a translator for the Germans, while Irène was busy writing her new book, *Suite Française*. On 13 July 1942, she was arrested and sent to Pithiviers. On 17 July, she was deported to Auschwitz, where she died of typhus on 19 August 1942. Her husband was arrested on 9 October 1942. He was sent to Drancy then deported to Auschwitz, where he was gassed on arrival in November 1942.[92]

In this dismembered France, a large part of which was occupied, Vichy tried to put its National Revolution project into practice. People who were branded as Jews were the first to suffer, and painfully so, due to numerous measures: the anti-Semitic laws called the *Statut des Juifs* of 3 and 4 October 1940, which barred Jews from holding posts of power and "influence" in the police, the courts, educational establishments and management positions in private companies; the creation on 29 March 1941 of the *Commissariat Général aux Questions Juives* (CGQJ— General Commission for Jewish Affairs) headed by Xavier Vallat, a politician well-known since the 1930s for his anti-Semitic convictions;[93] the second *Statut des Juifs* of 2 June 1941, which banned Jews from working in banking, the arms industry and advertising, and excluded them from various artistic and journalistic professions. Overnight, this cascade of measures caused enormous hardship for both individuals and families as the people they targeted found themselves jobless and thus without an income.

Variations in living conditions

Even in the Free Zone, Vichy interned many foreigners declared "suspect" in camps that had been created during the Third Republic to intern refugees fleeing the Spanish Civil War. A law passed on 3 September 1940 authorized the administrative detention of individuals deemed a danger to national defense or public safety. One month later, on 4 October 1940, the *Statut des Juifs* made it became possible to intern foreign Jews by a simple prefectural decree. In late 1940, some 50,000 people, most of them foreigners, were estimated to be interned in camps in France.[94] Among these internees were several thousand Jewish immigrants. The best known of these internment camps were Gurs (Basses-Pyrénées) where the Mayers were imprisoned, Rivesaltes (Pyrénées-Orientales), Vernet (Haute-Garonne), Bram (Aude), Argelès and Saint-Cyprien (Pyrénées Orientales), and the Camp des Milles (Bouches-du-Rhône) for foreigners pending their emigration. There were many other camps, operating under different regimes, which brought together diverse categories of internees.[95] Living conditions in these places were usually very harsh, and often degrading. Supplies were often short and sanitation inadequate, leading to a number of epidemics. Over 3,000 people died during their internment, over 1,000 in the Gurs camp alone, with the largest number of deaths occurring during the winter of 1940–1941. Among them was Fred and Heinz Mayer's grandmother. These internment camps served as "human pools" for forced labor, as much for the occupying forces as for Vichy. As of late 1940, thousands of male internees were transferred to *Groupes de Travailleurs Étrangers* (GTE-foreign labor units), which were closely linked to the system of internment camps.

Living conditions in the Occupied Zone and the Free Zone differed considerably. While the same discriminatory laws against Jews applied in both zones, the political contexts of their enforcement were different on either side of the demarcation line, which is why the flow of migration from the Occupied to the Free Zone grew over 1941 and 1942, right until Germany invaded southern France on 11 November 1942. This movement of people—not only Jews—fleeing occupation and persecution is sociological and quantitative proof of the attraction of the Free Zone to people living in the Northern Zone. The illegal and hazardous crossings gave rise to a lucrative and risky business of smuggling people over the demarcation line.[96]

At least three reasons explain the migration of Jews to the Free Zone. First, the Free Zone symbolized what remained of French sovereignty after the Reich's victory. Vichy France was still France, in other words, a great nation that was trying in vain to retain a semblance of dignity, embodied in the person of the elderly Marshal Pétain, and some level of effectiveness in government. One unmistakable sign was the swift transfer by the main Jewish organizations of their headquarters to the Free Zone. The chief rabbi of France, Isaïe Schwartz, followed Marshal Pétain to Vichy; the Central Consistory set up its offices in Lyon; the Consistory of the Bas-Rhin left Alsace-Moselle and set up in Vichy as well. The highest density of Jews in the Southern Zone was in the Mediterranean area, which saw its pre-war Jewish population swell to eight or ten times its size between 1940 and 1942.

Another reason had to do with how Jewish immigrants in Paris imagined the Free Zone. As their situation gradually deteriorated, they were happy to believe that life was better and above all that one ate better on the other side of the demarcation line.[97]

The third and most specific reason was that the increase in anti-Semitic persecution began earlier and was more brutal in areas placed directly under Nazi control. This was made manifest in Paris in early 1941, when group arrests and roundups began; similar operations did not begin in the Free Zone until a year later, at the end of August 1942.

The occupying forces tried to stem these departures by seeking to keep Jews from moving from where they lived. Starting on 10 December 1941, any change of address within the Seine department (including Paris and its immediate suburbs) had to be reported to the nearest police station in both the place of departure and the place of arrival. Permission was required to leave the department, which was granted only in exceptional cases. Scarcely two months later, on 7 February 1942, the even more draconian sixth German military ordinance came into force, imposing a curfew on Jews between 8 p.m. and 6 a.m., and decreeing that it was "forbidden for them to change their current place of residence." It is likely that these measures intending to keep Jews from leaving the Occupied Zone were fairly effective, but they did not dissuade the most determined to flee to the Free Zone.

Causes and evaluation of southward migrations

Although it is impossible to calculate the precise number of departures, certain characteristics of the migration from north to south can be identified. Firstly, there were those who decided to move to the Free Zone independently of any measures of repression that had been instituted—they wanted to leave, if they could, because they had somehow fallen foul of the *Statut des Juifs*, for example they had lost their jobs.

The case of Vidal Nahum differs somewhat from this model, for he found himself "trapped" in the Free Zone: he had returned to Paris despite the ban on doing so after the armistice, and was "doing well" there. With a laissez-passer that he had obtained, and his passport—which, unlike his identity card, was not stamped with the word *Juif*—he was able to make several trips to Toulouse to visit his son Edgar between May and August 1941. On 23 July, traveling south, Vidal was subject to an identity check on the train. He showed his passport and his *Ausweis*, but the Germans, who were looking for a man of Vidal's appearance who was smuggling money, searched him further; they made him empty his suitcase, ripped the lining out of his beret and his overcoat, and examined his shoes. The anxiety this created was such that once he got to Toulouse he decided not to return to Paris. This extended stay had not been planned and Vidal regretted not having brought all his money with him, which would have enabled him to open a store in the city.[98]

Physical repression was also a factor that prompted people to flee Paris, which alerted people even more to the danger of the situation. However, few people in Paris foresaw the catastrophic scenario of the mass arrests of both foreign and French Jews which were soon to take place: "Between May and December 1941, three major police operations took place in Paris, each with a different *modus operandi*, but they had in common the fact that they were ordered by the German military command in France (MBF) with the support of the administrative and police machinery of the French Prefecture of Police (PP)."[99] The first roundup occurred on 14 May: the Paris police arrested 3,500 Jewish immigrants who had been summoned to have their "status examined." Most were Polish, but there were also a number of Czechs and stateless persons living in the 11th, 20th, 10th, 17th, and 4th arrondissements. All were transferred to the camps in Pithiviers and Beaune-la-Rolande (Loiret). Another operation took place on 20 August 1941: the 11th arrondissement in Paris was entirely sealed off in the wee hours of the morning. This operation resulted in the internment of 3,000 foreign Jews between the ages of 18 and 50 in the Drancy camp. In the days that followed, another thousand or so arrests were made in eastern Paris. Finally, on 12 December, in retaliation for a series of anti-German attacks, the *Feldgendarmerie*, with the aid of the SS and the French police, arrested another 743 prominent Jewish figures, all male, almost all of them French citizens, living in the wealthy neighborhoods of the capital. They were first rounded up at the École Militaire, then later transferred to the German-run camp in Compiègne.[100]

This series of mass arrests not only took the individuals and their families entirely by surprise, but it had not been anticipated by Jewish organizations in Paris either. As long as the repression remained on an administrative and economic level, it was still possible to cope with it and manage things after a fashion. But once the repression became physical, in the form of the incarceration or the "disappearance" of family members or friends, it called for a different response. An arrest was often the factor that triggered the decision to leave for the Free Zone. Perception of the danger nevertheless remained subjective, which explains why in 1941 there were still many potential victims who had not yet decided to make the move.

It is very hard to gauge the migratory flows during the year 1941 with any precision. Most of the available data comes from the CGQJ and must be considered with caution. There has been a great deal of historical analysis of the relevance, limitations, and bias of the data collected by the Vichy administration, which were compiled on the basis of those who either voluntarily declared themselves as Jewish or who were denounced as such. For reference, the map below localizes the "Jewish presence" in France using the results of the census ordered by the law of 2 June 1941 in both zones. The map shows the distribution of Jews in France after the migrations that followed the fall of France, according to the administrative divisions in effect at the time, in other words, in the nineteen provinces that came into being with the law of 19 April 1941.

In autumn 1941, nearly 150,000 Jews were counted in the Occupied Zone, 125,000 of them in the Seine department alone. This figure includes the 7,000 Jews interned in camps (Drancy, Beaune-la-Rolande, Pithiviers) as well as the other 20,000 Jews in other departments of the Northern Zone. Of this total, there were 92,864 Jews over the age of 15 in the Seine department and 15,061 Jews over 15 in the other departments of the Occupied Zone.[101]

In the Free Zone, the CGQJ recorded the presence of 109,244 Jews on 15 September 1941, of whom 57,000 were French and 53,000 foreign (including 9,250 internees). As in the Occupied Zone, these statistics do not appear to take into account either the total number of Jewish internees or children under the age of 15. Unlike in the Northern Zone, this population was more dispersed, although over a third of these hounded Jews were located in just three departments: Bouches-du-Rhône, Rhône, and Alpes-Maritimes, largely because cities such as Marseille, Nice, and Cannes had become the temporary home for a significant number of Jewish refugees after the fall of France in 1940. Furthermore, between 15 and 20 per cent of those counted were interned at the time in camps in the Southern Zone, which explains the high figures for the departments of Basses-Pyrénées, where the Gurs camp was located, and the Pyrénées-Orientales, where the Rivesaltes camp was located.[102] The influx of Jews to cities such as Lyon, Marseille, and Nice was not surprising, given the existence of Jewish communities in these cities prior to 1939 (Map 1). One of the primary effects of the flow of departures towards the Free Zone was to cause an increase in the size of the Jewish population in these cities and their outlying areas.

Several departments that had very few—under 100—French Jewish inhabitants before the war saw a considerable rise in the number of Jewish refugees in this period. Studies of these areas have highlighted this phenomenon. It is likely that migration towards the Free Zone evolved in a similar way between the second half of 1941 and the early months of 1942, with those who had already made it to the Free Zone able to offer refuge to those who were trying to leave the capital. In this way, individuals and families might join forces, or became part of an informal web of relations in towns and villages.

The largest wave of departures, during the summer of 1942, probably intensified two parallel trends: the densification of the Jewish population in cities or regions where Jews were already living before the war; and the increasingly widespread dispersal of the Jewish population into rural areas that had previously had virtually no Jewish inhabitants.

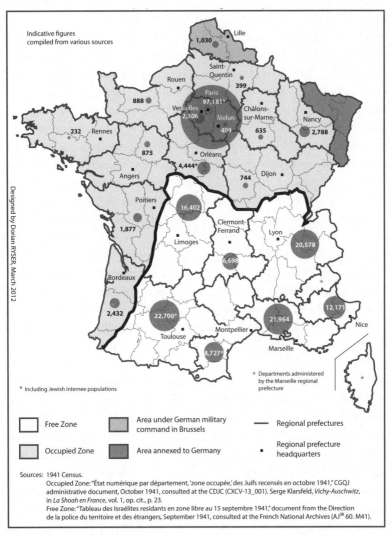

Indicative figures
compiled from various sources

Lille
1,030
Saint-
Quentin
Rouen   399
888   Paris
Versailles 97,181*   Châlons-
2,306   Melun   sur-Marne   Nancy
Orléans 409   635   2,788
232   Rennes
875
4,444*
Angers   Dijon
Poitiers   744
16,402
1,877   Clermont-
Ferrand   Lyon
Limoges   20,578
6,698
Bordeaux
2,432
22,700*   21,964   12,171
Toulouse   Montpellier   Nice
8,727*   Marseille

Designed by Dorian RYSER, March 2012

* Departments administered
by the Marseille regional
prefecture

* Including Jewish internee populations

☐ Free Zone	☐ Area under German military command in Brussels	── Regional prefectures
☐ Occupied Zone	☐ Area annexed to Germany	▪ Regional prefecture headquarters

Sources: 1941 Census.
Occupied Zone: "État numérique par département, 'zone occupée,' des Juifs recensés en octobre 1941," CGQJ
administrative document, October 1941, consulted at the CDJC (CXCV-13_001). Serge Klarsfeld, *Vichy-Auschwitz*,
in *La Shoah en France*, vol. 1, op. cit., p. 23.
Free Zone: "Tableau des Israélites residants en zone libre au 15 septembre 1941," document from the Direction
de la police du territoire et des étrangers, September 1941, consulted at the French National Archives (AJ[38] 60. M41).

Map 3: Distribution of the Jewish population, September–October 1941

Occupied Zone prompted a new wave of departures among those to whom the measure applied, especially since Vichy did not impose the wearing of the yellow star, which was one more reason to be tempted to try and reach the Free Zone. This new migration was limited to the last two weeks of June and the first half of July 1942.

The situation changed radically after the mass arrests of stateless foreign Jews on 16 and 17 July, known today as the "Vel' d'Hiv' roundup."[103] This event struck terror into the population, as no one had ever imagined women and children being arrested, despite rumors circulating in the days leading up to the operation, which was carried out by the Paris police. How could they possibly pose any danger to the occupying forces? The operation targeted not only Jewish women and children who were foreign or stateless, but also French Jewish children with foreign parents. This unthinkable expansion of the targeted "undesirables" provoked considerable outrage. Even as the arrests were taking place, some people were inspired to help, hiding children and their mothers. Nevertheless, 12,884 Jews, most of them foreign, were caught in the net and deported in the following weeks.[104] This tragic event jolted the Jews into action, whether they were foreign or French. Some changed address but remained in Paris. Others tried to take their children to safety if possible in the Free Zone, and to leave themselves. A new wave of departures southward—several thousand people— began in the following weeks, peaking in the months of August and September 1942.

Sophie Krajcer was one of the people arrested during the roundup. Her husband Simon was working as a laborer on a farm in the Ardennes run by the Germans, but even so his name appeared on the list the two police officers had in hand when they came to her door on 16 July 1942. Sophie's daughters Annette and Léa were not on the list, presumably because they were French citizens. Nonetheless, they refused to be separated from their mother and all three were sent to the Vel' d'Hiv' and then, three days later, to the Pithiviers internment camp. Simon Krajcer, who arrived in Paris two days later with authorization from his German supervisor to move his family close to him, was unable to obtain the release of his wife and daughters. Sophie was deported on 3 August in a "convoy of mothers," and their daughters were transferred to Drancy on 15 August 1942.

Having been warned of the danger, the Becker family agreed to separate and were not at home. As the family had long been French citizens, no one came to arrest them. Jean-Jacques explains that his parents had already made up their minds to leave the city. They had taken a long time to reach this decision and planned their departure on around 20 July 1942 in minute detail:

> On the given day [...] the whole family set off. The evening before, we had made a memorable meal—there were soft-boiled eggs, it was extraordinary, it was such a luxury—to use up some of the food we couldn't take with us. We gave the rest to our neighbors. Our feelings, mine at least, were not completely clear. [...] On the one hand, there was heartache that we were being forced to leave our home, sadness that we were leaving the neighborhood where I'd always lived, knowing I would not be going back to school in September; but the main thing, given everything that had happened, was relief that we were leaving the Occupied Zone.

They left by train and went down to Saint-Pierre-Le-Moutier to stay with a family who knew a smuggler. They walked a few kilometers to reach a swimming area in the Allier River, which served as the demarcation line, but found themselves faced with an unexpected problem: the Germans had forbidden people to swim in this area, having realized that people were pretending to go for a swim but were actually getting across the line. A German soldier in bathing trunks came over to tell them that swimming was forbidden. According to Jean-Jacques, he simply walked away, whereas Annie recalled being shot at.[105] Despite it being forbidden, the whole family jumped in eventually and swam across to the other side.[106]

Crossing the line was dangerous, but not impossible. In some places, the internal border was more like a "sieve."[107] During the summer 1942, many Jews managed to cross over into the Free Zone more or less under cover, though they were never safe from denunciation or an unfortunate combination of circumstances. For some, attempts to cross went badly awry, and they found themselves trapped. Some illegal immigrants were arrested as suspicious foreigners. In such cases, they would be taken to an internment camp or a GTE, and from there were most likely deported. In the summer of 1942, being arrested at the demarcation line carried a much heavier risk than in the autumn of

1940. If they were foreign or stateless Jews, their lives were endangered during this period, with the French government actively involved in deporting foreign Jews to Poland. Moreover, as of 18 April 1942, a ministerial circular imposed special rules requiring all Jews—French, foreign or stateless—to report any change of residence. They were required to declare any change of address of more than thirty days to the city hall or police station at both their place of departure and arrival, or else be punished by internment or house arrest. Being caught taking the train to cross the line illegally was proof of contravening the new legislation.

On 26 August 1942, Vichy conducted a large-scale operation against stateless Jews on its territory: 6,584 people were arrested and immediately sent to Drancy, and 4,700 Jewish internees in the camps of southern France met with the same fate. Altogether, in August and September, twenty-two convoys left Drancy for Auschwitz.[108]

While greater clemency reigned in the Free Zone than in the Occupied Zone, it was in no sense a safe haven for Jews. A person's fate could change in a matter of minutes. Making it to the Free Zone was a new stage in their turbulent and uncertain itinerary; they no longer had to wear the yellow star, which meant that they could more easily blend in with the crowd. But while they had for the time being managed to escape danger, they were far from safe. They had only just fled the Northern Zone when the Wehrmacht invaded the south. The Germans were once again on their heels.

The Attraction of the Italian Zone and Dispersal into Rural Areas

In reaction to the Allied landing in North Africa on 8 November 1942, three days later, on 11 November, the Wehrmacht invaded the Free Zone. Mainland France was now entirely occupied by foreign armies, with Italy simultaneously taking control of the departments located east of the Rhône. Hitler nevertheless still claimed to recognize Vichy's sovereignty and that the armistice convention of 1940 remained in effect. This meant that the former "Free" Zone was not technically an "occupied" territory: it was called instead a "militarized zone." Berlin still needed the administrative and authoritarian instruments of the French state to manage and control the newly conquered territories in the former Free Zone, now called the "Southern Zone."

Overnight, the outlook became even more worrying for Jews: now the Nazis had arrived in the heart of the very regions of southern and central France where the Jews had taken refuge. Their situation nevertheless remained at once exceptional and paradoxical. On the one hand, Vichy policies hewed to those of the occupying forces. For instance, as of 7 December 1942, anyone identified as a French or foreign Jew was prohibited from traveling. This measure was aimed at keeping them in place, thereby making them more vulnerable to arrest. On the other hand, the Vichy government still refused to make wearing the yellow star mandatory, having decided not to implement the measure six months before. However, it did pass a new law on 11 December 1942, requiring the word *Juif* to be stamped on ration and identity cards as well as residence permits. This distinctive mark could have serious consequences in the event of an identity check. It was nevertheless more discreet and less demeaning than wearing the yellow star, as was required in the Northern Zone. This considerable difference between the Northern and Southern Zones continued until the end of the occupation: though they remained in great danger, Jews could hide among the local population more easily, even after the Germans occupied the south.

Another particularity of the Southern Zone was the behavior of the Italian occupier towards the Jewish populations living in the eight departments now under its control: Haute-Savoie, Savoie, Isère, Drôme, Hautes-Alpes, Basses-Alpes, Var, Alpes-Maritimes (as well as parts of Ain and Vaucluse). The Vichy government did not take kindly to this further loss of sovereignty and still sought to impose its authority over these territories. But the Italians saw things differently and began pressuring Vichy prefects not to enforce the measure of stamping *Juif* on identity cards. Beginning in December 1942, conflicts between these two sources of authority multiplied, to the benefit of the Jewish refugees.

The German authorities soon expressed their discontent with the Italians' attitude and began to pressure the Italian authorities to arrest Jews. In late March 1943, Guido Lospinoso, appointed for the occasion to inspector general of the Racial Police, was sent to Nice to organize the transfer of foreign Jews to inland regions. The Germans believed that this operation would be the last step before deportation. But they were wrong. As soon as he arrived in Nice, Lospinoso proceeded to move hundreds of refugees to Megève, Saint-Gervais, Saint-Martin-de-Vésubie, Vananson, Barcelonnette and Vence under the surveillance of his *carabinieri*. The transfer of some 4,000 people was organized with the help of the synagogue's Jewish committee. Once they arrived at their destination, the refugees were officially placed under house arrest but were actually taken care of by Jewish organizations.[109]

The Italian safe haven?

After the war, these various measures of protection were interpreted as the expression of a humanitarian policy on the part of the Italian occupying forces towards Jews living in the French territory under their control. This is the thesis promoted by Léon Poliakov, who became one of the very first researchers in France to study anti-Semitism and the persecution of Jews under the Occupation immediately after the war.[110] Some years later, Serge Klarsfeld, drawing on archival sources, put forward a similar argument.[111] How does this analysis fit in with the fact that the fascist Italian government had passed anti-Semitic laws as early as 1938? New light was shed on the subject in the first decade of the 2000s with research uncovering Mussolini's specific foreign policy goals during that time.[112] By refusing to hand over Jews living in the French territory placed under its control, it was argued, Rome wanted to demonstrate that it was sovereign in its decision-making, even with respect to its German ally. The Italian military preferred to imprison them in camps under their control rather than hand them over to the Nazis. But living conditions in these camps were appalling, and foreign (non-Italian) Jews were still in danger. In fact, Rome sought only to "protect" Italian Jews, using non-Italian Jews as bargaining chips in its relations with the Reich and the more or less puppet governments in the occupied countries. "In July 1943, on the eve of Mussolini's overthrow, Italy was just about to hand over the German Jews residing in the zone it occupied."[113]

Whatever the accuracy of these interpretations, it did not take long for the rumor to spread that the Italian zone was a safe haven for Jews. We do not have precise figures for how many reached there. Between 20,000 and 25,000 Jews, most of them with foreign (non-French) citizenship are believed to have been in the Italian zone on 1 January 1943, mostly concentrated in the area around Nice.[114] It is impossible to know how many of those were people who were already living there prior to 11 November 1942 and how many arrived afterward. As noted previously, by summer 1940 the region was already attracting a large number of both French and foreign Jewish refugees. After the exodus, the Hoffmanns left Lamalou-les-Bains to settle in Nice, while Alfred Grosser and his sister left Saint-Germain-en-Laye, in the outskirts of Paris, by bicycle, and eventually reached the area where they settled in Saint-Raphaël. One year later, the Klarsfeld family did the same, arriving in Nice in the autumn of 1941.

Jewish refugees went to many other cities in the southeastern region, in particular Grenoble, which was also in the Italian zone. As with Nice, this migratory movement began well before the Italian occupation.

Liliane Lieber and her mother were forced to leave Vichy in late 1941. "Despite our five generations of French citizenship, which we could document, we were 'invited' to leave Vichy in November 1941. Pétain's government presumably wanted to 'purify' his city. So we went to Grenoble, where another branch of our family had settled after the war of 1870. I was also delighted to be reunited there with my second natural family, the EIF [*Eclaireurs Israélites de France*—Jewish Scouts of France]."[115]

The Beckers, who had fled Paris after the Vel' d'Hiv' roundup, also headed for Grenoble in late summer 1942. Once they made it across the demarcation line, they spent the night with some friends who had a farm, and then were driven by car to Bourbon l'Archambault (Allier). The family stayed there for a month while the father sought longer-term accommodation. For the children it was a very enjoyable time: there was no food rationing, they could go swimming or walking in the forest, and play soccer. Other refugees taught them to play bridge. Then came the journey to Grenoble. The family spent a few days in a boarding house, before moving into a rented apartment in the Cours Berriat. Henri was enrolled at Lycée Champollion in an intensive university preparation class, Jean-Jacques in the same school, in the penultimate year of secondary school, Annie at Lycée Stendhal for her final year of secondary school, and Françoise in primary school. According to Jean-Jacques, "life returned to a semblance of normality, except for one tiny detail—it was impossible for my father to find work. We therefore had to live extremely frugally, which was in fact not very difficult, as there was virtually nothing left to buy."[116]

In the early months of 1943, another wave of Jewish refugees arrived in southeastern France, who knew by word of mouth that the Italians were more lenient with the Jews. The Italian zone first drew those living in nearby areas that had fallen under German control; they came from neighboring cities such as Montpellier and Marseille, for instance, after the mass arrests of Jews at the Old Port of Marseille on 22, 23 and 24 January 1943, as well as from more distant areas such as the Massif Central, Limousin, and Toulouse and its environs.

The Dreyfus family had been living in Limoges since late 1939. "In April 1943, my father decided that we would go to Haute-Savoie," Gérard Dreyfus remembers:

> Because Savoie and Haute-Savoie were occupied by Italian troops, and we knew they protected Jews. We left on trucks with benches, which were being used as buses. One had a coal-fired engine. It was a very bumpy ride. I remember going through Lyon, which was deserted. The city was terribly bleak; there was no one in the streets. We got to Annecy. We had moved during the Easter vacation because I couldn't miss school. We stayed in Annecy till the end of term, in a small hotel called the Hôtel du Lac, near the prefecture, and I went to school at the Lycée Berthollet.

In 1942 Léon Poliakov left his position as personal secretary to Rabbi Zalman Schneerson in Marseille and went to Saint-Étienne to join his friend Oswaldo Bardone, whom he knew from the army. Poliakov, who was becoming increasingly active in the Resistance, went to Grenoble just after the Germans took over from the Italian occupiers. He describes the atmosphere there as "explosive." Rabbi Schneerson also headed to Grenoble in early 1943 with his group of children and adults and moved into a château 30 km outside the city.[117] Vidal Nahum chose to live in the Italian zone as well: he settled in Nice where several other family members had taken refuge.[118]

Those who lived through it generally have good memories of this Italian period. Liliane Lieber describes her time in Grenoble as "wonderful," because the Italian soldiers did not enforce anti-Semitic policies. Jean-Jacques Becker recalls that, "Compared to the Occupied

Zone, the Free Zone—which hardly changed when the Italians were occupying the region—seemed like an oasis of liberty." Spending the 1943 Easter vacation at his cousins' home in Nice, he had the impression that the Jewish community of the city was under the protection of the Italian occupying forces.[119] Other accounts strike a similar tone, though these memories are perhaps too idyllic compared to what the situation for the Jews was really like. The Polish writer Oser Warszawski, who arrived in Grenoble around June 1943, recorded his impressions as he got to know the city and incorporated them entertainingly in a novel through the eyes of the character Naphtali. The picture he paints is very different: overcrowded hotels, slum landlords, anti-Semitic graffiti on the sidewalks, Jews gathering in cafés where Yiddish, Russian, and Polish could be heard around the tables.[120]

After the German invasion of the Free Zone, Jews dispersed deeper into rural areas. On top of these unprompted departures, the German authorities ordered the evacuation of foreign Jews who were placed under house arrest in the departments along the Mediterranean coast and on the Spanish border. Those living in the vicinity of Toulouse headed to the department of Creuse, those around Montpellier to Corrèze, those in Marseille and its environs to Cantal and Haute-Loire, and those in Nice to the Ardèche and the Drôme.[121] About 650 newcomers went to the Creuse.[122] Many of those who left of their own accord generally headed for small villages in the Aveyron, Lozère or Isère. This was a huge upheaval. Chief Rabbi Schwartz described it to the Central Consistory on 28 February 1943 as "the disappearance of three communities along the Mediterranean coastline: those of Montpellier, Béziers, and Perpignan."[123]

On 25 October 1943, Albert Lévy, a member of the Consistory, took stock of the trips he had undertaken since April of the same year to the all the different places where Jews had gathered. He noted two major trends: one saw Jews migrating "to the zone occupied by the Italians. The other saw them leave the city and spread out through rural areas."[124] A Vichy government inspector for the Marseille area noted, "The Jewish element migrates so much that about 30 per cent of the information from the census is already out of date."[125] In fact, according to one German report, which was probably fairly accurate, by mid-July 1943 nearly two-thirds of France's Jewish population was living in the Free Zone.[126]

The "Jewish presence" in the Southern Zone

How was this population distributed over the various regions? Can any internal patterns be detected? People did not settle down once and for all in one particular place, but nor were they constantly on the move. Between arrests, rumors of roundups, expulsion orders, local support networks, and the search for means of subsistence, it is very difficult to assess accurately what proportion of Jewish refugees was settled in one place and what proportion was on the move at any one time. Information collected by the CGQJ's *Section d'Enquête et de Contrôle* (SEC—Section for Investigation and Control) in 1943 offers an administrative snapshot of the "Jewish presence" in the Southern Zone. The data indicate the number of people who, in accordance with the new law of 11 December 1942, presented themselves in order to have their identity cards stamped with the word *Juif*.[127] The figures compiled by the regional prefectures thus make it possible to draw up a new map of the "Jewish presence" in the former Free Zone in early 1943. By using the same reference (the regional prefecture), it is possible to attempt a cautious comparison with the 1941 data.

The Vichy government recorded a significant rise in the Jewish population in the Southern Zone, which rose from around 110,000 in 1941 to 140,000 in 1943. The increase was probably even greater than 27 per cent, given the arrests in the zone of over 10,000 Jews in August 1942. It may seem surprising that these figures are relatively high, given that official Vichy figures did not include those who had managed to avoid being registered as Jews.

One might imagine that many people who had been caught by the 1940 and 1941 censuses would have decided go underground in 1942 and 1943 to avoid the trap of having their identity cards stamped with the word *Juif*. The truth is more complicated. The figures were probably a little inflated to correct the fact that a good many people sought to avoid having their papers stamped, but at the same time there were also many who went along with the procedure out of a desire to have their papers in order. They often had no other choice, in fact, if they hoped to buy food. Formal compliance with the law did not, however, prevent many of them from also obtaining forged identity cards. During the last two years of the Occupation, legality and illegality tended to coexist in everyday survival tactics.

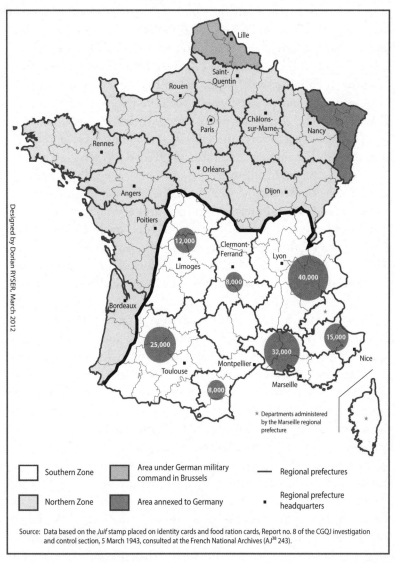

Designed by Dorian RYSER, March 2012

Legend:

Southern Zone	Area under German military command in Brussels	— Regional prefectures	
Northern Zone	Area annexed to Germany	■ Regional prefecture headquarters	

★ Departments administered by the Marseille regional prefecture

Source: Data based on the *Juif* stamp placed on identity cards and food ration cards, Report no. 8 of the CGQJ investigation and control section, 5 March 1943, consulted at the French National Archives (AJ[38] 243).

Map 4: Estimated distribution of the Jewish population in the Southern Zone, February 1943

The map thus shows a significant increase in the Jewish population, especially in southeastern France. The largest number of Jews was to be found within the prefecture of Lyon (+19,400), followed by Marseille (+10,000), and Nice (+3,000). In the southwest, the prefecture of Toulouse also recorded an increase (+2,300). Meanwhile, there was a drop in the Limoges area (-4,400). After the migration from north to south in the wake of the Vel' d'Hiv' roundup, these figures suggest a new trend: people living in the center-west, not far from the demarcation line (such as around Limoges), left the area, either to move farther down towards the southwest (Toulouse), or, more probably, towards the southeast, towards the Rhône-Alpes region and the Mediterranean rim. In all, an estimated 67 per cent of the Jews registered in the Southern Zone were to be found in the southeast (Lyon, Marseille, and Nice). In terms of surface area and number of departments per prefecture, the small region of Nice, made up of only two departments (both entirely under Italian occupation) had the highest Jewish population density. The Alpes-Maritimes department alone harbored nearly all the Jewish refugees in this area. Such a concentration would prove to be a cause for concern.

The end of the summer of 1943, around the time of the Allied landing in Italy, saw new waves of migration in various directions. The changing military front forced Mussolini's forces to desert the zone they were occupying in France, and the Wehrmacht immediately took over the regions that were formerly under the control of the Italian army. At first the Germans allowed Italy to keep a parcel of territory in the district of Nice. The Italians tried to gather as many Jews as they could into the area: "Forty trucks transported some 1,800 Jews from Saint-Gervais and Megève to Nice on September 6 and 7."[128] Some decided not to wait and left for Nice under their own steam. Various plans for the evacuation of these refugees were put forward during the forty-five days of the Badoglio government's rule in Italy. An Italian Jewish banker, Angelo Donati, aided by Father Pierre Marie-Benoît, sought to obtain their transfer to North Africa, but the plan failed to materialize. On 8 September, General Eisenhower announced Italy's surrender to the Allies. The news caused instant panic among the Jewish refugees. Suddenly southeast France went from being a safe haven to a trap.[129] This led to some Jews following the Italian troops in their retreat, in the hope that they would thus be protected—a decision that would prove fatal to some who, weeks or months later, were arrested and deported by the Germans. Among them was Oser Warschawski, who was arrested in Rome in May 1944 and deported to Auschwitz, where he was killed in October that year.

In Nice, the situation was worsening. At the beginning of September, SS Aloïs Brunner arrived from Drancy to lead a special commando in charge of rounding up Jews. It did not matter to Brunner whether they were French or foreign: a Jew was a Jew, to be arrested and deported. Brunner relied on the help of informers and "physiognomists" who sowed terror in the streets of the city. Men were made to drop their trousers and if they were circumcised they would be arrested on the spot. Brunner extended his manhunt from Nice to other towns in what had been the Italian zone, including Grenoble. After five months of roundups, he left the area in March 1944, having arrested some 2,000 people. To the Nazis this tally was disappointing: they had been counting on deporting tens of thousands.[130]

At the same time, Jewish and Christian organizations were mobilizing in an attempt to frustrate Brunner's roundups. With the help of Bishop of Nice Monsignor Paul Rémond, Moussa Abadi, a Syrian Jew, took as many children as he could under his wing, sending them mostly to Catholic institutions of the diocese. Individuals and families were trying to leave the area, fleeing to other parts of France. Some scattered to the Provençal hinterland or went farther north into the Alps. Others escaped to the Massif Central or to the southwest, or headed to the Paris region.

Stanley Hoffmann and his mother had been living in Nice since autumn 1940. After the Nazi invasion, Stanley's closest school friend, the French-born son of Hungarian Jewish émigrés, was arrested in September in front of his mother, who elected to go with him. For that moment on, Stanley and his mother lived in constant fear of being picked up. After three nerve-wracking months, exhausted by anxiety, they decided to leave. They retraced the path they had taken three years before, returning to Lamalou-les-Bains, where they remained until the end of the war.[131]

The Klarsfelds were directly affected by the persecution. During a roundup that took place in their building, the father was arrested as his wife and their two children were hiding in a closet in the apartment. The father was deported a few weeks later. How does one react to and survive such an event? After a few very difficult months, in early 1944 the wife and two children managed to leave Nice for Saint-Julien-Chapteuil (Haute-Loire), where they remained until the end of the war.

During the final year of the war Léon Poliakov moved constantly from one city to another. After Mussolini was overthrown, he left Grenoble for Nice where Rabbi Schneerson had now settled with his group. But after the Germans entered the city the situation became extremely dangerous and it became urgent to evacuate as many Jews as possible. Léon helped organize this evacuation with the network of safe houses he was involved with, known as the "Service André," led by Joseph Bass. Every evening he went to bed in a different hotel, convinced that the odds were one to seventeen that he'd be picked up during the night, since there were 170 hotels in the city and the SS were cleaning out ten hotels a night. Because of informers, his comrades were being arrested one after the other. Léon helped organize the escape of the children of members of the *Association des Israélites Pratiquants* (AIP—Union of Orthodox French Jews) and some of the rabbi's close associates, but once it became clear that Rabbi Schneerson himself refused to leave Nice, Léon gave up and went to Paris to try to get a friend out of Drancy. Once there, he discovered that his friend had died during the transfer, so he turned around and went back down to Marseille, the city where he had originally spent time when he first reached the Free Zone, and resumed his activities with the Service André. After the network's headquarters were relocated to a café-restaurant run by his friend Oswaldo Bardone in La Ricamarie, not far from Saint-Etienne, Léon returned there to stay with his old friend. He often visited Chambon-sur-Lignon (Haute-Loire), the Protestant village famous for taking in many Jewish refugees, closely associated with the Service André. Léon lived out the last years of the war in the nearby village of Tence, where he began studying Jewish thought with a philosopher who was in hiding there.[132]

The decision to return to Paris during the last year of the war may seem surprising. Poliakov returned only briefly, but others went back to live there. This migration ran counter to the general trend, all the more as supplies were very hard to come by in Paris. But there were always the suburbs, where it was possible to find eggs and vegetables; the out-skirts of Paris were still semi-rural, with farms, gardens, and fields.

Léon Werth, who had remained since 1940 in his country home in Saint-Amour (Jura), decided to return to Paris in the early months of 1944. In the diary he had kept since he first arrived in the countryside, he clarifies this decision by explaining that the area was becoming increasingly dangerous due to resistance operations and reprisal actions. His entry for 7 December reads: "Derailment at Moulin-des-Ponts. Only one carriage went off the rails. 'They arrested the station guards,' Laurent's son told me. 'They searched them. One of them was smoking a cigarette. A German snatched it out of his mouth and threw it to the ground. He called the guards dirty Frenchmen.' Another, who was drunk, grabbed one of the Frenchmen by the throat and nearly strangled him." After another rail sabotage at Sainte-Croix and the blowing up of a grocery store in Don belonging to a member of the Milice, a Gestapo raid was expected any day in Saint-Amour. Arrests were becoming increasingly frequent and Léon lived in constant fear of being denounced. After some *réfractaires*, men who had refused to be drafted into the STO, were arrested, he left for Paris on 6 January 1944, arriving there on 15 January.[133]

In fact, the return to Paris had been made easier because now that the whole of the country was under occupation, there was a relaxation of the inspections at border checkpoints between zones. The demarcation line became a sort of customs barrier. As of 1 March 1943, it could be crossed without having a permit, but merely by showing an identity card. As the differences between the zones were diminishing, people began to return north. Jews who decided to return to the Northern Zone were obviously acting outside the law however. It was not only residents of Paris who had fled to the Southern Zone who were return-ing to the capital. At her father's insistence, Francine Weiller also left for Paris with her stepmother and her two sisters, Nicole and Danièle, in December 1942. The family lived in Strasbourg before the war, but the three women had remained in Saint-Malo, in northern Brittany, where they spent their summer holidays, since 1939.

Since it was impossible to escape the occupying forces and their collaborationist allies by moving from one French region to another, people began to make other plans. They wanted to get across the border, either east to Switzerland or south to Spain, risking everything, including their lives.

Reaching Safety in Switzerland or Spain

The Swiss authorities had maintained good relations with their German neighbors since Hitler's rise to power. In keeping with its policy of neutrality, Switzerland believed that its role on the international stage was to remain on good terms with every country even, or perhaps most of all, when they were at war. But was it possible for a country to remain neutral, and even passive, in the face of the rise of Nazism in Europe? The guiding principle of Berne's foreign policy seemed indeed to be "to adapt and defend the interests of the Swiss confederation."[134] This policy took the shape of a substantial economic and financial collaboration, from which both countries benefited. Afraid of being overrun by thousands of refugees fleeing Nazism, Switzerland also had an extremely restrictive asylum policy for foreigners, a policy of refoulement, turning away refugees at the border. In the wake of an agreement with Berlin, as of 1938, "J" was stamped on the passports of all German Jews, a harsh measure of political and economic discrimination. After war was declared between France and Germany, Berne made visas once more compulsory. A decree dated 17 October 1939 ordered the refoulement of all foreigners without a visa, apart from soldiers.

Despite the initial severity of its policy of refusing entry to refugees, in late August 1942, the Swiss government softened its stance somewhat, opening what historian Ruth Fivaz-Silbermann has termed "breaches of humanity."[135] This noticeable change of heart came as a result of the pressure of hundreds of refugees at the border trying to enter Switzerland. Jews from the Netherlands and Belgium had begun arriving in the region even before deportations began in July 1942, clandestinely crossing occupied France as they headed for the northern Swiss border, along the arc of the Jura mountains.

Initially this first influx of around a hundred refugees, however small, prompted the authorities to close the border, for fear of a mass exodus into Switzerland. On 4 August 1942, the Federal Council ordered that refugees be denied entry, denouncing the actions of human smugglers and reiterating that Jews did not have the right to claim the status of political refugee, a rule that remained in effect throughout the duration of the war.

But the order sparked protest among the Swiss. Journalists and public figures raised their voices in opposition. People on the left as well as representatives of the church began to speak out in support of the duty of giving asylum as opposed to the sovereign right to refuse it. This wave of public disapproval overcame the policy of shutting people out, at least for a time. While officially the border remained closed, on 23 August cantonal police forces received orders "to procrastinate and to turn away as few people as possible," and not to hand anyone over to the Germans.[136] Those who were allowed to enter the country were men and women over 65, children under 16 with or without their parents, pregnant women, and the sick.[137] Although the criteria for entry were classified, many refugees heard about them from those who had made it across, and attempted to use them when they in turn were trying their luck to get into the country.

The persecution of Jews in France played a decisive role in the various stages of development of this sporadic immigration into Switzerland: first, the mass arrests organized by Vichy throughout the Free Zone on 26 August 1942 prompted a large flow of Jewish refugees towards the border. The German invasion of the Free Zone on 11 November 1942, followed by the retreat of the Italian military from the Italian administered Zone, prompted a new wave of refugees to head for the border. And finally, in the spring of 1944, a smaller exodus was triggered by German reprisal operations in reaction to resistance actions.

In a moving testimony written a few months after she arrived in Switzerland, in February 1944, as part of her application for financial support from a refugee relief organization, Cécile Klein-Hechel described her successful attempt to cross the border. Of Polish extraction, she had lived in Switzerland and later in Alsace. She and her husband, Charles Klein, were both naturalized French citizens. During the exodus she found herself stranded in Vichy with her 12-year-old daughter Berthe and her baby son Claude, born in November 1939. Her husband caught up with them there. Eight months later, they were obliged to leave the city and moved to Montfleury, near Grenoble. After the roundups of summer 1942, she looked for a way to get her daughter, now 14, into Switzerland,[138] which Berthe finally did without any complications on 1 December 1942. It was not so straightforward when Cécile tried to cross into Switzerland a few months later with her husband and their young son Claude, now aged 3. They decided to go in September 1943, immediately after the Germans entered Grenoble. Theoretically, there was no legal obstacle to their entering Switzerland, which, as of 29 December 1942, was allowing in refugee families with a child under 6. But they were afraid that they might be arrested at any time by German soldiers or French gendarmes who lay in wait for refugees approaching the border, "people who had been declared fair game, when all they wanted to do was to save their lives," in Cécile's words. A preliminary attempt to reach the border by train failed and the family ended up spending a night in an old wooden shack in the forest to dodge the gendarmes' flashlights.[139]

After that night spent in the woods, they found their way to a village where a local farmer took them to an elderly priest who agreed to help them. They made another attempt to cross with the aid of a smuggler. After walking for 25 km they reached a barbed-wire fence. To cross it, Cécile had to undress:

> Finally, I made it through and, dazed by the passage, I began to run because the actual border was apparently another 40 meters away. The smuggler called me back and told me to get dressed again, which I quickly did. Together, we headed towards the Swiss border we so yearned to reach. The hilly terrain made our night-time progress difficult. We were so close to complete exhaustion it was as though there were great chasms ahead and the forest was virgin forest. Suddenly we found ourselves on level ground again, walking through a field. We could see lights and as we went towards them our hopes revived, but to our horror we realized that we had been going around in circles in the dark and here we were again in front of the barbed wire. We heard gunshots. We ran like mad back into the forest. We sat down, on the verge of passing out, and rested on the damp moss. We decided to wait for morning. I was feverish, distressed by what we had just gone through and everything we had recently experienced. More gunshots. We spent the night there, pacing back and forth until daybreak, our little boy in our arms. In the distance, we heard the beating of a Swiss drum and the sound of trumpets. We walked for fifteen minutes and ran into a Swiss soldier who greeted us politely and took us to the nearest guard post. After having provided the requested information, we were given something to eat. A group of soldiers helpfully led us to

the first reception camp, Les Charmilles near Geneva, where we met about 400 people who had been through similar hardships.[140]

In early 1944, Liliane Lieber and her mother had also planned to reach Switzerland. Again it was fear of the Germans that prompted them to leave Grenoble, because of Liliane's resistance activities. After earning her baccalaureate, she wanted to become scout leader in the *Éclaireurs Israélites de France*. In reaction to the mass arrests in late August 1942, the movement's leaders had encouraged youths Liliane's age to take care of the children of foreign Jews and find them shelter. Thus was born the underground wing of the EIF, known as "*La Sixième*." The young scouts' mission was to find these children shelter either with host families or in institutions for children who had until then been placed in children's homes. They also supplied them with basic necessities and psychological support. From the beginning of the 1942 school year, Liliane devoted her time to this work in Grenoble and the surrounding region, but once the area came under German control her activities became much riskier. "My mother and I moved to Uriage, a small village in the mountains," she remembers:

> German Jewish friends leaving for Switzerland let us have their apartment. The situation had become much more dangerous for "escorts" like myself. Several of us had been arrested, and I trembled when I ran into Germans in the street or when I was asked for my papers. My mother was very afraid for me. So in March 1944 we decided to leave France, and we were lucky enough to get into Switzerland illegally. When we arrived, we were held in prison for two days, but as we had family in Geneva, we were eventually released. Once we had found somewhere to live, I carried on my job of finding shelter for refugees, only now I was working on the other side of the border.

The Dreyfus family was also hoping to reach Switzerland. They had left Limoges in the spring of 1943 for the Italian zone, eventually settling in Saint-Jorioz, on Lake Annecy. When the Germans took over from the Italians, the family moved again, deeper into the countryside, to a small village called Naves above Annecy. They arrived in late 1943, but just a few weeks later there was the attack carried out by the Glières resistance and the terrible crackdown that followed (12 February–28 March 1944). On 7 April the Milice arrived, wreaking havoc and fear. "At this point my father realized we had to leave," remembers his son Gérard. "The situation was becoming more and more dangerous. [...] So he arranged our departure for Switzerland."

From 1942 to 1944, Switzerland maintained its policy of refoulement, although the refusal rate dropped below the rate of admission.[141] A total of 51,129 civilian refugees entered Switzerland without a valid visa between 1 September 1939 and 8 May 1945.[142] Not all were Jews; some were young French who refused to be drafted into the STO. The number of Jewish refugees arriving from the French side was somewhere between 14,000 and 15,000, 13,500 of whom were actually admitted.[143] These figures contradict the image of a closed and xenophobic Switzerland. But the overall picture is more nuanced: the decision to admit or turn someone away was often a matter of arbitrary power exercised locally. Swiss authorities continued to turn away Jewish refugees until the spring of 1944. As of 12 July 1944, they were admitted without restriction.[144]

In the south of France, other refugees, fewer in number, tried to reach Spain. The mountainous barrier of the Pyrénées made this journey much more difficult than the paths that led across the plains to Geneva. Although there is no research comparable to the research on the Swiss border crossings, the influx of Jewish refugees at the Spanish border undoubtedly increased after the Southern Zone was invaded. Madrid was tempted to expel all those who entered the country illegally, for Franco did not want Hitler to accuse him of sheltering Jews. Nevertheless, until the end of the war the British and Americans kept the pressure on Madrid to leave the doors open to combatants who wanted to join the Allied forces. This policy certainly worked to the benefit of Jewish refugees and in general they were not turned away. But one should not forget the fate of those who were unlucky enough to be jailed once they reached Spanish territory. They were usually interned at Camp Miranda de Ebro for various lengths of time while a solution was sought to force them to leave the country as soon as possible, and some refugees, even though they had made it into Spain, were turned away: "A certain degree of administrative opacity and German pressure led to arbitrary expulsions to France or even deportation to Germany."[145]

The fates of so many people often hung by no more than a thread. They could not predict what might happen if they tried to escape from

France, though this did not stop them trying their luck. Even when they believed they had everything planned down to the last detail, a minor hitch could ruin everything. Perhaps they were sure they had all the necessary documentation to get across, only to reach the border and realize something was missing. The German philosopher Walter Benjamin was turned back at the Spanish border on 26 September 1940 because he was missing the exit visa that he needed to enter the country. In despair, he took his own life. Only a few weeks later, Madrid no longer required this document. In another tragic example, the administrative regulations for admission into the country changed literally the day before the attempted crossing. As the people who were hoping to get across had obviously not been informed, they found themselves caught in a bureaucratic trap.

This seems to have been what happened to Saul Friedländer's parents in 1942 at the Franco-Swiss border. In the letter he received from his mother after her arrest, she told him sadly: "We were misinformed."[146] In fact, the rules about who was allowed in had changed a mere 48 hours before the Friedländers arrived at the border. If they had arrived there two days earlier, they would have been let in even without their son, whom they had left behind in France. But the day they hoped to make the crossing, they were required to have their son with them in order to be allowed in.

Once again, this reminds us how precarious individual destinies were. Many accounts suggest that people were painfully aware of their extreme vulnerability.

Staying Home, or Close By

Although the years 1942–1944 were characterized by the increased dispersal of Jews around the country, one should not conclude that everyone who was at risk of arrest was now living in southern France or had crossed the border to take refuge abroad. Some remained at home or at least nearby. Individuals and families who were already living in what would become the Free Zone were the least likely to move away. Little research has been done on them. They did not move much during the exodus, if at all, and did not have to flee the occupying forces. These French nationals of Jewish heritage were able to live an almost normal life in the so-called Free Zone up until November 1942. Although they were not spared by Vichy's anti-Semitic policies, they did not feel the need to leave the area where they were living, where they were on the whole well integrated. Indeed, it was in their interests to stay and survive with the help of the local community. Pre-war friendships and professional contacts were the best antidote to discrimination. Furthermore, their children could continue their education without risk of being excluded from their primary and secondary schools. Why would they move? They were not directly affected by the roundups organized by Vichy in August 1942, which specifically targeted foreigners. This changed, however, after the German invasion of 11 November 1942, when they were now in danger of arrest, though it remained a possibility rather than a certainty. If they avoided going out there was less chance of being arrested. Today we tend to imagine an automatic causal connection that led directly from identification as a Jew to social and economic exclusion and then to arrest and deportation. In France, the majority of Jews, in particular those who were French, were not caught up in this tragic sequence. To be identified as a Jew living at an address known to the prefecture did not necessarily mean that the police or gendarmes would receive an order to take action. Even so, in 1943 and 1944, no Jew, French or foreign, was safe from denunciation or a Gestapo operation. When someone in their entourage or family was arrested, some were persuaded to leave their homes and either seek shelter with non-Jewish friends in the same city, or else flee into the surrounding countryside to stay with a relative or a farmer they knew. Often, though they left their homes, they did not move far, in some cases only a few hundred meters away, or more commonly a few kilometers or a few dozen kilometers. Most would remain there until the end of the war. It is very difficult to make a quantitative assessment of these non-resettlements or short-distance resettlements.

The largest number of Jews who did not leave their homes were those living in Paris and its surrounding suburbs. This is hardly surprising, as before the war broke out the largest community of French Jews and Jewish émigrés was living in the capital. According to the October 1940 census, the Paris police prefecture counted 149,734 Jews (85,664 French nationals and 64,070 foreigners) in the department of Seine alone. Of them, 133,451, of whom 57,791 were foreigners, were living in Paris proper.[147]

But as we have seen, mounting persecution sparked several large waves of departure to southern and central France. Below is a table summarizing the various migratory flows out of the Seine department between 1940 and 1944 and the number of those still living in Paris and its outlying areas at the end of Occupation. These figures are naturally an approximation, particularly as it is impossible to know how many returned to Paris and its suburbs in 1943–1944.

These figures show that despite denunciations and mass arrests, tens of thousands of Jews were still living in Paris in the summer of 1944. In a report submitted on 16 September 1944, Maurice Brenner, a representative of the American Jewish Joint Distribution Committee (commonly known as the Joint), estimated that at least 40,000 Jews remained in the capital, around 10,000 of whom were in need.[148] Chief Rabbi Jacob Kaplan reported 30,000 "legal" Jews in Paris in August 1944 and a similar number of Jews in hiding, in total around 60,000 at the Liberation.[149] Once again, little research has been done on these French and foreign Jews who remained in Paris.

Table 1: Estimated numbers of unforced departures from the Seine department between 1940 and 1944

Seine Jewish population (October 1940)	Arrests in the Seine department (1941–1944)	Estimated Jewish population in Paris (August 1944)	Estimated voluntary departures
149,734	33,141	60,000	56,593

Source: Camille Ménager, "Roundups, Rescue and Social Networks in Paris (1940–1944)," in Semelin, Andrieu and Gensburger (eds), *Resisting Genocide*, 2011, pp. 411–432.

Some remained because they it was not possible for them to leave; in other words, staying in Paris was the consequence of a non-choice. Various obstacles prevented them from leaving: socioeconomic factors (age, the size of their family, elderly dependents, limited financial resources) or the impact of the administrative measures taken by the occupying forces and the police prefecture to restrict Jews' mobility. It is impossible to say to what extent these restrictions and prohibitions dissuaded people from leaving. But none of the testimonies surveyed for this study suggest that any plan to escape to the Free Zone was postponed, still less abandoned, because of threats hanging over Jews who dared to move away from their homes.

There were also those who stayed in Paris, even under Occupation, because they did not see any reason to leave. Since they were French and often had a war veteran in the family, they believed their citizenship protected them, in spite of the fact that they were Jewish. Unable to foresee the rise in persecution, they adapted to the situation. The more they delayed the decision to leave Paris, the less likely it was that they would be able to leave. This was the case for the Lefschetz family.

Denise Lefschetz's parents were both French citizens of Russian extraction. They had arrived in France with their families at the very beginning of the twentieth century. Denise, who was born in 1926, spent her time between two homes, on rue des Martyrs and rue Notre-Dame de Lorette, as her parents had separated three years after she was born. Her mother lived with the cabaret artist Jean Lec, whom she married later on during the Occupation. Her father ran a sports club for young Jewish athletes. Denise was a member of the *Éclaireurs Israélites*. During the Occupation, Denise's father was made director of the UGIF office on rue Claude-Bernard (5th arrondissement), while Denise herself became a counselor:

> My family never considered leaving Paris. In 1941, my maternal grandfather and my father were convinced that their status as war veterans would spare them. After that, it was too late. On top of this, my father had his 82 year-old mother to take care of and she wasn't in fit shape to travel. My grandparents did everything they could to maintain a semblance of normalcy in their life: they continued to host friends on Sundays to discuss politics. As for me, I was a teenager, and at that age one is less affected by fear than adults are.

Among the Jews who remained in Paris, a significant portion fell into the category mentioned in Maurice Brenner's report: the needy. These were foreign Jews with no means of subsistence, as well as the elderly and children whose parents had been deported. These people required ongoing assistance. The *Union Générale des Israélites de France* (UGIF—General Union of French Jews) provided food through its network of soup kitchens. In summer 1944, about 31,000 meals were served monthly, enabling several hundred Jewish families to survive. For example, 300 strictly kosher meals were prepared daily, except on Saturdays, at the soup kitchen on rue Villiers-de-l'Isle-Adam.[150] The flip side of this subsistence aid was the huge vulnerability, not only of the people benefiting from UGIF relief but also of the people who worked there, for the soup kitchens and children's reception centers could easily become treacherous traps.

This should not obscure a startling historical fact: thousands of Jews were living both in the open and underground in Paris, in the midst of the occupying forces and their collaborationist allies. In this regard, the situation of the Jews in Paris in 1944, though far from enviable, was a far cry from the plight of their fellow Jews in other European capitals such as Warsaw and Amsterdam. The Jewish population in these major cities had been virtually annihilated over a year previously.

A more detailed description of the distinctive situation in Paris during the final months of Occupation can be found in another report filed by Maurice Brenner after his stay in the capital between 3 and 17 May 1944.[151] Coming from a zone where the yellow star was not mandatory, Brenner discovered with a fresh eye what life was really like in the capital and his report offers a valuable analysis of the situation. He identified three "profiles" of Jews then living in the capital.

According to his report the largest category was made up of those "who were perfectly legal, registered with the authorities and sleeping in their own beds." This group was "by far the strangest and most improbable," which is why Maurice Brenner, intrigued, devoted the longest section of his report to them. Among them, notably, was the group of "legitimates," in other words those who had a UGIF 'legitimation' card that was handed out to nearly all the organization's employees.[152] This card protected the bearer, along with his or her immediate family and children, from deportation and the requisition of their home, except if the person was betrayed for having broken the law [...] There were about 800 legitimation cards which provided protection to about 3,500 people."

The second category was made up of "those who wore the star during the day, but who slept elsewhere at night, or who did not wear their star and permitted themselves to do things forbidden to Jews, thanks to Aryan papers that were more or less in order ... They

[were] people who, under the influence of *La Sixième* and the *Mouvement des Jeunesses Sionistes* (MJS—Movement of Young Zionists), had become 'synthesized' and used these documents to [remain safe] or travel."[153]

The last category identified by Maurice Brenner was those who were "synthesized," i.e. in possession of "Aryan" papers. This group of people was fairly large relative to the others, composed of young people who had been living in the Southern Zone and had been coming up in dribs and drabs to Paris. They avoided being seen with people from the other categories. Some of them got by like the Aryans in their respective social classes, the rest of them belonged to the *Sixième* youth section and the MJS.

Maurice Brenner might also have included in his typology the category of Jewish communist militants who were living underground in Paris and its suburbs.

A few biographies illustrate the profiles described in Maurice Brenner's report. In the category of legal Jews, there were those who worked for the UGIF such as Denise Lefschetz and her father.

Madeleine Grunfeld was also living as a legal Jew. A French Jew, she was born in 1920 and spent the entire period of the Occupation in Paris. She lived with her mother on Avenue Mozart, in the 16th arrondissement, but she often spent the night with her aunt and uncle, Monsieur and Madame Preis, in the 11th arrondissement. After registering with the authorities in October 1940, she did a course to qualify as a UGIF counselor beginning in November 1941. After the Vel' d'Hiv' roundup, she was employed at the rue Lamarck center, along with her cousin Annette, who could no longer work as a schoolteacher. Both of them had legitimation cards. In June 1942, Madeleine began wearing the yellow star, as did all the other members in her family until the Liberation.[154] None of them sought to leave the Paris area. Reflecting on that period today, Madeleine said:

> At the time, I was oblivious. I didn't realize I could be arrested at any moment. I thought that my UGIF legitimation card protected me, especially as I was not doing anything illegal. [...]. The children and I were only vaguely aware of the danger hanging over us, and we sometimes engaged in activities that I only realized much later were totally reckless [...]. My mother and I never contemplated leaving Paris. We didn't

know anyone in the provinces, and in any event I didn't want to abandon the children I looked after. And my mother was loath to leave her shop.

Those working for the UGIF were a minority. There were many others who also adhered to this rationale of obeying the law. They adapted to the legal requirements and went to work wearing the yellow star.

As Asher Cohen points out, compliance with the law was anything but systematic. Individual accommodations were numerous. In fact, each person had his or her own relationship with the law: some wore their yellow star during the day and, depending on how bold they were, took it off in the evening. In this second category, young people were most likely to risk removing their star on certain occasions, as Denise Lefchetz makes clear:

> Sometimes, we were overcome with the need to go out in the evening. We gave in to temptation and took off our yellow stars before going out in defiance of the curfew imposed on Jews. I remember one evening when I went to meet some friends at the Pleyel concert hall. Like me, they couldn't resist coming out to hear Alfred Cortot play the piano. For those of us who were young it became a game: defying the law was a way of overcoming our anxiety, and daily life prevailed over tragic circumstances.

Joseph Minc is a good example of the third category Maurice Brenner described, the "synthesized." In 1942, he refused to wear the yellow star. He and his wife went underground and obtained forged identity papers. As the documents were poorly done, he learned to make them himself. With his prosthetics instruments, he managed to forge an official government stamp. Armed with his real-fake identification, he writes, it was impossible to get caught, "unless they checked the card number with the prefecture, which never happened."[155] Many resistance fighters lived in a similar situation of "overt" clandestinity.

Another kind of underground existence, which could be described as physical, involved withdrawing from the world entirely. In that case the person lived as a recluse in a confined space, remaining in hiding for months, if not longer.

This was how Albert Grunberg, the Romanian hairdresser who lived on rue des Écoles (5th arrondissement), survived. He did not move far from his home, but he went completely underground. On 24 September 1942 he just managed to escape the police who had come to arrest him at his home at 14 rue des Écoles. He immediately went into hiding in a maid's room on the top floor of 8 rue des Écoles, in the same building as his hairdressing salon. He had been sleeping there every night since December 1941, when the prefecture had declared him Jewish (not being a practicing Jew he had not registered, because he assumed the obligation to register did not apply to him). Now he confined himself day and night to a room 7.5 square meters in size. He spent his time reading the newspapers, listening to the radio, and keeping a diary. His brother Sami joined him in July 1943. They did not come out of hiding until 23 August 1944.[156]

Albert Grunberg's story is in some ways comparable to the more tragic story, known throughout the world, of the Frank family in Amsterdam, as told by their daughter Anne to her diary.[157] However, the situation illustrated by the Romanian hairdresser was unusual and thus not really representative of what Jews experienced in France. One of the most tenacious clichés about the anti-Semitic persecution during this period holds that Jews had to hide in basements or attics to escape arrest. In light of what we have seen, this notion is simplistic to say the least.

In this first chapter we have seen the remarkable diversity of situations and the high degree of mobility that people demonstrated to avoid arrest. Next we will examine how, on a day-to-day basis, individuals and families managed to avoid a tragic outcome. To understand this better, the personal accounts of several people describing their years of suffering during the war will now be examined in greater detail. Indeed, surely there is no more justified and necessary point of departure than their own words. Those who were involved are certainly qualified to tell the story of what they lived through, even if their accounts must be cross-referenced and verified against other historical facts. This is the aim of the following chapter: to explore a different memory of the period, not only the one that describes the stigmatization and deportation of the Jews, but also the memory of their daily survival.

2

IN THE FACE OF PERSECUTION

STRATEGIES FOR SURVIVAL

In the late 1970s, the memory of the deportation of the Jews became increasingly present in the public arena in France, superseding the heroic commemoration of patriotic resistance to the German occupying forces that had previously held sway. Those who recounted their experience in the concentration camps started being known as "survivors."[1] In the 1990s, another memory gradually began to be heard in the United States as well as in Israel and France: that of the "hidden children." Today there is one other voice too seldom taken into account: that of all those, both adults and children, who might have been deported but who managed to avoid it. In France, they make up a larger group than those who were deported, but finding a way of naming them has always posed a problem. They are often designated with some sort of circumlocution: "those who survived the persecution," or "those who escaped the Holocaust." Bob Moore has suggested calling them "survivors" as well. But to use the same word to refer to those who returned from the camps and those who were spared that experience leads to confusion. I would simply describe them as constituting a broad group of non-deported Jews. Whatever term is chosen to designate them, the fundamental issue is how to explain that, although they were, in theory, condemned to die, they in fact somehow escaped that fate. There is obviously no simple explanation.

It should always be borne in mind that the persecuted were not equal in the face of danger. Deportation figures attest to this. Among the some 330,000 people categorized as Jews according to Vichy's criteria in 1940, the social circumstances of Jewish immigrants, who were usually poor and isolated and whose families were decimated if not entirely destroyed, were clearly far more precarious than those of French Jews, who were able to rely on family and personal relations to help them cope with the situation. Personal accounts dating from the period[2] reflect this distinction, since then corroborated by the figures compiled by Serge Klarsfeld. Everywhere in Europe where the Nazis tried to deport Jews, those who were considered foreigners according to the various governments' categories paid the heaviest price, as their rate of extermination was higher than that of Jews who belonged to the national community.[3] Among the Jews deported from France who perished in the gas chambers, there were nearly twice as many foreigners as French nationals (46,500 compared to 24,500).

Aside from nationality and the degree of social assimilation, financial resources were also a factor that had a major influence on the fate of the persecuted. Recent immigrants to France, who had generally been obliged to leave everything behind in their country of origin, experienced a brutal drop in social status. This was the case for Saul Friedländer's family, for instance. In 1939, the Friedländers left Prague in haste just as the Nazis were about to occupy the city, and soon arrived in Paris. The father, who had occupied a distinguished position in Prague, found himself jobless in France. He took a number of courses, while his wife trained to become a beautician.[4] Inequality of living conditions was already noticeable at the time of the fall of France, between those such as Léon Werth or the Lindon family, who were able to flee Paris by car, and those who boarded crowded trains, left on foot or if they were lucky by bicycle, like the young Alfred Grosser and his sister Margot.

There were similar inequalities when it came to having the means to procure food, as with war and occupation came serious food shortages. Those who could afford to buy decent food on the parallel black market were highly privileged.

Age-related factors also played a role in a person's ability to cope with persecution. The elderly, who were less mobile and quicker to resign themselves to the situation, were, along with children, the most vulnerable. At first caught off-guard by a level of aggression no one had imagined, families and organizations subsequently managed to devise specific means to shelter these defenseless people.

It is important to avoid any distortion of the memory of this period. The term "hidden children" is often used to refer to the children of foreign Jews who were taken into the care of Jewish and non-Jewish organizations. But the figures show that only about 10,000 children of the 70,000 Jewish children still alive at the end of the war had survived in hiding. Where, then, did the 60,000 others go who were not taken under the wings of the various relief organizations? As Vivette Samuel writes, most of these Jewish children, many of whom must have been French nationals, were sheltered by members of their own families outside major cities, most commonly in the countryside.[5] Between the two age extremes (the very young and the very old), single young adults were the most likely to adapt to the persecution or flee their pursuers, given their youth, their mobility, and their physical health.

Lastly, "family situation was also a major differentiating factor."[6] Having a family was not an insurmountable handicap, but the larger the family, the more difficult it was for all its members to travel as a unit. One solution was to move separately, which happened fairly often, as we will see. As a rule, however, it appears that the larger the family, the more inclined they were to stay put and consequently the more in danger of arrest they were.

Whether family members stayed together or separated, every story is unique. Some trajectories were marked by tragedy from the start; others attest to a degree of calm, even lack of awareness of the danger. Still others were characterized by dramatic episodes, improbable encounters, or extraordinary twists of fate. Beyond these major differences, what these stories share is the protagonists' will to live and to survive. Even when they were forced into isolation, devastated by the loss of a loved one, or worried about the future, they were often driven by a sort of inner resistance to persecution, even when they were imprisoned in a camp.

Obeying the Law and Legal Recourse

The stages of the persecution of Jews in France, from mandatory registration in 1940 to mass deportation starting in 1942, have been reviewed above. In the Occupied Zone, it is clear that in accordance with the German ordinance of 27 September 1940, the overwhelming majority voluntarily identified themselves as Jews in a special register opened at the sub-prefecture where they lived. To conclude that they were naïve in doing so, walking straight into the trap set for them by their soon to be executioners, is an anachronistic perspective. No one in 1940 could imagine what was to happen in 1942, for the simple reason that the Nazi leadership itself had not yet devised its plan for the extermination of the Jews.

The argument that claims that the more people had a clear awareness of the danger, the more prepared they were to cross the line into illegality or go underground must also be qualified. In this regard, the mandatory census instituted eight months later in the Free Zone (law of 2 June 1941), is instructive. Since concrete measures of persecution and professional exclusion were already in effect, one might think that individuals would have been more likely to be on their guard. A very large majority nevertheless came forward to register as Jewish after that date. Why were so many of them willing to go through with this administrative procedure, a tangible sign of their stigmatization?

The first explanation, a political and psychological one, lies in the very widespread human inclination to obey the law. Fear of punishment is one of the principal motives for people's submission to authority. In this case, non-compliers exposed themselves to extremely severe sanctions: the first census of the Jews in the department of Seine in October 1940 already led to for fines and imprisonment for those who contravened. These measures were toughened in the law of 2 June 1941 and the provisions associated with the second major census ordered in Paris in October 1941, which authorized administrative detention.[7] All governments wield threats to secure people's allegiance. But voluntary consent to obey is an equally fundamental pillar of power. This observation in no way implies a value judgment on the conduct of the Jews at the time; most people are more inclined to obey than to disobey. Education and upbringing within the family and the community, both religious and civil, are of decisive importance. Disobeying the law is never a straightforward or automatic course of action, and rebelling against authority does not usually become the norm, except in exceptional or tragic circumstances. This was without doubt the case in France between 1940 and 1944; it is unsurprising to note that illegal behavior became more and more common, but obedience and compliance with the law did not entirely vanish. One of the aims of the present study is to point out the inevitable and ambiguous entwining of obedience and disobedience.

Those who maintained their trust

Individuals react differently to legal prohibitions depending on their own cultural experience. In this regard, the respective behavior of French Jews and Jewish immigrants was rooted in different histories. In 1940, the former still had faith in France and many supported Marshal Pétain, like the overwhelming majority of the French. In Paris, the Beckers agreed to be registered. As Jean-Jacques writes, "as well as a natural inclination to obey the law, when they were summoned, Jews went to the police station to declare themselves as Jewish." He points out that, "Among French Jews, *Israélites*, there was hardly a family in which the older men were not veterans of the Great War, often decorated [...], as was the case in most French families. They considered themselves, despite certain irritations, untouchable."[8]

In the Benayoun family, French Jews from Algeria, the father seems to have hesitated to register, Simon explained: "At first my father did not want to have us registered, but he got a call from our local police chief who persuaded him. Unlike many Algerian Jews, we were not stripped of our French nationality in October 1940, because our father was a war veteran.[9] He long remained convinced that his status as a war invalid would protect him from the worst. As a supporter of Pétain, he believed that the laws against the Jews were the work of the Germans." This conviction was shared by a number of French Jews of foreign extraction whose parents or grandparents had fought in the First World War, including Denise Lefschetz's family. They felt quite different from the "Polacks" and other Central European Jews who had arrived in France more recently. "Both branches of my family considered themselves to be French," Denise points out. "And, with a certain snobbishness, I understood that we had little in common with the Yiddish-speaking Jews who had arrived more recently from Eastern Europe." Edgar Morin also reports that his father Nahum, after some hesitation, eventually registered, in compliance with the law.[10]

Even when French Jews agreed to register with the authorities, many of the letters they sent to Marshal Pétain at the time attest to their disapproval of the requirement the French administration imposed on them. In these often very moving letters they mention the members of their family who died on the battlefield and speak of their patriotism and love for France. They decided once again to obey, to prove their loyalty, but this time with great bitterness. One of the most famous letters was sent by the lawyer and politician Pierre Masse, at the time a senator from the region of Hérault. On reading the decree stating that "*Israélites*, even those of strictly French lineage, could no longer be officers," he wrote to the Marshal:

> Kindly inform me whether I must remove the insignia from my brother, a second lieutenant in the 36th infantry regiment, killed at Douaumont in April 1916; from my son-in-law, a second lieutenant in the 14th division of the dragoons, killed in Belgium in May 1940; from my nephew J.-F. Masse, lieutenant in the 23rd colonial regiment, killed at Rethel in May 1940? May I leave my brother with the military medal he won at Neuville Saint-Vaast with which I buried him? May my son Jacques, second lieutenant in the 62nd mountain infantry battalion, wounded at Soupir in June 1940, keep the stripes he earned? Can I be assured that the medal of Sainte-Hélène will not be retroactively taken away from my grandfather? It is important to me to obey the laws of my country, even when they have been dictated by the invader. Please be assured, sir, of my deepest respect.[11]

Reading these words, it is not hard to imagine the inner torment and personal tragedy of a man who had been a close associate of Pétain since serving with him on the War Council in 1917. That did not protect Masse from being arrested on 21 August 1941, along with fellow lawyers, and interned at Drancy.

Rabbis urge Jews to obey the law

Several rabbis also protested, at the same time as urging Jews to obey the law:

> On 22 October 1940, the chief rabbi of France, Isaïe Schwartz, issued a long protest against the Jewish Statute. He lashed out against the set

of racial laws on which it was based and against the accusations of inter-
nationalism: "It is in the very nature of all civilized religions to be uni-
versal." He demanded equality before the law and endorsed the motto
of Vichy's new order of things, "Work, family, country" [...]. He cited
Jews who were heroes in the First World War and those who died fighting for their country. Finally Schwartz concluded, "Our response to this
special law shall be one of unswerving devotion to our country. At the
same time, we remain faithful to the belief in the one and only God and
to the revelation of Mount Sinai." Chief Rabbi Schwartz's letter was not
even acknowledged. On the next day, 23 October 1940, the chief rabbi
of Paris, Julien Weill, assured Marshal Pétain that French citizens of the
Jewish religion remained faithful to their country, "whatever the rigors
of the new law may be." In his response dated 12 November 1940,
Pétain emphasized the importance of obeying the law and spoke of the
spirit of sacrifice that he expected from all his fellow citizens "whatever
their particular circumstances may be."[12]

In response to anti-Semitic propaganda, the Consistory made several
requests among its members for reliable information attesting to
Israélite roots in the national community. A survey was conducted on
their participation in the war of 1914–1918, followed by another study
on their participation in the battles of 1939–1940. The Consistory
asked its members to retrace the genealogy of their own families in
order to "counter inaccurate figures expressed by our opponents with
precise figures, no more, no less." On 13 August 1941, in response to
the Consistory's survey, inspector-general Jules Isaac, author of several
well-known history textbooks, drew up a genealogical chart going
back to 1747.[13] In his memoirs the historian Pierre Vidal-Naquet
describes the quest his father, lawyer Lucien Vidal-Naquet, undertook
to prove his own family's longstanding roots in France.[14]

The fact of going to register as *Juif* could also be construed as a means
of defying the anti-Semitic press that made "Yids" out to be a bunch of
forgers and smugglers with no respect for French law or values. The
philosopher Henri Bergson made it a point of honor to register as Jewish
after having refused the honorary Aryan status[15] that the government
wanted to grant him.[16] Although he was philosophically attracted to
Catholicism, he wrote in his will in 1937 that he had always refused to
convert out of solidarity with his persecuted co-religionists.

To register as Jewish was also a show of courage. It was in a spirit
of solidarity with his fellow Jews that the writer Léon Werth, who

took refuge in the Jura mountains, justified his own decision to register on 9 July 1941. The scathing humor of his words betray his anger at Vichy:

> And so it was that the Marshal and Xavier Vallat forced me to declare myself citizen of a Jewish homeland to which I feel no attachment [...] the most basic sense of dignity requires me to identify with it. [...] What cowardice it would be for me to wonder whether I or not I consider myself a Jew. If you insult me by calling me Jewish, then I am Jewish, passionately Jewish, Jewish right to the roots of my hair, viscerally Jewish. After that, we shall see [...]. I made my declaration at the prefecture, I cried out the word "Jewish!" as if I were about to sing the *Marseillaise*.[17]

Identity-based affiliations

Jewish immigrants recently arrived in France could not prove any such patriotic rootedness. No doubt few of them deluded themselves regarding how the situation was evolving now that the Germans occupied two-thirds of the country. Many had been facing persecution in their own country since the early twentieth century, which is what prompted them to leave. Their own history most likely made them more wary. The proportion of people who refused to comply with the order to register was probably therefore higher among these Jewish immigrants. However, foreigners tended in general to comply with inspections so as not to "run into trouble" and many probably also registered to be in compliance with the new law. In October 1940 they lined up in front of police stations to register and emerged with the word *Juif* stamped on their identity card. One of these was Joseph Minc's wife, Lisa, who was registered in Paris, an act she came to regret when the obligation to wear the yellow star came into effect. During the June 1941 registration, the Markscheid family, newly arrived in the area of Toulouse, also went in to fill in the forms.[18] Some foreign Jews had already been identified by the administration prior to the mandatory census. For instance, the residence permit Sal Kanner, Mia's husband, received when he was expelled from Germany to France in January 1939 indicated that he held German citizenship and that he was Jewish.[19]

For some, the desire not to disown their origins played an essential role. For them, the obligation to register was fully embraced and asserted as a form of identity affiliation with a particular group. This is how Léon Poliakov justified registering in his memoirs:

> My family name ended in -*ov*, my birth certificate was in Leningrad and I had no enemies. So it would have been impossible for the Germans to verify my racial affiliation. "'Don't go," [Alexander] Kojève insisted. "In my village, when the statistics office undertook a census, everyone knew it was a bad omen, and went and hid in the woods. I beg you to follow their example." But with a characteristic mixture of conflicting motivations—the refusal to deny my origins and the habit of obeying the law—I ended up doing what the others did. [...] My sister Olga, on the other hand, decided to break the law, to the great benefit of her husband, a veteran of the White Army whose only offense was to be called Rabinovitch. There could be no mistaking his origins.[20]

In the context of the times, this administrative procedure was not generally perceived as a trap laid for the Jews. Edgar Morin believes that his father did not experience this self-registration as a threat to his life. It was even the opposite: "Vidal was very optimistic during the fall of 1940. His business was doing well, and the 'Jewish' stamp on his identity card reassured him more than it worried him, because he felt that he had his papers in order with the law."[21]

Some people mistakenly believed that the census did not concern them. Albert Grunberg, a Romanian Jew, saw no reason to register because he did not practice Judaism. Nevertheless, anxious to be on the right side of the law, he went to the prefecture for information and for unknown reasons came out without the stamp. It was only fifteen months later that he received a summons from the "Jewish service" that had been set up at the prefecture, instructing him to go to the police station to have his documents put in order, at which point his identity card was stamped with the word *Juif*.[22]

In 1941, Jewish immigrants were not any more suspicious when over 3,700 of them received a "green slip" notifying them to report to their local police station for an "examination of their status." Why should they not have gone? They were used to police inspections. Over a thousand of them, however, did not comply, including David Diamant, who recalled, "many people had suspicions about their future destination."[23] They were right to be suspicious: those who showed up for the summons would not return.

This first mass arrest of Jewish immigrants in Paris, on 14 May 1941, organized by the French police at the Germans' request, resulted in the imprisonment of 3,710 Jews, most of whom were Polish. In this specific case, their compliance was all the more under-standable as no Jewish organization had instructed them not to answer the summons. Contextual factors have also been suggested: the fact of being known and identified as a Jew living in a particular neighbor-hood obliged these people to register: "How could we not declare ourselves as Jews, when we were born in Poland, hardly spoke any French and were garment workers making pants on rue des Immeubles-Industriels?" one of them said.[24]

What induced some to register and others not, sometimes within the same apartment building? Nicolas Mariot and Claire Zalc carried out a sociological study on Jews in the city of Lens to try to shed light on the factors that weighed in this decision. "Self-registration was not a homogenous phenomenon," they point out. "Those who were younger, unmarried, spatially isolated, born in France, or those who had entered the country more recently, were among the least likely to register."[25] While socio-professional status scarcely played a role, age was a determining criterion. The unregistered population included more young adults, who were, relatively speaking, less compliant with the order. It also included more children: some parents attempted to protect them by not registering them. In any event, the unregistered were not socially marginalized individuals or families.

While the majority consented to the registration, letters sent by those who registered reveal the many misunderstandings regarding the definition of "Jewishness." The first texts issued by the occupying forces defined a Jew according to his religion, whereas for Vichy it was a ques-tion of "race" (*Statut des Juifs* of 3 October 1940). But for many Jewish immigrants from Eastern Europe, Jewish identity was a nationality. The French government hardly pondered these semantic subtleties: anyone who declared himself to be Jewish was considered to be Jewish.

Who is a Jew? Nationality versus Jewishness

Registering as a Jew could in and of itself constitute an attempt to protect one's family. It amounted to declaring, "Yes, I'm Jewish, but my wife and my daughter are French." The vagueness of the legal definition of who was a Jew opened several avenues for possible administrative redress. In the area of Lens, Daniel Galuneff managed to have his name removed from the lists of Jews drawn up by the municipal authorities on the grounds that his nationality was Russian.[26] The procedure involved proving one's nationality to escape one's Jewishness and was fairly widespread throughout the Occupation. Proof of a nationality that offered diplomatic protection in the eyes of the occupying forces and Vichy theoretically insulated one from physical persecution as a Jew. This protection, entirely relative, varied over the course of the war. It did, however, offer an initial form of legal recourse. Before Germany invaded the USSR in June 1941, for instance, Polish Jewish immigrants could go to the Soviet embassy in Paris to obtain Soviet citizenship, according to Jacques Biélinky's entry for 19 August 1940: "More than 50,000 people have signed up for repatriation with the Soviet consulate. They are Jews who have automatically become Soviet citizens following the annexation of half of Poland, Lithuania, Latvia, Estonia, Bessarabia, and Bucovina by Russia. Apparently repatriation is to begin on 1 September."[27]

After the May 1941 arrests, Poliakov recounts that his contact at the Soviet embassy, deputy secretary Tarassov, issued certificates to several Poles who had been arrested, attesting that they were born in the Soviet Union (which had become true since the modification of the borders).[28] Joseph Minc was also able to take advantage of this godsend of an opportunity. Summoned to the police station because he was a Polish Jew, he realized that those who answered the summons were being arrested, so he decided not to go. Meanwhile, he had managed to get Soviet identity papers: "A doctor friend, Dr Senikes, advised me to go to the Soviet consulate before answering the summons. That is what I did, and what a stroke of fortune it was: in accordance with the new border that made Brest-Litovsk part of Russian territory, I was issued a Soviet identity card. I was officially a citizen of a country allied with Germany, which enabled me to escape the first roundups of foreigners."

Spanish Jews living in France did the same, requesting protection from the government in Madrid by virtue of the Franco-Spanish treaty of 1862 and the royal decree of 1924 granting Spanish subjects resident in France the same rights as if they lived in their native country. "In answer to the concerns of these Sephardim, the Consul assured them that they need not register, given the absence of any Spanish legislation discriminating against Jews."[29]

Italian diplomats, for their part, took steps to protect their own nationals. Mussolini had enacted anti-Semitic legislation in Italy in 1938, and the Italians intended, as we have seen, that they alone would decide the fate of Jews who came under their authority, thus asserting the primacy of an individual's nationality over Jewishness. "On 4 August, the Italian consul general issued a statement making it clear that no anti-Jewish measure would be applicable to Italian Jews without his prior consent."[30]

Conversions, exemptions, legal recourse

Some, unable to prove they belonged to these "protected" nationalities,[31] tried to claim religious status: another means of circumventing the *Statut des Juifs* laws was to prove one had become a Catholic (provided that the person had only two Jewish grandparents). According to Annie Kriegel, "the provision of the second Vichy statute that accepted as a criterion of Aryan status proof of conversion to Christianity prior to 25 June 1940 led to an epidemic of conversions."[32] But that required the complicity of a priest prepared to issue a fake baptism certificate. The new converts would have been somewhat like the Marranos—Spanish Jews in medieval times who were forced to convert but secretly continued to practice Judaism. Many mixed couples who had children during the war years would have had them baptized as Catholics to protect them from anti-Semitic persecution. These children were often given names that unequivocally attested to their Frenchness, like "Jean-Pierre" or "Marie-France."

The extent of conversions remains unverifiable. In any case, the procedure, which was frowned upon in Jewish circles, was rarely effective once the deportations began. Stanley Hoffmann and his mother, both baptized Protestants, clearly never felt that their baptism, despite being genuine, protected them from persecution.

For French Jews, the legal possibilities for being exempt from the *Statut des Juifs* were in reality very slim. Vichy made an exception for some high-ranking personalities who had given outstanding service to

France in the scientific, literary, or artistic fields. But this did not release them from the obligation to register as Jews. The Council of State granted this dispensation sparingly; in all, some fifty names are listed, including the historian Marc Bloch and the internationally renowned physician Robert Debré, whose official exemption from the statute did not prevent either of them from active involvement in the Resistance.[33] Senior Vichy officials considered no figure in the industrial or business sector worthy of exemption. Without being officially exempted, a few especially well-known foreign Jews living in France enjoyed some form of protection by the authorities. Among them, the most famous example is probably the writer and art collector Gertrude Stein.[34]

There was also a chance that men and women with a non-Jewish spouse could avoid being deported. They had to obtain a certificate stating they did not belong to the Jewish "race," issued by the "personal status bureau" of the CGQJ. The application to be sent to the administration needed to include the baptism certificates of both parents and grandparents. An estimated 10,000 certificates were issued by Vichy and 3,000 were on hold by the time of the Liberation.[35] In fact, while Vichy had its own criteria for defining Jewishness, it was the Germans who ultimately decided who was to be deported and to which destination. The Nazis, however, even in Germany, were not really sure how to deal with the case of mixed couples and their children. Their fate was discussed at length at the Wannsee Conference of 20 January 1942, when the "Final Solution," the plan to exterminate some 11 million Jews in Europe, was planned. The matter, however, was never settled. Ultimately, these spouses of Aryans were not deemed "deportable."

During the entire period of the war, various attempts at legal recourse, thus involving the courts, were undertaken in France, either in order to escape the severity of anti-Semitic persecution or to obtain the release of people who had been incarcerated. These legal procedures might seem surprising today, as the French were living under the yoke of a dictatorship, which was itself under the rule of what for most of the population was a despised occupier. One might therefore think that they no longer had any faith in their country's judicial system and thus were reluctant to assert their rights. This was not always the case.

Judiciary collusion and the arbitrariness of the German authorities

Examples of this recourse to the law do not contradict the oppressive reality: judicial institutions took part in enforcing Vichy laws. The term "law" is in fact inappropriate, since, as Pétain had dissolved parliament, there was no longer a representative assembly in France with the function of debating and passing legislation. General de Gaulle maintained that the so-called Vichy laws had no legal force. The judiciary, through its magistrates and lawyers, adapted to the new situation by showing itself to be completely submissive to the political executive.[36] A form of legal hair-splitting, which legitimized and rationalized in legal terminology the arbitrariness of the Pétain dictatorship, became the norm. The judiciary thus contributed to normalizing the ignominy of official state racism: a new discipline was born, known as "anti-Semitic law," that was taught at university and debated in academic journals.

Those who fell foul of the law still appeared in court to assert that this legislation did not apply to them, either attempting to ignore the reality or seeking to exploit its loopholes. The cases to be tried were sometimes incredibly complex, all the more as there was of course no precedent in French anti-Semitic law that dated from before 1940. No one knows how many such cases came before the judges and what their outcomes were. In an exercise bordering on the surreal, magistrates had to reconstruct family trees to make their learned decisions as to the Jewishness of the applicants.[37]

Jurisprudence developed as months passed, with certain cases reaching the Council of State, which handed down its first rulings in February 1942. While it recognized the validity of the anti-Semitic legislation, it also served to some extent as a regulating force.[38]

Alongside French law, the Germans applied their own categories to determine who was Jewish and who was not, thereby deciding who could be deported. Theoretically, those who were transferred to Drancy had little legal recourse left to them. Some of them, however, were able to try another tack, as the German authorities at the camp classified the internees by different categories, not all of which were equally "deportable." The following classification was formalized by Aloïs Brunner when he took up his post at Drancy in 1942:[39]

A) "Aryans" arrested for having helped Jews, the Jewish spouses of Aryans, and half-Jews (not deportable);

B) the majority of Jews, with no protection;

C1) camp administrators, nearly all of whom were French citizens, who headed the various services and offices (and were theoretically not deportable);

C2) foreigners protected by their country: Swiss, Turks, Spaniards, Greeks, Romanians, Hungarians, Yugoslavs, and Argentines (they met with various fates, the protection offered generally being only temporary);

C3) wives of prisoners of war (not immediately deportable);

C4) Jews awaiting family reunification, who actually were used as an incentive to convince other members of their family to give themselves up: when an entire family was sent to Drancy, its members fell into category B and were deported;

C5) inmates in a position to be released if they could prove they were not Jewish.[40]

Those married to an Aryan spouse were among the most protected inmates, at least theoretically. They had to prove that they had been transferred to Drancy by mistake or that their request for a certificate attesting that they were not a member of the Jewish race was being processed. Some people in that category were lucky enough to be allowed to work outside the camp and thus avoided being deported.[41]

From the beginning of 1944 onwards, however, Aloïs Brunner, who was having increasing trouble filling trains bound for Auschwitz, began applying vague, not to say arbitrary, selection criteria,[42] with complete disregard for the documents and certificates produced by prisoners, and even for international law, which theoretically protected wives of prisoners of war from deportation.

Financial and Dietary Subsistence

Among the raft of new regulations whose purpose was to exclude Jews from French society, those pertaining to finance, business, and employment were immediately and drastically put into effect. Many Jewish business owners were dispossessed or robbed of their property, and forced to give up the management of their business. Public service employees lost their jobs, and thousands of employees in the private sector were dismissed. How did the 200,000 or so Jews who were still in France at the end of the Occupation manage to survive despite a policy of wholesale pauperization? No overall study has been made of this nevertheless fundamental question.

Two main reasons explain the dearth of research into the issue. First, analyses naturally turned first to the mechanisms of public policy of pillage (by the occupying forces) and spoliation (by Vichy) of Jewish property. In addition to ground-breaking studies by historians such as Joseph Billig,[43] we must also note the remarkable work of the Mattéoli Commission between 1997 and 2000, which was in charge of proposing procedures for returning seized assets and compensating victims. Second, it is virtually impossible for a historian to retrace the trajectory of the tens of thousands of people who, in order to escape a legal vice intended to crush them, often sought to leave as little trace as possible of their unlawful activities. Researchers nonetheless have some means of inquiry: with experience in exploring archives, they can sometimes detect clues in the files, examine detailed figures, analyze local monographs, and draw from a variety of testimonies. The present work offers such a synthesis.

As the noose tightened, Jews had to demonstrate a spirit of initiative, resourcefulness, and cunning to wiggle out of it. They tried to survive the best they could in spite of laws and regulations meant to keep them in an economical and financial stranglehold. Several types of reaction can be identified:

– holding on to their own resources for as long as possible so as to "live off their savings," either money withdrawn from the bank or valuables that they sold for cash. Additional sources of income from before the war were also of great help;
– circumventing the anti-Semitic legislation to continue their business activities in a roundabout way. Some were able to turn to legal ruses, especially to get around the law on the Aryanization of businesses;
– keeping an official full-time job, or finding another one, thus maintaining a legal source of income, by working for a Jewish organization recognized by Vichy, for instance, or even for the occupying forces. Children aged 14 and over were sometimes able to find a job and bring additional income into the household;

– when forced out of the system, people had to look for odd jobs, living by their wits, the black market and bartering. Their primary concern became survival in terms of the daily search for food, with the constant fear of identity checks and arrests;
– a fifth, very different reaction—because it made individuals more passive than active—was to rely on aid from the state or from charitable organizations.

The following pages attempt to give a sense of these highly contrasting situations, by examining individual trajectories that are fairly representative of the various paths that people took, and once again showing considerable differences between French Jews and foreign Jews.

For those who had some financial resources, the first means of dealing with the situation was to keep their money somewhere easily accessible, ready to take it with them if necessary. This was not specific to Jews. In 1940s France, cash was still often stashed at home: hidden away with valuables under the mattress, in the wardrobe, or in the garden. Transactions were frequently made in cash. It was far from the case that all adults had a bank account, and even when they did, the amounts deposited were usually quite small. The idea of opening a bank account did not necessarily occur to Jewish immigrants. People driven from their homes because of war were probably going to be carrying fairly large sums of money on them, if they had it. Some also took their valuables—jewelry and gold coins—that they would sell off as the need arose. Thus the Hanaus, who had been allowed to take thirty kilograms of personal belongings each with them, left with clothing, silver, and most of their money. Craftsmen and shopkeepers would sell off all or part of their stock, fearing that their merchandise would fall into the hands of the occupying forces, which meant that they might have substantial liquid assets.

When the Germans invaded in 1940, one might have thought that French people who did have a bank account would rush to withdraw their money, as happened in 1914, forcing the banks to impose a moratorium on withdrawals. In 1940, to the relief of the banks, that did not happen. However, the situation soon became alarming for Jews who held a bank account. Article 4 of the second German ordinance against the Jews, issued on 18 October 1940, stipulated that "any legal operation performed after 23 May 1940, disposing of the assets of the people named in paragraph 3 [the Jews], can be annulled by the head of the military administration in France."[44] Steered by the Nazi fantasy about the Jews' financial power, the determination to impede any transaction by Jews who held bank accounts, to investigate their accounts and later seize their assets, was already clear. The most affluent Jews were living in the Northern Zone, in Paris and its suburbs, where three-fifths of the nation's wealth was concentrated. The Mattéoli Commission report determined that "the use of banking services among the adult Jewish population in the occupied zone was about 45 per cent: there were nearly 60,000 depositors for an estimated population of just over 120,000 Jewish adults."[45]

Well-informed Jews were no doubt aware of the threat implicit in this German ordinance and quickly took appropriate action. As the demarcation line had just been established, a practical solution became obvious: to have as many funds possible transferred to the Free Zone. This was the decision made regarding the company owned by the Louis-Dreyfus family, one of the richest families in France, which in 1940 moved its headquarters to Marseille, where it already had a branch. In a symbolic move, the CGQJ took over the company's vacated Paris offices. In the Southern Zone, the bank accounts belonging to Jewish individuals and companies were not blocked, and so Pierre Louis-Dreyfus was able to continue to do business, including banking.[46] Non-Jewish account holders no doubt had the same idea. The transfer of funds to French territory not directly controlled by the occupying forces appeared to be a way of keeping money safe. It was theoretically illegal, however, for Jewish account holders to make such transfers.

The general climate of anti-Semitism and the instructions issued to banks could make bankers suspicious of their Jewish clients, which led some Jews to withdraw their money. Jean-Jacques Becker remembers what happened in his family: one day his mother went to get money from the bank and the teller asked her if she happened to be an *Israélite*. His mother refused to answer, emptied her account, and left. From then on money was stashed away at home. One day Jean-Jacques counted it: there were 1 million francs.[47]

Some foresaw the measures to "Aryanize" Jewish property and freeze bank accounts. Withdrawing money as fast as possible was the last resort to avoid disaster. Annette Krajcer describes what her father did in 1941; the family owned a women's apparel store on rue Saint-Antoine in Paris. In March 1941, the store was placed under the management of a CGQJ-appointed provisional administrator. Anticipating that his accounts were about to be blocked, her father went to the bank to withdraw all his money. He took it to the Poirots, a retired couple who were their neighbors in the countryside where they had a house. Throughout the war, Monsieur and Madame Poirot acted as bankers for Annette and Léa, sending them money as they needed it. In September 1945, the Poirots gave Monsieur Krajcer back the remaining funds together with a detailed account of the money with which he had entrusted them.[48]

The fear that accounts would be frozen was perfectly justified. On 28 May 1941, a new German ordinance obliged banks to set up such measures.[49] With grim foreboding the well-known playwright Tristan Bernard quipped: "All accounts are blocked, all the Blochs are accounted for!"[50] Actually the formula was flawed: since it had been issued by the occupying powers, the measure did not apply in the Free Zone and was never enforced, even after the German invasion of the Southern Zone. Bank accounts operated there as usual throughout the war, beyond the control of the CGQJ. The Mattéoli Commission was unable to ascertain how many bank accounts were held by Jews in the Southern Zone. In the Northern Zone there were an estimated 79,000. The amounts deposited were usually quite small: a few hundred francs in current accounts and a few dozen francs in savings accounts. Hardly great fortunes, despite the legend of Jewish wealth.

The term "blocked accounts" is misleading, however. The measure meant that an account was placed under surveillance, that all transactions required special authorization, and that they could not be emptied. This was of course to prevent the flight of this supposed Jewish capital. But in practice, so-called blocked accounts continued to function. What was referred to as "blocking" or "freezing" an account did not amount to confiscating the funds deposited. Account holders still had the right to withdraw a fixed monthly amount as stipulated in article 3 of the same ordinance, enabling them to meet "routine expenses." These measures remained in effect until the end of the Occupation.

Aryanization of Property, the Statut des Juifs, *and Ways Around the Law*

Many tragic situations nevertheless resulted from the obligation to "Aryanize" companies declared to be under Jewish ownership. The measure imposed by the German ordinance of 18 October 1940 in the Northern Zone was intended to eliminate supposed Jewish influence in the French economy, but was actually a "legal" means of despoiling them of their property and assets. All "Jewish" businesses were to be placed under the management of an "Aryan" provisional administrator. Once an administrator was appointed, the Jewish owner was dispossessed of his property. The managing administrator was in charge of handling the forced or voluntary sale of the business or simply liquidating it.

Vichy nevertheless succeeded in preventing the proceeds of these sales from coming under the direct control of the occupying forces. As head of the CGQJ, Xavier Vallat managed to convince the Germans that the proceeds from the sale of Jewish property be deposited in the *Caisse des Dépôts et Consignations* (CDC—Deposits and Consignments Fund), in an account opened in the name of the former owner. But the effort to keep Jewish assets in France soon came up against obstacles. In August 1941, the communist resistance began wounding or killing German soldiers and officers. One of the retaliation measures demanded by the Germans was a fine of a billion francs to be paid by the "Jewish community," even though there was no evidence that these actions had been organized by Jewish resistance fighters. To come up with this exorbitant sum, Vichy had to agree to the emptying of the best endowed accounts held in the CDC by Jews. Among the victims of pillage by the Germans is the well-known case of the Camondo family, wealthy Levantine bankers who had lived in Paris since the late nineteenth century.[51]

Such economic Aryanization measures were introduced a little later in the Free Zone, by the law of 22 July 1941. Due to cumbersome administrative procedures, they only came into force nearly a year after the Northern Zone, which marked another major difference from the French areas under German control. Nonetheless, the fact remains that the Vichy administration enforced the specifically French measures with zeal and efficiency, as is highlighted in Tal Bruttmann's detailed investigation of Grenoble and its surrounding area.[52]

The Mattéoli Commission revealed the scope of this Aryanization policy: "Just over 31,000 dossiers for the department of Seine, and over 11,000 for the other departments in the Occupied Zone: a large number. If one includes the Aryanizations in the Free Zone, probably between 7,000 and 8,000, files were opened and an administrator appointed for about 50,000 properties, companies or buildings," writes Antoine Prost.[53] Relative to the overall size of the Jewish population, estimated at 330,000 (including children), the figure is indeed high, particularly considering the significant proportion of small businessmen and artisans.

However, not all the proceedings initiated by the CGQJ resulted in the sale of property. In practice, a range of scenarios was possible, from the most brutal form of dispossession to the complete absence of enforcement. Jewish commercial districts in Paris, such as around the Carreau du Temple, were among those targeted by the most severe actions: "At ten o'clock on 24 April 1941, several provisional managers showed up, closed down the shops, and immediately proceeded to take inventory of the merchandise on display. At four in the afternoon, each one of the Jewish storeowners got his official red placard posted in the window after paying a fee of 200 francs. Some 225 stores had just been Aryanized."[54] Provisional administrators out for personal gain also misappropriated funds and committed other abuses after the property was sold. As appointed managers, they sometimes paid themselves large fees out of company funds. The Aryanization of Jewish property was an opportunity for some to make very lucrative business deals, which could only encourage denunciation.

A number of cases dragged on and were never conclusively dealt with. The Mattéoli Commission determined that, depending on the sector of activity, "anywhere between 20 and 80 per cent of the cases opened had not been settled by the end of Occupation, the two extremes being textiles and leather goods on one hand (very "Aryanized"), and real estate on the other."[55] A number of reasons might explain this: cumbersome bureaucracy, differences between legislation in the Occupied Zone and the Free Zone, where legal actions were not as punitive, the absence of the Jewish owner who had in all likelihood fled, and the passivity of provisional administrators, in whose interest it was to let things drag on so as to continue collecting their fees for as long as possible.

In actual fact, the future of a business placed under provisional administration depended primarily on the administrator himself. Every case was different. Some administrators showed understanding towards the Jewish owner, allowing him to continue to run his own business. Sometimes an administrator and owner were in collusion and put together a fake dossier for the CGQJ. It is impossible to know how many such cases there were, but this was certainly one way of getting around the Aryanization laws so that the Jewish owner could pursue his professional activity. Such situations sometimes arose out of employee loyalty to their employer, as was the case with the industrialist Gustave Nordon who, although officially divested of his business in Nancy on 3 August 1941, nevertheless continued to run it with the help of members of his board of directors.[56]

An example of a case that dragged on until the Liberation was the hairdressing salon in Paris run by Marguerite and Albert Grunberg, whose adventures were recounted in Albert's diary. While Albert went into hiding, his wife managed for a time to prevent the Aryanization of the business, since the premises were in her name and she was not Jewish. However, on 22 August 1943 she received a visit from a man who told her that as someone who had been "under Jewish influence," her assets were to be liquidated. Shortly after, a letter arrived from the CGQJ informing her that an administrator had been appointed. The Grunbergs' lawyer, Monsieur Rivierez, did his best to stall the case for as long as possible.

In October, the CGQJ asked Marguerite for her professional license, which she did not have. She asked for help from the chairman of the hairdressers' association, who at first refused, but then promised to help for a 3,000-franc fee. According to Albert, the chairman and the shop administrator connived to squeeze as much money as they could out of his wife. The administrator gave Marguerite until 25 January 1944 to find a buyer for the salon. Sale to the first potential buyer she found, Madame Chabanaud, the wife of one of Albert's neighbors whom they had befriended, fell through because she was contractually barred from opening a business in Paris. The Grunbergs then attempted to have the salon purchased by friends who would continue to employ Marguerite. Eventually it was Marguerite's nephew Henri who lent his aunt the required amount (40,000 francs) to arrange the fictitious purchase of the salon in the name of his wife Denise. In March–April 1944, the sale, which was authorized by the hairdressers' association, was rejected by the CGQJ on the grounds that Marguerite knowingly underestimated the value of the salon. Meanwhile, both the hairdressers' syndicate representative and the administrator continued to extort money from Marguerite. But the expert appointed to assess the value of the salon told Marguerite he would declare whatever value she wished. The case was still pending when Paris was liberated.[57]

The German ordinance of 26 April 1941 further limited employment opportunities for Jews. From that date onwards, they were permitted to work only in subordinate positions and were not allowed to have any contact with the public.[58] Madeleine Grunfeld's mother, whose toy store was Aryanized, repaired dolls off the books to make a little money. The ban on contact with the public was not, however, strictly respected everywhere.

Large companies were expected to dismiss their "Jewish managerial staff." Annie and Jean-Jacques Becker's father, who managed a factory belonging to the "Jouet de Paris" toy company, was dismissed after the *Statut* was published.[59] But some managers did what they could to outsmart the new legislation. The Banque de France, which in 1940 was a private institution, tried to keep its Jewish employees in the back offices in order not to create trouble. Those who had no choice but to leave either took retirement, were transferred, or were laid off and given a graduated salary decrease.[60] If company directors were forced to dismiss a Jewish manager, they could still hire them back in a subordinate position that had no customer contact. Putting aside moral considerations, this was in the executives' best interests if they wanted to retain an experienced employee at a time when there was a serious dearth of qualified personnel (many of whom had become prisoners of war). Such solutions had the advantage of continuing to provide an income, however modest, for these employees. The new German ordinance did, however, undoubtedly increase the unemployment rate among Jews and led to increased levels of impoverishment.

The economic and financial situation of the Jewish population also deteriorated in the Free Zone, though seemingly to a lesser degree and with a lag behind the areas under German occupation. In autumn 1940, going to the Free Zone—or remaining there—was for some a way to keep their job or look for another one, as a number of businesses had moved their headquarters there. The city of Lyon "served as a fall-back base for many Jewish bankers who had left the capital."[61]

But Vichy's second *Statut des Juifs*, issued on 2 June 1941, followed by the Aryanization law of 22 July, caught up with Jews who had gone south to try to escape the more drastic restrictions already in effect in the Northern Zone. This *Statut* considerably broadened the ban on professional activities. It excluded Jewish persons from the entire civil service (article 2), the professions, commercial and industrial activities, artisanal work, the press and the service sector (articles 4 and 5). Certain exemptions were provided for: Jews could continue to work for strictly scientific or Jewish publications. The 22 July Aryanization law affected a host of shops and companies, including those that had moved their headquarters to the Free Zone precisely to escape the German ordinances. To get around them, the main response by Jewish owners, as in the Northern Zone, was to arrange fictitious sales. Elie Scali, Arlette's husband, joined her in Graulhet (Tarn), where he ran a tanning factory. To escape the Aryanization of the factory, he arranged a fictitious sale with the collusion of Monsieur Duverger, who had also moved to Graulhet with his family. Elie Scali was thus able to continue to operate his business. Monsieur Duverger's daughter Simone sent him files every day via her maid, Odette, who hid them in her baby carriage. Simone was taking a huge risk, especially since she was married to the prefect of Montpellier, Roger Hontebeyrie.[62]

As months went by, it became increasingly difficult for Jews to continue their normal business activities. There was still a significant distinction, however, between the two zones: unlike the Germans, Vichy did not bar Jews from coming into contact with the public. This difference was not insignificant in everyday life and made it possible to preserve a few pockets of employment. Some people were able to continue working, in the banking sector for instance, for a fairly long time.[63]

Continuing to Live By One's Trade

The public service: Pensions, exemptions and odd jobs

It is important to read in detail all the articles of the *Statut* of 2 June 1941 to understand in full the consequences of Jews being excluded from the civil service. The exclusion measures, in themselves scandalous, unfair, and humiliating for the men and women who fell victim to them, nevertheless did not leave former civil servants without any income at all: article 7 of the statute stipulated that civil servants affected were "entitled to claim their rights" to "pensions and allowances" after fifteen years of service. Those who were ineligible "would receive a salary for a duration that would be fixed by a decision of the public administration." In other words, civil servants who were now barred could continue to receive their state pension or an allowance that might enable them to make ends meet. The specific amount of these stipends and their duration is unknown.

Situations probably varied considerably. There is no doubt senior officials received privileged treatment, like Philippe Erlanger, purged from the Ministry of Public Education and Fine Arts, who wrote in his memoirs that his salary continued to be paid for two years.[64] Depending on their age, some civil servants were able to take early retirement and thus receive a pension. According to the ministry, "administrative arrangements" were set up to soften the blow of exclusion, in all likelihood with the complicity of certain department heads.

The 2 June 1941 *Statut* listed those categories that were exempted from the new provisions: holders of a veteran's card, bearers of the Croix de Guerre or the Legion of Honor, recipients of war decorations, or "wards of the nation or the forebears, widow or orphans of a soldier who died for France" (article 3). The statute also did not apply to "prisoners of war until their return from captivity" (article 7). The large number of exemptions raises a number of questions. The law seemed to be based on a paradox. On the one hand, it redefined the legal framework of state anti-Semitism in 1941. But on the other, it exempted Jews who had shown bravery in combat against a victorious longstanding enemy that was now occupying two-thirds of the national territory. According to the logic of patriotism, the supreme value attributed to giving one's life to the nation somehow transcended anti-Semitic categories.

The question remains as to whether the two *Statuts des Juifs* were enforced with equal rigor by the various French state administrative institutions. No research appears to have been done that both examines the situation in each ministry and also takes into account possible differences in enforcement of the law between the Northern Zone and the Southern Zone. To what extent did civil servants drag their heels in applying Vichy's instructions; did they twist the rules or even protest? One of the rare studies providing an overall picture of Aryanization within a specific ministry is Claude Singer's research on the national education ministry. According to him, 0.5 per cent of the teachers employed by the ministry in 1940 were *Israélites*. A CGQJ memo dated 2 April 1942 estimated that 986 of them had been suspended in accordance with the first *Statut* and 125 in accordance with the second.[65]

Nearly three-quarters of those who lost their jobs were primary school teachers. At secondary level, Jacqueline de Romilly (née David) and Simone Veil were both frozen out by the *Statuts des Juifs*. In the universities, famous names such as Marcel Mauss and Léon Brunschvicg were fired. Some administrators complied and enforced the orders, in spite of their disapproval.[66] Others refused to do so. Gustave Monod, then 55 years old and inspector general for the Académie de Paris (Paris school board), refused to draw up a list of Jewish teachers. He informed the rector of the Académie of this fact in a report dated 4 November 1940. Demoted and then forcibly retired, Monod joined the Resistance, becoming a member of the *Défense de la France* movement.[67]

Most university teachers who were dismissed from their posts did not inform their students beforehand; they simply bade them farewell on the last day of class without uttering any complaint about what had happened and urged them to remain loyal to their country. This dignified attitude, according to Claude Singer, was the result of a sense of disbelief among the teachers dismissed, who could barely grasp what was happening to them.[68] A few exemptions were granted, for instance to scholars of international renown, including Louis Halphen and Marc Bloch. But such measures happened only in the rarest of cases, because of the German authorities' hostility to the very principle of exemption. By late 1942, all Jewish professors who had been reported or discovered to be Jewish (barring a few exemptions) are believed to have been dismissed.

Deprived of a job, how were teachers able to survive? Some received a retirement pension, compensation that was proportional to their seniority, or an advance of a few months, while the wives of prisoners of war continued to receive their husband's salary until the statute was applied to them when they came home. But many soon found themselves with no regular means of survival. In that case, most sought to make a living by giving private lessons or taking odd jobs. Some were lucky enough to find a teaching job in an educational institution in the Free Zone. This was the unusual case of Samuel Abrahamovitsch at La Roseraie, a Catholic secondary school in Dieulefit (Drôme), a town that would become known for its spirit of resistance. The school's principal, Monsieur Arcens, made no secret, even to the authorities, of his opposition to Vichy. When he received a letter from the CGQJ instructing him to dismiss Samuel Abrahamovitsch, he tore it up and acted as though he had never received it. Samuel Abrahamovitsch continued teaching there up until the Liberation.[69]

Discriminatory measures also targeted students. On 21 June 1941, Vichy instituted a quota for Jewish students, limiting them to 3 per cent of the student body in universities and institutions of higher education. But no instructions were given as to how the 3 per cent was to be calculated.[70] As it turned out, institutions did not apply this legislation consistently.

The medical field

A number of Jews were excluded from the medical field. At the outset, these exclusions targeted doctors of foreign origin, most of whom were Jewish. The law of 16 August 1940 reorganized the medical profession, stipulating that "no-one [could] practice as a medical doctor in France if he [did] not have French nationality by virtue of being born of a French father." Nonetheless, the *Statut des Juifs of* 3 October 1940 authorized Jews to practice medicine, and they were not banned from doing so by the 2 June 1941 *Statut* either. It was first those working in the public sector and education who were barred from professorships, clinical directorships, and assistantships. By autumn 1940, some fifty Jewish university hospital professors and seventeen doctors and surgeons were excluded.[71] Robert Debré was an exception. The second *Statut* on 2 June 1941 and its associated enforcement decree instituted a quota restricting the number of Jewish practitioners to 2 per cent per department, with the same exemptions as those applied in the civil service.

It was soon clear that these exemptions posed a problem for the CGQJ, because the number of Jewish doctors who met the conditions for exemption often exceeded the permitted 2 per cent. In fact, a medical inspector had to choose who was allowed to continue practicing according to a list drawn up by the French Ordre des médecins (medical board) newly established by Vichy. It all depended on the zeal with which the directive was enforced.

Some Jewish doctors continued to practice, as attested by the report written by Léo Hamon in 1941.[72] Hamon, a Parisian Jewish lawyer who had taken refuge in Toulouse, was involved with the first resistance groups to set up in the city. Since he was in contact with the Joint, he agreed to conduct a survey for them on the situation of Jews in Paris, where he went in the winter of 1940–1941. Writing about the doctors' situation, Léo Hamon said, "While Jews continue to practice quite normally, maintaining their list of patients intact, by contrast in professional gatherings they are given to hear hostile remarks [...]. Generally speaking, [...] the medical world is certainly one in which the elimination of a certain number of colleagues is accepted with the greatest satisfaction."[73] As it happens, following the publication of the second *Statut*, the first chairman of the medical board, Professor René Leriche, managed to stall the procedures initiated against certain colleagues.[74]

The paramedical professions do not appear to have been forbidden to Jews, as is apparent from the story of Henri Opoznov's father, a blind Jewish physiotherapist who worked in Paris and later in Megève.[75] Joseph Minc, a Jewish immigrant of Polish origin, also managed to make it through the years of the Occupation earning a decent living as a dental prosthetist. In 1939, he earned his degree as a dental surgeon and volunteered for the army. He was taken prisoner, but he managed to get rid of all his papers except his diploma. In September 1940, even though he was Jewish, he was released on the grounds that he was a member of the medical profession. Minc returned to his family and his Paris apartment and resumed work in his dental laboratory. In 1942, given the difficulty of obtaining supplies, he found it "more profitable" to be hired by another laboratory, owned by Dr Perrault in Neuilly-sur-Seine. Thanks to his job and the fake identity papers that he forged himself, Minc was able to live more or less normally, at the same time as being active in the Resistance. It is likely that his degree in dentistry was one of the factors that enabled him to survive.[76]

IN THE FACE OF PERSECUTION

The Need for Labor

It would be impossible to detail the experiences, profession by profession, of all those who managed to legally hold down a job that was in some way related to their training. Most of those who did were French Jews, although some, like Joseph Minc, were Jewish immigrants. Foreign Jews who held down a job were far more exposed, since from the beginning of the Occupation they were considered suspect and at risk of being interned. For them, the priority was no longer to find a job in French society, to which most of them never really belonged. As soon as the deportations began in summer 1942, Vichy was delivering foreign Jews to the German occupiers. By late 1940, although they had no way of imagining the tragedy to come, Jewish and Christian groups had already begun working to rescue as many as possible, starting with children.

Given the need for labor, the Vichy government released some able-bodied internees from the camps and assigned them to work crews. Usually they joined one of the foreign labor units (GTEs) created by the law of 27 September 1940 pertaining to "supernumerary foreigners in the national economy." In early 1941, 50,000 men, most of them Spanish republicans, filled the ranks of 200 GTEs and were employed, often in very difficult working conditions, by the state or by private companies in agriculture, industry or in the mines. They were joined by smaller numbers of foreign Jews, forming so-called mixed GTEs made up of Jews and non-Jews. [77]

To be assigned to a GTE meant to have a legal, supervised job that was often backbreaking but still preferable to being interned in a camp. But for how long? Starting in summer 1942, many foreign Jews in these units could no longer escape deportation. Within a GTE, people were obviously under direct government surveillance and could therefore be transferred to Drancy at any moment. This was, however, not the case for all of them, as in the Lot-et-Garonne department, for instance, there were still dozens of foreign Jews in mixed GTEs at the Liberation. [78] Others were not so lucky, especially those who were grouped in "unified" GTEs, in other words, made up solely of foreign Jews, strangely referred to by Vichy as "Palestinian" units. Nearly all of them, numbering about a thousand, would be deported. [79]

113

Work in a Jewish Organization

There was another legal employment sector open to the Jews, and that was to work for one of the Jewish organizations officially recognized by Vichy. The regime's attitude towards the Jews was not only one of stigmatization, exclusion, and repression. That would be too simplistic a view of a government that was marked by contradictions. Though Vichy ostracized Jews, it nonetheless allowed them a legal perimeter, granting them the right to assemble within their own organizations, whether to practice their religion, educate their children, or provide medical and social assistance.

Jewish religious observance thus remained possible throughout the Occupation. This was more difficult in the Northern Zone, where many synagogues were targeted by attacks and acts of vandalism. However, "the practice of Judaism was not prohibited by any legal measure and so could continue unrestricted in areas entirely under German domination, even if it was necessarily obliged to remain discreet."[80] The chief rabbi of Paris, Julien Weill, remained in the capital throughout the entire Occupation, where he did his best to protect his congregation. In October 1943, on the eve of Rosh Hashanah, a police blockade was set up to inspect identity papers after the service. Julien Weill took it upon himself to hide all those whose documents were not in order in the choir changing room, thus enabling them to escape arrest.[81]

In the Free Zone, synagogues were not closed and the practice of Judaism could be continued more openly, at least until the German invasion of November 1942. Consequently, rabbis were able to continue legally to conduct services and, for those who came under the Concordat in Alsace-Moselle, to receive their salary from the Vichy ministry of religion.

Vichy also recognized the Jewish Scouts organization, the *Éclaireurs israélites de France*, (EIF), and, at least in the early days of the regime, provided it with material and financial support. There was a somewhat paradoxical dovetailing of the values of the EIF—founded by Robert Gamzon in 1923 and still headed by him during the war—and those of Vichy. The "return to the land" theme championed by the EIF before the war was quite in line with what the Vichy government itself was trying to promote. "It did not seem dishonorable to the EI to receive help from the French state, any more than it seemed strange to the various ministries to grant aid to a Jewish youth movement."[82] This meant that the EI received equipment and even financial subsidies from the government, at least until 1941. Not only that, but the EIF was seen by Vichy to be an exclusively *Israélite* and French movement, even though young Jewish immigrants were included in their activities. The EIF was one of the six scouting federations recognized by the state, which on 1 October 1940 established the umbrella organization *Le Scoutisme français* at the Château de l'Oradou in Clermont-Ferrand, all of whose members took part in the Leadership School in Uriage, without prompting anti-Semitic reactions.[83] The future of the EIF was, however, called into question when the UGIF was set up in November 1941. Although Xavier Vallat, head of the CGQJ, assured Robert Gamzon at meeting in December that Jewish scouting activities could continue, this tolerance on the part of Vichy was not to last. In January 1943, his successor as head of the CGQJ, Louis Darquier de Pellepoix, ordered the EIF to be disbanded, forcing the movement to take its activities underground, a precaution it had already set in motion in the summer of 1942.[84]

As regards medical and social aid, the *Œuvre de Secours aux Enfants* (OSE)—the Children's Welfare Organization—was also recognized by the Vichy authorities. This international organization, founded in Russia in 1912 to provide relief for Jewish people in need, opened a branch in France in 1934. Its first president was the non-Jewish politician Justin Godard. During the 1930s, the OSE focused its efforts on Jewish immigrants in the poor neighborhoods of Paris and its suburbs. It set up a children's day camp in Montmorency and a free clinic in Paris, as well as a young people's psychological observation center for the treatment of the traumas of immigrant children.

After the armistice, the OSE split into two branches. The organization headquarters were moved to Montpellier, in the Free Zone. There the OSE focused its efforts on obtaining the release of as many internees as possible, starting with children, from the camps in southern France. Other associations, such as the Cimade and *Amitié Chrétienne* (Christian Fellowship), worked alongside it towards similar goals. The OSE operated out in the open at the time and necessarily cooperated with the prefects, as they issued residence permits in their department. In the Southern Zone, "with 230 employees, doctors, teachers and social workers, the OSE created health and social welfare centers in provincial towns as well as children's homes, nurseries, sanatoriums and day care centers to ensure the protection of several hundred orphaned children or needy refugee families."[85] Among its staff, the OSE employed a number of foreign Jews, regardless of whether their documentation was in order, as was the case for Amalia Kanner who, as we have seen, after being hired legally as a cook for a children's home in Eaubonne, was not permitted to follow the children when they were evacuated to Montintin. She managed to make her own way to Montintin, where she was hired back by the OSE at their new establishment, even though she did not have the proper documents. Sal, her husband, was also employed there illegally as a handyman.[86] Mia and Sal were later transferred to the Le Couret home, still illegally. After they managed to obtain forged identity cards, Mia was employed in a fourth children's home, the "Pouponnière" in Limoges. In September 1943, she was released from the Nexon camp, where she had been interned. Now, with her papers in order, she worked in an OSE orphanage in Broût-Vernet, near Vichy.[87] Jewish organizations thus could provide work and shelter for people who had no means of subsistence or anywhere to go.

Like the EIF, the OSE was confronted with the obligation to join the UGIF. In April 1942, its secretary general, Joseph Millner, joined the UGIF as head of its health directorate. However, a few months later, a new OSE member, Georges Garel, a French engineer of Ukrainian Jewish stock from Lyon, formed an underground network for hiding children in that city (see chapter 3). Now, both legal and underground, the OSE entered a difficult period of its existence that lasted until the end of the Occupation.

Whatever changes were imposed upon it, from its founding in November 1941 at the instigation of the German occupiers, the UGIF was expected to bring under its umbrella all existing Jewish organizations, with the exception of the Consistory. The organization, which grew out of the *Comité de Coordination des Œuvres de Bienfaisances Juives* (Committee for the Coordination of Jewish Charitable Organizations), founded on 2 January 1941, counted over one hundred member organizations.[88] The Rothschild Hospital was incorporated in October 1942. It was the official institutional framework, recognized by both the occupying forces and by Vichy, within which Jews could work legally and receive a salary for their labor. Relative to the size of the Jewish population identified by the CGQJ, the staff of this organization remained fairly small: in 1944, it employed approximately 800 people in the Northern Zone and 650 in the Southern Zone. In a time of severe shortages, the opportunity to work for the UGIF was far from insignificant, however. The salaries earned by Denise Lefschetz and her father during the Occupation, for instance, as a counselor and director of the center respectively, were the only financial resources they had to draw on. According to the pay slips kept by Madeleine Grunfeld, who became deputy director of the Vauquelin office (Paris 5th arrondissement), in October 1943 she earned 3,946 francs.

Those who worked at the UGIF were constantly in danger of arrest, even though they had legitimation cards, which theoretically protected them and their families. In 1943 and 1944, several members of the UGIF staff, mostly French Jews, were arrested and deported. These arrests did not target low-grade staff, who were largely spared, but rather the executive staff, particularly those involved in relief efforts in Southern Zone.

The role of the UGIF, obliged to cooperate with the occupying forces and Vichy even as its members were carried off to their deaths, has been severely criticized by eyewitnesses and observers of the period. In the 1980s, for instance, both Maurice Rajsfus and Jacques Adler maintained that the Jews, via this organization created by the Nazis, were caught up in institutionalized collaboration, leading them in a manner of speaking to participate in their own extermination,[89] a thesis that was fervently disputed by Serge Klarsfeld.[90]

In the first decade of the 2000s, Michel Laffitte's work opened new avenues for research. In a detailed study of the evolution of the structures and staff who worked there, he demonstrates, first of all, the different phases of development of the UGIF, showing how its very centralized organization in the Northern Zone is to be distinguished from its operations in the Southern Zone, where its leadership was more dispersed. He also makes it clear that this French organization can in no way be compared to a *Judenrat* ("Jewish council," imposed by the Nazis, predominately in the ghettos in Eastern Europe), which may have been the Nazi intention. On the other hand, there is no doubt that the UGIF, because of its legal framework, was involved in the process of deporting Jews and thus was indeed caught up in the fatal chain of events.[91] This was clearly the specific intention of its Nazi instigators. However, several members of the UGIF worked to undermine the Nazi plans by playing a double game, using their official roles to cover for or even aid underground networks protecting Jewish children and adults. Between the legal framework and the illegal activities of some of its members the UGIF thus navigated an ambiguous situation that requires nuanced and detailed contextual analysis.

Working for the Occupying Forces

There has been no overall study of those who worked for the Germans in France. As it is impossible to provide a complete view, a number of trajectories will serve to illustrate the diversity of these cases. Some professions were more useful to the occupying forces than others, such as furriers who supplied the German army, which faced freezing temperatures on the eastern front. Jewish furriers were confronted with the question of whether or not they were prepared to work for the occupying forces, although it could be argued that they did not really have a choice. As anti-Semitic measures were increasingly impoverishing Jews, such work enabled some of them to preserve a source of income.

It also, in theory at least, saved those who dealt in furs from the worst. But only in theory. In fact, the UGIF secured relative protection for furriers and their children up until the end of 1942. But in 1943 some were deported.[92] The usefulness of their work, or what could be called its functional rationality, was swept aside by the radicalism of Nazi anti-Semitism.

Others worked for the occupying forces without necessarily having chosen to, for example those who before the war worked for a company which then found itself manufacturing products to be sent to Germany. The weight of circumstance, the unforeseen escalation of the situation, and the urge to protect one's own family all go towards explaining why people might have ended up working for the Germans. The trajectory Simon Krajcer, Annette Krajcer's father, is a good example. After the roundup of foreign Jews in the 11th arrondissement in August 1941, he decided to leave Paris and was hired as a lumberjack in one of the Vichy government's civil construction projects located in the Landes in southwestern France. For a time this work offered him relative protection, as well as allowing him occasional leave to visit his family in Paris. But in late December, all the Jews working in the Landes were arrested and interned in the Mérignac camp. In March 1942, this group of Jews agreed, as part of a program set up by the UGIF, to work on a German-run farm located in Bulson, in the French Ardennes mountains. They and their families were promised a degree of protection, but this turned out to be nothing but a lure: Sophie, Simon's wife, was arrested during the Vel' d'Hiv' roundup in July 1942 but in spite of her husband's protests she was not released, and she was deported in early August. Simon Krajcer remained in Bulson until January 1944, when he decided to escape.

Others used cunning, concealing the fact of their Jewishness in order to be hired by a German company. They walked straight into the lion's den, so to speak, betting that such an unlikely situation offered them the best possible protection. This was the wager of Boris Schreiber, a Russian Jew with Polish citizenship who used his German-sounding name to devise a subterfuge. Using a fake passport, in 1943 Boris pretended to be Russian Orthodox and was taken on by the Organisation Todt, a Nazi engineering corps, in Marseille.[93]

Jews who were subjected to forced labor at Todt, or other Reich engineering projects, were not always so lucky. Sal, Mia Kanner's husband, described for her the grueling work conditions on the Atlantic Wall site he was assigned to:

> Sal was in a group of cement carriers. A worker placed a hundred-pound sack of cement on his back. It took him and the other men of his detail five minutes to reach the cement mixer. They put down their sacks and returned to the starting place for another load. Mid-day there was a lunch break—a cup of soup. Then the men went back to their labor. […] Work ended at sundown; Jewish men were forced to labor seven days a week. […]. [One day], on the road back from the fortification site, Sal saw a man's legs buckle under him. Two Jews picked him up, placed his arms round their shoulders and dragged him back to the barracks. The next morning he could not stand up. When twenty-nine Jews returned to the barracks that evening, he was gone.[94]

At least 1,552 Jews assigned to this detail were deported to death camps.[95]

Job Retraining

Surviving in the countryside

Between these two extremes—working for a Jewish organization or for the Germans—other less exposed areas of legality or semi-legality were available for many Jews in France. While the laws promulgated by the occupying forces and Vichy set out everything that was forbidden to Jews, they also indicated, by omission, areas that were not forbidden to them. First among these was agricultural work, which was not on the list of banned occupations. The omission was obviously not unrelated to Vichy ideology, which sanctified labor of the land. This "opportunity"—which was minimal but at the same time very broad (France at the time still had a largely agricultural economy)—offered many people a means of subsistence, and explains why Jewish organizations such as the EIF or *Organisation Reconstruction Travail* (ORT—Professional Retraining and Reorientation Organization) developed occupational training courses for rural trades—sometimes with Vichy government support, as we have seen.

Denise Gamzon, the wife of Robert Gamzon, in 1940 the head of the EIF, recalled that her husband "had a dream, perhaps a utopian one, of training crews of French Jewish farmers who knew how to farm land while remaining true to Jewish traditions."[96] The first sustainable rural center was set up in the commune of Lautrec (Tarn), between Albi and Castres, with some forty young people aged between 16 and 25. It was well accepted by the local inhabitants, and developed a Jewish educational program.[97]

There were various reasons why Jews moved to rural areas: some were looking for food or affordable lodgings, some were trying to get away as far as they could from the persecution. As almost all came from the city, their transplantation to the countryside was not easy. In his remarkable study on Jews in Auvergne, the anthropologist Martin de la Soudière describes the arrival of some of the refugees. "And so they settled into their temporary little house. A garden might be made available to them, the husband would work there, often clumsily, as with other tasks. [...] Hired as farmhands, a few others learned the trade quickly, bundling firewood and carrying bags of grain."[98]

Many people either tried to cultivate a small kitchen garden or get themselves hired for various types of farm work, or both, in order to survive. The Friedländers began farming a plot of land in Néris-les-Bains, and also resorted to occasional crop picking. Upon arriving in Vienne, the Hanau family farmed different plots of land the mayor made available to them, and later rented a garden in Loye-sur-Arnon. After the family took refuge in Blot-l'Eglise (Puy-de-Dôme) in 1943, Denis Lindon studied for his baccalaureate by correspondence and herded cows and learned to work the fields. Arlette Scali left Graulhet with her children around the same time to hide in an isolated house in the small village of Murat (Tarn). She survived thanks to the vegetables she grew in her garden, which she bartered with local farmers.

Some accounts show evidence of complete professional retraining. Jean Samuel's father had been a pharmacist in Alsace. In 1940, the Samuels fled to the southwest where they bought a large house, Villa Marie, in the village of Dausse, 25 km from Agen. Jean's parents, aunts and uncles, brother, and cousins established a sort of agricultural commune there. Jean, the eldest child, was sent to study to be a pharmacist in Toulouse. But, in 1943, fearing for his safety, he moved back to Villa Marie. His memoirs give the impression of a prosperous, almost idyllic life:

> Photographs from the period attest to our peaceful, rural life. In one you can see the women in the family sitting on the porch of Villa Marie, in front of the handsome balustrade, smiling. [...] In another, my uncles are posing in front of our ox cart, like real farmers. The family had rediscovered the country life it once knew. More than that: we had become farmers. [...] We cultivated in all twenty hectares of land, mostly wheat fields. Like all the farmers in the areas, we grew plums and peaches, and we had innovated by starting to dry pears. [...] We had a very large meadow where we put our eight cows out to pasture. [...]. Madame Marty, the grocer, bought most of our produce and sold it on the black market.[99]

This kind of success story of "farming Jews" in the countryside is fairly unusual, and it turned to tragedy on 2 March 1944. Men from the Gestapo circled Villa Marie, no doubt in search of resistance fighters. Among those arrested were Jean Samuel, his parents, his brother, and his uncles. All of them were part of convoy 70 that left Drancy for

Auschwitz. Of the men in his family, Jean Samuel was the only one to survive. Assigned to the chemistry commando, he met a certain Primo Levi, whom he befriended. Levi, who nicknamed Jean "Pikolo," mentions the importance of their friendship in *If This Is a Man*, published in 1947.

Plying one's trade in a rural area

Many felt much less apt for work in the fields or did not even wish to try. Rather than do nothing at all, they tried to ply their original trade in the countryside. Sometimes there was an opportunity to be seized, such as was the case for Jacqueline Feldman's father who moved from Paris to settle with his family, all Polish Jews, in the village of Noirétable, in the hills of Forez (Loire). They rented the second floor of a house. "At first," she remembered:

> My father went to work in Saint-Étienne during the week and came home on weekends. Then he requested permission from the mayor to replace the village tailor, who was a prisoner of war. The mayor, a churchgoer and supporter of Pétain, who was forced out of his post after the Liberation, approved his request, although he knew full well that we were Jewish. That is what enabled us to fit in: my father was valued for his work, all the villagers put orders in with him, including the gendarmes and the countess. He hired several village women to help him.[100]

There is also the case of a dental surgeon who had studied in Nancy. Standing in for his local colleague, he made house calls in the mountains, all the way to the Creuse, the next department over: "He went off on his bicycle. He treated resistance fighters too. [...] He was paid with meat, cheese and eggs."[101] Nearly all the time, services rendered were paid for in kind, in other words, in food.

House arrest and the perils of idleness

This kind of integration into local life through work was far from being always successful and sometimes it was even possible. When that was the case, Jewish refugees remained in the village doing little or nothing. Such enforced idleness could only be damaging. The ones who suffered the most were those under house arrest.

House arrest did not begin with the war and did not only apply to Jews. The measure had been instituted during the Third Republic by the Daladier government to isolate foreigners, if deemed necessary, as they were increasingly regarded with suspicion. This exclusion policy immediately became a central feature of Vichy's anti-Semitic strategy. The internment or house arrest of foreign Jews, by decision of the prefect, was authorized by the law of 4 October 1940.[102]

One of the main purposes of house arrest was to keep "undesirables" separate from the "healthy" part of the population, and to that end, some were forcibly relocated to very remote rural areas. The town of Lacaune, in the Montagne Noire range, was a perfect candidate to receive these "undesirables," since it was far removed from all the large urban centers in the area (Castres, Albi, Toulouse) and poorly served by the road network. Between 1942 and 1944, Lacaune's original population of 2,500 grew by 648 new inhabitants, including 128 children. Approximately 100 of these new arrivals would be arrested in the roundup of 26 August 1942 and deported. They were mainly Polish and Dutch Jewish immigrants, but there were also Austrians, Russians, Romanians, Belgians, and Czechoslovakians, the vast majority of them of modest means: "80 per cent of them were poor people who had no money at all."[103]

Enjoying a limited degree of freedom of movement, those who were under house arrest had to fulfill a number of requirements, including regular check-ins with the gendarmerie. Many were condemned to spending their days in idleness, which induced boredom in some and exasperation in others, and created friction between the two populations.

Some did manage eventually to find employment, usually in agriculture. They helped out in the fields or on farms, while offering their skills as shoemaker, tailor, or seamstress. Such offers of service, often paid in kind, helped considerably to acquaint the two populations—at first worlds apart—with one another. Whether or not they managed to find work, the people who were forcibly relocated to Lacaune seem to have shown a certain level of solidarity with each other, organizing themselves so that the most destitute were given some support: "A mutual aid fund was set up by those who had sufficient means and could help those in need, the poor people who had nothing left to their name."[104]

Among those under house arrest were the Markscheid family, introduced earlier, who had fled Belgium during the exodus and arrived in Grenade, near Toulouse. Meir and Taube Markscheid were forced to move to Lacaune in April 1942. They lived there with their daughter Léa, while their elder daughter, Fanny, remained at boarding school in Toulouse. The family rented a two-bedroom apartment on the second floor of an old house in the center of town. The Markscheids were under constant surveillance by the police, who made sure that accommodation and furnishings acquired by those who were forcibly relocated were limited to what was strictly necessary. They were also required to pay a visitor's tax. According to Léa, "humiliations were heaped upon us, for instance when we went to the public baths. Most of those under house arrest had to take their showers or baths there, because the majority of lodgings did not have a bathroom. Jews were only allowed to use them once a week, to avoid any possibility of contact with Aryans. It was always crowded, we had to wait for hours and then bathe very quickly." Because she did not settle in the local school, where the children of relocated Jews were grouped together in a special class, Léa was tutored along with the daughter of a local aristocrat who had a private teacher. Up until summer, "life was almost normal." Léa tells how her father made friends among the other German Jews under house arrest. He gave private lessons to support his family, but in June 1942, he was conscripted into an agricultural work crew. Shortly afterwards, rumors of arrests reached Lacaune. Meir Markscheid tried to put his daughters in a convent to ensure their safety, but the strategy failed because the mother superior insisted that they be baptized immediately, an act the father found too significant to be undertaken lightly.

Most of the Jews in Lacaune were aware that a roundup was imminent, Léa writes. Some decided to escape. They left on foot, alone or in groups, and hid out on neighboring farms or in caves, or managed to escape farther afield. Her father hatched a plan to cross the Pyrenees into Spain with his whole family. But a sudden deterioration in his wife's health made him change his mind. On the evening of 25 August, Taube was too ill to try to flee. Her husband decided to remain by her side. Léa and Fanny were meant to leave for Carcassonne the morning of 26 August, but it was too late:

It was very early. I was awakened by loud banging on the door of our apartment. Gendarmes burst in. They spoke French with the local accent. They had come to arrest us because we were Jewish. I could not imagine what horrible crime we had committed. [...] My mother was very ill, in bed, unable to get up. My father packed a suitcase. He had to leave. I knew they would take us as well. He said goodbye to my mother. She screamed, clinging to him with her arms around his neck. [...] Everything stops, the rest is a black hole. My memory has retained nothing else about that day and the weeks that followed.

Only the father was taken, as it was concluded that his wife could not be transported and was dependent on her two daughters, who were therefore allowed to remain with her. Meir was interned at Saint-Sulpice before being transported to Drancy and then in mid-September deported and murdered. After her husband's arrest, Taube Markscheid made a little money knitting for a hosiery shop. As she was very frail, most of the household chores fell to Léa. They both remained in Lacaune until the Liberation, and Fanny continued to join them during school holidays.[105]

An infinite variety of trajectories

Whether they lived in rural areas or not, many Jewish refugees tried to make a living by seeking odd jobs, or even tried to retrain. Some managed to find employment, often in a lowly position, in a different sector, using a fake name. This gave them a minimal source of income, but rarely lasted for long. They moved from one region to another, hoping that they would also move from one job to another, which was anything but sure. Such living conditions required an ability to move and adapt that not everyone was capable of, especially if they did not speak French, or spoke it poorly. But for those able to face changing situations, especially if they were young, departure spelled not only uncertainty and danger but also the promise of a different future.

Léon Poliakov's path between bread and butter work and his resistance activities illustrates how fluid these trajectories often were. He left Paris and arrived in Marseille in October 1941. Although not religious, he became secretary for Rabbi Zalman Schneerson's *Association des Israélites Pratiquants*. At some point in 1942, having already been arrested once, he succeeded in obtaining a forged identity card. On the advice of a friend, in late 1942 he went to work in a paper plant not far from Saint-Étienne. During this time, he became increasingly involved in hiding Jewish children. Russian by birth, Poliakov took French lessons to try to conceal his accent that made him roll his 'r's. His involvement in the Resistance led him to leave Saint-Étienne for Grenoble in 1943 where he managed to find a day job as secretary for a kitchen-gardening association.[106]

Alfred Grosser was a young man, born in Germany, who left Saint-Germain-en-Laye on his bicycle in 1940 at the time of the fall of France. He ended up in Saint-Raphaël, where his mother joined him. He studied for his baccalaureate by correspondence and passed it in 1942. He subsequently found a job as a mathematics teacher in a private school while his mother found a job as deputy director of a children's home in Cannes.[107]

Edith Hanau, who left Alsace with her family, was living in Chauvigny, near Poitiers in western France, in 1939. She initially found work in a tent canvas factory, and then in a factory making powder puffs. These jobs did not last long. She was then taken on at a wholesale grocery, bagging coffee. But when war broke out she lost her job because there was no more coffee. Through a friend who lodged at the home of the head accountant for a company that produced feed meal for livestock, Cérélactos, she found a job in the billing department after she learned how to type. In the final months of the war, she often left to hide out in the surrounding countryside for a few days, and then returned to work.

People had to seize whatever opportunity they could to make a little money, usually under the table, or be paid in kind. Wood turner, milk truck driver, newspaper peddler, traveling salesman: the list of odd jobs done by Jews during this period is as endless as it is varied.

An overall trend emerges from these varied situations: more and more people were sidestepping the law and transgressing the rules and regulations. They can hardly be said to have had a choice: if they wanted to make some kind of a living, they had to accept work off the books or be hired legally, but under an assumed name. Increasingly therefore, they entered the world of deception and scheming, the entwining of official life and unlawful practices. It would be an exaggeration, however, to claim that everyone practiced illegal behavior. Many people were afraid to break the law, as will be seen when it came to complying with the obligation to wear the yellow star. It was more a matter of the increasingly frequent overlapping of legal and unlawful behavior, which became characteristic of much of the population at the time, not only Jews.

Increasing Pauperization of the Jews and Vichy Government Handouts

As the months passed, specific and complementary policies implemented by the occupying forces and Vichy resulted in the increased pauperization of the Jews. This was a common goal of both powers: to make the Jews pariahs and thus to destroy the "Jewish influence" over society once and for all.

For their day-to-day survival, most of these Jews—the majority of whom were foreign families who found themselves in critical situations of poverty—depended at the time almost exclusively on support from relief agencies, starting with the UGIF. This state organization was funded by the Jews themselves, in accordance with the instructions from the Nazis to the Vichy government in 1941. The Nazis were applying the same policy they had already implemented in Germany: make the wealthiest Jews pay for assistance to the most needy. In that way, the "Aryan" state was relieved of the obligation to provide aid to the Jews, the wealthiest among them being obliged to use what money they still had to help the others.

In France, however, this policy came up against a number of difficulties. In order to increase the UGIF's operating budget, on 11 May 1943, with approval from the German authorities, Vichy decreed that, "an annual capitation tax would be levied on all Jews aged 18 and over, 120 francs in the Northern Zone, 360 francs in the Southern Zone [...]. In addition, banks were to charge a fee of 5 per cent on each subsistence withdrawal the Jews were permitted from the 80,000 blocked accounts listed in the Occupied Zone."[108] Although several major obstacles limited the effectiveness of this self-financing mechanism, the funds thus collected partially enabled the UGIF to pay its staff, provide relief for the internees in the camps, operate its canteens and children's centers, pay allowances for Jews in need, and so on. The funds were not sufficient, however, to meet the growing needs of a population whose resources were gradually drying up, among whom a substantial number of French Jews were soon included. To meet these expenses, relief organizations in the Southern Zone, operating under the UGIF umbrella, secretly received funds from a different source entirely: the United States. The American Jewish Joint Distribution Committee came to the aid of Jews persecuted by the Nazis in Europe. This support from abroad contributed substantially to the development of underground networks for protecting Jews in France.[109] In this way, up until the Liberation, UGIF continued to provide relief for thousands of Jews in both the Southern Zone and the Northern Zone.

In addition to this aid, many Jews were also able to receive allowances from the state, which were granted as part of its welfare policy, dating to well before the UGIF was established. This page of Vichy history is too little known, even though recent research has demonstrated its importance.[110] Marshal Pétain's government did not call into question the principle of public assistance as it had been known in France since the end of the nineteenth century. As a "national solidarity program," it was recognized as "a right for those who cannot work and have no resources. It is essentially administered by local municipalities, except for the insane and children in care, who come under departmental administrations."[111]

For this reason, in the aftermath of the armistice, Vichy attempted to meet the specific needs of categories of the population particularly affected by the war, in the first place refugees, casualties, and victims of bombing raids. Many measures were based on the experience of the First World War. For instance, as early as fall 1940, the government enabled hundreds of thousands of French and foreign refugees to receive a daily subsistence allowance. Tens of thousands of Jews were as entitled to it as anyone else, given that they were part of the huge cohort of refugees in 1940. To benefit from it, a person had to have been forced out of the area where they lived due to the war, and, unable to return, to be in a "state of need."[112] Those who received this allowance were primarily inhabitants of the Occupied Zone, evacuees and refugees from the Forbidden Zone, as well as refugees from Belgium and Luxembourg. An allowance was also established for victims whose homes had been destroyed. The amount was allocated according to the number of dependents and the number of inhabitants in the host town. A head of household was allocated 10 francs per day in a town of fewer than 2,000 inhabitants, and 14 francs in a city with a population of over 30,000—very small amounts indeed. Edith Hanau, who had left Bouzonville (Moselle) with her family for Chauvigny, remembers that they received an allowance of 200 francs, but she cannot recall if this figure was the amount for the entire family or for each of its members. The day and place of distribution was announced in the newspapers for allowances that were handed out by the city hall or the local tax office. As soon as a refugee found work, he was theoretically no longer entitled to an allowance. But not everyone declared their employment, seeking to combine the two sources of income. Refugee cards came into circulation in 1940, which soon afterwards prompted the beginning of trafficking in forgeries.

The system for granting this allowance to refugees and war victims changed several times during the Occupation, particularly the means of calculating the amount depending on salaries and the local economic situation. Proof that it was impossible to return home was also required. Foreign refugees would see their allowance withdrawn by decision of the prefecture. Starting in summer 1941, refugees who changed their place of residence without prior authorization lost their allowance, a measure designed to control population movements and combat trafficking in forged cards. In 1943, in reaction to growing economic difficulties, Vichy allowed the concurrent drawing of several allowances: the refugee allowance could thus be combined, depending on the case, with the single salary allowance, military allowances, allowance for care of the elderly and the disabled, people with incurable diseases, and so on.[113]

Upon the establishment of the UGIF, payment of the allowance to refugees who declared they were Jewish was called into question. The threat that it would be canceled hovered throughout the whole year 1943, on the pretext that the UGIF was henceforth the only organization empowered to take care of them. A circular dated 19 May 1943 pertaining to "putting *Israélites* back to work" made provisions for withdrawing this allowance from able-bodied men between the ages of 16 and 60. To what extent and as of when was this measure enforced, and where? While demands to end the refugee allowance for Jews were voiced, most seemed to have continued receiving it up until December 1943.[114] But in the final months of the Occupation, the only resource available to the most impoverished was the aid from the UGIF.

Refugees and war victims were not the only people eligible for mandatory resource-based public relief benefits: destitute families, "undesirables," and administrative internees, in other words, the families of those in camps in Gurs, Rivesaltes, Drancy, and so on, were also eligible. By decree of 27 February 1940, the Daladier government had already established an allowance for families of administrative detainees, essentially communists who had refused to condemn the German-Soviet Nonaggression Pact. Vichy extended this aid to families of foreign Jews by ministerial circular of 23 June 1941. As Jean-Pierre Le Crom points out, "This measure seems so incongruous that it is worth examining. Vichy put its opponents in prison or in an internment camp, and used its administration and police force as Gestapo auxiliaries in the deportation of Jews, yet at the same time paid their families relief benefits," however small they may have been.[115] It is indeed striking that such "humanitarian" concerns could be reconciled with anti-Semitic policies in the realm of public welfare. Even as it was passing anti-Semitic legislation, Vichy pursued and even expanded its social protection policies, developed during the Third Republic, although its official rhetoric was one of making a clean break with the republican legacy. Social protection thus increased for all sorts of population categories under Vichy, especially wives of prisoners of war,[116] without distinction between Jews and non-Jews. That being said, the meager amount these benefits paid was out of step with the expenses that had to be met and was not enough to live on.

The Miserable Conditions of Internees

Those who remained in the most vulnerable situation were the internees Vichy left to rot in the camps. For a person who was persecuted as a Jew in France, there were a few fall-back solutions and other schemes to survive, as has been discussed. But to make use of them, even if they were registered and under surveillance, people had to be able to move around more or less freely. Such was not the case for those held in an internment facility. They had no room to maneuver, no means of skirting the law or doing some sort of professional retraining. Kept behind barbed wire, they were nailed to the spot, penned in almost like animals that were hardly fed. Condemned to idleness, they were prey to physical and mental decline. Vichy was not concerned with them and offloaded its responsibility onto different relief organizations that did their best to improve the internees' living conditions.

Among those who arrived in the Gurs internment camp in the Pyrenees in 1940 were the Mayers, a German Jewish family from the little village of Hoffenheim (Baden region). As it did with several thousands of their co-religionists, Berlin expelled the family into the brand new Vichy France in October. Caught off guard, Vichy sent them to this camp, already crammed with Spanish, German, and Austrian refugees. The Mayers' life fell apart in a matter of days. They had been expelled to a country whose language they did not speak which then imprisoned them in a camp in appalling living conditions. Cold, hunger, lack of privacy, and rats, were facts of life for some 11,500 internees from December 1940 onwards. Most of them were Jewish. Several hundred of them did not make it through the winter of 1940–1941, which was particularly harsh.

The two Mayer sons have horrific memories of their time spent at Gurs. They described the rain, the wind, the damp, and the cold in the completely empty barracks they were confined to, the constant wailing of children and the elderly, washing in cold water that ran out of pipes drilled with tiny holes, and the outbreaks of diphtheria, typhoid fever, and dysentery. And most of all, the mud and the hunger:

> When the two of us—eleven and eight years old—went outside in the morning, we immediately sank into the mud, because the entire camp was build on swampland. There were no sidewalks, no pavement or vegetation, just a sea of squelching mud. I do not exaggerate when I say that it came up to my knees [...] We were always hungry. [...] It is impossible for anyone who has not experienced true hunger to understand how important food became to us, and how central it was to our lives.[117]

Several aid organizations attempted to bring relief to these thousands of foreigners who had lost everything. Their efforts focused primarily on food, but also on hygiene and health, including vaccinations. Improving internees' lives also meant supplying care packages and clothing and making sure they reached the hands of the intended recipients. Such items were sometimes confiscated by the camp administration, and it was not unusual for guards to take part of the package contents for themselves. One of the main goals of relief organizations was to get the children released from the camps, as long as the parents agreed. That is how Fred and Heinz were able to leave Gurs in January 1941. They would never see their parents again.

Some 200 camps were scattered throughout both the Occupied and Free Zones. Conditions of detention varied from one internment center to another. Every camp had its own history depending on its supervisory authority and the types of people who were interned there. It is hard to imagine today just how squalid conditions in such camps could be. In Mia Kanner's account she describes the camp in Nexon (Haute-Vienne), where she ended up in January 1943; it is utterly horrifying. After nearly being arrested at the home in Le Couret, Sal and Mia were separated from their daughter Léa—luckily for Léa, for her parents were caught by the police and interned. Nexon was officially called a transit camp and had a capacity of between 1,300 and 1,600 internees. It was from there that trains left for Drancy after the mass roundups of August 1942. Living conditions were terribly harsh. It was almost entirely emptied in March 1943, but activity resumed there after Gurs was closed in November 1943.[118] Mia Kanner recalls:

> As we neared a large pit, the smell of human waste reached my nostrils. I felt ill, but I followed my companion to the edge of a depression in the ground. Overwhelmed by the horrendous odor, I staggered back towards the barracks. I could not rid myself of the awful stench and discovered I had fouled my shoes. I had been terrified, exhausted and in pain. Now all those feelings evaporated into fury. [...] Our existence was worse than anything I could have imagined.[119]

After Sal volunteered to work outside the camp, he was sent to Muret, while Mia left Gurs for La Meyze. If she chose this little-known camp, it was because, as a camp managed by the body responsible for GTEs (foreign labor units), La Meyze was designed for families of foreign workers and men unfit for work. It was a "free camp," without barbed wire and with great freedom of movement, according to a UGIF camp commission report dated June 1943. In fact, it was more a center for the forcibly relocated than a camp, as the inhabitants could come and go at will, as long as they returned for the night.[120]

Aside from the outside help some internees were given, their chances for survival also depended on their mental and physical resilience. The elderly were by definition the most physically vulnerable and among the most likely to die. At Gurs, in the winter of 1940–1941, 700 people died, including Fred and Heinz's grandmother, Mina.[121] Religious observance was one way for some to keep up their morale: "'I have attended religious services in the camps at Gurs, Noé, Recebedou [Haute-Garonne],' wrote Rabbi Kapel in January 1942, 'and I can say that never in our French synagogues have I observed as much piety and religious fervor as in these cold, humble, ramshackle buildings used as makeshift places of worship.'"[122] The Mayers almost certainly also attended services. In a letter their mother sent to her sons, she told them their Hebrew names, which they did not know, so that Fred could celebrate his bar mitzvah: Fred's name was Maier and Heinz's was Menachem.[123]

Whether religious or not, the internees had to keep their hands and their minds busy to try to distract themselves from the horror of their situation. Finding a way to occupy oneself was a means to combat boredom and sometimes even to make a little money. At Nexon, Mia Kanner volunteered to help a Red Cross nurse who was overburdened with work. It was thanks to this job that she survived the winter, Mia writes, as it allowed her to focus on other things than the constant diarrhea she was plagued with. Mia also wanted to help the rabbi's wife prepare the dead for burial, but the work made her so ill that she had to stop.[124] In Rivesaltes, where Madame Mayer was transferred, she made a few francs by doing laundry for other internees while her husband was sent outside the camp to work for several months.[125]

Thus, little by little, what Denis Peschanski has called an "internee society" developed,[126] a society organized according to barracks and nationalities, where individuals helped each other even though they were in competition, in particular in the search for food. Spanish refugees, who had been there the longest, would help newcomers find their feet in the camp. In spite of illness, insalubrious conditions, and malnutrition, men and women from different backgrounds and cultures managed to live together in these terrible conditions. Local people and businesses also profited from the existence of these camps, which generated some economic activity. The entire area took advantage of the availability of free labor that could be exploited at will. The authorities were also able to select able-bodied men from the camp population and assign them to GTEs. This system of internment and exploitation of foreigners had developed and expanded since 1939.

But at the beginning of summer 1942, another "rationale" brutally took hold. Although it was not conceived in France, Vichy very soon became involved in it. This "rationale," grounded in the Nazis' genocidal anti-Semitism, is still utterly unfathomable. It no longer aimed merely to corral and detain human beings or exploit them economically. Its primary aim had become to destroy them. This agenda would claim around 6 million Jewish lives throughout Europe.[127]

3

BLENDING IN TO AVOID ARREST

Who could have possibly imagined at the start of summer 1942 that the persecution of Jews in France would be transformed into a genocidal enterprise? The word "genocide" did not even exist. Yet the plan to annihilate the Jewish "race" had already been underway in Eastern Europe since the previous summer. On 20 January 1942, the Wannsee Conference took place just outside Berlin, where plans were finalized for the "Final Solution," or the plan to exterminate some 11 million European Jews, including those in the United Kingdom. At the same time, gas chambers were being built in Poland to carry out the mass murder of Jews, a killing method already tried out on Soviet prisoners and the mentally ill.

In Western Europe, the implementation of this genocidal enter-prise was not yet on the agenda in early 1942. Though the first train-load of deportees had left from Compiègne for Auschwitz on 27 March, mass deportations from France had not yet begun. The definitive impetus came a few weeks later, from Berlin. The decision was taken following the 4 June murder in Prague of one of the high-est-ranking Nazi leaders, Reinhard Heydrich, in charge of organizing the genocide alongside Heinrich Himmler. On 11 June, Himmler issued the terrifying order to accomplish the "Final Solution" in one year, throughout occupied Europe. The obligation to wear the yellow star that had just been imposed by a German ordinance in the

Netherlands, Belgium, and occupied France marked a new phase in the stigmatization of Jews in Western Europe. The initial plan was to deport 15,000 Jews from the Netherlands, 10,000 from Belgium and 100,000 from France. This last figure was deemed unrealistic, however, and was lowered to about 40,000.

In terms of which sectors of the population were viewed as a priority for deportation, negotiations in France stumbled on the issue of nationality: Vichy was unwilling to evacuate French Jews to the East. A serious crisis emerged between the German and French negotiators in late June. Adolf Eichmann came to Paris in person to find a solution. Finally, Vichy agreed to take responsibility for evacuating to the east all stateless Jews in the Occupied and Free Zones. The operations were conducted by the French police and gendarmerie.[1]

The future victims of this plan were obviously completely unaware of the fate that awaited them. German and French officials had come to an agreement about implementing procedures for mass arrests. They had time to make their preparations, while those targeted would have to react on the spur of the moment to escape arrest. They could only respond to events as they occurred, often with no help. The power struggle between persecutors and victims, if it can even be described as such, was totally unequal.

The mass arrests that began in summer 1942 contributed, however, to altering the state of mind of the persecuted Jews. Whichever zone they were living in, they had to resort to a variety of strategies to avoid getting caught. In view of the repressive measures being enacted by the French government and the occupying forces, Jews were now highly vulnerable. Individuals had in effect only two means of fighting back. In the first place naturally was physical escape: flight. They scarcely had any other choice if they were to avoid the clutches of their pursuers. The other means was to conceal oneself socially: to blend into the population to "become, as far as possible, invisible," as Simone Veil wrote.[2] Both of these reactions implied a considerable effort of adaptation. To struggle through the ordeal, Jews had to agree to enter a different world, so to speak. First in the literal sense, as many of them headed to the countryside, an environment they were almost totally unfamiliar with. But also in the symbolic sense: they at least partly ventured into illegality, learning to act, concealing their true identity, passing themselves off as Catholics and so on. Some were able to demonstrate this physical and psychological agility, but not all of them.

In spite of everything, their accounts often express their determination to carry on with their lives, even in the face of fear. In the last two years of the Occupation, the political climate dramatically deteriorated. Anyone who was a Jew or a resistance fighter was in grave danger. And yet life went on: children still went to school, young people got married and soon had the joy of greeting their first child. They continued to practice Judaism even when the occupying forces were nearby. Were people oblivious to the danger? Or was this simply the expression of an inner resistance, deep down inside a threatened human being? Whether or not they had a sense of the fate that awaited them, it was as if people activated a form of vital resistance, a resistance of survival, so as to maintain their dignity and their identity, despite the deadly plans laid out for them.

The Yellow Star or How to Defy the Forced Wearing of a Stigma

Following the measures of internment, professional exclusion, and property expropriation, the process of Jewish persecution crossed another particularly humiliating line in June 1942: Jews living in the Occupied Zone were now required to wear in public a distinctive sign of their social degradation. Caught up in their anti-Semitic delusions about the supposed concealed influence of the Jews, the Nazis decided to make them highly visible. On 29 May 1942, ordinance no. 8 of the German military command in France required that "all Jews over the age of 6 are forbidden to appear in public without a Jewish star. The Jewish six-pointed star, drawn in black, shall be made of yellow fabric the size of the palm of a hand. The word *Juif* must be printed on it in black letters. It must be visibly displayed on the left side of the chest, firmly sewn to the piece of clothing." The yellow star of David was reminiscent of the "rota" or the yellow hat that Jews were required to wear in certain places, including France, in the medieval Catholic world, by application of Canon 68 of the Fourth Lateran Council (1215) called by Pope Innocent III and which ruled that Jews had to wear distinctive dress.[3]

Jews were thus from then on obliged to exhibit the stigma of their own banishment, the mark of their collective disgrace. Some, if they were citizens of neutral countries or allies of the Reich, managed to escape this new measure. Those obliged to wear the star were individuals with French, Dutch, Belgian, Slovakian, Romanian, Croatian, and Yugoslavian nationality, and stateless Jews.[4] The measure was extended to Hungarian Jews on 16 July 1942.

The wearing of the yellow star, imposed by the occupying forces in the Northern Zone—but rejected by Vichy in the Free Zone—was the most humiliating law passed against the Jews within French territory under German domination. The obligation had already been introduced throughout the Reich as of September 1941. In June 1942, it was extended to all the countries of Western Europe under Berlin's rule. To implement the measure in France, the Germans relied on the French police and the UGIF. This organization was expected to pay to have the yellow stars made and to inform all Jews of the new German ordinance. An overwhelming majority of them complied with instructions: in the Paris area, for instance, if official figures are to be believed, "out of the 100,455 individuals obliged to wear the badge, approximately 80 per cent have come to their local police station to pick up the three stars reserved for each person in exchange for a stamp on their clothing and textile ration card."[5]

The UGIF leadership decided at the time to campaign to encourage Jews "to wear the badge openly and with dignity," a decision that still earns this organization criticism decades later from former Jewish communist activists such as Adam Rayski.[6] In its newsletter of 10 July 1942, the UGIF informed its readers of the serious consequences of not fulfilling this obligation: fines, imprisonment, or internment in a camp. Those caught not wearing their star, or not according to specifications, usually ended up in a camp. This was the case for Gilbert Benayoun, Simon and Guy's older brother. A typographer by trade, he was arrested in the street in November 1942, on the grounds that he was wearing his star on his jacket and not his gabardine. He was deported in February 1943.

Other violations could also be reason for arrest. In addition to the obligation to wear the star, new restrictions and prohibitions were introduced that weighed heavily on everyday life: the obligation to board the last car in the Paris metro, and then, in early July, the ban from public places (cinemas, theaters, swimming pools, public squares) and stores except between 3 and 4 p.m. when there was nothing left to buy. Through this cascade of measures, of which the yellow star was merely the most visible, the intention of the occupying forces could not have been clearer: to make sure the Jews were singled out in public, to bring them even more to their knees so that they would feel entirely ostracized from society, completely unwanted, physically branded like cattle, in short so that they would end up being ashamed of themselves. But it also happens that human beings, when the object of serious persecution, can find inner resources to save face and a little of their dignity. In those early days of summer 1942, that is what was at stake for the Jews, under pressure from all sides because of the unrelenting burden of these stigmatizing measures.

"I held my head high"

In Paris, according to Jacques Biélinky's notes, the general reaction was to show bravery and dignity. In his diary entry of 1 June, he wrote, "No one will give in or feel ashamed about being Jewish. The rare examples of those who advised others not to present themselves at the police station or not to wear the badge were accused of cowardice."[7] An unfair judgment on those who did not intend to wear it, given the risks they ran. But this entry emphasizes the determination to react with a sense of pride to an objectively humiliating situation. Biélinky often uses the expression "decorated Jews," as if he wanted to transform their humiliating situation into a sort of honorary distinction. In fact, it occurred to some veterans of the 1914–18 war to go out in the street wearing both their military decorations and their star.

A World War I veteran in a Zouave regiment, Joseph Benayoun was wounded and decorated seven times. "We took this ignominious stigma very hard," his son Guy recalled. "I have a memory of my father walking in the street with his decorations and his yellow star. [...] He tried to walk proudly by the people in the street as if to remind them of his sacrifice and his status as a Frenchman. He was not oblivious or reckless. He was courageous."[8] The Germans theoretically forbade wearing the yellow star together with military decorations. "Monsieur Bloch, a surgeon in Paris hospitals, learned it the hard way: for having displayed his decorations along with this yellow star, he was sent to Drancy and deported a few days later."[9]

It is difficult to peer into the thoughts of these men, women, and children who suddenly had to expose themselves in public with this sort of "decoration." There are very few historical documents that enable us to do so. The diary of Hélène Berr is one of them. She was a 21-year-old student of English at the Sorbonne, from an upper middle class family living in the 16th arrondissement of Paris. When her father, vice-chairman of the Kuhlmann group, fell victim to economic Aryanization, she started a diary that she would keep regularly from 9 April 1942 until 7 March 1944, the date that she and her parents were arrested. It makes for terribly moving reading: this finely written document introduces us to a young woman raised on music, literature and poetry. The early pages speak of her love of nature, which gave her great strength and filled her with awe. They are soon followed by her notes about wearing the yellow star. Hélène Berr does not seem to have been affected by anti-Semitism until then. But in early June 1942, what was she going to do? Wear the star or refuse to? Almost daily, her entries attest to her hesitation and then her decision and her first impressions: "Monday evening [8 June 1942]: My God, I never thought it would be so hard. I was very courageous all day long. I held my head high, and I stared at other people so hard that it made them avert their eyes. But it's difficult."[10]

Her first comments about the star introduce a theme that recurs throughout the pages of her diary: the rejection of cowardly behavior and thus a display of courage. She believed it would be cowardice to abandon those who were suffering more than she. As a young woman from a wealthy family, she was certainly thinking of the impoverished Jewish immigrants in the eastern part of Paris. Prevented by Vichy legislation from sitting for the prestigious *agrégation*, a competitive teaching exam, in late June 1942, Hélène Berr volunteered to work for the UGIF in its offices on rue de Téhéran.

Another particularly poignant theme that runs through her diary is the sense of being somehow estranged from herself and the internal suffering it caused: "If they only knew what a crucifixion it is for me. I suffered there, in the sunlit Sorbonne courtyard, among my comrades. I suddenly felt I was no longer myself [...], that I'd become a foreigner, as if I was in the grip of a nightmare. [...] It was if my forehead had been seared by a branding iron."[11]

The young woman writes movingly about the importance of how people wearing the star looked at those who were not. Much depended on this fleeting exchange of glances with passers-by. It was a moment of defiance, as if to say, "Look at me the way I look at you. See how I assert my dignity despite this public humiliation. Have the strength to look me in the face as I have the courage to detest this abomination."[12]

In this search for a fleeting glance from others, there was much more than defiance; there was a desperate quest for humanity. Marked by a stigma imposed by the Nazis that was supposed to set them apart from others, people wearing the star anxiously sought to lock eyes with those who were not wearing it to ensure that they were still part of the human community.

The force of habit

The diaries of both Jacques Biélinky and Hélène Berr confirm that right from the start, when wearing the star became mandatory, Parisian Jews received many signs of compassion and sympathy from non-Jewish Parisians. Similar spontaneous compassionate reactions were also reported in Brussels during the same period when "the introduction of the star of David sent a shockwave through public opinion."[13] When Hélène Berr began wearing her star, she did not encounter signs of hostility in the street, but rather the opposite.[14] Such spontaneous compassion probably helped Jews accept their new public status. If the occupying forces wanted fingers pointed at them, the policy fell short of its aim, with some exceptions. Feeling that the population did not reject them even though they were compelled to exhibit the sign of their ostracism in the street helped many Jews to cope.

In any event, in some neighborhoods it was unthinkable not to wear the star unless one moved away. In the eastern districts of Paris, especially, where many Jewish immigrants lived in poverty and crowded conditions, the yellow star quickly became a visible symbol for and by everyone, at once ordinary and familiar. Anyone who dared not to wear it put himself in danger.

This group effect contributed over time to making the yellow star to some extent a banal feature of ordinary life. As the months went by, Hélène Berr alluded to it less and less in her diary. The fear of punishment communicated by the UGIF should nevertheless not be underestimated; in late June 1942 Hélène Berr's father fell foul of the law and was sent to Drancy for having his star attached with snaps rather than properly sewn on. He was released on 22 September. Others did not have the connections needed to get out of Drancy and were deported. Everyone had to incorporate this symbol of hatred into his or her routine, or risk being taken in.

Nor should the pressure to obey the occupying forces and the French police be underestimated. For anyone who wanted to avoid trouble, the easiest way was simply to wear the star. It was also the best way to try to quell the anxiety of the situation. And so the force of habit stepped in to curb apprehension, which ultimately led many Jews to cease their soul-searching and simply obey the law by donning the star. Thus thousands of Jews in the Northern Zone wore the star until 1944.

Recalling this period in her life, Madeleine Grunfeld, who worked in the Paris branch of the UGIF, expressed it in these terms: "I was living on a cloud, coping day by day, and I didn't realize the magnitude of what was going on. I walked around with my star, without ever really being worried, even one day when in the metro I found myself sitting between two German soldiers, who paid no attention whatsoever to me."[15]

Obliged to live with a badge that was supposed to symbolize their public degradation, many Jews had to simply get used to it. But can one truly become used to something like that? Watching her mother shed tears as she sewed stars onto her children's clothing, Annie Becker recalls her older brother clowning around. "Luckily never lacking ideas, he very successfully demonstrated, by various contortions, a thousand ways to conceal the despicable symbol with an arm, a satchel, a book, a cap and so on. Everyone laughed and we sat down for dinner a little less glum."[16] And to make the best of things, why not give it some style and make it into something pleasant to look at? "My grandfather the admiral had one made up in silk that he flaunted like a decoration," Pierre Lyon-Caen remembers, "to transform what was meant as a symbol of opprobrium into a symbol of pride."

Occasional removal of the star

Others were bold enough to remove their star entirely, but only from time to time. They learned to wear or not wear the star depending on the circumstances. Young people in particular would take off their star to go out to a show in the evening or meet up with friends. The need to live normally gave them strength for a time to break out of the shackles of their stigmatization. Denise Lefschetz, aged 16 at the time, recalled this period when, with a group of friends, she wavered between obeying the law and her desire for freedom: "We proudly sported our star with a degree of foolhardiness [...]. In my class, six or seven of us wore it. [...]. Sometimes, we were desperate to go out on the town. We gave in to temptation and took off our stars before braving the curfew imposed on Jews."

Francine Weiller, who was also 16 years old in 1942, recounts a similar experience. From a very wealthy Alsatian family, she was on vacation with her sister Nicole in Saint-Malo when the war broke out. They continued going to school there until 1942 and then joined their father who had fled Alsace for Paris. Before leaving, he advised them to have an identity card made up. In fact, "in Saint-Malo, the municipality issued normal identity cards [without the *Juif* stamp] to everyone." While her sister Nicole left for Clermont-Ferrand to continue her studies, Francine stayed behind in Paris to attend the Lycée Fénelon. To comply with the law, she went to her local police station where she was issued a new identity card with the word *Juif* stamped on it and was thus suddenly obliged to wear the star. "I now had two identity cards, both with the exact same information, but one stated my religion and the other didn't." During the last two years of the war, Francine would then use these two identities depending on the circumstances. "I often removed my star. Everything that was forbidden held enormous appeal for me."[17]

Individual behavior was not always the same within one family, as Jean-Jacques Becker, Annie's younger brother, points out: "Attitudes in the family were very diverse. [...] I don't recall any family council being held to decide what we should do." His father never wore the star, but walked in the street clutching a briefcase to his chest to cover the place where it should have been. Their mother wore it with ostentation, like an act of defiance. Henri, a boarder at the Lycée Louis-Le-Grand preparing for competitive university entrance exams, did not have to wear it. Annie said she did wear it, but Jean-Jacques did not remember. His was sewn on a pullover that he wore to leave the house but that he took off as soon as he left the neighborhood, because it was humiliating and also to be able to enjoy activities that were otherwise forbidden to him, such as going to the theater.[18]

A "bag of marbles"

Children were obliged to wear the yellow star from the age of 6, but since it was sewn on to outer garments, it was generally not worn inside school. It is hard to imagine how they experienced, were affected by, or understood the requirement. It certainly depended first of all on the way their parents or relatives talked about it. The attitudes of their teachers and schoolmates mattered as well, for children can be mocking and even cruel to each other. Again, accounts reveal a great diversity of reactions: depression that could even lead to suicide,[19] rebellion and refusal to wear the star,[20] or on the contrary the badge might be flaunted in the spirit of a game. That was the angle taken in Joseph Joffo's famous story, *A Bag of Marbles*, in which the author, in adulthood, tells of his adventures with his big brother Maurice in occupied France. On the first day that Joseph wore the star, his best friend, Zérati, trades him a bag of marbles for it, because to him "it [looked] like a medal or something."[21] A child's world burst into an adult tragedy, thwarting the efforts of the Nazi persecutors: the vile meaning they intended to give a scrap of yellow fabric was destroyed by the power of a child's imagination.

From refusal to deliberate transgression

A minority of adult Jews refused from the beginning to wear the star. Most of them were the same people who did not go to register as Jews in the 1940 census. By 1942 some of them had already fled to the Free Zone, where *de facto* they dodged the requirement to wear the star. Those who remained in the Northern Zone had no reason to come forward and go pick up their stars. They were indeed wise in October 1940 not to identify themselves as Jews, since it increased their chances of not having their names figure in any files or on any lists. Initial behavior vis-à-vis the law has to be taken into account here: when disobedience has been chosen once, it is easier to make the same choice again. Conversely, the more one remains within the confines of the law, the harder it becomes to step outside it. In June 1942, this was the challenge Jews who were "legal" in 1940 faced if they wanted to avoid wearing the star entirely.

Some experienced this new legal obligation as the ultimate and unbearable humiliation. Others believed that it was still possible to be granted exemption. They wrote to the authorities requesting not to be subject to wearing the star. They remained within the boundaries of the law, hoping to see their request granted. Such procedures were generally a waste of time. To avoid having to wear the yellow star, the only effective solution was to move away from one's home as quickly as possible. In some rare instances, departure was not necessary, at least at first, as in the case of Professor of Medicine Robert Debré. In view of his exceptional services to the state, he informed the authorities in June 1942 that he had no intention of wearing the star. He was intent that his statement be put on record with the police. He did not believe it would put him more in danger as such an attitude, he wrote, was shared by many, including by two other male members of his family who had also remained in Paris.[22]

Depending on their means and their connections, those who sought to go elsewhere, by definition in a hurry, decided either to move to another neighborhood where nobody knew them or to attempt the journey to the Free Zone. Joseph Minc took the first option:

> In June 1942, I refused to wear the yellow star, but Lisa (my wife), who had registered as Jewish, found herself obliged to wear it to go out shopping. That is when we decided to go into hiding: with the help of one of our friends, Sylvie Vidal, we moved into a studio apartment on rue des Sablons (16th arrondissement), taking with us only a few clothes so as not to attract the concierge's attention. That is how we escaped the Vel' d'Hiv' roundup, which took place a few days later, and which I witnessed from the metro.[23]

Others, in greater numbers (but how many were they?), made up their minds to go to the Free Zone immediately after the Vel' d'Hiv' roundup, thus freeing themselves of the obligation to wear the star. So as not to draw attention to themselves during their escape, they unstitched it from their garments. Once they crossed the demarcation line, they would no longer be required to wear it. Annie Becker remembered getting rid of hers in the days preceding her family's departure: "I no longer wore the yellow star. It was clear that on the other side of the demarcation line, we would conceal the fact that we were Jewish. There was no time like the present to start."[24]

Some people's behavior would radicalize over time. Those who put on the star in 1942 in the Northern Zone were not necessarily still wearing it in 1944. For instance, Annette and Léa Krajcer, fearing arrest after their father escaped, stopped wearing the star as of January 1944. This was also the case for those who engaged in resistance activity. Since her job as a counselor at the UGIF center and her participation in the *Sixième Nord* children's rescue network put her in danger, Denise Lefschetz decided to go underground. She who had begun wearing the star in 1942 also removed it in 1944. The question of wearing the yellow star or not thus can be seen as a seismograph of individuals' relationship to the law and the possibility of transgressing it.

Escape

The yellow star requirement imposed on Jews, followed by mass deportation, were two associated measures taken by the Nazi leaders to implement the "Final Solution" in Western Europe. It was for this reason that the most elementary reaction among the persecuted—physically to escape their persecutors' clutches—was so vital. There was no need to know what the end destination of the "journey to the East" was. Very few people indeed knew what was happening there. The main thing was to avoid arrest at all costs and flee as fast as they could. But not everyone was able or willing to demonstrate such resourcefulness in the face of danger. It may seem that the decision to flee was the obvious course of action to take, that each person would weigh the pros and cons, choose the right moment, and so on. But that would be to misjudge the factors hanging over people that limited their room for maneuver. The decision whether or not to leave depended on sociological variables, especially age (younger and older people were less mobile) and family status (people with children were more likely than others to stay).

These objective factors do not entirely explain individual conduct, however. More qualitative elements also need to be taken into account.

Again, Hélène Berr's case is illustrative in this regard: although young and from a wealthy family, she did not leave. Other members of her family and her close circle had already moved to the Free Zone. Her father had fallen victim to persecution. His internment at Drancy should have alerted her about her own safety. Reading and rereading her diary, it is clear that a sense of responsibility kept Hélène Berr in Paris. Insofar as she wanted to help "internees and the wretched poor," for her to leave would have been "an act of cowardice." The same argument prompted her to reject the idea of not wearing the yellow star.

Besides, in her new position as volunteer counselor for the UGIF, she found reasons to live and to fight.[25] Her diary also suggests another motive for remaining in Paris: she had become increasingly attached to a young man by the name of Jean Morawiecki, a Catholic student from Saint-Cloud. She mentions the man she affectionately refers to as "J.M." frequently in her writing, and it is clear that his presence brings her happiness. The relationship between the two young people was apparently growing more serious.

How can we differentiate between a deep emotional reason and her "moral principle" of staying, to explain that she did not want to leave Paris? Both were undoubtedly factors, and Jean's presence gave her the strength to fight. But when Jean joined the Free French Forces of North Africa in November 1942, Hélène still did not leave Paris even as more arrests affected her inner circle. After Jean's departure, Hélène ceased writing her diary for nine months. When she picked it up again on 25 August 1943, her style became even more sober and her day-to-day entries gradually transformed into a meditation on suffering.

It may seem remarkable that Annie Becker also mentions the theme of cowardice in her memoirs at the moment when her parents were preparing to leave Paris in the wake of the Vel' d'Hiv' roundup. "My personal reaction was odd," she remembered. "I saw cowardice in my parents' decision to leave and at the time I was angry with them. I had no notion of the idea of a balance of power and I had not yet experienced the foolishness of engaging in direct confrontation when the situation is hopeless." However, Annie went with the crowd, and left for Grenoble in the Free Zone with her family. "Of course I kept my objections to myself. There is no doubt that the fury and sense of humiliation provoked in me by our hasty departure, which can only be called a flight, contributed to bringing closer the moment when I decided to join the Resistance and the armed struggle."[26]

In addition to these moral misgivings, there was psychological resistance, beginning with the force of habit and the fear of the unknown. It is never easy to tear oneself away from a familiar environment and to abandon home, friends, and possessions at a moment's notice. People are also sometimes very reluctant to recognize the risks hanging over them. It is tempting to believe that life will go on as usual. But at any moment the hatred driving the occupying forces, a civil servant's zeal, or the baseness of an informant neighbor could spell doom. Just when it was least expected, violence would raise its ugly head and strike. By good fortune a person might avoid it by the narrowest of margins, but it was time to act and leave as quickly as possible. A police raid or the arrest of someone close could thus trigger the decision to flee.

Yet there was often no direct causal link between mounting persecution and the decision to leave. Family-related reasons sometimes stood in the way of such plans, as Denise Lefschetz explained. Her own family never considered leaving Paris. Certainly, "in 1941, my maternal grandfather and my father were convinced their veteran status would spare them" but, she added, "my father had his 82-year-old mother to care for, and she was not in any condition to travel." The family was obliged to split up in 1944. They were unscathed by the time of the Liberation. Even those who had already been through the ordeal of arrest and internment, if they were lucky enough to be released, did not necessarily take flight, even with every reason to do so.

The young Stanley Hoffmann had great difficulty leaving Nice in the autumn of 1943, even though Aloïs Brunner and his henchmen had been hunting down Jews in the city for the previous two months.

The brutality of the arrests in summer 1942, which targeted entire families, from infants to the elderly, triggered spontaneous, desperate survival responses. Before then, the dominant belief in Jewish émigré circles was that only the men had anything to fear. This is why in northern France, for instance, there were those who left for the Southern Zone in 1941, often to scout locations with the intention of bringing their family down later.

The belief that only men were in danger, but not women and children, was prevalent on the eve of the police operation in Paris on 16

and 17 July 1942, the Vel' d'Hiv roundup. Despite rumors about further arrests of Jews circulating in early July, no one could imagine the
scenario of mass murder, whatever the victims' age and gender. The
authorities had in fact informed the UGIF that the operation was in
preparation, and that information was leaked, giving the communists
just enough time to distribute a notice encouraging Jews to go into
hiding. It is not known how many they were able to warn. Those who
received the news had to take the information seriously and act accordingly. It was primarily men who rushed into hiding. In too many cases,
basing their decision on previous police operations, only the men
sought cover, leaving their wives and children at their legal address,
which was on file with the police. It was unimaginable that women and
children would also be targeted.[27]

The consequences of these mass arrests, which would begin a few
weeks later in the Free Zone, were shattering: in some cases entire
families disappeared, in others several members of a single family were
taken. Some people might, for instance, have been absent for some
reason, or managed to hide when the roundups took place. A mother
and her children might have been caught while one of the youngsters
managed to escape at the last minute; or only the parents were
arrested, leaving the children alone; or one parent and one child were
arrested. And it all depended on the attitude of the police and gendarmerie, who might decide for some reason in the course of an operation
not to take one person or another away.

There were many different scenarios, but all had one point in common: the suffering and distress of the victims. Those who escaped
arrest were still in danger. Several organizations, mostly Jewish or
Christian, sought to take them under their wing, especially children
who had lost their parents overnight. A foster home had to be found,
quickly, either in a non-Jewish family or in an institution. For those
who had the most trouble adapting—who spoke no French, or whose
features were too visibly Eastern European—the aim was to get them
out of France, usually via Switzerland.[28] But this undertaking was never
simple to organize and was always in danger of not succeeding. Because
of this, in reaction to the anti-Semitic brutality of a regime that targeted primarily foreign Jews, regardless of their age and sex, various
children's rescue networks were created, thereby forming one of the

most important components of civil resistance in the country. According to Bob Moore, the earliest acts of rescue in Western Europe of Jewish children took place in France.[29]

The most remarkable of the underground networks was the one founded in the Southern Zone in late 1942 by Georges Garel, inspired by OSE doctor Joseph Weil. It aimed to transfer children placed in OSE homes to "non-Jewish environments," setting them up with a fake identity. Some dozen Catholic, Protestant, and secular organizations thus helped out by taking in Jewish children via a network that covered as many as thirty departments.[30]

Ensuring the Safety of One's Children

Among the families that were still unharmed, people were beginning to realize that it had become urgent to get their children to safety. Some parents thought that, should anything happen to them, if they had already found somewhere safe for their children, the youngsters would have a greater chance of pulling through. Such a decision was by definition painful and in addition difficult to put into practice. Not everyone took that route. As Simone Veil noted, "Separating from one's children was a terribly difficult decision to make when one instinctively has a tendency to think that by sticking together nothing could happen or rather that they could support each other. [...] Parents themselves did not always seize the rare opportunities they had to leave their children, afraid of letting them go and themselves handing them over to the police."[31] After reading several accounts, it becomes clear that many parents were often at a loss. Those who managed to find a solution for their children generally had the help of a work colleague, a friend, a neighbor they could trust, their children's teacher, or even someone encountered by chance.

The most frequent solution was to place a child with a family (usually, though not always) in the Southern Zone, typically in a rural area. Others were put in a private Catholic or Protestant institution or in a UGIF or OSE children's home. Living conditions varied according to the people and the institutions that agreed to take them in. Some children fit in to their new home, some were not at all happy in their new environment, and some were even mistreated by their foster family. In any event, they had to adapt to a new living environment, one that in general was totally unfamiliar to them, but that in many cases they were happy to discover, as will be seen below. However, such placements did not always last long, for multiple reasons, which meant that many children lived a kind of itinerant existence, shunted between different places. For instance, a child may have had to leave a foster family to go to an accommodation center, and then later be placed with another family, or a different institution.

These children did not always realize what was happening to them and were already suffering from being separated from their parents. Meanwhile, the parents had to find ways of coping with persecution; some managed to escape while others ended up being caught during a police raid or following a denunciation. If they were unable to save their own lives, at least they had theoretically managed to save the lives of their children.

In 1940, Saul Friedländer and his parents arrived at Néris-les-Bains (Allier), a spa town where other Jews had found refuge. The Friedländers spent two "quiet years" there, though they were living from hand to mouth. Alarmed by the arrests of summer 1942, the parents decided to place their then 8-year-old son in a Jewish children's home near La Souterraine (Creuse). But in late August, gendarmes came and took away foreign boarders over the age of 10. Saul, who at the time was called Paul, was brought back to Néris-les-Bains and his parents had to find another solution. His mother wrote to a woman in town, Madame M. de L., the director of the library to whom Saul's father gave German lessons, to ask for her help. Saul Friedländer later found this letter, written in late August 1942. In it one senses a mother on the verge of exhaustion and yet still level-headed, who wants to save what is most precious to her: her son. She wrote:

> In my despair I am turning to you, for I know through my husband that you have pity for us and understand what is happening to us. We have succeeded, for the moment at least, in protecting our boy… but I do not want to leave him where he is, for today one can no longer have any confidence in any Jewish institution. I beg you, dear Madame, to agree to look after our child and assure him your protection until the end of this terrible war. […] The little one has plenty of clothes, underwear, and shoes, and there is also enough money for him. I will bring everything over to you if you will have the great kindness to say yes to me. We can no longer exist legally.

Madame M. de L. dealt with finding Saul a place in a Catholic boarding school, Saint-Béranger, in Montluçon. He was admitted on the condition that his parents agreed for him to receive a Catholic education and that he be baptized. They gave their consent. But Saul did not like the boarding school at all, at least not at first. Once his parents had handed him over to this institution, they looked for a place to hide, and then tried to flee to Switzerland. But their attempt failed: on 30 September 1942, they were arrested at the border and handed over to the French police. Interned at Rivesaltes, they were deported on 5 October.[32]

The parents of Fred and Heinz Mayer also managed to get their children to safety in February 1941. The whole family had been interned at Gurs, and to get their sons out of that horrible situation the parents agreed to entrust them to charities that were working to get children out of the camp. Convinced it was the only way to spare them the state of near famine that prevailed there, they gave permission for Fred and Heinz, aged 12 and 9 at the time, to be placed in an orphanage. In his memoir, Heinz described his parents' agreement to be separated from their children as an act of "heroism," saying that most internees contacted at that time refused to let their children leave without them.[33]

After the Vel' d'Hiv' roundup, Lisa and Joseph Minc, who were living in Paris, decided they had to get their 4-year-old daughter Betty to safety. She went to live with some communist farmers in the Yonne department. Joseph Minc remembers:

> We sought out friends who could take us in. It happened that Paula and Joseph Epstein had given birth to a baby boy a few months before. Joseph, a resistance fighter who commanded the Francs-Tireurs Partisans (FTP) in the Paris area under the alias 'Colonel Gilles', had to take considerable precautions and so sent Paula and the baby to Yonne. It was a safe hiding place with friends, and they agreed to take in Betty. Out of necessity, we let our daughter go there on her own. At least we were sure she was in good hands.

Once she had left, Lisa and Joseph became actively involved in the *Mouvement National contre le Racisme*. But Betty did not remain with her first foster family.

> Our main concern was our daughter Betty. For several months she stayed with our friend Paula, but then she had to return home. A friend of ours contacted a concierge she knew, Mme Roulin, who was origi-

nally from a little village in Cher, Neuvy-Deux-Clochers. Some people there agreed to take in our daughter. We did not tell them our true predicament. We told them that Betty's health required her to spend some time in the country.

Betty again changed families but this time she was accompanied by her mother, for in February 1944, Joseph narrowly escaped arrest in Paris. "After this scare, we hid out at the home of some friends in the 18th arrondissement, then we parted ways: Lisa and Betty went into hiding in Montillot (Yonne), while I went to Villeneuve-Saint-Georges and then to the 17th arrondissement."[34]

Some also managed to send their children abroad, often an intensely heart-wrenching decision. While Mia and Sal Kanner were living in an OSE home with their three daughters, the director proposed to include them in a group of 200 children who were being sent to the United States. Mia could not imagine giving up her children and declined, whereas her husband saw the offer as "wonderful luck." There ensued a heated, painful argument, with each hurling accusations at the other, as Mia remembers. "You are asking me to give up my children," she told him. Her husband instead saw it as an opportunity to put an ocean between the Nazis and their daughters. In light of his insistence as well as their daughters' pleas, Mia finally gave in. But she decided to keep Léa with her, convinced that she was too young to bear the separation.[35] Léa was later placed by the OSE in a convent.

Although as of 1941, it was largely the families of foreign Jews who were destroyed, that does not mean that French Jewish families were spared: in the eyes of the Nazis, a Jew was a Jew and was therefore to be captured, whatever his or her nationality. Nevertheless, French Jews were less affected by persecution, or rather later in the day, and in lower proportions. Thus, some of the families whose biographies are evoked here managed to stay together throughout the whole war, though not without difficulty and countless upheavals. The Beckers left the capital for Grenoble with their children, just as the Lindons went to Aix-en-Provence in the Free Zone. Coming from Alsace, the Dreyfuses went to Limoges, and then left for the Italian Zone.

In the chronology of persecution, some French families were hit very early, as there were some French Jews on the first train that left France for Auschwitz on 27 March 1942. But the arrests and deportations that followed, in summer 1942, targeted stateless Jews, in accordance with deals made between Vichy and the German authorities. 1943 and 1944 were more dangerous years for French Jewish families, for several reasons: the constant pressure the occupying forces put on Vichy to step up arrests of Jews of any origin, the invasion of the Southern Zone after 11 November 1942, and the radicalization of relations between occupiers and the occupied as resistance movements grew in scale. Knowing they were in danger, French *Israélite* families tended to split up to avoid a possible collective arrest. They only rarely put their children in the care of a Jewish organization or placed them in a foster family (unlike foreign Jews). If these children were sent to the country, it was usually to join grandparents or other family members, or else friends of their parents. This is, of course, because French Jews were generally more assimilated into society.

Preparing to Flee, Hide, or Be Arrested

In this climate of fear and possible denunciation, people learned to be increasingly cautious, to be careful about what they said in public, and to be wary of people they didn't know. People lived one day at a time, without ever really being able to let their guard down. Trying to cope with an often difficult daily routine, they would be overcome by worry and dread. As arrests became more frequent all around them, they were afraid above all of succumbing to the same fate. For that reason, some made preparations to leave at a moment's notice and even practiced doing so. In Limoges the Dreyfuses had a plan to leave by a door at the far end of the garden in the event the Germans came to arrest them. In Nice, Stanley Hoffmann and his mother practiced leaving their apartment over the rooftops. Claude Lanzmann has described how his father, after they had moved to Brioude (Haute-Loire) in late 1941, trained him, his brother, and sister for their escape. The children would be woken up in the middle of the night; they had to dress and run outside to a hiding place that had been dug at the far end of the garden without making a sound and as fast as they could.[36]

In Nice, Serge Klarsfeld's father, instead of a plan to flee, prepared a hiding place for the entire family inside their own apartment, behind a double dividing wall in the entrance hall closet. On the night of

30 September 1943, the German police swarmed the building. Serge was 8 years old at the time and remembers, "They opened the closet door. [...] I can still hear the rustle of clothes being shuffled along the rod."[37] His father, who remained outside the hiding place to divert attention, was arrested, transferred to Drancy on 2 October and then deported to Auschwitz. He would never return. His wife and two children managed to leave the city, probably in February 1944, to settle in Le Puy-en-Velay (Haute-Loire). They remained there until the end of the war.

The story of Albert Grunberg, the Jewish hairdresser in Paris, also of Romanian origin, is a very different case. Narrowly avoiding arrest on 24 September 1942, he managed to flee and reach a hiding place he already knew well. He remained there for nearly two years thanks to the unwavering support of his family and friends. We know how he lived through this long period of isolation by keeping a daily diary, a regular activity that also helped him cope psychologically. The result is a major historical document, some 1,200 pages long, in tiny handwriting, from which his son Roger selected passages for publication.[38] The narrative begins with the arrival of three police inspectors at his home on 8 rue des Écoles, in Paris's 5th arrondissement, as Albert was having breakfast with his wife Marguerite. He realized instantly that they had come to arrest him and immediately sought a way to escape, as he knew that, if he went with them, he would probably never return. Albert told the police officers that he was going to get some blankets, and then went around to the back of the apartment and left without being seen. Albert went straight to 14 rue des Écoles, the building where his salon was located, to hide in a maid's room owned by the building's concierge, Mme Oudard. He had in fact been sleeping there for the past year, ever since his brother Sami was arrested in a roundup in the 11th arrondissement. Now he found himself confined to a room of only 7.5 square meters, but that was nonetheless comfortable. Albert knew that he wasn't alone, and that to stay there long term, he was able to count not only on his wife Marguerite, but also the concierge, Madame Oudard, a widow whom he describes with great affection. Other tenants were also in on the secret: the Maillards, the Ouvrards and Monsieur Bon, who all knew that he was living on the top floor. Monsieur Bon, who was living in the Free Zone, agreed to hook Albert's room up to his kitchen so that he could have electric light and listen to the radio. People in the neighborhood thought he had fled to the Free Zone, as his wife tried to persuade him to do numerous times, but he refused, assuring Marguerite that he was not in the least bit bored.

This was when Grunberg started keeping a diary. His daily entries provide a wealth of information on the life of this Paris neighborhood during the Occupation, and help to understand what and who enabled him to remain in hiding and, despite some difficult periods, cope with the life of a recluse: "It's terrible to feel hunted. Sometimes you hope for the worst. It's stupid, but that's how it is."[39] During the Liberation of Paris in August 1944, the neighborhood was barricaded, and Albert tried to find the best way to go outside without running into anyone in the building. Finally, on 23 August, he went down into the rue des Écoles with his brother, twenty-two months and a day after escaping from the police.[40] Sami and Albert were given FFI armbands but there were no weapons for them. On 26 August, Albert stopped keeping his diary.

Accounts such as this, of people hiding in enclosed spaces, without ever leaving and for such a long time, are rare in France. On the other hand, many more Jews went into hiding for shorter periods, intermittently, in hideouts or "*planques*," a term often used by witnesses of the period. This was, of course, the case for people engaged in resistance activities, but they were not the only ones. Those not involved in such subversive activity also had to learn to conceal themselves. This did not necessarily mean hiding out in an enclosed space. They would go to live somewhere else for a while, often with friends, or friends of friends, or find a place through work colleagues. As discussed previously, many Jews were constantly on the move in their efforts to disperse during the Occupation.

Being prepared to move from place to place requires a certain psychological capacity to adapt that not everyone has. It involves changing one's state of mind, for instance being able to trust a person who has come to warn of danger. The decision not to sleep at home anymore had to be made very quickly. In Paris, the young Francine Weiller was not involved in any movement. And yet, in the years 1943–44, she suddenly found herself threatened: "One day, while I was at a café with friends, one of them warned me that while he was in the bathroom he had heard someone say that I had been denounced. From that day on, my father and I stopped sleeping in our apartment. I spent nights at a friend's and my father slept in the attic of a building that belonged to a neighbor. I would go home in the morning to wash and get my school books."[41]

It is difficult today to understand that some chose not to flee even though they were in danger of arrest. They became even more vulnerable to being denounced by a neighbor or to being caught in a police raid. As a researcher I found this fascinating, as we tend to believe it is possible to explain human conduct by rational factors, within the historical and psychological context of their time.

Is it because they were highly reluctant to leave familiar surroundings and even more to be separated from people they cared deeply about? At the start of 1944, Hélène Berr's diary illustrates such dilemmas within her own family concerning the question as to whether they should leave their apartment, stay there, or leave for a while and then return.[42] Despite their reluctance to split up, the Berrs did not sleep at home in the days to follow. On 14 February, Hélène noted, "I carry on sleeping at Andrée's, and my parents at the L[oiselet]s'." But it would appear that this new routine still posed a problem, as she added, "Every evening, when we are on the point of leaving, a question hangs in the air [...]. It's just fatigue, the temptation to spend the evening at home, to sleep in our own beds, which reawakens an opposition that has already been considered and consciously rejected."[43]

What happened after that 14 February? Does this last entry mean that they continued to meet at home during the day? The diary does not say. In any case, on the evening of 7 March, they returned home to sleep. That night would prove fatal: the next morning they were arrested and transferred to Drancy. They were deported in the convoy of 27 March 1944, never to return.

Sometimes, physical and psychological exhaustion could lead people in danger to let themselves be arrested. After being separated from their children, the Kanners were targets for an attempted arrest at the children's home in Le Couret. As a result, during the summer of 1942, they went into hiding in the nearby mountains, and then, as winter closed in, they came back down to Limoges. Totally worn out, living in constant fear, Mia and Sal decided to go back to the home, hoping the police had forgotten about them. When they came to arrest them in

January 1943, the couple put up no resistance. Mia had a chance to escape: one of the policemen sent her to get her ration card from the center's director. Mia obeyed and when Madame Krakowski told her to take the opportunity to escape, she replied that she refused to be separated from her husband again. She ran to catch up with the policemen who had gone down the road with her husband without waiting for her.[44]

So the terrible moment of arrest arrives, the point when everything falls apart, when all seems lost. Whether it comes as a surprise or was anticipated, it seems that life has been suddenly turned upside down and time has stopped. The awful paradox is that arrest can be experienced as a relief precisely because it seems like everything is over: the unbearable marginalization, the wandering, the fatigue, the exhaustion, the manhunt. Only the words of a former deportee can convey such a state of resignation: "Life had become so precarious and so dreadful," noted Simone Veil, "that when the trap snapped shut, we reacted with a sort of fatalism, almost relief, that brought an end to the constant anxiety, even if deep down we knew that we had come to the end of the road and that the course of our life had been halted, probably forever. All that is unimaginable today, as it was for us even at the time."[45]

Conversely, in others arrest sometimes triggered the spontaneous reflex to flee, or at least attempt to. Hardly had they been caught or were on the verge of being captured than some, like the hairdresser on rue des Écoles, were already working out how to escape. A person's fate could be played out in a flash, and perhaps luck would shine on him or her. Whether or not they already had a *planque*, the survival instinct was so strong in some people that they found a kind of audacious courage. Young Léon Poliakov, for example, having just been arrested by two policemen, took advantage of a moment when he was left unattended to give them the slip. During the arrest of a group of Jews from the Ardennes, Simon Krajcer managed to escape from the WOL camp in Bulson. Some children also seemed to have an instinctive awareness of danger and tried to flee or hide. Such behavior was rare but it did occur. Consider the account of the neuropsychiatrist Boris Cyrulnik. Aged 7 at the time, he managed to escape after being arrested in a roundup in Bordeaux. Taken to the city's synagogue where all the arrested Jews were being held, he intuitively realized that if he boarded one of the sealed freight cars, he would die. Taking advantage of his agility and small size, he managed to hide in a urinal and then climbed up to the ceiling by bracing himself against the walls. As his pursuers did not think to look up, the boy escaped the convoy heading to Drancy.[46]

These sometimes incredible tales of manhunts, arrests, and escape bids, whether successful or not, are part of the story of the Occupation and persecution. There are infinite variants to them. Nonetheless, the number of those who had neither the opportunity nor the ability to react in time was far higher, all the more so as the means deployed by the police and gendarmerie were sometimes so vast that it was pointless to even try. Added to that was the brutality of the persecutors' action, in the face of which the victims' cries and weeping eventually gave way to resignation and despair. Already socially excluded and publicly humiliated, arrest and internment confirmed that they no longer had the right to exist. It ended up destroying their spirit. Some of them came to an immediate, final, and irrevocable conclusion: overcome by complete despair, they preferred to end their life. "Out of all the camps, Les Milles registered the highest number of escapes and suicides; Les Milles had not been completely sealed off from the outside world. It was at Les Milles during the single day of 12 August 1942, that there were ten attempted suicides and about eighty escapes during the first round of deportations."[47] Perhaps in such circumstances suicide can be seen as an ultimate display of freedom.

After Arrest, the Attempt to Escape

Some tried to break out of the prisons or camps. They plotted their escape even when they had little chance of success. Managing once on the outside would prove difficult for those who spoke little or no French. That did not discourage them: deprive human beings of freedom and they will do anything they can to try to regain it.

Escape attempts were reported from most internment camps, but they were rare and almost always failed. They were relatively frequent in 1941 in the camps in the Loiret: between July and September, "82 internees broke out from Pithiviers, and 377 from Beaune-la-Rolande. They took advantage of the few hours they were out to meet their wives or friends outside the camp. [...] Other escapes were more spectacular, such as Zalman Korenblut's, who left the camp concealed beneath a pile of garbage."[48] Afterwards the authorities took the necessary measures to tighten their grip over the internees.

Sal Kanner managed to escape from a camp near Calais. Assigned to working on the construction of the Atlantic Wall, he fled with a fellow detainee, using as an excuse that he needed to relieve himself during the morning march to the work site. The two men waited until the line of prisoners passed by, tore off their star, and then went to the nearest village and got on a train. During an identity check they hid in the toilets and thus managed to escape.[49]

In Paris, those who wound up confined in the Vélodrome d'Hiver following the mass arrests of 16 and 17 July 1942 had practically no chance of escape, short of a miracle or an extraordinary combination of circumstances. The topography of the place made it almost impossible to get out, all the more as several checkpoints had to be navigated. Even so, a young woman, 20-year-old Anna Traube, did get out, thanks to her tenacity as well as the spontaneous help of some of those who performed the arrests.[50]

Escapes from Drancy were also extremely rare. Only about thirty internees managed to break out by the end of March 1942. In the middle of September 1943, a group of detainees began to dig a tunnel starting from the basement under the office of the Jewish commander of the camp, Robert Blum. Approximately seventy men worked on it for two months, managing to dig a tunnel 32 meters long. But the camp authorities were eventually informed of the project. Robert Blum was deported, as were nineteen of the men who took part in the endeavor.[51] The project shows that escape, which earlier on was only a succession of individual initiatives, had by 1943 become a group effort. In the case of the Drancy escape attempt, communist inmates from the Francs-Tireurs Partisans (FTP) were involved in digging the tunnel. Up until May 1942, the communists had instructed their militants to remain in the camps and put up resistance. But after the first eastward-bound train left Drancy, the party had the following order circulated: "Kick down the gates of the camps! Don't let yourself be deported!"[52] No resistance organization, however, communist or otherwise, seems to have made helping Jewish prisoners escape its priority.

The same observation applies equally to the deportees' attempts to escape from the trains carrying them eastward, their last chance to flee while physically in France. No resistance organization tried to prevent the departure of these trains filled with Jewish deportees, nor did they attack them to let the prisoners get away. The only operation of this sort in Western Europe was carried out by the Belgian resistance on 19 April 1943. Ignorance as to the fate that awaited them is probably the main reason that explains the limited number of escape attempts from Drancy and from the trains carrying the prisoners eastward. Many accounts show that the detainees believed or wanted to believe that they were going to "work hard in the East," an illusion that was maintained by the Germans.[53]

The historian Ahlrich Meyer has collected the scant amount of reliable information concerning the few attempts to escape from the trains carrying Jews from France.[54] In all, between 1943 and 1944, out of some 32,000 Jews deported to Auschwitz, very few were able to escape, most of them young men. Most attempts met with ruthless responses from the Germans and from the heads of convoys, who were always finding new ways to prevent escapes. Out of the 120 attempts reported, just over half succeeded.[55]

Breaking the Law

Resistance to the genocide was played out first and foremost through the physical strategy of evasion, in other words, the capacity of individuals to find ways of avoiding arrest. There was, however, another form of resistance, which began in the period before the roundups started. Insofar as genocide is predicated on identifying the "undesirable elements" to be killed, anything that hinders the process of identification is by nature a hindrance to the enterprise of murder. The efficiency of the individual's response thus depends on one's ability to avoid being identified, in this case as a Jew, and then on one's ability to blend in as far as possible into the surrounding society.

The dynamic of immersion into local society is made up of several complementary elements. The first inevitably drives the persecuted towards illegality if they hope to enhance their chances of not being arrested. Many people tried to obtain forged identity cards, but the process of erasing one's formal identity cannot be reduced to a simple technique of camouflaging it. It requires a simultaneous effort of adaptation to a new environment, especially for city dwellers who relocated to the countryside.

Procuring forged identity cards

There was no specific moment when people thought of themselves as having crossed the line from a legal to an illegal status, as though they had weighed the pros and cons before making such a decision. It was imposed on them with the urgency of a situation where their lives were already in danger. Just as some people had already begun to circumvent the law to be able to continue working and thus ensure their economic survival, people also found themselves forced to take on a new identity to evade administrative checks and police searches to avoid arrest when the roundups began. The initial impulse to escape prompted them to break the law. To pass through the net, they believed that the solution was to procure forged identity cards attesting to their French citizenship. This procedure was somewhat paradoxical, since it basically consisted in resorting to illegal means in order to obtain the legal protection that French nationality ought to guarantee them. By 1942, foreign Jews, many of whom had already had an experience of illegality in their own countries, believed that it was a risk worth taking. Once again they needed to procure "real" forged identity cards that conferred on them legal status.

During this period, a French person might have held half a dozen cards and administrative documents: an identity card, military papers, a demobilization card, ration cards for food, clothes, and tobacco, as well as a work certificate. The identity card, which had been compulsory for foreigners since 1917, was the most important of these documents, and was usually sufficient to get through most inspections and searches. Under the Vichy law of 27 October 1940, it became obligatory for every individual of either sex over the age of 16 to possess a French identity card.

This new law was the translation, among a number of other measures, of the policy of monitoring the population, which dovetailed with the general public's wish for everyone to be able to obtain certain basic necessities (hence the institution of cards for food, clothes, and tobacco). The identity card came into force progressively. From 1943 onwards, it had to show the number under which the person was registered on the National Directory for the Identification of Natural Persons (RNIPP). That meant that the card was "registered"; it had more value than a card that was not, which was considered to be "unregistered."[56] By requiring that the word *Juif* be stamped on the identity card of a person declared to be Jewish as well as French, Vichy managed to exploit the widespread issuing of the identity card to identify and track those who the regime had ascertained were Jewish, thus instrumentalizing the identity card for anti-Semitic purposes. Jews were swift to recognize the advantage of obtaining a false French identity card that lacked the fatal stamp.

By autumn 1940, some Jews had managed to obtain false baptism certificates; however, they were often not accepted as proof of non-Jewishness. By 1942, when roundups were mainly targeting foreign Jews, the possession of an identity card appeared to provide fairly solid protection. For that reason, from summer 1942 onwards and increasingly by the autumn of that year, hundreds, if not thousands, of foreign Jews were trying to get hold of this valuable administrative document. Léon Poliakov was one of them. At the beginning of the chapter in his memoir that recounts his adventures of a Jew in hiding, Poliakov describes his experiences with forged identity cards. It is crucial to bear in mind, he writes, "the incredible confusion that reigned within the Vichy administration. The card might have been registered at the town hall, at the prefecture, at the police station, or by the National Police. The photograph, accordingly, might be face on, in profile, or partially facing away. The card itself was sometimes supplied by the administration, but more often was provided by the individual concerned; cards could be purchased at a tobacconist, but each tobacconist had a different model. This diversity introduced a certain amount of arbitrariness into the police machine and probably saved thousands of lives, since it made checking the cards singularly complicated."[57] The "crowning ingenuity," he continues, was to have a card that was legally registered, bearing "the name of a real person, preferably a prisoner of war, along with its owner's birth certificate: that gave you full security, even in the case where verification of place of birth was required."[58] Poliakov goes on to describe how he obtained his first (unregistered) forged identity card at the OSE in Marseille.

Several weeks later, he set out to try to get hold of a registered card. In Lyon he met Father Michel, the chaplain at the detention center, and confided in him what he was after. The following day he was put in contact with a certain Monsieur Bourgeois from the police station on the Place Bellecour, who made him the "card of his dreams."[59] In spring 1942, a forged identity card was still a rare commodity; from autumn onwards this became less and less the case. In 1943, after he moved to Grenoble, Poliakov himself began forging identity cards.

Joseph Minc's experience was similar. After the Vel' d'Hiv' roundup, he too managed to obtain a forged identity card. But it was of such poor quality that he decided to make one himself, with the help of a photographer friend of his called Malek. Minc recounts:

> Malek and I had the idea of obtaining real identity cards that had been issued by the Seine Prefecture, and to falsify them. We washed them to erase the original names, then altered them by changing the photograph. The problem was what to do about the embossed mark that straddled the photograph and the card. Among my dentistry tools I had a sort of stamp. Metal with a low melting point was poured, along with a very hard wax that softened when it was heated. [...]. Once that problem had been resolved, we needed to get hold of some cards. A friend's sister, Sylvie, who ran a hairdressing and beauty salon in her apartment, helped us. Her clients would leave their handbags in the waiting room, and Sylvie would sneak in and steal their cards. Her clients were completely unaware of the theft, and once they discovered it they never imagined that it had taken place at the hairdressing salon. This was how we began to produce "real" forged identity cards. A certain Joseph 'Mine'—then 'Dacquemine'—whose identity I took, was apparently born in Pessac.[60]

In Toulouse, Edgar Morin's father, Vidal Nahum, also managed to obtain a new identity card without declaring himself Jewish. This multiplied administrative "guarantees" and thanks to his Livornian ancestry he was able to obtain a certificate of Italian nationality. In 1943, he managed to procure forged French papers and used several different identity cards in the names of Nicolas Vidal, Georges Leuzot, Eugène Barré (the father-in-law of one of Edgar's friends) and Louis Blanc (the deceased husband of Madame Blanc, his mistress). He held on to a stack of other forgeries.

Reading through numerous testimonies, it is clear that in 1943 it was relatively easy to obtain or to make oneself forged French papers.

From that point of view, the situation is not remotely comparable with the contemporary invention of the digital ID card that is impossible to falsify. In 1943–1944, a kind of resourceful genius began to develop in France, with the forgery of all kinds of papers that enabled people to circulate freely as French citizens. If the Vichy dictatorship sought to strengthen its control over the population with a flood of new laws and decrees, that same population knew how to use tricks and countermeasures, exploiting bureaucratic loopholes and contradictions to circumvent this control.

During this time, resistance organizations—including Jewish rescue organizations—were becoming increasingly adept at producing forged documents. Within the Jewish rescue organizations certain figures epitomized the increasing professionalization of the forger's craft. The story of Adolfo Kaminsky, who was born in Argentina in 1925 to Russian parents, and came to France with his family in 1932, settling first in Paris then in Vire, in Normandy, exemplifies this evolution. At the age of 14, Kaminsky began working as an apprentice to a dyer, where he developed a fascination for chemistry. When he first joined the Resistance he was helping to make explosives, before becoming the technical supervisor of a clandestine laboratory in Paris known as la *Sixième*, whose methods he revolutionized. With his small team, Adolfo was soon producing 500 documents a week.[61]

In 1943 and 1944, French Jews also began to procure forged papers. At the end of the Italian occupation, the Dreyfus family left Annecy for a small village near the town of Nâves. With the return of the Germans and their raids on the local resistance, the region was becoming increasingly dangerous. The whole family acquired forged identity cards and the father, with his Alsatian accent, tried to pass as Flemish. The Lindons moved to the Berry region and they also managed to acquire forged identity cards, taking the name Ladant.

In Graulhet, Arlette Scali realized the necessity of obtaining forged identity cards when her husband, who was being pursued by Vichy, went into hiding. Using connections, she made an appointment with the prefect of the town of Albi who agreed to provide her with a forged card but urged her to leave the area as quickly as possible, which she was already planning to do.[62] For those involved in resistance activities, the need to taking on a false identity was even more urgent. This was the case for the Beckers, who were living in Grenoble, and Annie in particular, since she had joined the Jeunesse Communiste (MOI). It was similarly vital for Liliane Lieber, who was part of a network that hid Jewish children.[63]

Edgar Nahum, who by 1943 had become actively involved in the communist resistance, took the name of Gaston Poncet, who was at the time a prisoner of war in the Stalag. One day he went to a meeting in Toulouse. "I was greeted by a comrade to whom I introduced myself as 'Manin,' but she misheard the name and introduced me to the meeting of this group of Toulouse resistance fighters with the moniker Morin, which I didn't have time to correct."[64] And so Edgar Nahum alias Poncet began to call himself Edgar Morin.

Even so, many French Jews never took the key step of obtaining a forged identity card. They remained "legal Jews" [*Juifs légaux*] as Maurice Brenner described them in May 1944, those in the Northern Zone wearing the yellow star and those in the Southern Zone carrying identity cards stamped with the word *Juif* as the law required.

Assuming a dual identity

The fact that someone obtained a forged identity card did not necessarily signify that they were then plunged into a completely clandestine life, although this was certainly the case for those who were actively engaged in resistance activities. For most of those who held forged identity cards, the range of everyday activities was actually fairly broad. They maneuvered in ways that were semi-illegal—or, rather, semi-legal. They did things that were legal and things that were illegal, causing them to lead double lives, so to speak.

The case of Francine Weiller is interesting in this regard because she learned to "use" the law without actually contravening it. By 1943 she held two legal identity cards, both identical except for one crucial difference: one, issued in Paris, bore the stamp *Juif*, while the other, which she had obtained earlier from the town hall in Saint Malo, did not. She used the cards interchangeably depending on the situation.

It was common for people to use either genuine or forged papers, depending on the circumstances. They would use them to verify a false or a real identity in the same way that they judged whether or not it was necessary to wear the yellow star in a given situation. It was crucial not to get picked up in possession of a poor quality forged identity card: anyone caught breaking the law might soon find themselves in Drancy and be deported. But the pressure on people was too much. They desperately needed to "breathe," which meant contravening decrees that had been ratified by the regime as "laws," whose specific purpose was to exclude them. This explains why patterns of behavior led to "incoherent combinations of obedience and disobedience."[65] People being stigmatized as Jews increasingly became part of an in-between world that necessitated not only disobedience but in some cases recourse to criminality.[66]

Crossing the line into this world of deceit, or semi-deceit, was not insignificant. Some were unable to do so, or even to imagine doing so, even though it was in their interest to defy the law as a matter of sheer survival. Transition to the mode of transgression and disobedience was not self-evident. It led people into a new realm where they lacked clear points of reference, and while some found it exhilarating, for others it was deeply unsettling. They had literally to learn to become someone else, to play a role.

Indeed, some talked about their wartime experiences as if life under occupation had been a magnificent, tragic costume ball.[67] In this theater of appearances, there were Jews who pretended to be Christian, whether Orthodox like Boris Schreiber or Catholic like Vidal Nahum. People who were actively engaged in resistance activities had to disguise themselves. After narrowly avoiding arrest at his office, Robert Debré went underground, shaved off his hair and beard, and started dressing differently.[68] Joseph Minc realized he was being followed and hurriedly left Paris in February 1944. When he returned, he moved to a new apartment and changed his physical appearance: he grew a beard and never went out without a full-length raincoat.

This was not merely play-acting: the lives of all these men and women, pursued for who they were and what they did, depended on how well they played their roles. Playing a role well, during this great civil tragedy, was so vital that some even began to partially identify with their character. Learning to become another person is to actually become that person, to a certain degree, if only by taking on another name. To go under a false name is, in the literal sense of the word, to change one's identity. Everything depends on the use one makes of it, and what significance the individual gives to that "other self." The effect can be profound, to the extent that at the end of the war, some, like Edgar Morin, elected to keep their *nom de guerre*.

Adapting to Rural Life

Endeavoring to blend in with the local population cannot be reduced to a straightforward double game of shunting between legality and illegality. Whether or not they took on a false name, or were using forged identity cards, the incomers' survival depended first and foremost on how they presented themselves in daily life. In the city they could pass relatively unnoticed. But what about in the countryside, where many escaped to? How did they blend in there? Being a chameleon was rather more difficult, if not impossible, in the countryside, where social convention tended to be much more of a constraint. The ideal solution was to hide out on some remote farm, as some chose to do, particularly towards the end of the war. But for the majority of Jewish refugees, physical concealment in the countryside was simply not possible.

The challenge for their survival was to be able to adapt to a rural environment—with which, with the exception of a very few, they were quite unfamiliar—without disrupting the way of life of the local people.

Every region of France, every administrative department, has its own distinctive features. Even within a given department there can be noticeable differences. It is therefore difficult if not impossible to generalize about the ways in which the refugees slipped into life in the French countryside and the degree to which the local population accepted their presence. Both sides prospered from the relationship: the refugees found shelter and food, while the often-impoverished local people were able to make a little money from the newcomers. Caution, suspicion, and self-interest were characteristic of the modes of encounter between these two groups of people who were strangers to one another. Newcomers were often given some kind of provisional accommodation: a small house a short distance from the village, an unoccupied building rented out for a pittance, an apartment, or just a room.

Many local men were prisoners of war, had been enlisted into the STO, or had joined the Maquis, so there was certainly room for newcomers in these villages. And, of course, because so many men had gone away, any addition to the workforce, however lacking in experience, was especially welcome in certain sectors. In spite of that, however, the refugees tended to remain as inconspicuous as they could, aware that their survival depended on keeping a low profile. "If villagers knew, they said nothing, but the Jews were better off if they didn't. And so the daily life of the refugees unfurled like Ariadne's thread, with a structure and tempo according to set rules of time and place, dictated by codes of appearance which gave rise to multiple tactics of precaution and the avoidance of danger."[69] The refugees were never able to be entirely comfortable; they were always aware that anything might happen, suddenly and without warning, even in a place that seemed perfectly safe.

Martin de La Soudière, author of a detailed study on Jews who found refuge in the Auvergne, highlights the double imperative inherent in this integration effort. It was crucial that the refugees never gathered in large groups or made themselves too visible; they had to avoid the kinds of places where people tend to gather, such as markets and festive public gatherings. But at the same time they also had to do the normal things that everyone did: enroll children in school, line up for food vouchers, apply for residence permits. In some cases, physical appearance (blond hair, blue eyes, particularly for women) and not having an accent made things easier. "Fitting in meant not talking too much, keeping a low profile and trying to adapt to local village life."[70]

Having children enrolled in the local school was an important way of getting roots in the community, and it offered families a means to integrate local life. Children were enrolled under either real or assumed names in both public and private local schools. While private Catholic schools were able to insist that certain conditions be fulfilled in order for children to be registered, there are no recorded cases in mainland France of children being refused a place in a village public school, whatever their background.[71]

Parents often instructed their children to speak in school as little as possible in order not to stand out. Children would be regularly admonished for failing to keep quiet and in some cases for forgetting their assumed name. They were enjoined not to talk in class. But it is clear that the integration of Jewish children into the school system renders the notion of "hidden children," which became current in the United States in the 1990s, not really pertinent when discussing France. It is much more appropriate when discussing Poland, for example, where anti-Semitic persecution was exceptionally brutal and widespread.

For city children, moving to the countryside meant discovering nature. For the first time in their lives these children found themselves in close proximity to animals. They were obliged to adapt to the rough rural lifestyle typical of the time, which was not without its difficulties. Saul Friedländer describes how he was sent to a Catholic boarding school in the countryside in the Indre department of central France at the age of 9, where he was given many odd jobs to do, including looking after the cows, which "frightened [him] more than all the rest."[72] One 7-year-old girl, newly arrived in the Auvergne, "objected to having to relieve herself in a pile of manure in the barn, which was a still a widespread practice at the time in the region."[73] There were certainly cases of children being abused or exploited by unscrupulous farmers. "But it is important not to generalize," Martin de La Soudière insists, "for if nature was a 'hostile environment,' it was also fascinating to the refugees, as studies of different regions corroborate." The encounter with rural life in Auvergne was fairly uncomplicated. In his autobiography François Stupp barely mentions his precarious situation, preferring to focus on a narrative redolent with images of rutted country lanes and infused with the lyrical style of the rural novel, in which he extols the harmony of village life, the beauty of the landscape, and the cycle of the seasons.[74]

For many Jewish children who escaped to the countryside, this was not an unhappy time of their lives. Marie-Claire recalls the time she spent in the Auvergne: "The farm really left an impression. We played with the children who lived opposite. We went for long walks in the forest where we learned to identify mushrooms. Sometimes we children did our own version of resisting, where no one could hear us. We would sing aloud when we were out in the middle of the countryside." One object, symbolic in more ways than one, seems to have made a particular impression on the children: the bicycle, which provided both the opportunity and the means to explore the district, to escape their hiding places, and to enjoy an instant of solitude. For young people displaced from the city, nature was more than merely a compensation for the uncertainty of their situation or a source of wonder and enthusiasm; it brought them consolation: "Even in the most discouraging moments, nature offered us freedom and beauty and gave us inner strength."[75]

Becoming Catholic

Jewish refugees understood that they had to give up every manifestation of their faith in order to facilitate being accepted by the local villagers. Deep in the French countryside, they were surrounded by Christian families and living in the heart of parishes that were for the most part Catholic. In this part of their lives, as in all other areas, their stance was one of caution and concealment, although this did not eliminate danger entirely. Many parents went even further to protect their children, enrolling them in catechism classes or allowing them to be baptized. Some let their children be placed in religious institutions (schools, boarding schools or monasteries) where they were in theory safe from police checks and inquisitive prying. Male children of Jewish families who lived outside these institutions were particularly vulnerable to a specific danger, as noted by a refugee who lived in the Auvergne during that period: "There was one constant risk we had to deal with, physical and intimate, that wasn't immediately visible, but meant that we could find ourselves imperiled at any moment: we were circumcised," Albert recalled.[76]

The majority of refugees from central Europe, many of whom were communists, were not practicing Jews. They had few qualms when it came to taking the decision to send their children to catechism classes or church services. Since France was a majority Catholic country, the social immersion of foreign Jews was based on the assumption that they would take on the other sign of Frenchness: the dominant religious culture of the country. Jacques and Simon Benayoun, who were sent to live with a Normandy farming family in 1944, dutifully attended mass, just as they had uncomplainingly attended synagogue in Paris. They explained their ignorance of the liturgy by claiming that their father was Muslim. Some children were forced to convert to Catholicism, a subject of intense controversy in the post-war period, particularly around the time of the Finaly affair.[77] Research on the subject has shown that cases of forced conversion were rare. Nonetheless, many of those who lived through the persecution have testified that when they applied to enter a Catholic institution, it was on condition that they be baptized, as was the case for both Alfred Grosser and Saul Friedländer. These children's experiences of becoming Catholic often left them with striking memories. Often their identities were unsettled, as was the case for Saul Friedländer, who was placed in a Catholic boarding school in Montluçon at the age of 9. This experience, coming at the same time as the abrupt separation from his parents, was deeply trau-matic. Desperately worried about the safety of their son, his parents had agreed to send him to live in a Catholic institution, after his father had signed a letter allowing his son to be baptized and to receive a Catholic education. "As I entered the portals of Saint-Béranger, the boarding school of the Sodality where I was to live from now on, I became someone else." Pavel became Paul-Henri Ferland, "to which Marie was added when I was baptized, so as to make it even more authentic, or perhaps because it was an invocation of the protection of the Virgin."[78]

But boarding school life was very hard: strict discipline and "revolt-ing" food. He ran away and managed to rejoin his parents, who, for want of any other option to keep their son safe, made him return to the school. In October 1942, Paul-Henri was placed in another Catholic boarding school in Montneuf (Indre), deep in the countryside. He was no happier there. He fell seriously ill and nearly died. He eventually recovered, in April 1943, supported by the "kind" head of the school, Madame Chancel. He returned to Saint-Béranger in September 1943, and slowly began to adapt to boarding school life. He became a "good little Catholic" and began to make friends. Young Paul-Henri served at mass and excelled academically; it was thought that he would become a Jesuit and he considered training for the priesthood. He loved the adoration of Mary, who put him in mind of his mother. During his whole time at the school he never stopped hoping for a letter from his parents, but none ever arrived. "Because I received no letters or visits, and because I never went on vacation, my schoolmates realized that I was different. In their eyes, I suppose I was already an orphan. I had only one recourse: religion. I threw myself into it with a passion [...]. I embraced Catholicism, body and soul." After the war it was his godmother who had to break the news to him that his parents had been deported and killed; while he was away at boarding school, the Milice had come to arrest them at their old address. At the beginning of 1946 he went to see a Jesuit priest in Saint-Étienne to tell him that he had decided to join his community. The priest realized that his visitor knew almost nothing of the Nazi extermination of the Jews, and he decided to tell him about it. It was a terrible shock to the young man, who, as he listened to the priest's words, began for the first time in his life to feel Jewish. Paul-Henri was determined to find a way to reconcile his new identity with the Catholicism that he did not want to abandon. In 1947 he began studying at the prestigious Lycée Henri IV in Paris, where he first became interested in Zionism.

Such a precocious commitment to religion was, however, highly unusual.[79] Most of the young Jewish children who found themselves in a Catholic environment did not have the same experience. Martin de La Soudière, who spent some of his childhood in the Auvergne, remembers how he, like Annette, loathed going to church: "I hated the atmosphere in church, the disturbing statues of Christ, having to learn the catechism by heart, having to submit to it. I have very bad memories of that time of my life, almost like an adolescent trauma." He suggests that those who experienced similar distaste for Catholicism were often the same as those who hated living in the countryside, "as though the two aspects of the local culture that were imposed on them were two sides of the same coin, which they either rejected or embraced wholesale. To my surprise, I have only heard a few statements in that vein."[80]

More commonly, people recall that period of their childhood in a positive tone. "I found church beautiful, there was a poetic element to it, Jesus and all that. I loved going to church. At Christmas there was a little Jesus who sang. You put in a coin and he sang. I remember it all, processions, picking flowers in May for Corpus Christi,"[81] Marie-Claire remembered.

For some of these young and impressionable children, this immersion in Catholicism often seemed like a magical form of religion, at the very least a compensation for their parents' absence. Others, by contrast, remained completely indifferent, and went off to catechism like they went off to school in the morning.

Going to School, Studying, Gaining One's Freedom

In most cases, parents continued to send their children to school, with or without their yellow star. If they were not living with their parents, there were other adults who took on the responsibility of keeping the children in the education system. Going to school helped them maintain a semblance of normality in their daily lives. Many were enthusiastic to learn; the children of immigrants wanted to learn to speak perfect French and to succeed academically, despite, or perhaps because of adversity.

The acceptance of Jewish children—including foreign-born Jewish children—into public schools in France was, along with Denmark, unique in Nazi-occupied Europe.[82] In Italy, the 1938 anti-Semitic laws excluded Jewish children from school. The integration promised by school in France sometimes worked actively in favor of foreign children, who had previously been interned. Children freed from camps in southern France were able, with the help of aid associations, to move in with foster families and attend local village schools. Obviously these children ran the risk of arrest. But assuming that they were fortunate enough to avoid this, they were able to remain in the school system throughout the entire duration of the war, even when they had to move around from place to place.

Annette Krajcer's story is extremely unusual. On 16 July 1942, her mother was arrested in Paris during the Vel' d'Hiv' roundup. Her father's name was also on the list but he had already been taken to a German work camp in Bulson (Ardennes). Annette, who was 12, and her 14-year-old sister Léa were not targeted for arrest, but they refused to leave their mother and so they too were taken by the police. After several days in the Vel' d'Hiv', all three were transferred by cattle car to the Pithiviers camp. On 3 August their mother was deported to Auschwitz, where she was gassed on arrival. On 15 August, Annette, Léa, and several other children were sent from Pithiviers to Drancy. They were supposed to be part of the second convoy of children that left Drancy for Auschwitz on 19 August, but by an extraordinary stroke of luck, one of their mother's cousins, Berthe Slezger, who had also been arrested on 16 July, had been made assistant to the camp's Jewish commandant.[83] When she saw their names on the list, she erased them and then managed to have the two girls transferred to the block where she and her mother were housed, for internees who were not due to be deported imminently. Berthe removed their names from several subsequent lists, desperately hoping that her strategy would not be discovered. All this time, one of the girls' aunts, Berthe Libers, a social worker at the UGIF, was working to have them freed, on the basis that their father was working for the Germans. After several setbacks, on 29 September 1942, Berthe Libers at last succeeded: Annette and Léa left Drancy, the only two of the thirty-two children whom their aunt had managed to free who would avoid deportation altogether. The girls were sent to a Parisian UGIF center, again thanks to their aunt; they were later authorized to leave the center to go and live with their maternal grandmother, where Berthe and her sister Fanny also lived.[84] The girls' lives now began to follow an unexpectedly "normal" path; having been on the verge of being deported in August, Annette and Léa returned to school in October 1942. This was an extraordinarily unusual outcome for two girls who had spent their school holidays in horrific conditions in Pithiviers and Drancy. Annette, an excellent student, was in her fourth year of secondary school at the Lycée Victor-Hugo in the rue de Sévigné, in Paris's 3rd arrondissement. She recalls that although she was obliged to wear the yellow star on her way to school, she was permitted to take it off once she arrived. She had the comradeship and support of her friends, who chose to travel in the last metro car with her. Only the headmistress, Madame Maugendre, a few teachers, and her closest friends knew that she and her sister had been arrested the previous summer with their mother. The two girls were still suffering from the after-effects of their internment, during which they had become infected with scabies and lice. Léa was extremely weak from the dysentery that she had contracted in Drancy, to the extent that at one point they feared for her life. The sisters were in constant dread of being rearrested and suffered terribly from the absence of their mother, about whom they had received no news whatsoever.

Many of the witnesses whose stories are told in these pages also continued their schooling during the war; some even took their baccalaureate, the French secondary school examination, which was taken in two parts, at the end of the penultimate year of school, and at the end of the final year of school. All the Becker children went back to school after the family returned to occupied Paris. Henri and Jean-Jacques started school in October at the Lycée Charlemagne; their parents encouraged Henri, who was more interested in literature, to study for a science baccalaureate (known as "Matelem," meaning "elementary mathematics"), because "in these worrying times in which we are living, it might be useful to have a scientific qualification." Following a similar logic, Annie, who was at the Lycée Victor-Hugo, took extra lessons in typing and shorthand, and Jean-Jacques took his secondary school certificate so that he too would have a qualification.[85] In July 1942, after the family moved to Grenoble, all the children again returned to school: Henri and Jean-Jacques to the Lycée Champollion—Henri to do advanced science in preparation for university, Jean-Jacques to do his penultimate year of secondary school, Annie to the Lycée Stendhal to do her final year, and Françoise to primary school.[86] Jean-Jacques took the first part of his baccalaureate in July 1944.

When the young Alfred Grosser arrived in the town of Saint-Raphaël on the Riviera, he began preparing for the baccalaureate with the help of a teacher who was also a refugee. Grosser passed the two parts of the baccalaureate in June 1941 and June 1942, in mathematics and philosophy.[87] Denis Lindon, whose family went into hiding in 1943 in a remote village in the Puy-de-Dôme region, was unable to go to school. Nonetheless, he set about preparing for the second part of his baccalaureate, taking a correspondence course with a former philosophy teacher who occasionally passed through the village. "We had forged identity cards with the name Ladant, but I had to register for the exam under my real name. I ended up getting a good grade, but I think the examiners must have been being particularly indulgent." In Paris, Denise Lefschetz went underground again in 1944 after her grandfather, with whom she was living, was arrested at their home. She stopped wearing the yellow star and managed to obtain a forged identity card. But in June 1944 she had to wear the star again in order to sit the first part of her baccalaureate exam, which she had registered for under her real name. The future Edgar Morin passed his baccalaureate in 1939. In 1940, after the fall of France, he enrolled at the University of Toulouse to study history, geography, sociology, philosophy, and economics. He was enrolled simultaneously in the faculties of literature, law, and political science. In October 1940 he registered in both the history department and second-year law and economics. He completed both degrees during the war.[88]

Not everyone was lucky enough to be able to continue at school or study at university. The children of immigrants often had to get by on their own to survive, sometimes from a very young age. It was not uncommon for children as young as ten to find themselves alone, forced to get by on their own devices, moving from place to place in search of assistance and shelter. This is the story told in *A Bag of Marbles*, by Joseph Joffo, an ode to the life and youth that triumphed over violence and hatred. But many of the other experiences of Jewish children are much more troubling, bearing all the hallmarks of loneliness and insecurity.[89] These children were deprived of their childhood. Who knows what psychological scars they bore from repeatedly having to move around from place to place?

The exceptional circumstances of war and persecution were by their very nature likely to bring about young adults' independence prematurely. Often the age hierarchy within the family was reversed, with children becoming responsible for their parents, who found that they were less able than their children to cope with new and unfamiliar situations. Alsace-born Edith Hanau, aged 20, was living near Limoges with her family: "My parents spoke no French. I had to deal with everything." She found work locally. Many accounts testify to the fact that children often spoke better French than their parents, which was a vital asset for a family seeking to be understood and accepted. This was the experience of Stanley Hoffmann, who left Austria for France and was living with his mother in Nice until December 1943. Their status as foreigners meant that they were very vulnerable. He recalled how, at the age of 15, "we had no papers, as my mother had always refused to become German after Austria was annexed. But we had a sort of substitute: the fact that I spoke excellent French helped us enormously."

In other cases, this emancipation manifested itself through young people moving away precipitately from their families. What is an entirely natural development during peacetime was often accelerated during wartime. The search for work and the stepping up of persecution meant that some young people had no choice but to move away; this was on top of the fact that during this period of war and occupation, with the floods of refugees and displaced people, it was not at all uncommon for families to be separated. Some young people experienced this break from parental protection as a newfound freedom. After the exodus from Paris, Edgar Morin remained in Toulouse, where he began a new life after his father went back to the capital. Writing of himself in the third person, he says: "In Toulouse, Edgar was free, happy; he looked after student evacuees, made all sorts of friends, had his first girlfriend, met writers whose work he had read in the NRF.[90] He met a family who adopted him, offering him everything he loved and admired [...]. Disaster had freed him from the permanent tutelage of his father, and the Occupation was to be his liberation."[91]

Undoubtedly this newfound independence helped young people to brave the stigmatization that they endured as Jews. Many accounts describe the desire to live as normally as possible: they were young, and they wanted to enjoy themselves, even if it meant flouting the law by concealing their yellow stars, carrying forged identity cards, violating the nighttime curfew, going swimming, to a café, a concert, or a fair. "For those of us who were young, it became a game: defying the law was a way of overcoming our anxiety, and daily life prevailed over tragedy," says Denise Lefschetz. Edith Hanau, who lived in Chauvigny, recalls her zest for life as a 20-year old: "I went places. I went dancing, camping, swimming in the River Vienne, I was the only girl to swim across it. I had lots of friends."

Clearly for many Jews in France life was nothing like this. Many were trapped, psychologically worn down by persecution, reduced to poverty, forced to keep moving from place to place, imprisoned. But the difference in their experiences was also a consequence of the differences between the generations. While parents were often broken by the persecution, their children seemed to have had more resources to confront it. The urge to carry on living was for them the best way to ward off the horrors they faced. Whether consciously or not, these young people, drawing from deep within their innermost selves, sought to stand up to the threat of violence, to find ways to ensure that it would have as little impact on them as possible. These young adults were the main vectors of the notion of living resistance, which they manifested in their desire to simultaneously rebel against their parents and defy the anti-Semitic laws and regulations, and thus to live how they pleased.

Falling in Love and Having Children

The desire to continue to enjoy life also manifested itself in the flowering of love affairs during the Occupation, some of which culminated in marriage. Couples were frequently split in wartime (the man was killed or taken prisoner), but wartime also enabled brief affairs to blossom, as well as more serious relationships that might be secret or in some way forbidden.[92] To continue living and loving was a way of defying the enterprise of persecution. It was another form of inner resistance, a way of reaffirming the indestructible humanity of a stigmatized section of the population.

During the Occupation many relationships were kindled, some brief and others lasting. In some cases both halves of the couple were Jewish, while in others one was Jewish, the other not. Why consent to the racial segregation imposed by state anti-Semitism? Many men and women refused to accept being divided along such lines—whether the person with whom they had fallen in love with was Jewish or not was of no consequence; there was no reason not to get to know someone, to fall in love, even to marry. It is as difficult to know how many relationships of this kind were formed as it is to know how many "arranged" marriages took place, for a marriage between a Jew and a non-Jewish French citizen, an "Aryan," in theory provided a safeguard against deportation. This appears to have been the rationale that led Denise Lefschetz's mother to marry her long-time companion in 1942, the singer known as Jean Lec, whose real name was Fernand Lecoublet. Since no specific research has been done on the subject, it is impossible to know how widespread this phenomenon was.

Within Jewish organizations too, there were romantic relationships and some marriages during the Occupation. "There were plenty of budding romances at the Jewish scouts center in Moissac."[93] How should we interpret that some managed to imagine a future life, even thinking about marriage, during these years of persecution, and despite the risk of arrest? Why did some Jewish partisans who were actively engaged in underground activities take the risk of getting married in the open? Were they unaware of the danger, or was it a calculated risk? Or was it an indication that they did not feel that they were directly threatened? It is hard to know.

Some couples had their first children during the Occupation. Arlette Scali, who remarried before the war, gave birth to her first son, Philippe, in October 1939. After she and her husband escaped to the Free Zone they had two more children: Eric, born in December 1940, and Pierre Francis James (Jimmy), born in December 1941. In her memoir, Arlette relates that she also aborted a fourth child before the end of the war.[94] The decision not only to marry but also to have children was an even greater expression of faith in the future, and of defiance in the face of current events. The fact of becoming parents was yet another demonstration of inner resistance by Jews threatened with death, which went even further than the instinct to keep on living normal lives. To be sure, it is not clear whether these young couples were aware of the fate that the Nazis had planned for the Jews, or if they knew that those who had been deported would never return. But now that we know what happened at Auschwitz, we can surely say with hindsight that the children born to Jewish couples were the most defiant response, by definition filled with life, to the Nazis' genocidal undertaking.

Vivette Herman and Julien Samuel met while they were both working for the OSE, and married at the Marseille city hall on 6 October 1942. Vivette muses in her memoir, "To be united in such circumstances was perhaps a way for us to face adversity. Compelled to live in a somber present, we put our trust in the future."[95] The name they gave to their first baby suggests that they wanted to believe in France as well: "In order to emphasize the hope we still placed in France on this 14 July 1943, we gave our daughter the first name of Françoise."[96] But the happiness of the young family was cruelly interrupted: in January 1944 Vivette's father was arrested in Limoges and deported, and later that year, in May, Julien was captured in Lyon during a mission. Somehow Vivette found ways to cope with the double loss of her father and her husband; though she does not tell how hard it was emotionally, she comes across in her memoir as a fighter who would not give up easily. Knowing she could count on the help of her friends in the OSE, she set about the risky business of trying to get them freed.

In Paris, another young woman found herself in a similar situation. Jacqueline Mesnil-Amar learned of the arrest of her husband, André Amar, a member of the *Organisation juive de combat* (OJC—Jewish

Combat Organization), who was caught in an ambush on 18 July 1944. With no news of André, Jacqueline began writing a diary as a way of dealing with her distress. The first words she wrote were, "André didn't come home last night." In her writing, we see how she tries to come to terms with her predicament, wondering whether to abandon herself to her grief, or continue to enjoy life.[97] On 10 August, Jacqueline learned that her husband was being held prisoner in Fresnes; still alive but at risk of torture and deportation. In such a situation of uncertainty and waiting, carrying on with normal life seemed to her simultaneously a form of betrayal and of resistance. Writing became for Jacqueline a personal form of resistance; keeping a diary was a way of coping with her anxiety and remaining steadfast. In the end, Vivette and Jacqueline were lucky: their husbands both managed to escape from trains that were carrying them towards their deaths. Julien Samuel managed to free himself from the convoy that was taking him from Lyon to Drancy, while André Amar escaped from the last convoy to leave Drancy on 17 August 1944.

Praying And Religious Practice

There was a vast range of different elements of Jewish life in France under the Occupation, beginning with expressions of religious faith. During times of persecution, religion has always offered a refuge and comfort for the victims, with praying becoming a form of profound inner resistance. For the believer, prayer builds an internal resolve that helps those being persecuted stand strong in the face of adversity. In addition, continuing to perform religious rituals, in whatever place and circumstances, becomes another form of resistance at a community level.

In Judaism, any room can be transformed into a place of collective prayer; all that is needed for a service is a quorum of ten men to make a *minyan*, and a Torah scroll. In France, rabbis were free under Vichy to continue to lead religious services. At no point during the Occupation did Marshal Pétain order the closure of synagogues. This decision has not been subject to any detailed research.[98]

If Jewish freedom of religious observance was legally respected under Vichy, what was the situation in the Occupied Zone? The

Germans were not especially concerned with forbidding religious practice, presumably in order to avoid outraging public opinion.[99] In Paris, "synagogue services continued to be held and were even discreetly protected by the French police [...]. Synagogues were full throughout the high holy days during the autumn of 1940 [...]. Though placed under the control of provisional managers, businesses connected with Jewish religious practice—including Jewish butchers and delicatessens (174 identified in Paris), eight Jewish bookstores, and two ritual bathhouses—were not closed. [...] When Passover drew near, Jews could purchase their matzo in exchange for bread tickets; they could even buy what they needed on the black market."[100] According to Philippe Landau's research, during the four years of the Occupation in Paris the Consistory registered two conversions, sixty-nine bar mitzvahs, fifty-five marriages and 2,294 burials.[101]

Nonetheless, after the July 1942 roundups, synagogue attendance fell significantly, due to the wave of Jews who escaped the capital for the Free Zone. Hélène Berr, who remained in Paris, noted in her diary that she attended the Rosh Hashanah services in October 1942, and lamented the fact that there were so few people in attendance: "It was depressing. Not a single young person. Only old folk."[102] The Benayoun family continued to attend weekly Shabbat services throughout the war, first at the rue Popincourt synagogue and then, from Passover 1942 onwards, at the synagogue in rue Buffault. Simon and Guy both recall how few people there were in attendance; there was rarely a *minyan* and they were almost always the only children there. The family never stopped going to synagogue, even after there was an attempted roundup at the entrance to the synagogue on Yom Kippur 1943, when worshipers managed to escape through a hidden door.

During the Occupation five rabbis, including the Grand Rabbi of Paris, Julien Weill, continued to lead services in the capital, assisted by various other ministers, some of whom were foreign. In other cities and regions, many people continued to attend synagogue, particularly in Nice (at least until September 1943), in the Périgord[103] and around Toulouse.[104]

Did this insistence on continuing to hold services become irresponsible when worshipers were exposed to the risk of arrest at the height of the deportations? Members of the Central Consistory were certainly warned in advance of the mass arrests in the Free Zone that were being prepared by Vichy for the end of August 1942. They met on 23 August to compose a formal protest against the deportations, which they argued was an unacceptable violation of the right to asylum, and against the inhumane conditions in which this policy was being conducted. The petition was sent to Marshal Pétain. "The declaration of 25 August was extremely well written," according to Serge Klarsfeld. "It was a text whose vehemence was entirely proportional to the events that the Jews of France were being subjected to. The authors of the document risked reprisals from Laval and his police, and their courage must be emphasized, because the core of their criticism was directed at the French government. Their clarity of thinking is also striking."[105] The tone and content of the declaration could not have been more clear or vivid; it was entirely commensurate with the impending tragedy.

So it is not clear why, following on from this, they did not order the closure of synagogues in order to protect worshipers. It is true that some people wished to continue their religious practice regardless of the circumstances. Even so, the Consistory could have given the order to hold services in unofficial locations given that synagogues were clearly the perfect hunting ground for capturing Jews. In 1943 and 1944, several synagogues were the target of raids by the Gestapo, the Milice, and the French police, in actions organized on synagogues in Lyon, Marseille, Nice, Grenoble, and Toulouse. During this period, several well-known French Jews were arrested, including the president of the Consistory, Jacques Helbronner, who was arrested with his wife on 23 October 1943. Several other rabbis suffered the same fate. All were deported. The Chief Rabbi Isaïe Schwartz narrowly escaped arrest on 9 January 1944 and went underground. In response, on 11 January 1944, during an assembly of French rabbis, Rabbi Jacob Kaplan argued in favor of closing all synagogues. Even though a few days later he would be chosen to stand in as interim chief rabbi, he was unable to persuade the rabbis to agree (5 votes to 9). It was, however, a decision "in principle," since the assembled rabbis left the decision to close their synagogues to the rabbis themselves.[106] "Most synagogues continued to function, and closures were gradual. Closures tended to follow rather than anticipate the roundups, which, up until July 1944, led to the deportation of many religious Jews. After the roundup at the

Quai Tilsit synagogue in Lyon on 13 July 1944, the Consistory finally decided to close its offices. Those who had opted to live as practicing Jews in the open struggled with the decision to break with their traditions. Some felt that they were abandoning responsibilities that must be shouldered in any and all circumstances. More often, though, it stemmed from a kind of political myopia."[107]

In the countryside, where the Gestapo was less present, active religious observance was not as risky, though rabbis who settled in the countryside had to expend a great deal of energy to keep their communities' activities alive. This is seen in Léa Markscheid's study on the religious life of Jews forcibly relocated to Lacaune.[108] Markscheid draws on the August 1943 to September 1944 correspondence between two rabbis, Ephraïm Kleerekoper, who was living in Lacaune, and Robert Sommer, his hierarchical superior, who was living in Montauban. There were 648 Jews in Lacaune, a remote village in the Tarn department. They represented nineteen nationalities, mostly Polish and Dutch, who had arrived there between 1942 and 1944. Only three were French. Although there had already been two waves of arrests, the two rabbis were doing all they could to maintain Jewish life there in all its aspects, including organizing religious services, providing traditional foods and ritual objects for festivals, carrying out circumcisions, officiating at *bar mitzvahs*, and so on. A cinema was used as a synagogue and activities were organized for young people (book lending, Hebrew classes, *bar mitzvah* preparation). This impulse to maintain a religious life at any cost was the manifestation of a defiant form of religious resistance in the face of persecution.

Becoming Conscious of Jewish Identity

Attending classes given by a rabbi was liable to crystallize awareness of Jewish identity. For some young people on a path of self-discovery, reading the Bible led to a personal revelation of their roots. At a time when they were wondering what their future might hold, this awakening of an awareness of Jewish values helped them to construct a Jewish identity in a dangerous environment. Living under Occupation, this incipient awareness gave a profound meaning to their lives. In direct contrast to their assimilated parents, some experienced this as a spiritual journey. In 1943 Jeanine Hemmendinger was in her penultimate year at a Catholic secondary school in Valence. "At the time," she recounts:

> I was highly influenced by Rabbi Henri Schilli, who was from Montpellier. He was also in hiding in Valence, and had become the de facto rabbi of the Jewish community. I began practicing and joined the *Eclaireurs Israëlites* (EIF). I joined the Jewish study group that the rabbi had set up, and the term "Jewish" finally made sense to me: it was now associated with specific ideas and values, whereas before I had never understood the reason why a part of the population was persecuting us.

The EIF's founder, Robert Gamzon, involved the organization in various youth activities in the countryside, a project that was in accordance ideologically with the "back to the land" ideas extolled by Vichy. These EIF farm schools were boarding schools for teaching young people, whether French or immigrants, about Jewish values and Zionism.[109]

Involvement in Jewish movements inevitably led some young people to want to become involved with the Zionist project. Some tried to reach Palestine, encouraged by the EIF or other organizations such as the *Mouvement des jeunesses sionistes* (MJS, Young Zionist Movement). The voyage was risky but they did not want to wait for the hypothetical end of the war in Europe. Claude Hemmendinger, Jeannine's brother, was four years older than her. He had also heard Rabbi Schilli speaking in Montpellier. He became religious and joined a farm school in Taluyers (Rhône) in order to prepare to go "back to the land." He managed to reach Spain in May 1944 after a spell in prison, from where he embarked on the journey to Palestine. Some immigrants, like Saul Friedländer, would do the same after the war. Friedländer had become a passionate Zionist, and in June 1948 he decided to emigrate to Israel. Once again he changed his name: he abandoned Paul-Henri, the name he had been given at his Catholic boarding school, and adopted the Hebrew name Shaul. Later he changed it to Saul, "a compromise between the 'Saül' that French requires and the 'Paul' that I had been."[110] However, it was very rare for a French Jew to emigrate to Palestine, as Denise Caraco did. Though her Marseille family was fiercely secular, she discovered at the age of 8 that her father, whom she had believed to be dead, had in fact emigrated to Palestine. Having learned about Judaism through her participation in the Jewish scouts, she was persuaded after the Liberation by her fiancé, Polish-born Zeilig

Siekierski, to leave for Palestine. The couple married and left for Palestine in January 1947 with their six-month-old son Jacob.[111]

Whether or not they had received some kind of Jewish education, many young people only become conscious of their Jewish identity because of the war and the persecution of the Jews. This evolution impacted first and foremost on French Jews whose connection with Judaism was often tenuous. It was anti-Semitism that reminded them of their Jewish roots, especially during the 1930s. In this sense, "it is the anti-Semite who creates the Jew,"[112] as Jean-Paul Sartre wrote in his famous essay of 1944, published in 1946. "The Jew is one whom other men consider a Jew. That is the simple truth from which we must start."[113]

In her diary, Jacqueline Mesnil-Amar attests to a similar metamorphosis, clearly showing the trajectory by which in the course of the Occupation someone came to identify as a Jew. She belonged to the intellectual Jewish bourgeois elite, and understood how she had become victim—both theoretical and actual—of the regime. While the word "Jew" is barely present in the early pages of her diary, she soon begins talking about the "drama of the Jews, our drama, my drama."[114] It would appear as if the racial policies imposed by the occupying forces and Vichy in 1940 had been internalized. There is no doubt that Nazi oppression was at the heart of this process of self-identification.

Adolfo Kaminsky had absolutely nothing in common with Jacqueline Mesnil-Amar, neither in his origins nor his nationality; and he had barely ever considered the question of his Jewishness. But when he arrived at Drancy the shock triggered a sudden awareness: "The camp could be jam-packed one day and almost empty the next, until the inevitable processions of prisoners came to fill it up again. Jews, short, tall, with blond hair, brown hair. [...] It was not until I was at Drancy that I realized I knew nothing about them. [...] At Drancy, I discovered the Jews in all their diversity. I loved them, and through them I came to love myself—I felt I was a Jew, and I never lost that."[115]

For both foreign and French Jews, political struggle was the crucible for a committed anti-Nazi and anti-Vichy engagement. From summer 1941 onwards, after the Soviet Union had been invaded by Hitler and joined the war, it was the communist resistance that constituted the main force of attraction for young Jewish immigrants and native French Jews committed to fighting the Nazis and Vichy.

This was the path followed by the young Annie Becker, who at the end of 1942 joined the Jeunes Communistes-Main-d'oeuvre immigrée (JC-MOI: the Young Communists-Immigrant Workers Union). For her, joining the communist resistance was a commitment to a patriotic political struggle. The historian she became, going by her married name Annie Kriegel, wrote, "Adherence to communism broke the vicious circle in a way that was in the first instance fairly trivial: it was better to perish for having voluntarily belonged to a subversive movement than to die for having been included by a coincidence of birth in a category—a so-called race—which was nothing less than absurd. But the point was not so much the desire to take action as to be subject and master of both their lives and their deaths. For those Jews who were not religious and thus did not have a theology of persecution, the point was to give some meaning to Jewish existence."[116] In addition, according to Kriegel, for many foreign Jews, the Communist Party was a kind of conveyor belt for integration in France. The participation of Jews in the major resistance movements was also a way for them to assert themselves as French.

However, this brutal confrontation between individuals and anti-Semitic persecution did not mean that everyone suddenly considered themselves Jewish. For some it was quite the opposite: they had never accepted a description that they considered to be imposed on them by anti-Semites. But whether they felt Jewish or not, they were now concerned. It was a personal, private decision. It was not up to anyone else to tell them whether they were Jewish or not, and above all it was not up to anti-Semites. "It was the Germans and Vichy who told me I was Jewish," Stanley Hoffmann explained to me, "Something I have never accepted." Thinking back on that period during the 1970s, he now defined himself as a "partly Jewish alien,"[117] since his mother had converted from Judaism to Protestantism and had him baptized at birth as a Protestant.[118] As for Jean-Jacques Becker, he recalls how at the end of the war, seeking to turn the page, he wanted to "stop being Jewish."[119] Choosing to rid themselves of something that they considered a "label" could also be seen as an act of personal resistance, in order to "forget" as swiftly as possible the grim period of Nazism and Occupation.

Thousands applied to change their names after 1945, a phenomenon that has largely been forgotten today. In an important study on the subject by Nicole Lapierre, one of her interviewees was a man with the surname Finkelsztajn. "My wife and I wanted to be done with this label. When someone said Finkelsztajn, it was like the yellow star, we'd had enough of it." They experienced the name Finkelsztajn, with its distinct overtones of "central Europe," as an unendurable stigma. After the war, "without any hesitation or regret," he decided to change his surname to Félix, the first name of a close friend. While the name conserved his first initial as a nominal reminder, he simply liked the way it sounded.[120] For some Jewish immigrants, changing their name constituted a symbolic act that enabled them to break with a painful past. "Between 1945 and 1957, 2,150 decrees (passed by the *Conseil d'État* [Council of State]) were granted to Jews at a sixfold greater rate than during the entire period between 1809 and 1939, most of those concerned changing surnames of Eastern European origin. [...] Bearing in mind that these changes of name applied equally to spouses and underage children, they concerned between eight and ten thousand people out of a Jewish population estimated at around 200,000."[121]

The applications were mostly made by Ashkenazi Jews who had immigrated to France—which they saw as country representing freedom, modernity and cultural openness—before the war. After the war there were those who still wanted to show their loyalty to France, to the point of changing their names; changing one's name was primarily a way of "protecting their descendants against a possible resurgence of anti-Semitism," but it was also a way of affirming an attachment to France and to express a continued faith in the country.[122] These Jewish immigrants did not share the sentiment of French Jews, who felt bitterness and resentment towards the France that they had so loved before the war, who had been humiliated and excluded by the Vichy regime, and in some cases arrested and deported. This was entirely legitimate, though it was at odds with the actual deportation figures, for almost nine out of ten French Jews survived the war, as opposed to six out of ten Jewish immigrants. In theory, therefore, immigrant Jews should have felt the greatest sense of betrayal. Yet Nicole Lapierre notes that paradoxically many foreign-born Jews managed to uphold their devotion to France. "A major factor which explains the persistence of this sentiment was that the *Statut des Juifs* and the measures of persecution were enacted by the State and its administration, [...] but unlike for example in Poland, these discriminatory and repressive measures were not matched by the widespread support and active participation of the population. Many fugitive Jews were able to hide thanks both to the life-saving activities of organized Resistance networks and to the initiatives of individuals who helped them, among other things, to obtain forged identity cards."[123] In short, the aid given to Jews by non-Jewish French citizens, who had no scruples when it came to defying the pseudo-legality of the regime, both embodied and preserved the cardinal values of France, which were otherwise so compromised by the state's collaboration. It is for this reason that understanding the range of random acts of solidarity that were spontaneously carried out by non-Jewish individuals towards persecuted Jews is so important.

4

RANDOM ACTS OF SOLIDARITY
TOWARDS THE PERSECUTED

Almost all say the same thing, in almost identical words: "We felt protected by the local people." In December 1943, Stanley Hoffmann and
his mother arrived in Lamalou-les-Bains, having fled Nice, where the
SS captain Aloïs Brunner now held sway. Arriving in the spa town, a
place they had already visited as tourists, they found that around a
thousand German soldiers were stationed there. And yet they felt safe:
"I have no example of people behaving badly towards us. They behaved
like human beings."[1] Jacqueline Feldman had a similar experience when
she and her Polish parents were living in the village of Noirétable
(Haute-Loire): "I felt protected by the local people, who were very
'anti-Boche.'"

The list goes on. So many witness accounts attest to similar experiences, even as they were plunged into such different situations and
found themselves living in different regions. It is important to consider
whether, beyond the facts that they report, their words might be the
expression of a memory effect, rather than objective testimony. Are
these the words of a generation of Jewish witnesses who were not
deported, who were children or adolescents during the war, and who
realized as adults that they owed their survival to an individual or a
family who had once welcomed them into their homes? Many of these
victims of persecution felt intense gratitude after the fact. As adults

191

they frequently returned to the places where they had once lived, to see the faces of those who had once taken them in. Some feel ashamed for not having done so earlier.

Pierre Sauvage was thirty-six and living in the United States when he first learned that he had been taken in as a baby, along with his parents, by a farming family in Le Chambon-sur-Lignon (Haute-Loire). He decided to make a documentary paying homage to the inhabitants of the Protestant village in the mountains of the Haut-Vivarais, which has since become known throughout the world for having hidden hundreds of Jewish refugees, both adults and children, at the instigation of pastors André Trocmé and Édouard Theis.[2]

The testimonies of Jewish witnesses who avoided deportation cannot simply be put down to the simple urge to acknowledge their gratitude. Their words are not univocal, and, moreover, they do not fail to note instances of denunciation or attempted denunciation of which they or their relatives were sometimes victims. Their accounts do not describe an idealized vision of life under the Occupation but rather—and it is no small matter—relate that the French population displayed tacit and often lifesaving goodwill towards them. Their claims are corroborated in a range of archives, beginning with reports from the CGQJ which, particularly after 1942, "complained constantly of the 'stupidity' of the French, who were in their eyes too prompt to take pity on the suffering of the Jews and to come to their aid," according to Jean Estèbe, pointing to the region around Toulouse as an example.[3]

So why is it that one can still read and hear it said that during this period the French were overwhelmingly anti-Semitic? The British media was swift to claim, for example, when the film La Rafle (The Round Up) was released in May 2010, that the help received by Jews came from a tiny minority of the population.[4] The image of the majority of the population as being anti-Semitic, with a heroically courageous but tiny elite of "good" people devoted to saving Jews, is an unadulterated cliché. That a particularly virulent strain of "traditional" anti-Semitism prevailed during the years of the Occupation is undeniably true. That there existed among the French a certain indifference regarding the early anti-Semitic measures taken by Vichy and the Nazi occupying forces is also well documented. Yet the interpretation of this "generalized indifference" is not straightforward, and historians are not wholly in agreement about what it meant. Indeed, as many Vichy documents attest, the population showed distinct hostility to the mass deportations that targeted Jews from 1942 onwards. It needs to be acknowledged that the anti-Semitic policies that were instituted by the occupying forces and Vichy did not spread through the entire body of society. Studies on the evolution of public opinion are highly illuminating, in for example the work of Pierre Laborie.[5] Jews received various forms of concern and protection, whether passive or active, from the wider population. Recognizing the extent of this phenomenon does not mean rehabilitating the myth of "resistance-ism" from the 1950s and 1960s, which propagated the claim that all the French took part in the Resistance.[6] The discreet support shown by the wider population between 1942 and 1944 to Jewish refugees, to those forcibly enlisted in the STO who refused to obey, and to other victims of the regime, cannot be defined as a resistance movement in the conventional sense of the term, i.e. as a coordinated and structured organization fighting against the occupying forces and Vichy. It indicates rather the wide range of small gestures of aid and protection offered to Jews by individuals, whether or not they already knew each other. These small gestures in some cases had large, lifesaving consequences. Having seen how Jews struggled to survive, with ingenuity and resourcefulness, it is time to explore a remarkable social phenomenon which developed in France during the last two years of the Occupation especially. In fact, the two go hand in hand, for it would have been impossible for so many Jews to have survived if they had found themselves living among a hostile population. This was a highly variegated social world, diverse and complex, where the lines were often blurred between self-interest, non-consent, and disobedience.

Anti-Semitism, Indifference and Compassion

It is not necessary to describe the anti-Semitic policies of the Vichy government again: there are hundreds of books and articles which explore this area from a wide variety of perspectives—their inspirations, their targets, the stages in which they were set in motion. Nonetheless, the adoption of official anti-Semitic policies by the Vichy regime does not prove that a large majority of French people suddenly became virulently anti-Semitic.

193

Propaganda and its limits

The sudden change in the political situation of the country exposed the population to the parallel propaganda of Vichy and the occupying forces. From one day to the next, the anti-Semitic ideas that a portion of public opinion was stirring up before the war had now been hoisted to the rank of official ideology of the regime. While Marshal Pétain never raised the "Jewish question" in his speeches to the French people, even as his government was drawing up anti-Jewish legislation, the collaborationist press was flourishing, propagating claims that the "Jew" was a traitor and a profiteer and had to be relegated to the margins of society. French radio also contributed to spreading the regime's ideology, increasingly so in the wake of Pierre Laval's return to power in 1942. As they read and listened to such messages, people were indeed convinced that there was a "Jewish problem," an expression that had gained currency in the 1930s. Meanwhile, propaganda spread by the occupying forces was even more aggressive and destructive.

In the streets of Paris a pedestrian might catch sight of a poster showing an unknown soldier rising out of his grave to cut the throat of "Jewry" and Freemasonry; on the metro, commuters might see the image of a man with a hooked nose, stretching out his arm towards a crown and scepter, a classic depiction of "the Jew Süss", the protagonist of the film of the same name. This 1940 film was the quintessence of Nazi anti-Semitic propaganda. It portrays Jews as obsessed with sex, money, and the Promised Land, by definition swindlers and manipulators, and contemptuous of non-Jews. The film advocates locking Jews up in ghettos and slaughtering their elites. But nothing suggests that this vile propaganda persuaded the French that they had to rid themselves of the Jews once and for all, and research on public opinion of the time demonstrates that the French population rapidly showed themselves to be recalcitrant, if not actively hostile, when faced with both German and Vichy propaganda. The sociology of communication has amply demonstrated that the impact of propaganda must never be overestimated: broadcasting a message is one thing, the way it is received is another. The public that was targeted had its own interpretation filters, and did not always necessarily decode the message in the way intended by the sender.[7] In other words, academic studies of Vichy propaganda aiming to show that French society at the time was deeply anti-Semitic are based on debatable assumptions.

It would nonetheless be naïve to believe that such propaganda had no impact on people's thoughts and behavior. As an official ideology, it decreed how to talk about Jews in public. The sudden change in the political regime, accompanied by newly introduced censorship and surveillance, obliged individuals to be prudent, forcing them to hide their real beliefs. As Elisabeth Noelle-Neumann puts it, a "spiral of silence" began to develop. In research focusing on Nazism, she suggests that public opinion is "the opinion which can be voiced in public without fear of sanctions and upon which action in public can be based."[8] Public opinion determines what an individual can openly declare, such as "I don't like Jews." Noelle-Neumann points out that even though an individual may not necessarily have believed such a statement, it could nonetheless be used to prove that it represented majority opinion. In fact, while it may have accurately represented the most extreme wing of opinion, it is likely that most of the population rallied around such statements through the habit of conformism and the fear of retribution.

The public stigmatizing of a group, turning it into a popular scapegoat, also increases the likelihood of the unleashing of violence—spontaneous or ordered—against members of that group. Anti-Semitic state policy created a climate of impunity favorable to those who wanted to attack Jews and their possessions. It is important to distinguish between different degrees of intensity in the evolution to actual violence, depending on the political context and the level of integration of Jews into society.

In Nazi Germany, in the years after Hitler came to power in 1933, there were countless acts of violence against Jews, including murder; the violence reached a peak with *Kristallnacht* on 9 November 1938. The Kanner family had to learn to live with the intensification of anti-Jewish legislation. On 28 October 1938, Markus, Sal's father, was deported to Poland. Ten days later, during Kristallnacht, Sal was arrested and his clothes shop was vandalized; he was sent to Buchenwald.[9] The same day, the synagogue in the village of Hoffenheim, in the state of Baden where the Mayers lived, was destroyed.[10] In Poland, in July 1941—at the very moment when the Wehrmacht launched its assault on the USSR, invading and occupying eastern Poland—the non-Jewish villagers of Jedwabne took advantage of the situation and burned their Jewish neighbors to death.[11] Such horrors, either instigated by the local population or with its willing participation, did not take place in France. When the occupying forces arrived, partisans of Jacques Doriot's *Parti Populaire Français* (PPF— French Popular Party) ransacked and pillaged Jewish-owned shops in Paris and provincial cities. But Jacques Biélinky, an astute observer of everyday Jewish life in Paris at the time, remarked that these kinds of activities fizzled out quickly and that Parisians were more likely to demonstrate sympathy with the Jews, a tendency confirmed in Léo Hamon's account, written during the same period between 1940 and 1941.[12] Spontaneous physical attacks on Jewish people and property were quite rare in France, occurring only sporadically during the Occupation, and carried out almost always by right-wing extremists and members of the Milice.

The lure of material gain

There were plenty of people who, while they did not resort to physical violence, had no compunction when it came to exploiting the many anti-Jewish laws and restrictions to turn a profit. Lawyers, doctors, and journalists were perfectly happy to see their Jewish colleagues forbidden from practicing their professions under the impact of these new laws. A shop owner might denounce a Jewish competitor in order to expand his own clientele, or try to buy the business when the order had been given for it to be "Aryanized." A concierge would make it known that foreign Jews were living in the building, and they would subsequently be arrested: she would either take their furniture, or organize for a "real" French family to move in, from whom she in turn would receive a nice commission. A thoroughly respectable gentleman might take it upon himself to denounce the owner of a Jewish business and later arrange to become the provisional manager, for which he would receive substantial payment. A teacher would accept a post left vacant after a colleague was forced to leave as a result of the new legislation. Is it fair to call those who benefited from the persecution of Jews anti-Semites? There were people, of course, who were convinced that "Jewry" presented a genuine threat to France, and that it was thus essential to eliminate their malign influence in order to "regenerate" the defeated country. There were others who were solely motivated by the promise of material gain. Committed anti-Semites were certainly not indifferent to the potential benefits of their actions: anti-Semitism and profit went comfortably hand in hand.

An urban phenomenon?

The exclusion and persecution of Jews tended to take place in towns and cities; up until the war Jews mostly lived in an urban environment, particularly in Paris. It is possible that these phenomena were essentially urban, for rural populations seemed almost completely unaware of the "Jewish problem." Though many Jews fled to rural areas after 1940, prior to the fall of France few Jews were living in the French countryside. There were exceptions, such as Claude Lanzmann's grandparents, French-born Jewish farmers, who lived in Groutel, a hamlet in Normandy,[13] and the Feldman family, who spent the summer of 1939 in central France, in the town of Noirétable, thanks to the Yiddish Arbeiter Sportif Club (YASC), the Yiddish section of the communist Fédération Sportive et Gymnique du Travail (FSGT).

The flow of refugees into the Free Zone did sometimes provoke hostility in the areas where they settled, but is not clear that such reactions were the expression of anti-Semitism or merely resentment of the new arrivals in a context of increasing shortages. People recalled not anti-Semitic harassment or insults, but being mocked for their city ways: "*Parigots, têtes de veau*" ("Parisian meatheads") or "*Parisiens, têtes de chien*" ("Parisian mongrels").

Vichy's anti-Semitic propaganda did not appear to have much impact in the countryside, where, according to Léon Werth, people rarely read a newspaper, unless it was to look up agricultural commodity prices. In fact, the Pétainist press rarely talked about the situation of the Jews. By contrast, the Catholic Church at the time was very much a vector of traditional anti-Jewish sentiment, which had more of an impact on the mentality of rural populations and made them more liable to be drawn to anti-Semitism; traditional Catholic education had already instilled a negative image of Jews, even though for people living in the countryside it would have been an entirely abstract notion, since few would have ever met anyone Jewish. Serge Klarsfeld recalls how, having arrived in the small village of Saint-Julien-Chapteuil with his mother and sister, his sister got into conversation with a local woman who was convinced that "Jews had cloven feet and little tails."

As a result, the rural population who witnessed these people arriving from the city did not see them as Jews, but rather as refugees and victims of war. While coexistence was not always effortless, in general it was not because of anti-Semitism. When local village people found out that the new arrivals were Jewish, this information was apparently of little significance to them.

Pétainism and anti-Semitism

However, the paradox was that people living in the countryside, and the French in general, largely supported the actions of Marshal Pétain, at least in the early years of the Occupation. Since one of the first actions of his government was to take discriminatory measures against Jews, one might conclude that the French were naturally in favor of such policies. This conclusion would follow the same kind of reasoning as has frequently been seen in studies on propaganda, which assumes that the actions of the elites were a reflection of dominant popular opinion. Researching in the archives of public policy is easier than analyzing the evolution of public opinion, which is by definition less tangible. This has led some historians to focus their research on those in power rather than on broader public opinion, basing their conclusions on the hypothesis that the actions of the former largely determined the evolution of the latter. This general tendency underpins Michael Marrus's and Robert Paxton's *Vichy France and the Jews*, which has been the inspiration for much other work on the subject since the 1980s. Such a historiographical perspective gives rise to some major reservations.

As Paul Thibaud points out, "The new *Statut des Juifs* was not accompanied by mass expressions of anti-Semitism. It was relayed to the public in hypocritical speeches, which presented the new legislation as moderate and necessary, but it aroused such little enthusiasm in the population that some of the major newspapers in the Free Zone (*Le Figaro*, *La Montagne*, *Le Progrès*) did not even pass comment on it."[14] Indeed, if the French were so anti-Semitic, why is it that the publication of the *Statuts des Juifs* did not occasion any manifestation of public support either in the Occupied Zone, or later on in the Free Zone? Marrus and Paxton claimed to have revealed a great wave of popular anti-Semitism in the Free Zone, based on their analyses of reports by a large number of prefects who, after the publication of the second *Statut des Juifs*, "commented on the influx of additional Jewish refugees from the Occupied Zone and on the sharp hostility these newcomers provoked."[15]

Marrus and Paxton were well aware that they were exposing themselves to criticism by basing their conclusions on potentially biased sources. It is important to consider to what extent Vichy representatives were reporting what their political leaders wanted to hear, but Marrus and Paxton qualify this objection, and conclude that "the most striking revelation of a study of Marshal Pétain's own intelligence sources is a powerful surge of popular anti-Semitism in the Free Zone during 1941–42."[16] It is not hard to understand why the authors chose to focus on the Free Zone, since that was where in theory Vichy had full authority.

The claim that there was a widespread anti-Semitism in the Southern Zone might be considered surprising, given that we know from Jacques Biélinky's independent observations of daily life, as well as Léo Hamon's account, that it was not at all uncommon in occupied Paris for non-Jews to show discreet sympathy towards Jews during that period. The idea that the French in the Free Zone were more anti-Semitic than those in the Occupied Zone is surprising, to say the least.

Indeed, an entirely different perspective was offered thirteen years later by Asher Cohen in his book *Persécutions et sauvetages*. After critiquing the sources used by Marrus and Paxton, Cohen used his thesis to explore attitudes in the Free Zone, drawing on departmental archives from several prefectures, the CGQJ, and the PQJ (Police for the Jewish Question); in other words, he used archives that were "closer to the people, including reports that surveyed public opinion."[17] In conclusion, Cohen writes, "the reports of the PQJ and the CGQJ constitute a precious source of information on opinions and attitudes that could not be expressed openly. The Commissariat agents were extremely sensitive to these underlying attitudes, which focused only on Jews and largely contradict the thesis that there was a hostile or even an indifferent attitude towards Jews before the mass arrests that took place in the summer of 1942. The Commissariat agents had a quite different perspective to that of other sources in terms of how they interpreted the opinions of 'neutral' observers, which they took as evidence of 'indifference' in the face of attacks on Jews, while for the agents of the CGQJ, a lack of cooperation was proof of 'incomprehension' and even 'hostility' [to anti-Jewish measures]." In support of his thesis, the author cites an autumn 1940 memo from the intelligence services in Lyon,[18] which sounds like a warning to historians: "It would be a grave error to interpret the current silence as tacit support or approval."[19] Cohen concludes, "This is the heart of the problem: the unexpressed attitude of the majority of the French, prior to the mass arrests. It is specifically on this point that the literature must be revisited."[20] It is not the first time that historians have drawn different conclusions from different archival sources, or indeed from the same ones.

Some historians interpret the passivity of the population as a kind of tacit acquiescence. Silence can be read as approval and acknowledgment of the fact that they did believe that there was a "Jewish problem" in France. In short, silence was consent. This is the position taken by Renée Poznanski, who observes that although Jews often received expressions of sympathy in private from non-Jews, public opinion remained silent in the wake of the promulgation of the *Statuts des Juifs*.[21]

Only the Catholic Church was in a position to be able to formulate a critical response to the promulgation of the laws. But the Catholic faithful, just like the broader French population, were extremely pro-Pétain. In this "new" Vichy France, the Catholic hierarchy broadly accepted the status of Jews as second-class citizens. The Catholic Church, like the general public, accepted that Jews were to be marginalized from this point on precisely because they were perceived as a "problem." In her diary, Hélène Berr was highly critical of the Catholic Church for this attitude.[22]

However, it is highly unlikely that all those, whether or not they were Catholic, who considered that the Jews were a "problem," reasoned in the same way. Even the expression "Jewish problem" is somewhat ambiguous. How can we differentiate between xenophobes ("there are too many foreigners in France") and anti-Semites ("The Jews are responsible for all our problems")? Not everyone who spoke of a "Jewish problem" was anti-Semitic. In September 1941, a group of

Protestants who were actively aiding Jewish internees in the camps of southern France tackled this question in a foundational text, the "Theses of Pomeyrol," in which they stated that when it came to the Jews, "the state faces a problem to which it must find a solution" (§ VII). One might thus be tempted to detect anti-Semitism in this passage. But given the pioneering commitment of these Protestants to helping the persecuted, is this so clear?[23]

An incipient opposition

There is an alternative way of interpreting the silence of public opinion in the early period of the persecution of the Jews in France. To understand it, "it should first be placed in the context of the defeat of 1940," as Pierre Laborie points out. "Attitudes towards the persecution of the Jews cannot be dissociated from everything else, including the way in which the French saw their relationship with the wider world in autumn 1940 and how they reacted to the events themselves," he writes. "Yes, as shocking as that may seem to our contemporary sensibility, with hindsight, and with what we know today about what would later take place, the question of the exclusion of the Jews was not seen as being a key issue by non-Jews. It was a minor issue relative to the huge impact of the fall of the country to the German occupiers, and the profound feeling of humiliation that accompanied it; it was a minor issue relative to concerns about prisoners of war, to the disruption of daily life and the material problems that resulted from chronic shortages; it was a minor issue relative to the chaos from the fallout of the exodus from Paris and the multiple uncertainties about what would happen to the refugee population. It was, moreover, drowned out by the measures of repression that impacted other persecuted categories (communists, Freemasons, partisans working for the Front Populaire)."[24] What is more, any fallout there might have been as a result of the publication of the *Statut des Juifs* on 3 October was quickly overtaken by the political events of autumn 1940 and the momentous meeting that took place in Montoire on 24 October between Pétain and Hitler.

One event came hard on the heels of another. The photograph of the famous handshake between the two men, symbolizing the beginning of their "collaboration," certainly struck the imagination of the French rather more than did the passing of the first *Statut des Juifs*, which went scarcely noticed by the press. Those newspapers that did comment on it stated, wrongly, that the racial discrimination instituted by Vichy was in direct response to German pressure. Acknowledging the context— which does not, of course, excuse public apathy—does go some way towards understanding the reasons for it, especially as the press was by now muzzled by censorship.

In a radical critique of Robert Paxton's work, Pierre Laborie takes issue with his assumption that French passivity regarding Vichy policies equates to approval of these policies. As an expert in the field of public opinion and the Resistance, Laborie insists that Paxton's approach is far too perfunctory and deplores the fact that the "Paxtonian vision" is now dominant in the study of the period. While acknowledging Paxton's vital contribution in demonstrating the French government's collaboration with Berlin, he rejects the historian's conclusions about the collective behavior of the French. Laborie disputes Paxton's premise "that those who did not actively oppose authority were *de facto* supporters of that authority."[25]

There were people who raised their voices, actively defying the generalized apathy. Such isolated protests were even braver, considering that they went against prevalent public opinion. In Paris, the curate of the Saint-Médard parish spoke from his pulpit on 28 November 1940 to condemn "all hatred and hostility towards non-Catholics";[26] in London the spokesman for the Free French, Maurice Schumann, spoke out on BBC radio against the promulgation of the *Statuts des Juifs*.[27] Moreover, even though their voices—unsurprisingly—went almost unreported in the press, there were many individuals and organizations who were actively helping Jews, beginning with the aid provided to foreign internees in the camps in the south of France—for instance Madeleine Barot and the Cimade (Protestant), Christian Fellowship (*Amitié chrétienne*, an inter-confessional organization based in Lyon) and Abbé Glasberg. In the Northern Zone, there were priests and pastors who were forging baptism certificates on their own initiative, without consulting their superiors. From the very first months of the Occupation, non-Jewish French people—admittedly a minority— were working in support of those who found themselves being persecuted because they were Jews.

Was this the legacy of the struggle against racism and anti-Semitism that had emerged in the 1930s, as described by Ralph Schor and Vicki Caron?[28] Jews living in Paris were aware from the beginning of manifestations of sympathy from the wider population. Furthermore, a simmering opposition to the anti-Semitic legislation began to be expressed in Catholic circles from the summer of 1941.[29] The CGQJ knew that priests were forging baptism certificates. Quite often the counterfeit certificates managed to deceive the authorities.[30] Abbé Henri Ménardais, parish priest of Chalmaison, was responsible for a series of forged baptism certificates that saved the lives of at least five people imprisoned in Drancy.[31]

This aid and protection gradually expanded and spread in the second half of 1942. Historians agree that there was a shift as public opinion became increasingly hostile to the brutal and inflammatory measures that Jews were now subject to. In June 1942, the introduction of the yellow star in the Occupied Zone triggered spontaneous demonstrations of sympathy on the part of Parisians, as we have seen.[32] The journalist Jacques Biélinky was witness to such behavior, and throughout his testimony emerges a range of spontaneous gestures of support by anonymous Parisians, including: the wearing of the yellow star in solidarity; verbal expressions of sympathy; purposeful greetings from strangers; expressions of disapproval of anti-Semitic attitudes; priority service in shops.[33]

As we know from other testimonies, such as that of Georges Wellers, some young people started wearing stars emblazoned with inscriptions such as "Zoulou," "Swing," or "Papou."[34] Some of those who wore these stars were arrested and imprisoned for up to three months in Drancy, though they were not deported. During their imprisonment, they were forced to wear a yellow star inscribed with the words "Friend of the Jews."[35]

Compassion and solidarity

In the wake of the Vel' d'Hiv' roundup on 16 and 17 July 1942, public hostility became even more marked. The spectacle of entire families being picked up at their homes by French officials was by its very nature deeply upsetting. That August, similarly negative reactions spread among people in the Free Zone who witnessed both the transfer of Jewish internees towards Drancy and the arrests of foreign Jews in villages and towns throughout the region. In Lacaune, Léa Markscheid recalls how the local inhabitants, shocked by the arrests that took place on 26 August 1942, became increasingly disposed to offer aid to Jews who had been placed under house arrest.[36] In just a few months public opinion had gone from indifference to the persecution of Jews to the expression of a genuine compassion for them. This arose primarily because the nature of the persecution had changed. It was now both more violent and more conspicuous, affecting not only men but also women and children. Reflecting this widespread public hostility, several senior prelates from the Catholic Church became mouthpieces of this sentiment in sermons they gave at the end of August and the beginning of September 1942. We know who they were and when they delivered their sermons: Mgr Jules Saliège in Toulouse (23 August), Mgr Pierre-Marie Théas in Montauban (30 August), Cardinal Pierre-Marie Gerlier in Lyon (6 September), Mgr Jean Delay in Marseille (6 September), Mgr Joseph Moussaron in Albi (20 September). The protest made by Mgr Saliège, archbishop of Toulouse, already known for having condemned anti-Semitism in the 1930s, unquestionably had the strongest impact. His pastoral letter, entitled *Et clamor Jerusalem ascendit*,[37] was read in the churches of the diocese of Toulouse on 23 and 30 August:

> That children, women, men, fathers, mothers should be treated as a wretched herd, that members of the same family should be separated from one another and embarked for unknown destinations, was a sad spectacle reserved for our times to see. [...] In our diocese moving scenes have been enacted in the camps of Noé and Récébédou. These Jews are men, these Jewesses are women; these aliens are men and women. All is not permissible against them [...]. against these fathers and mothers. They belong to mankind.[38]

The letter was reproduced extensively in the underground press. It was also read on air on the BBC on 30 August and was the subject of a *New York Times* article published on 9 September.[39] Public protests from Catholic officials, while limited in terms of the number of bishops, had significant consequences for worshippers: "There was then a shift from a kind of passive complicity to forming active and silent chains of solidarity in predominantly Christian milieus."[40]

This sympathy towards the predicament of Jews was just one element of a more general political evolution: a growing rift between the general population's position and that of Vichy. Other factors contributed to intensifying that evolution: in April 1942, Pierre Laval returned to power, declaring that he hoped for a German victory, then in September 1942 the worker-for-prisoner exchange program, called the *Relève*, was set up even though prisoners of war were still not being sent home. This was followed by the German occupation of the entire country (with the exception of the Italian zone) in November 1942, and the establishment of the extremely unpopular STO forced labor program, in March 1943. In a general climate of defiance, a variety of behaviors that were more or less rebellious and illegal began to emerge in most strata of French society.

While there were French people who wrote letters informing on Jews to the CGQJ, there were others who did the opposite. Asher Cohen has analyzed letters addressed to Marshal Pétain and Pierre Laval[41] and published a sample of 152 letters written between 1941 and 1944 (21 of which are anonymous). The chronology of persecution shows that there were two main types of letter. In the 1941 to 1942 period there were correspondents—who made sure to emphasize their status as war veterans and members of the Catholic Church—intervening on behalf of individual Jews. Beginning in summer 1942 the content of the letters became more general and critical, expressing disapproval for the inhumane treatment reserved specifically for Jews. "France has condemned and dishonored itself by meting out such cruel and disgraceful treatment to people who believed they had found asylum in our country. It brings shame upon us as Frenchmen, Christians, as men; and the admiration surrounding the image of the Marshal has been shaken, if not completely swept away," François Ditte-D'Arrien wrote in a letter to Marshal Pétain dated 30 August 1942.[42]

With the entrenched radicalization of the relationship between occupiers and occupied characteristic of the years 1942 to 1944, the issue of the anti-Semitism attributed to the French population appears to have been settled. With the exception of a minority of ideologically driven extremists, the general conduct of the French suggests that they were not hostile to Jews, in fact quite the opposite. Nonetheless, this assessment does not satisfy some historians, who insist that even those who came to the aid of Jews might nonetheless have been anti-Semitic. Renée Poznanski suggests as much when she writes, "Individual compassion was not a new thing and it has always and everywhere been compatible with deep-seated anti-Semitism."[43] So it was with the priest from Saint-Secondin (Vienne), who told Marthe Hoffnung when she came to him seeking help, "I'll help you because it's the right thing to do. But you should know this from the outset—I'd never trust a Jew."[44] Compassion, in this case, overcame prejudice and stigmatization.

There is no doubt that the figure of the "anti-Semitic rescuer" existed both in France and elsewhere in Nazi-occupied Europe.[45] The fact that some people who saw in the "Jew" the figure of Judas betraying Jesus nonetheless helped Jews in desperate straits is in itself an important element for understanding the widespread mobilization against their persecution in all parts of French society: we will return to this. But the assumption that most of those who helped Jews held anti-Semitic opinions is based on a gross generalization. If that were the case, what does it mean to be anti-Semitic, as a way of thinking and acting? The word becomes devoid of meaning. Every non-Jew (with a few exceptions) is potentially anti-Semitic. This hypothesis of a diffuse and widespread anti-Semitism, when applied to an entire society, is more than fragile when considered with hindsight, once we acknowledge that three-quarters of the Jewish population survived the war in France. This does not, of course, alter the fact that the ways in which human beings behave can be riven with paradoxes.

One thing, however, is certain: in seeking to understand how and why French non-Jews helped Jews to survive, it is important to focus on their behavior rather than their beliefs, since stereotypes and prejudices are often transcended through the lived experience of an actual encounter.

Betrayal and Self-Interest

It is vital to avoid presenting an idealized image of human relationships. Prejudice is highly tenacious and the experience of getting to know an individual does not always work its magic. Thus it was when the opposite scenario played out, with catastrophe turning into tragedy; when fear and mistrust won out, and the victim was delivered to his executioners. During the Occupation, thousands of French people turned informer, denouncing Jews, whether neighbors or strangers. Even as we try to understand how it was that so many of the Jews in France survived, it is important not to forget the reality of human baseness. It is clear that there was a broad span of behavior, ranging from informing to selflessly and fearlessly offering aid.

The informer embodies one of the most unpleasant figures of the period of the Occupation. It is a vector for clichés, and serious research on the subject has been rare, at least in the case of France. Several examples of informing have been recounted by some of the witnesses whose stories are told in this book, whose families or comrades were targeted. In 1943, while helping with the evacuation of Jews in Nice, Léon Poliakov recalls that members of his rescue network were arrested one after another after a series of denunciations and that he was afraid that he too would be picked up.[46] Denise Lefschetz's grandfather was denounced in 1944 in Paris by an unnamed boy for having shopped for groceries outside the hours reserved for Jews; some communist friends procured forged documents that attested to the fact that he was married to an "Aryan" woman, and so he was sent to a camp reserved for the spouses of Aryans and thus avoided deportation. The pages of Albert Grunberg's diary are suffused with the constant fear that he would be denounced. He was particularly afraid of the Ls, a couple who lived in the building where he was in hiding.

In general the informer used the laws that were in effect to denounce to the authorities a person known to be flouting them. Jews were subject to so many different prohibitions that it was not hard to find a reason to denounce them. The informer became an auxiliary to authority, presenting himself as a "good Frenchman." Informers were also guided by more personal motivations, such as jealousy or the lure of profit. In France, during the Occupation, denunciations were conveyed in anonymous letters to the authorities as well as orally. Informing was practiced against all enemies of the regime, communists and other resistance fighters, Jews and Freemasons alike. It also targeted "economic crimes," including procuring goods on the black market. Economic motives seem to have been the most frequent reason for informing.[47] Anti-Semitic denunciations were just one dimension of informing, something that was hardly new in 1940; fifty years earlier

Edouard Drumont, in the wake of the success of his book *Jewish France*, had added a section to his newspaper *La Libre Parole* (Free Speech), devoted to contributions from anyone who wanted to lash out against supposed "Jewish influence."[48] This longstanding practice of public denunciation in the press was taken up by collaborationist newspapers such as *Je suis partout* and *Au Pilori*.

Of all administrative offices, the CGQJ was the one that received the largest number of letters of denunciation. Laurent Joly has dug deep into its archives,[49] concentrating on cases of denunciation in Paris and the surrounding suburbs (the Seine department), where around half of those listed in the census as being Jewish—around 150,000 people—lived. Out of a total of 35,303 letters registered as having been received by the CGQJ, Joly found only 1,118 cases of anti-Semitic denunciations between 1942 and 1944, most often unsigned. Extrapolating from these figures, he estimated that the number of anti-Semitic denunciations was around 3,000 during the entire period of the Occupation. Such a low figure bears no relation whatsoever to estimate of 3 to 5 million letters of denunciation (all categories included) once put forward by the journalist André Halimi.[50]

While the denunciation of Jews was a marginal phenomenon in France, unlike in Poland where some 30 per cent of all the letters of denunciation targeted Jews,[51] its effects were certainly devastating. Several thousand people were arrested, most of whom were deported, whether as individuals or with their families, including young children and elderly relatives.

The victims of these denunciations were generally not fugitives, contrary to widespread belief. They were primarily people who had been living in the same neighborhood for a long time. Those who fell under the new regulations that came into force with the *Statuts des Juifs* and who then failed to obey them, or obeyed them only in part, might be denounced by a neighbor harboring resentment towards them because of some longstanding personal grievance.

In general, the informer was an anti-Semitic collaborator, of which there were broadly two types. The first was already an "initiate": he or she wrote with confidence to the head of the CGQJ, whose values they shared. The second was less sophisticated, sending anonymous letters without necessarily being knowledgeable about the apparatus of persecution. The utmost disgrace: there were some Jews who informed on other Jews whom they believed were not "obeying the law."

Anti-Semitic denunciations were, of course, encouraged by the German authorities, who were trying to orient the Paris police towards a policy of discreetly hunting and targeting the Jews of the capital. For the Nazis this was an essential weapon in their campaign to increase the number of Jews deported to the east from summer 1942 onwards. CGQJ dossiers attest to an increase in denunciations up until early 1943. After that the numbers fell, presumably because people sensed the wind was changing, with German military setbacks and Italy's surrender. Nonetheless denunciations continued in Paris until summer 1944, exploited by the zealous brigade set up by police chief Permilleu in November 1942 within the Police Prefecture.

While some denounced their Jewish neighbors, others sought to protect them from denunciation. In Paris, Francine Weiller was alerted by a friend who overheard someone bragging that they had informed on her. She escaped arrest thanks to her friendship with her concierge. The Lindon family, who had got as far as the tiny village of Blot-l'Eglise, were denounced by a housekeeper who had been let go by Madame Lindon, but the letter was intercepted by the postman.

Considering the many bans and prohibitions that burdened the daily lives of Jews, and which provided numerous opportunities for others to report them to the authorities when they failed to obey them, it is actually surprising that Jews were not denounced in greater numbers. The numbers were so insufficient that the Germans were forced to resort to paying informers, as was the case for example in Nice, where SS Captain Aloïs Brunner increased the premiums offered in the latter part of 1942.[52]

What can explain the spontaneous decrease in the rate of denunciations? Certainly not an upsurge in good intentions: nothing suggests that non-Jewish French people were suddenly overcome by philo-Semitism. It seems rather more likely that a significant number were beginning to reject the propaganda of the occupying forces and Vichy.

Nonetheless, this explanation, political in nature, is not on its own enough to explain what happened. By their very nature, economic and financial interests tend to discourage informing. Of course, within some professional areas, such as medicine, the legal profession, culture, and the jewelry trade, there were people who exploited the new *Statuts des Juifs* in 1940 to dismiss the competition. In such cases, economic interest and denunciations went hand in hand. But in other situations, denunciations worked against the economic interests of both the individuals involved and the wider population. Refugees, even when they were Jewish, were almost never denounced. Moreover, some of them found themselves highly appreciated for the help they provided to the local population, who naturally offered them protection in return.

As Shannon L. Fogg has shown in her study of the Limousin region,[53] while the flood of refugees into Limoges and the surrounding vicinity led to a housing crisis and subsequent related tensions, most of the local people revealed themselves to be more pragmatic than ideological in their relationships with the new arrivals. For both farmers and local craftsmen, some of whom were engaged in black market activities, the newcomers constituted an important source of income. This led to a sort of "alliance" between the two groups, and the local inhabitants were generally kind to the Jewish incomers. The everyday burdens of life— housing, feeding, and looking after oneself—took precedence over an ideological discourse that was extraneous to country existence. In another study, of the town of Châteauroux, Simon Ostermann shows that there, too, economic factors outweighed anti-Semitic sentiment.[54]

The aspect of self-interest that was so central to their survival leads prompts a re-examination of the initial issue of the newcomers' financial resources. For many non-Jewish French people whom Jews encountered in the course of their peregrinations through different regions of the country, "race" and religion were of no importance, as long as they had the means to pay. This key question of money was far more important in determining how they were treated than whether or not they were Jewish. Let us consider for example the problem of housing, which faced all those who had left their homes for a new place to live: where would they find a roof when they had neither family nor friends to house them? In April 1941, Philippe Erlanger, a senior civil servant who had fallen under the *Statut de Juifs*, found a room at the Grand Hôtel de Cannes.[55] His situation could not have been more different from that of the penniless Polish writer Oser Warszawski. When Warszawski arrived in Grenoble, a city already overflowing with Jewish refugees, he found a tiny room in a small, seedy hotel, owned by a slum landlord who pitilessly exploited the refugees' destitution.[56]

Financial resources also determined the kind of welcome refugees received in private homes. Some people had the money to pay for room and board. Others had few means, or none at all. When they could, they gave a little and offered services in kind, for example doing housework or, for those in the countryside, working on the farm or in the fields. This was what the Markscheid family did when they were taken in by the Duffauts, a farming couple living in Larra, a few kilometers outside Toulouse. In exchange for room and board, they helped out with daily chores: "Our hosts involved us very naturally in farm life, according to local custom: parents in the fields, children minding the animals. Because Fanny was afraid of the cows, she was assigned to the fields [...]."[57] Little detail is available about the conditions of accommodation and the financial arrangements in these cases. Witnesses rarely bring up the subject, probably because they were children or adolescents at the time, and would not have known. It is clear, however, that the search for private lodgings was based on arrangements that mutually benefited both Jews and non-Jews.

Financial resources also played an important role in parents' search for a safe place for their children to live, whether with a family or in an educational institution. Whether the children were Jewish or not, unsurprisingly those who took them in expected some kind of financial compensation in order to provide for the basic needs of the child. This meant paying an allowance to foster parents, who most often lived in the countryside and stood *in loco parentis*.

In general, French Jewish parents were able to find some sort of solution through their networks of family or friends. It was far more difficult for foreign Jews to find a host family, and they often also lacked the means to pay. The situation became even more dramatic when parents were deported, leaving behind one or more children. Voluntary organizations did their best to place these orphaned children with foster families, and assumed financial responsibility; the OSE, for example, paid a monthly allowance of between 600 and 900 francs to a host family when they took in a child.[58] Such a sum was far from negligible for impoverished farming families, who tended to prefer older children, between 10 and 15 years old, who could help on the farm or in the fields, rather than babies or younger children. The survival of Jewish children was based on what could be termed an "economic model" which met the needs of both parties. Here again, it is clear that fostering children went hand in hand with self-interest.

The conditions of these placements varied. Sometimes they were based on expediency: the child was employed, even exploited, on the farm, as was the case for Nelly Scharapan, who had to "sweep up, serve dinner, and look after the cows," and who believed with hindsight that the farmers had taken her in simply so that she could work for them.[59] Sometimes the child received a warm and loving welcome, as was the case for Rachel Zylberberg, who took to calling the elderly lady who took her in "grandmother."

The fostering of Jewish children had no specific characteristics: there were successes and there were also many failures, some of which led to children being removed from their host families to be placed with other families or in an institution: Annette and Léa Krajcer were asked to leave the Notre-Dame de Sion boarding school in Livry-Gargan after they complained to their parents about their life as boarders; they were then taken into Sainte-Jeanne-d'Arc in Maisons Laffitte. Sarah Kofman lived in seven successive placements, both in boarding schools and with host families, all of which ended badly.[60]

Public Assistance and Social Protection

The placement of Jewish children who were at risk was consistent with a longstanding tradition in France, which began with the wet-nursing industry, established in the wake of the French Revolution, and out of which was born the principle of public assistance for foundlings and destitute children.

There has been little focus on the practices inherited from the traditions of public assistance and social protection that were prevalent in France well before 1939, and which certainly contributed to the survival of many—it is impossible to know how many—Jewish children in France during the war. Jeannine Levana Frenk is one of the few historians to have drawn attention to this in her comparative research on France and Belgium.[61]

Public assistance and national relief

People living in rural areas in France had been taking in foster children for almost 150 years by the time of the Second World War. The law of

20 March 1797, a legacy of the French Revolution, affirmed as a duty of the state the placing of orphaned children in homes in the countryside. This commitment was reinforced by the law of 10 January 1849, which led to the creation of the *Assistance Publique*, whose mission was, among other things, specifically to offer support and foster homes, again usually in rural areas, for children in need.[62] The law of 27 June 1904 ordained that orphans under the age of 13 should be sent to live with families in the country and that the *Assistance Publique* would pay an allowance to the foster parents. Ivan Jablonka has made a study of the conditions of the fostering of young children from the nineteenth century to the interwar period.[63] The foster family would receive a modest allowance, which was not insignificant for families with very low incomes. The *Assistance Publique* supplied clothes and other necessities for the children and paid their medical costs. It was also responsible for "the financial and moral concerns of the wards," and sent round its own inspectors, who were supposed to visit them four times a year. Many children were also placed with families in and around Paris.

Ivan Jablonka describes a scale of situations for these children, which ranged from cruel treatment to the loving foster parent who became a substitute mother or father. There were three distinct types of host family: young childless couples, parents with young children, and older couples or widows. Many widows volunteered to take in children: the presence of a child filled the void left by an absent husband or children who had already left home.[64] This became increasingly common after 1940 as a result of the huge number of men who were being held in Germany as prisoners of war. The policy of placing poor and needy children in the countryside was expanded after the outbreak of war. Families that had fostered children through the *Assistance Publique* during the interwar years continued to take in children, both Jewish and non-Jewish, during the Occupation. Generally these foster parents were aware that the children they had taken in were Jewish, especially in the case of circumcised boys.

However, there were certain cases where the foster family knew nothing about the child's background, as was the case for Ariela Palacz. After a period being housed by the *Assistance Publique*, she was sent to live with a woman called Mémère in a village in Nièvre. Though Mémère did not abuse her, she forced her to do housework and did not hide her hatred of Jews. In autumn 1945, when her father arrived in the village to take her back to Paris, the little girl was ecstatic. But in spite of Mémère's lack of affection for her, she was unhappy to leave the village and found it difficult to adapt once she returned to live in Paris. As an adolescent she returned three times to stay with her foster family, where she felt most at home, before eventually emigrating to Israel.[65]

Some of those who fostered children through the *Assistance Publique* have been honored as Righteous Among the Nations, such as Yvonne and René Victor Maurice, a farming couple from the village of Parçay-les-Pins in the Loire Valley. Before the war, the couple fostered children through the *Assistance Publique*. In July 1943 they received a telegram asking them to take in 3-year-old twins, Guy and Geneviève Nepomiatzi. Their mother, Marcelle, who had obtained the couple's name and address through acquaintances, decided to send her two older children as well as the twins. The couple found themselves welcoming four children and their non-Jewish aunt. After an initial moment of surprise, the couple agreed to house the entire family, who stayed with them until the Liberation.[66]

Jewish children were usually sent to the countryside through Jewish or Christian organizations. Occasionally, as was the case for Boris Cyrulnik, they were taken in by the *Assistance Publique* itself, whether under their real or an assumed name. This continuity between the prewar fostering of children through the *Assistance Publique* and the fostering of Jewish children in the French countryside during the Occupation was so marked that, as he was researching the history of his own Jewish Polish family, Ivan Jablonka was able to show an almost perfect correlation between the map of where Parisian children were fostered through the *Assistance Publique* in the nineteenth century and the map of where Jewish children were sent to live by the Comité Amelot during the war.[67]

Measures set up by the French government to provide social protection also benefited to a certain extent people who were being targeted for being Jewish. Jews were able to claim, at least initially, various modest allowances paid by Vichy. The *Secours National* (national relief agency) played an important role in supporting the neediest members of the population for the entire duration of the Second World War, when Jews and non-Jews alike were struggling to find shelter, winter clothes, or simply enough to eat. Founded in 1914 by the mathemati-

cian Paul-Emile Appel, the mission of the *Secours National* was to provide aid to soldiers and their families as well as civilian victims of the
war. The organization raised money from the public, which it then
distributed to privately run charities for people in need. Having been
suspended between the wars, its activities were revived by Édouard
Daladier in 1939; the organization's objectives remained the same but
it now also received state funding, and the war charities that it funded
were subject to inspection.

On 4 October 1940 Vichy passed a law (which came into force the
day after the *Statut des Juifs*) broadening the mission of the *Secours
National* and placing it under the honorary presidency of Marshal
Pétain. Henceforth the organization was to have a monopoly on the call
for donations for civilian victims of the war. But, as Jean-Pierre Le
Crom points out, "this monopoly was far from being absolute, and
there was a good deal of competition from other organizations, notably
the French Red Cross and the Committee for Assistance for Prisoners
of War (Comité de Calan); and they often raised funds jointly. The
mission of the *Secours National* was to subsidize charities, which it
amply fulfilled. As of 1 August 1944, 12,000 charitable organizations
had received subsidies totalling 1,600,000,000 francs."[68]

Some 55 per cent of this amount came from state subsidies and
assigned revenue (from profits made on lottery ticket sales, a 2 per cent
tax on auctions, and a 1 per cent tax on *parimutuel* betting, as well as
from the sale of lost and found objects and the belongings of French
people—frequently Jews—who had been stripped of their assets).
Altogether, a sum of 20 billion francs was raised between 1939 and
1946. The other 45 per cent came from collections (of funds, food,
clothing) and donations (primarily from businesses, which benefited
from tax exemption on their donations).

Vichy propaganda made a great deal of the link between the activities of the *Secours National* and Pétain himself, who was presented as
being the people's benefactor, personally relieving their suffering. The
activities of the *Secours National* "went far beyond helping civil victims
of the war; in addition to bringing aid to refugees and war victims in
camps and prisons, it handled the expansion of different kinds of support for children (reception centers and summer camps), as well as
providing support for the elderly, wives of prisoners of war, and young

delinquents. The largest proportion of its funds went towards the fight against hunger, which represented 28.7 per cent of its total budget in 1941 [...]. The *Secours National* provided food for school canteens and ran soup kitchens."[69] To implement all these different measures, the organization had delegates and correspondents in every department, assisted by female inspectors and social workers, who traveled all over their assigned area. The *Secours National* employed three-quarters of all accredited social workers in France, who in April 1941 numbered over 6,000.[70] Considering the needs of the population, however, the number was insufficient.

This did not prevent the CGQJ from putting pressure on the *Secours National* to fire its Jewish employees. Its managers were sometimes forced to comply with these demands, although they seem to have tried as hard as they could to hold on to these persecuted individuals. It is worth noting that among the documents published by the *Secours National*, not a single one has been discovered that was in any way anti-Semitic.

Administrative schizophrenia?

Resources derived from this organization undoubtedly helped some Jews survive, or were at least used to help them. Vichy policies were far from coherent; they embodied surprising contradictions and it could even be argued that they expressed a kind of administrative schizophrenia. On the one hand, Vichy was committed to anti-Semitic policies of segregation and the spoliation of Jewish property. Yet at the same time the *Secours National* was subsidizing charities working in internment camps in southern France and itself set up in the region in January 1942.[71] This was in spite of the fact that 70 per cent of the internees in these camps were Jewish. It is as if Vichy's right hand was unaware of what its left was doing. Moreover, swept up in the great tide of refugees, Jews were able to solicit help from *Secours National* representatives just like anybody else. In 1940 and 1941, there were certainly many mayors, town hall clerks and social workers who were not going out of their way to check if the refugees that they were helping were Jews or not. The status of refugee was sufficient reason to find these people temporary shelter and food vouchers. Even if it was suspected that some of these refugees were Jewish, or if it was discovered afterwards, many people pretended not to know. With the increase in persecution, some supervisors and representatives of the *Secours National* went further, actively using their positions in the organization to aid Jews. Liliane Lieber, who became involved in rescuing children in 1942, pays homage in her testimony to "a wonderful man to whom [she] was introduced by some Protestant friends. Monsieur Dormoy was the director of the *Secours National* in the Dauphiné region. He provided me with many things without asking any questions. He also gave a reference to the head of a local secondary school who immediately made two places available in the boarding house for 15-year-old twin sisters."[72]

Jeannine Levana Frenk points out that several members of the *Secours National* have been recognized as Righteous,[73] including Louis Collet who, when he took over from the outgoing mayor of Varennes-sur-Allier, a town strategically situated south of the demarcation line, offered every conceivable kind of aid to the forty or so French Jews who were in hiding there: he provided them with identity cards and food vouchers (without the stamp stating that the bearer was *Juif*), showed them places to hide, and warned them of imminent police raids.[74]

It is clear that the *Secours National* was used by some of its own representatives in order to help Jews. A parallel can be drawn between this evolution, particularly noticeable between 1942 and 1944, and what was happening at roughly the same time in the UGIF. In both cases, the legal façade of administrative jobs provided cover for underground activities, as illustrated by the extraordinary case of the Sèvres children's home in a suburb of Paris. In 1941, Yvonne Hagnauer, a former elementary school teacher with links to the revolutionary syndicalist movement, became head of the *Secours National* children's home for orphans and abandoned children, and gradually transformed it into a place of shelter for children whose parents had been arrested or deported. These children made up two-thirds of all those who were taken in, while the staff at the home was almost entirely made up of people who were technically outlawed by the Vichy regime.[75]

As surprising as this might seem, this is not the only example of a group of Jewish children being hidden in a home that was subsidized by an official state organization during the Occupation. After several charities operating in the camps had alerted the authorities to the living conditions of Jewish children interned with their parents, in February 1941 the Quakers and the OSE, headed by Andrée Salomon, managed to get 48 children out of the Gurs camp and placed in a "Home for Wards of the State" in Aspet (Haute-Garonne). These orphanages, created after the First World War to provide homes for some of the hundreds of thousands of children of fallen soldiers, had long lain empty as their first wave of residents reached adulthood. Fred and Heinz Mayer were among a group of children who moved into the home in Aspet, which to their eyes seemed like a "palace" in comparison with what they had experienced at Gurs. They lived there until February 1943, when they were transferred to an orphanage set up in Château Larade in Toulouse. By then, although they did not know it, their parents had already been deported to Auschwitz, where they perished.[76] Once again, it is clear that the national strategy for the protection of children, which had been considerably reinforced after the demographic disaster of the First World War and was symbolized by the creation of the status of "ward of the state," was being actively exploited to provide aid to Jewish children targeted by Vichy laws.

Social welfare in the camps

Another little-known aspect of Vichy-funded social work was that done by the *Service sociale d'aide aux émigrants* (SSAE—Social Service for Aid to Emigrants) throughout the Occupation. Lucienne Chibrac has written a detailed history of its evolution before and during the war, with material drawn from the Service's own archives.[77] No longer in existence today, the SSAE played a crucial role in the history of emigration in France and the welcome afforded to foreigners. Its origins were in the work of an American organization, the International Migration Service, which, in the early 1900s, provided support to young girls going to live abroad. The organization went on to broaden its mission, including looking after immigrants when they arrived in France. In 1924, the *Service international d'aide aux émigrants* (SIAE—International Service for Aiding Emigrants) was created, which supported Polish emigrants in particular in the process of adapting to life in France. The SIAE's operations depended on private donations, but its directors sought to have the organization recognized as a key partner of public agencies.

In 1932, thanks to the dynamism of its president, Lucie Chevalley, the SIAE was recognized by the state as an organization promoting the public interest. It became the *Service social d'aide aux émigrants* (SSAE— Social Service for Aid to Emigrants) and was now eligible to receive state subsidies. The SSAE recruited social workers who spoke the immigrants' language and ensured, among other things, that commitments written into the immigration treaties negotiated between countries were respected. It also dealt with repatriating to their countries of birth individuals who failed to adapt to life in France. In 1938 the SSAE was incorporated into a newly formed Under-Secretariat for Immigration. It now received regular funding from the authorities, while remaining officially a branch of the International Migration Service.

With the establishment of the xenophobic Vichy government, what would happen to the SSAE? Would Pétain's *Secours National* continue to fund a service whose entire purpose was to support foreigners? "Logically, due to the government's xenophobia and nationalist sentiment, one expected aid for this group of people to be either significantly reduced or entirely cut," Lucienne Chibrac points out.[78] In fact, the *Secours National* continued to support the activities of the SSAE, which transferred its administrative headquarters from Paris to Lyon. Some social workers took charge of helping refugees on a regional level, while others began to work on the ground bringing aid to people interned in the camps. They were able to do this because of the close links between the SSAE and the Red Cross, which officially was the only organization authorized to enter the camps. Social workers such as Enéa Avernouh and Marcelle Valensi worked tirelessly to meet the basic needs of the internees, while at the same time trying to help as many as possible to get out of the camps.

To be able to continue their work, which, due to the appalling conditions in the camps, was increasingly a question of providing humanitarian aid, the SSAE had to "demonstrate an unwavering neutrality and refrain from any criticism of current events." Its representatives were expected to comply strictly with the new Vichy laws that authorized prefects to intern any foreigner considered suspect. The SSAE had no choice other than to obey these laws in order to continue receiving the public subsidies they needed to continue their work on the ground. The SSAE was also obliged to reject applications by French-born Jewish social workers and dismiss their Jewish staff.[79]

Such a requirement to obey the law naturally placed everyone involved in relief work in a situation that was highly constricting and fraught with ambiguity. As the persecution of the Jews increased, the SSAE became more and more ensnared in this legalistic net. As it became locked into a mechanism of contradiction and compromise, the purpose of its activities became increasingly unclear. Dependent on funding from Vichy, its mission was to relieve the suffering of the very people whom Vichy was persecuting, impoverishing, and imprisoning. Concretely, what did it mean to be doing social work in these conditions? Increasingly, from 1942 onwards, some social workers, aware of the legal limitations of what they were doing, decided independently to engage in resistance activities, discreetly, and obviously illegally.

Between 1942 and 1944 the SSAE underwent an evolution similar to that of other legal organizations such as the *Secours National* and the UGIF. Some SSAE staff members played a double game: using their legal status as cover, they acted as a front for illegal activities, sometimes becoming actively involved, particularly in protecting Jews. Their activities were not risk-free, all the more so as the occupying forces eventually uncovered what they were doing. In April 1944, the Gestapo turned up at the SSAE premises to arrest Grâce Brandt, who was in contact with a children's rescue network. The raid revealed to the Nazis that the SSAE's involvement in aiding Jews went rather further than Mademoiselle Brandt's personal initiative. On 12 June, Adèle de Blonay, the director of the Paris office, was placed in solitary confinement in Drancy. She insisted that the SSAE had never formally been prohibited from aiding Jews, and was released after twelve days, but the organization's premises were sealed shut. One of the consequences of the raid was that the SSAE was obliged to furnish a list of all the Jews whom the organization had helped. Meanwhile there were several other police operations in the provinces, with, in particular, a Gestapo raid on 27 June 1944 on the SSAE headquarters in Lyon.[80]

Individual Figures Who Aided Jews and the Notion of the "Righteous"

From summer 1942 onwards, helping Jews was no longer solely the domain of social workers, direct witnesses of the sufferings of Jews. It began to spread through the population, which was increasingly shocked by and critical of the mass arrests of stateless Jews, firstly in the Occupied Zone, and later on in the Free Zone. This is not to say that French non-Jews rose up as one to obstruct the persecution of the Jews. How would that even have been possible when the population was under the yoke of a regime of occupation in the north and a national dictatorship in the south? Any notion of a unanimous resistance makes no sense considering the circumstances. It was certainly not enough for the persecuted to simply knock on any door to find shelter. Nonetheless, a surprising social phenomenon was born that had not been anticipated by the authorities: without any kind of coordination, thousands of French people all over the country began to offer help and protection to Jews who were forced to hide or flee. It is impossible to do justice to the extraordinary diversity of these situations.

For the most part they stemmed from individual initiatives undertaken in often tragic circumstances. A man or a woman might offer help spontaneously to a person in danger. They did not check in advance before offering help where the person came from or what their religion was: they simply came to their aid, aware that here was someone not so different from them who needed some kind of support. The unique nature of each situation and encounter was reflected later on in the testimonies of Jewish witnesses who, thanks to these people, managed to escape arrest and therefore—as they only realized after the war ended—almost certain death. Their accounts frequently describe either an individual or a group of people to whom they owe their lives.

Cécile Klein owed her successful escape over the border to Switzerland to the decisive help of a farmer and a parish priest whom she encountered while still on the French side of the border.[81] In Paris, Albert Grunberg narrowly escaped arrest thanks to his concierge, Madame Oudard; he had no doubt that his survival depended on this woman's loyalty, whom he nicknamed "*Secours National*," which she embodied. In the preface to his diary, he wrote a "dedicatory epistle," in which he pledged his "eternal gratitude"[82] to her. Thirty years after the event, Stanley Hoffmann recalled his youth in occupied France, paying homage to his history teacher in Nice who, in December 1943, helped him and his mother to flee the city that was now under the yoke of Aloïs Brunner. "That one man," he wrote, "erased all the terrible moments, the humiliations and terror."[83]

Farmer, parish priest, concierge, teacher—just a few of the occupations of those who came to the aid of Jews. There were many others. Spontaneous help, as we shall see, is not always related to a particular line of work. When witnesses recall the people who gave them crucial assistance, they frequently choose to universalize their tribute. In their eyes the person to whom they are paying homage is an emblematic moral figure or a character who embodies French values. Recalling his experiences as a young boy in France, Saul Friedländer expresses his gratitude to Pascal Delaume, a generous-hearted family man who, with no personal relationship to the boy whatsoever, accompanied him to a children's home where his parents hoped he would find safety: "A quiet father of a family, probably close to fifty, a slightly ridiculous figure thanks to his plumpness, his toupee, and his clumsiness, has come to symbolize for me the good-hearted man in the full sense of the word: he scarcely knew us, and in any case prudence should have suggested that he do nothing [...]. Beloved Pascal Delaume [...], for me you will always remain an exemplar, and a far-off friend," he wrote.[84] Stanley Hoffmann's homage to his history teacher is even more stirring: "He and his kind wife were not heroes of the Resistance, but if there is a certain class of ordinary Frenchmen, then this man represented those people; and for that reason, France and the French will always merit our respect; I will never cease to love them."[85]

These expressions of gratitude to a non-Jewish person to whom a Jewish survivor owes their life partially explains the success of the honorific "Righteous Among the Nations" attributed on behalf of the State of Israel by Yad Vashem. Officially established by law in 1953, Yad Vashem's primary mission is to commemorate the Jewish martyrs and heroes of the Holocaust. It is also charged with bestowing the title of "Righteous Among the Nations" to non-Jews who risked their lives, with no compensation, to help Jews escape the genocide. This honor, the highest distinction bestowed on civilians by the state of Israel, has a religious connotation: the citation "Whoever saves one life saves the world entire," engraved on the medal given to the person being honored, is taken from the Talmud.[86]

Since the 1960s, Yad Vashem has, after establishing the facts, bestowed the title of "Righteous among the Nations" on thousands of non-Jews from countries all over Europe, each of whom has been nominated by at least two Jewish survivors. In addition to the duty of remembrance and recognition, the state of Israel has not been blind to the wider political significance of this award, as Sarah Gensburger has shown.[87] The first two French nominations to be accepted as "Righteous Among the Nations" were that of a Catholic priest, Father Jean Fleury,[88] in March 1964, who worked actively to rescue internees imprisoned in the Route de Limoges camp in Poitiers, and that of Alice Ferrières, a Protestant teacher.[89] Were the choices of who receives the honor deliberate or the fruit of coincidence, reflecting the reality of those who helped Jews in France?

Alice Ferrières was a 31-year-old math teacher at a girl's school in Murat (Cantal). From the start of the war she signaled her willingness to help her many Jewish friends and acquaintances. As well as offering moral support and help with obtaining food, she also made up packages with her pupils to be sent to Jewish internees and took in Jews who had fled to the area around Murat. After she offered her help to child rescue organizations, her home became a hub for children awaiting foster placements, adults on the run, smugglers, social workers and so on. She celebrated Jewish festivals along with her guests. She received the title of "Righteous Among the Nations" on 28 July 1964.

Several others cited earlier also received this honor, including Hélène Oudard, Albert Grunberg's concierge,[90] Madeleine Barot, the administrative head of the Cimade,[91] Father Alexandre Glasberg from *Amitié Chrétienne*,[92] and café owners Oswaldo and Léa Bardone.[93]

During the 1990s, the title "Righteous Among the Nations" was gradually integrated into the historical memory of the Occupation in France. This is when the notion of the "*Juste* (righteous) of France," which both echoes Yad Vashem's honorific and at the same time imprints it with a specifically French national character, first emerged. The expression was officially adopted by the Republic in a law passed on 23 March 2000. "The substitution of 'Righteous of France' for 'Righteous Among the Nations,' offered a framework for the reconciliation of the nation with itself."[94]

In addition to these various memorial usages, the most important aspect of the "Righteous" honorific is that it draws the historian's attention to the different types of help and protection offered to those who were persecuted because they were Jewish. Until the 1970s, the

Resistance was viewed in terms of the different political movements or individuals of the time, whether the Gaullist or communist resistance, the Free French, based in London, or individuals practicing inner resistance. In the 1990s, the increasing number of ceremonies honoring the Righteous of France had not yet begun to interest historians. In 2003, the *Dictionnaire des Justes de France*, edited by Israel Gutman, with a preface by Jacques Chirac, was published to wide acclaim.[95] But, in spite of its obvious importance, the book offers scant biographical details about the people whom it honors that might have cast light on the reasons for their behavior towards persecuted Jews.

Several factors help to explain the initial lack of interest on the part of historians when it came to studying the Righteous of France: the legitimate priority given to the study of the persecution and genocide of the Jews; the significant difficulty inherent in relying both on oral testimonies and on written archives; and the huge diversity of individual experiences, which inevitably imperils any attempt at classifying these behaviors. In addition, the decision to bestow the title of "Righteous" is based on the moral distinction of individual non-Jews, making such a historical memorialization complicated for historians to analyze.

It is worth remembering in this regard the debates that took place in Israel over how to define the honor: according to Moshe Landau, one of the three judges who presided over the Eichmann trial, the only person who could be declared Righteous Among the Nations was the non-Jew who saved a Jew for absolutely no compensation. The Righteous had to be defined according to strict rules which only acknowledged the conduct of someone who acted completely without self-interest, whether political, financial, sexual, and so on. But Moshe Bejski, whose life had been saved by the German factory-owner Oskar Schindler (in whose case the issue of economic interest could be argued to have been a factor), pointed out that if this argument were taken to its logical conclusion hardly anyone would qualify for the title of Righteous Among the Nations.[96] Bejski criticized Landau—who, having left Germany just before the war, had not faced the Nazi genocide—for a notion that Bejski claimed was both too abstract and too elitist. The debates about Schindler highlighted two ways of judging the person who became a rescuer: one position insisted that it be done in the name of a moral purity defined from the outside, while the other conceived of it according to rather more human criteria, inseparable from the historical context which gave rise to the rescue. In the end it was Moshe Landau, the most celebrated judge in Israel, whose position prevailed.[97]

As a result, the definition of the "Righteous Among the Nations" rests on a narrow representation of the rescuer. As Bob Moore points out, by shining a light only on individual altruistic and philanthropic motivation, and ruling out other motives for helping Jews, it also contributes to the minimization of the collective factors that led to Jews' survival. In other words, "the wider social context of rescue is often lost in the many narratives that focus on the heroism of individuals."[98] In a way, the moral categorization turns the individual "Righteous Among the Nations" into a noble hero, a knight in shining armor surrounded by a crowd of either indifferent or actively anti-Semitic people.

The elitist approach to defining the Righteous Among the Nations, implying someone of exceptional courage, taking up the struggle in a hostile environment, is not supported by historical analysis. It was certainly not always the case in France, as has already been seen. At the very least, it must be considered case-by-case, while also bearing in mind the fact that different countries witnessed different levels of anti-Semitism. The situation in Italy or Denmark was completely different from the situation in Poland or Romania, not to mention in Germany, and therefore the degree of risk taken by a non-Jew helping a Jew varied greatly according to the country.

Another consequence of this very strict definition of the "Righteous Among the Nations" is that it presupposes that the person acted alone. Yet, in most cases that simply would not have been possible. The person who helped would certainly have benefited from some degree of collusion, whether passive or active, from people in their immediate entourage, whether family, friends or colleagues. The concierge from rue des Écoles would never have been able to help Albert Grunberg hide for almost two years if she had not been supported by her two children and her own mother, and if the neighbors on the sixth floor, who lived in the apartment neighboring the room where the young Jewish hairdresser was hiding, had not kept silent about his presence. Helping someone to hide necessarily presupposes a limited support network, whether for obtaining food or other material aid, or simply moral support. It was much easier to have a Jew arrested than to protect him or her from arrest. All that was required to have someone arrested was one person whose information would trigger a police raid. Protecting someone meant that the person who was hiding was absorbed into a group of people who served as a kind of protective screen, which demanded the complicity of several people and an entourage prepared to remain completely quiet about that person's presence. It is essential to bear this in mind when comparing the proportion of Jews who were deported or who escaped deportation from different countries.

Some nominations suggest that the rigidity of the definition of Righteous Among the Nations was not always respected—indeed could not always be respected. It is apparent that the person being honored could not have acted alone, as in the case of Alice Ferrières who, in her school in the small town of Murat, enlisted several of her colleagues and pupils to help her. In her case, what Yad Vashem recognized is the combative dynamism of a young woman who managed to set up a chain of volunteers who helped her provide aid to Jewish refugees. Similarly, the requirement that an individual's commitment be completely selfless has not always been applied. Various couples have been honored with the title of Righteous Among the Nations for having taken in a Jewish child, even though some received a stipend to cover the costs of the child's basic needs. On this point Yad Vashem's position has evolved: it is now accepted that receiving an allowance to go towards the costs of caring for a child was justified and cannot be considered to have been acting for profit.

Regardless of these limits, the research undertaken by the Yad Vashem Institute for Holocaust Research since the 1960s remains unique and necessary. Without this extraordinary investigatory project, we would not have the database that brings together thousands of testimonies detailing the different kinds of help and protection given to Jews all over Nazi-occupied Europe. There was a huge range of situations and acts of rescue on the part of individuals towards their fellow human beings, whom the propaganda of the time defined as the enemy. These stories have come to light thanks to the desire of those who were saved to honor their rescuers: there are certainly many others whose identities will never be known. That is precisely the reason that it is interesting to look into all the cases that have been gathered by Yad Vashem. In *Histoire des Justes de France*, Patrick Cabanel demonstrates how fertile that path could be.[99]

Jeannine Levana Frenk's quantitative analysis of the files of 700 Righteous of France who were recognized between 2000 and 2005 has proved similarly fruitful.[100] Her sample confirms that Jews were living all over southern France, where 58.9 per cent of the Righteous were located, although it was a rather smaller area than that covered by the Occupied Zone up until November 1942 (41.1 per cent of the Righteous).[101]

One of the most interesting aspects of this research is that it gives a snapshot of the socio-economic profile of the Righteous (Fig. 1 below).

Without discussing this diagram in detail, it is worth noting that farmers make up the largest occupational category (40.8 per cent). If one adds to that figure the Righteous who were not farmers but nonetheless lived in rural areas of France in relatively sparsely populated regions, the percentage rises to 69 per cent.[102] Farmers and the working class combined make up 66.2 per cent of the Righteous.[103] All were people with very modest incomes. The paucity of their resources was partly compensated by the fact that they or their families often owned a smallholding in the countryside.

In the distribution of the Righteous by age bracket, it can be seen that those who were born before 1900 and belonged to the First World War generation make up just under half of the sample of Righteous (48.7 per cent). The significant proportion of the "generation of the trenches" suggests that there was a strong correlation between patriotic anti-German sentiment and the spontaneous help given to Jewish refugees.[104]

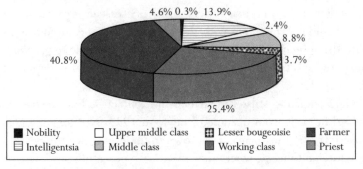

Fig. 1: Social status of the Righteous in France

Distribution of the Righteous by gender shows a somewhat surprising result: contrary to expectation, it was not only women who acted in this way: 46.4 per cent of the Righteous were men.[105] But this result may be an effect of the sources used. Cindy Biesse's later study of 649 Righteous in the Rhône-Alpes region shows that women made up half of the awardees. They were a majority in rural departments such as Ain, Isère and Drôme, as well as in the more urban Rhône department. These women were frequently surrogate mothers, and when a man was awarded the title of Righteous, it was very often due to the role played by his wife.[106]

Networks of Sociability

Another striking fact is that the majority of Jews who nominated an individual to be honored as a Righteous of France were foreign born. Knowing this, and bearing in mind the conditions of isolation of these foreign Jews, the notion of the Righteous takes on an entirely new dimension, not only commemorational but also sociological. Seen from this perspective, the title of Righteous is an indicator of the extent to which those making the nominations were not integrated into French society during the war. French Jews generally managed to use their own networks, which were much more diversified than those of foreign Jews. Looking at the different social and economic situations of the witnesses whose voices we have heard, we can learn a great deal from their recollections about those who helped them, and how.

The Mayers, German Jews from the Baden region who were transferred to France in 1940 and interned in the Gurs camp, were not at all integrated into French society. Only one rescue organization, the OSE, could provide them with aid, in the person of Andrée Salomon. With the agreement of their parents, the OSE was able to get the two sons, Fred and Heinz, out of the camp. Their parents were deported in August 1942.

The Friedländers also had virtually no contacts in France when they arrived in Paris from occupied Prague in 1939. Not long after, they moved to Néris-les-Bains, a spa town in the Auvergne region popular with foreign tourists, where they spent "two peaceful years" with their young son, Pavel. In summer 1942, as the situation of the family was deteriorating, Mme Friedländer wrote a desperate letter to the librarian, Madame M. de L., asking her to look after her son. She could not think of any other solution. Madame M. de L. agreed to take on the task of finding Pavel a place in a Catholic boarding school.

It would be, of course, be an exaggeration to claim that no foreign Jew had any contact whatsoever with French people. Everything depended on when they had arrived in France, what their occupation was, what kind of community life they led, and so on. The prewar years, and the first year of the war (1939–1940) also played a role in determining the extent to which they were able to depend on a friendship or professional network in the event of a difficult situation. The trajectory of the Russian citizen Léon Poliakov is illuminating. Enlisted into the army in October 1939 and captured with his unit in June 1940, he planned his escape. With a French comrade from the same regiment, Oswaldo Bardone, he managed to get to Paris. Poliakov's life could have gone in any one of several different directions, according to the people that he came across. Before the war he had built up a relationship with someone at the Soviet embassy, purchasing works of art for a diplomat collector called Tarassov. Tarassov suggested finding him a job as a doorman at the embassy of the former Baltic States, which would have allowed him to claim extra-territorial status. Poliakov was thrilled by this proposition, but the war between the USSR and Nazi Germany broke out before the plan could be put into practice. Realizing that the plan was no longer viable, Poliakov decided he had to find a way to cross the demarcation line.

Arriving in Marseille in October 1941, he contacted the Jewish community, "out of a curiosity," he later wrote, "to get to know [his] people."[107] He became the secretary of Rabbi Zalman Schneerson's *Association des Israélites Pratiquants*, while remaining in touch with his friend Oswaldo Bardone. At a chance meeting in Marseille, Bardone suggested that Poliakov come and join him near Saint-Étienne, where he and his wife ran a café-restaurant. Poliakov accepted the invitation and found work at a nearby factory. He had also become part of the Service André, an organization helping the Jews of Marseille to escape to the countryside, notably to Chambon-sur-Lignon. Bardone offered his help, and his café-restaurant, the Auberge des Musiciens, soon became a staging post for Jews from Marseille on the way to their new homes. It is clear that Poliakov's friendship with a Frenchman, with its wartime origins, had a significant impact on his life and his wartime activities.

The professional contacts of Joseph Minc, a Polish Jew who had arrived in France in 1934, were a huge help in enabling him and his family to survive. As a dental prosthetist, he had his own workshop, and obtained his dental surgeon's qualification in 1939. When war broke out, Minc, afraid of the bombing raids, sent his wife Lisa and their young daughter Betty to stay with a colleague, Dr Frenkel, who lived in Saint-Sever, near Mont-de-Marsan in southwestern France. In May 1941, another colleague warned him not to turn up to a summons at the commissariat to register as a Polish Jew.[108] In October 1942, he gave up his workshop for a better-paid job working for another dental prosthetist, Dr Perrault, in Neuilly-sur-Seine on the outskirts of Paris. "From then on, until the end of the Occupation, we lived more or less normally, apart from the permanent fear of arrest." In the meantime, both he and his wife joined the communist resistance, and he remained a member of the *Mouvement national contre le racisme* (MNCR—National Movement against Racism), and later the *Union des Juifs pour la résistance et l'entraide* (UJRE—Jewish Union for Resistance and Mutual Aid). The couple certainly took risks with their resistance activities, but in return they benefited from the protection of the communist network. It was through an acquaintance they knew through the network, Joseph Epstein (head of the FTP in the Paris region, who went by the name "Colonel Gilles"), that the Mincs found a foster family for Betty, in the Yonne, a farming region. Joseph and Lisa stayed in Paris, where they went underground and were obliged to move house several times. Joseph stressed later that it was thanks to friends that they were able to find places to live. Later on, in early 1944, a Gaullist resister called Jeanine found temporary shelter for Lisa and Betty in the Yonne. This particularly intricate web of friends and professional relationships proved extremely useful and certainly was part of the reason that Minc and his family were still alive at the end of the war.

Irène Némirovsky was close friends with her publisher, Albin Michel, who helped her and her family several times during this period. Throughout the Occupation she continued to be paid 4,000 francs a month in advances, as agreed in a contract signed in 1933.[109]

Many testimonies emphasize the difference good neighborly relations made during periods of mass arrests. Relationships with neighbors, the concierge, and local shopkeepers formed when immigrants arrived in the neighborhood might be recent or longstanding, or more or less "active" depending on whether the immigrants tended to keep to themselves or if they actively sought to create bonds with their neighbors. An informal network of friendships was more successful when the recently arrived immigrants understood how to be accepted in the neighborhood. The day the police arrived to arrest them, their neighbors did not hesitate: if it was materially possible they hid them or at least diverted the police's attention. It was a simple human reaction.

One example that illustrates the crucial intervention of a concierge during the Vel' d'Hiv roundup is recounted by Odette Meyer, née Melszpajz. Every day when she came home from school, the concierge would look after her until her mother arrived. On 16 July 1942 the police came to arrest Odette and her mother Berthe. The concierge knew what to do. She hurried them both into her living quarters and hid them in the broom closet. When the police entered she put on a show, welcoming them cordially, offering them a glass of wine, piling on the anti-Semitic comments and congratulating them on their anti-Jewish actions. Their trust having been gained, they believed her when she told them that "her" Jews had left Paris for their house in the country. After this episode, Berthe sent her daughter to the countryside to live with a Catholic family in the Vendée, in the small village of Chavagnes-en-Palliers. In 1943, she joined her.[110]

French Jews had much wider networks of friends and acquaintances than foreign Jews. For a start, they spoke French and were more likely to be able to rally both professional and other contacts as the persecution was stepped up. Some succeeded rather better than others.[111]

Gérard Dreyfus's brother, who had to leave Strasbourg for Limoges, got by fairly well. He was a leather merchant who represented the Maisonnier tanneries in Alsace, and in Limoges he became a partner in the local office of the same company, alongside a Monsieur Chabannier. Chabannier was a Petainist but, according to Gérard Dreyfus, he was not an anti-Semite. When the law on economic Aryanization came into force, Chabannier was formally made the sole manager, but he kept Dreyfus in the business. In 1943, when the Dreyfus family left Limoges, the father's personal contacts were key to them finding housing: the family went to Nâves (near Annecy), and moved into a village house that belonged the aunt of a local tanner, a Monsieur Verjus, with whom Dreyfus had worked before the war.

Student friendships were also very useful when it came to helping students and their parents to get by during this period of persecution, as we have already seen was the case for Stanley Hoffmann. Alfred Grosser had a similar experience: as a student, he received repeated help from his professors, both in public establishments at the University of Aix-en-Provence (where his professors gave him letters of recommendation) and private (when he was taken on as a teacher at the Catholic Saint-Joseph school).[112]

When Marthe Hoffnung was making plans to cross into the Free Zone, it was a friend from nursing school, Elisabeth, who told her to go and see her uncle, Christian de Chaunac, the parish priest of Saint-Secondin, a small village traversed by the demarcation line.

French Jews with origins in the colonies who had moved to mainland France, predominantly French Algerians, were another example. Their social resources were halfway between those of foreign and French Jews. Though they had had French citizenship since at least 1870 and spoke the language perfectly, many of them were recent arrivals to mainland France. Some had succeeded in building relationships with other families from similar backgrounds or simply with their neighbors. This was the case for the Benayoun family, who had arrived in Paris in early 1938, and had soon built up relationships with their neighbors in and around rue Popincourt in the 11th arrondissement of Paris. Their friends were of Turkish, Greek and Algerian origins, both Jewish and non-Jewish. They also had cousins they could lean on for help, one of whom, a farmer in the Péronne region, helped them to stock up on food, while another found a foster family in Normandy for the unruly Jacques and Simon.

These critical periods of persecution also disrupted social networks. Families who were at the top of the social ladder before the war found themselves, as a result of war and persecution, dependent for their survival on people of far more modest social backgrounds: nurses, domestic servants, and concierges. This was the case for the Lindon family who had moved from Paris to Aix-en-Provence. After the Germans occupied southern France, the father, a qualified lawyer without work, was desperate to move deeper into the countryside to find a safe place for his family to live. Denis Lindon recounts:

My father decided to consult the only one of his brothers who, like us, had stayed in France, my uncle Maxime. He discovered that when she left for England, my grandmother had sent a message: 'If you have any worries, ask Marie Nony-Pouzadoux for help.' She was the daughter of my uncle Maurice's former nanny, Annette Pouzadoux. Originally from a small village in the Puy-de-Dôme department, Blot-l'Église, she had lived for three years with my grandparents in Paris. During this period, and despite their very different backgrounds, Annette and my grand-mother had become very close. When Annette left their employ, my grandmother gave her a generous gift, and they stayed in touch. With the money she received, Annette was able to rebuild her farm, and she always remained deeply grateful to my family. My grandmother had been very affected by Annette's death in the 1920s, and sent one of her sons to represent her at the funeral. My father thus decided to ask Marie Nony-Pouzadoux for help. In January 1943, he traveled to Blot-l'Église and asked for directions to the Pouzadouxs' house, which was situated a little outside the village, in a hamlet called Les Berniards. Marie gave him a warm welcome. My father came back to fetch us, and we went to live with Marie and her family. There is no doubt that this saved our lives; a few weeks later we learned that the Germans had come to our house in Aix to arrest us.

There are many similar stories to be found among the nominations for Righteous of France.

Accounts of lifesaving interventions by concierges also appear in many narratives. Francine Weiller's father had to leave Alsace for Paris. Unable to work as a lawyer because of the *Statut des Juifs*, he scraped a living from his home on Avenue de Suffren doing translations from French to German. One of his clients owned a food-processing factory in Brittany and paid him in pots of jam. On 12 December 1941, the Germans came to arrest him during the roundup of French Jewish "notables." But "when they asked the concierge where they could find Monsieur Weiller," his daughter Francine recalled, "she told them that he was not at home, even though she knew perfectly well that he was in the courtyard inflating his bicycle tires."

Jean-Jacques Becker notes the role of concierges in his own family history. The Beckers had remained in Paris. His father was also targeted during the roundup of "notables" and was sleeping in the apartment of a former concierge. The day the police turned up at their apartment, their new concierge put them off the scent by telling them that the

Beckers' apartment was empty.[113] Concierges also looked after people's possessions and, through friends and family in the countryside, were able to give ideas about where to find families who would be willing to take in their children. When Annette and Léa Krajcer left Drancy, in September 1942, the girls first went to live with their grandmother, while the concierge from their parents' building protected their apartment from looting. In early 1944, Annette and Léa were sent to live in the Jeanne d'Arc boarding school in Maisons-Laffitte, and then, with the help of the niece of their grandmother's concierge, they were sent to live in Château-du-Loir in northwestern France.

Several witnesses tell of the spontaneous help given by their neighbors during mass arrests. Jean-Jacques Becker recalls how, during the Vel' d'Hiv roundup, one of his sisters, Françoise, spent the night with their neighbors, the Poublans.[114] There were also complex networks made up of groups of friends who helped each other, people who had longstanding friendships that dated from before the war or even from childhood, and sometimes lovers. During the Occupation, while Edgar Morin's father Vidal Nahum was living in Lyon without full-time work, he lived most of the time with one of his mistresses, Madame Blanc, and managed to procure a forged identity card in the name of her deceased husband.[115]

Some French Jews even had contacts in the Vichy government who helped them. For those who were able to benefit from such support, these relationships were compromising, but nonetheless very useful at critical moments, and in some cases they meant that people were spared the worst. Elie Scali, who owned several tanneries in Graulhet (Tarn), brought his young wife to live with him, and the couple, who went on to have three children during the war, lived a fairly normal life up until 1943. Elie Scali was able to continue his activities, even traveling to Paris for business, thanks to a Parisian friend he had met before the war, Colonel René Marty, who became private secretary to his cousin René Bousquet, secretary general of the Vichy police. Marty gave Scali an *Ausweis*, a pass that enabled him to travel freely between the Occupied and the Free Zones. An even more valuable consequence of Colonel Marty's friendship was that Scali was able to maintain a relationship with the local authorities. These personal relationships did not, however, completely shield Scali from persecution. The Vichy law on economic Aryanization that came into force in 1941 meant that he was no longer able to own the tanneries. He bent the rules to escape this proscription, going ahead with the fake sale of his business with the help of the person who became the provisional manager, Monsieur Duverger de la Roche-Jacquelin. By secret contract, the two men agreed that the ownership of the business would revert to Elie Scali at the end of the war.[116]

Scali continued to work at the tannery and visited Vichy occasionally to see his friend the colonel. He also joined the Resistance. In December 1943, a messenger from Colonel Marty came to warn Arlette that there was an arrest warrant out for her husband and his brother for "anti-government plots." Elie had just enough time to hide at the home of his foreman, who sent him to stay with his uncle, a farmer in Lambers.[117] He remained in this remote place until the end of the war.

The friendship between Xavier Vallat and Gaston Nora, a professor of medicine, is even more illustrative of the ambiguous relationship between a Vichy deputy and a French Jew. It was Vallat himself, as head of the CGQJ, who was the principal architect of the anti-Semitic policies of the French government. He and Gaston Nora were friends from as far back as the First World War. "They fought together in the Mountain Infantry," Pierre Nora explains. "It was my father who went to search for Vallat, who had been wounded [he lost his leg] under enemy fire, and Vallat was always profoundly grateful to him. Bound to each other by the solidarity of the trenches, Vallat and my father maintained cordial relations for many years. They were on familiar terms, and even exchanged the occasional correspondence. Their relationship deteriorated when Vallat, who had become a deputy in parliament, began to make anti-Semitism his stock in trade; my father ended up admitting that he regretted having saved his life."[118] During the Occupation, the professor of medicine chose to stay in Paris in order to continue running his department at the Rothschild hospital. "When he became head of the CGQJ, Xavier Vallat asked my father to become the director of the future UGIF. My father refused, which did not, however, prevent his former friend warning him when he was in danger. One day he told him, 'This evening you must leave the house, do not stay at home,' and my father escaped arrest." When Vallat left the

CGQJ, replaced by Louis Darquier de Pellepoix, he advised my father to go to Grenoble where his family was in hiding. However, rather than joining his family, Gaston Nora decided to stay in Paris, even though he had to wear the yellow star."

The Guardian Angel, the Host, the Forger, and the Smuggler

Reading and rereading the testimonies that illustrate this work, the same themes arise again and again. The same drama played out through the lives of these persecuted individuals, constantly repeated, just as in the theater, except that here the characters were acting out their own lives and often learned to play new roles.

This drama, as tragic as it so often was, was not only about fatality. Often the victims were unable to escape the fate that their persecutors inflicted on them. But others did manage to escape—and often the climax remained uncertain: the outcome depended on the different actors and locations as the drama unfolded. It was a drama of suffering and death, but also of life and survival, allowing for the unexpected resurgence of hope. A theater of small gestures, which often brings to life the same key characters. Who are these archetypal, symbolic figures, the central actors of compassion and rescue?

The Guardian angel

The first figure, and perhaps the least surprising, is the guardian angel. This figure is not a kindly spirit, constantly keeping watch over the potential victim; far from it. It is rather a person who, in the midst of a critical situation—most frequently around the time of mass arrests— becomes the guardian angel who brings help to individuals or groups of people being targeted. During a decisive period, whether lasting a few minutes or a few hours, this person might be all that stands between the hunter and the hunted. In general, the guardian angel has not decided in advance to take on this role. It is the intense drama of the moment, born of a threat hanging over friends or acquaintances, which turns them into a guardian angel. It was a guardian angel, with the features of a concierge, who intervened to save the lives of Odette Melszpajz and Francine Weiller's father. The role of the concierge or the housekeeper, at the fateful moment when the possibility of arrest looms, has been noted by Bob Moore.[119] In the heat of the moment, these women did not hesitate to resort to cunning and lies to trick the police, while the police themselves did not always want to appear overly suspicious.

The role of the guardian angel was not only taken by concierges, but by other acquaintances, including neighbors, as Françoise Frenkel recounts. Polish-born Frenkel opened the first French-language book-shop in Berlin in 1921. Forced into exile in 1939, she moved to Paris, before fleeing to the Free Zone in 1940. After much moving from place to place, she finally settled in a small hotel in Nice. On 26 August 1942: "After doing my groceries, I headed back to the hotel at a lei-surely pace. I had fallen into the habit of glancing up to the fifth floor to give a friendly wave to my Viennese neighbor. That morning she wasn't there, but I did notice my fellow countryman Monsieur Sigismond, on one of the third-floor balconies. He was waving his arms about strangely. I watched him, amused at first thinking he must be having a bit of fun. But I soon realized, astonished, that he was gestur-ing at me."[120] Thanks to her beneficent neighbor, who had been watch-ing out of the window for her return, she managed to escape the roundups that day. This story is very telling of an occupied population in which certain people became sentries, warning the persecuted of imminent danger.

With experience, people developed a system of alert, both for mem-bers of their own family and for their friends and neighbors. A sheet hanging out of a window warned of danger. The curtain in the con-cierge's lodge would be lowered to alert someone not to go up to their apartment. After they joined the Resistance, Joseph and Lisa Minc estab-lished such a strategy: "We had a sign that we would put outside our window. It was a pot of flowers. If it was outside, it meant, 'It is safe to come in,' and if it wasn't there it meant there was a problem."[121]

What began as a kind of hastily improvised safety net evolved into a full-time cottage industry of protective vigilance. This protection was often unplanned, and those who benefited were unaware of it. It really was as though there was a guardian angel invisible to those who bene-fited from its protective benevolence. Some only learned about their intervention afterwards. Denis Lindon tells of the period when he and his family were living in the Puy-de-Dôme region. In 1944, they were denounced by a former housekeeper whom his mother had dismissed. "Fortunately, the postman noticed the letter in picking up the mail, which he opened and didn't send. He came to warn us and later I learned that the residents of the village went to find the woman who had denounced us and threatened her with reprisals after the war if she dared to do such a thing again."

There has been little or no research done on employers who kept their Jewish employees on and offered them protection within their business. The story of Auguste Matringe, one of the directors of Saint-Gobain, is no doubt exceptional. Born in Switzerland in 1894, Auguste Matringe was the head of the Saint-Gobain factory in Saint-Fons, just outside Lyon. Since the early 1920s the factory had employed a large number of Moroccan Jewish immigrants. Auguste Matringe was a veteran of the 1914–1918 War and was initially a Marshal Pétain supporter, before breaking away. From 1943 onwards his factory began taking in many STO *réfractaires*. In May 1944, when an informer struck the region, Matringe offered shelter to his Jewish workers, setting up a dormitory in the factory where they could spend the night and stock up on food rations donated by their colleagues. He organized the evacuation of their families to Saint-Pierre-La-Palud, a village in the Monts du Lyonnais, some 20 km from Saint-Fons. From August onwards, the factory paid a stipend to the families who were in hiding. Matringe was arrested at the beginning of August, suspected by the Milice of hiding Jews and Spanish resistance fighters, but he was released three days later after the vice president of Saint-Gobain intervened. According to Yad Vashem, twenty-one Jewish families owed their lives to him—thirty-seven adults and fifty children.[122]

Sometimes the guardian angel's intervention had an immediate and decisive effect, saving Jews who were about to be arrested or deported. Mia and Sal Kanner escaped as they were about to be sent from the Nexon camp to Drancy, thanks to the camp nurse, Frau Meder, whom Mia had been assisting since her arrival, who persuaded the camp commandant that she would not be able to continue without Mia's help. The Kanners joined a group of twenty-three internees who were transferred from Nexon to Gurs rather than Drancy, where the other 5,000 residents of the camp were sent.[123]

The most paradoxical guardian angel figure, marking the limits of this character, is the policeman. It was sometimes he who was supposed to arrest someone but in fact became his protector. It is essential, of course, not to generalize: many law enforcement officers executed their disgraceful acts of power without hesitation. But this was not always the case, as was seen during the Vel' d'Hiv roundup. As the war and the occupation continued, the rate of such cases of disobedience increased.

Some people in positions of authority were able to reveal imminent plans for arrest. This was the case with Alphée Bonnaud, whose name features in Edith Hanau's testimony. When Hanau had to leave Alsace with her parents, they went to Chauvigny, in the Vienne region. Bonnaud, a policeman who had been posted before the war in Bouzonville (Moselle), was sent to the same town, where several other people from Alsace had relocated, including some French Jews. Bonnaud struck up a friendship with Armand Salomon, one of the Alsatian Jews now living in Chauvigny. Bonnaud left for Montmorillon (some 20 km away) in March 1944, where he had been appointed head of a motor patrol. In this new role, he found out several weeks later that the Milice was preparing a roundup of Jews in Chauvigny. The night before the operation he cycled to Chauvigny in civilian clothes to warn his friend Salomon, who passed on the news to the other Jews in the town. According to Yad Vashem, seventy-five people avoided arrest as a result.[124]

The host

After managing to avoid arrest, the first instinct for Jews was to flee in search of a new place to live. This was where the second character from the theater of aid, the host, enters. Generally this was a woman. Within a family, her position was pivotal when it came to deciding whether or not to take in a "stranger." If her husband was a prisoner of war, she was alone in taking such a decision, although other members of the family might, of course, influence her.

The character of the host symbolizes the idea of hospitality and giving. The gesture of hospitality is, in Christian culture, associated with the notion of charity, which consists in welcoming and providing sustenance to travelers and the poor without asking for payment. This is the origin of the word "hospice," a name given to an establishment, often run by a religious order, where strangers are given shelter. More generally, the host's welcome represents the possibility that the new arrival—particularly in the case of a child—would be embraced by the host family. When all went well, a foster child often became close to the host, who was sometimes already a mother or a grandmother. This was the case for Rachel Zylberberg, who was taken in by an elderly woman in the Berry region, whom she came to call "grandmother." Through her "grandmother," Rachel was absorbed into the family network of children, uncles and aunts, brothers, sisters, and cousins. Many of the nominations for the title of Righteous attest to the way that a child who had been absorbed into the wider family felt that they had truly become a part of this new family. This is evidenced by the affectionate names that they gave to their protectors (Papa, Maman, Pépé, Mémé, Tatie, Tonton, and so on) which they recalled in their nomination, as though the men and women for whom they were requesting the title of Righteous had succeeded in making up in part for their emotional abandonment during the Occupation. It is hardly surprising that after the war some chose to stay on with their host family (particularly if their parents had not survived), or remained in close contact with them.

Sometimes the bond was so strong that it led to a formal adoption or a similar process. After the death of Rachel Zylberberg's "grandmother" in 1963 and the sale of her house, her two daughters divided their inheritance equally with Rachel, whom they considered as their sister. Within the host family, close relationships sometimes developed with another member of the family, perhaps a brother or sister, or with family friends, which in a few cases even led after the war to marriage. In March 1941, Henri Steiner was taken on as a farmhand on the Douzal family farm in Tanus. Having survived deportation, he returned to Tanus and married Charlotte, one of the Douzals' neighbors, on 18 May 1946.[125]

Of course not all experiences turned out so well. The successful absorption into a host family also sometimes led to tragic consequences after the war when a child's birth parents returned to reclaim their children. There was a trial to determine who would keep Sarah

Kofman—her mother, who abused her, or her foster mother, "Mémé," to whom the little girl had become very attached. Mémé eventually won custody, but Sarah's mother then kidnapped the child.[126] It is clear that what began as a form of hospitality, whose success was primarily a matter of luck, and which was not intended to be a lasting arrangement, was as likely to turn the life of the host as much as the life of the person who was taken in upside down, to the extent that it even occasionally gave rise to an emotional attachment that continued long after the war was over. Even the most robust prejudices were sometimes shattered, as evoked in Claude Berri's 1967 film *The Two of Us*.

However, the emotional shelter provided by hospitality was not enough to ward off danger from the outside. Those who were lucky enough to escape an imminent arrest had to disguise themselves not only physically but also legally.

The forger

This is where the third character comes in: the forger. The forger played a double game, situated somewhere between the legality and illegality. He could be thought of as a criminal element, which effectively he was, since he broke the law. To view his actions through such a normative lens would be very shortsighted, however. In reality, the forger was the mirror image of this confused period, or its manifestation, in the sense that he possessed multiple facets, each relating to some key element of society. The shortage of food and the proliferation of new prohibitions gave birth to a cottage industry of forgeries of all types: forged ration tickets for food, textiles, and tobacco, and, more dangerous, forged safe conduct passes for crossing the demarcation line, and of course forged identity cards. Whether he worked as amateur or became professional, often charging a great deal of money for his services, the forger was one of the key players in this theater of appearances. It was vital to beware of the one who did not play his part with the utmost seriousness.

It is significant that there was a growth in the number of forgers at a political moment marked by grey areas and uncertainty, when it was unclear what the legal situation really was. What law counted? The law imposed by the occupying forces or by Vichy? They were not identical. Meanwhile the Gaullists claimed to be the legitimate representatives of

France, fighting to recover its freedom, which led them fiercely to oppose Vichy's claim of legitimacy. Two main types of illicit activity were born out of this radical conflict between legitimacy and legality. Insofar as the law as embodied by the state was no longer supported by the general consensus, individuals considered it legitimate not to obey all the laws, in particular those they considered to be especially unjust. This fracturing of the consensus created breaches that allowed the development of a culture of illegality, including the forging of identity cards. In the words of former resistance fighter Lucie Aubrac, "Every one of us entered the world of cheating and lies."[127] It was the development of this outlaw culture that was reflected in the refusal to be conscripted into the STO and the development of the Maquis.[128]

Forging identity cards for people being persecuted for being Jewish represents only one aspect of this outlaw culture. Some priests and pastors were among the first to become forgers after the publication of the second *Statut des Juifs*, in June 1941, in which Vichy demanded as a condition of being considered "Aryan" proof of conversion to Christianity dated no later than 25 June 1940. At this point some Jews realized that they could protect themselves by obtaining forged baptism certificates, issued by sympathetic representatives of the church. The development of forged identity cards came about a little later, beginning in summer 1942 with the rate of forgeries increasing during the autumn of that year, as a result of the surge in arrests of foreign Jews and stateless people. As French Jews began to be targeted in 1943–1944, they too began to equip themselves with forged identity cards, sometimes marked with a more "French" name and, of course, without the lethal stamp identifying them as Jewish. Most of those interviewed for this book were able to get hold of forged identity cards. Some, like Joseph Minc's friend, the hairdresser and beautician, resorted to theft to obtain them.

The ambiguous character of the forger was embodied by the person whose job it was to enforce the law. Who would suspect a Vichy functionary of trafficking in official documents when it was his responsibility to verify them? Yet this was precisely what happened when an employee of the town hall, prefecture or police station began fabricating forged documents for people on the run from the regime that he or she was supposed to be working for. Sometimes state employees tried to persuade someone coming in to register as a Jew that he or she might be exempt from this requirement. When Adolfo Kaminsky's father showed up at the commissariat in the Normandy town of Vire, an employee explained to him that he was not obliged to register as Jewish because of his Argentine nationality. Some came up with tactics that enabled people to avoid identifying themselves as Jews without actually breaking the law. Denis Lindon tells how "an employee of the Aix-en-Provence city hall, who was supposed to stamp our identity cards with the word *Juif*, was particularly beneficent: before he stamped the card he applied a layer of wax so that afterwards we could rub off the incriminating mark."

It is impossible to say how many town hall employees produced forged identity cards in 1943 and 1944. A former colleague of Marthe Hoffnung at the Poitiers city hall provided her with forged documents for all eight members of her family.[129] Claude Lanzmann pays homage to those "employees and secretaries at the town halls [who] had agreed, at great risk to themselves, to authenticate the false papers. Today they would be called 'Righteous Gentiles', but they weren't thinking about such things: I never knew their names, they didn't care about posterity, they did what they did out of solidarity, modestly, in the name of simple humanity."[130]

But being in possession of a fake history and a false identity was not always enough when roundups took place. As the danger—above all in cities—increased, the safest option was to escape to the Free Zone, preferably to somewhere deep in the countryside, or otherwise to try to get to Switzerland or Spain. This was when the fourth character appeared, whose services were indispensable when it came to crossing the demarcation line or getting across the border: the smuggler.

The smuggler

According to most accounts it seems that the smuggler, or border guide, was usually a man, though this role was also sometimes taken by a woman, for example a farmer's daughter. In witness accounts, the smuggler rarely has a name. The names of guardian angels, hosts, and forgers are often given, but the name of the smuggler almost never. This is probably quite simply because those they helped never knew their names: one characteristic of the smuggler was that he or she usually remained anonymous. The encounter with this person was necessarily short-lived. There was little interest in getting to know each other; the people trying to get across the border hoped that they would have no further need of the services of the smuggler and that the encounter would be over as quickly as possible. Though it was a transitory encounter, which usually took place at night, it was a determining factor in the survival of those fleeing danger. The smuggler was by definition a temporary actor in the drama being played out. The time spent in his company was tense, not least because it was by no means certain that the operation would be successful: they were not safe from a patrol, and an unexpected hitch could make the whole enterprise fall apart. This nervous, sometimes acute, tension generally meant that those involved were not left with fond memories of the experience.

The character of the smuggler inevitably raised doubts. Was he really reliable? Was he absolutely trustworthy? In Jean-Jacques Becker's account of the escape of his family to the Free Zone in the summer of 1942, he describes how his "parents found the services of a smuggler, who stayed with them throughout the journey and was completely honest";[131] this suggests that not all smugglers were so trustworthy. There are frequent references to the question of remuneration. While some smugglers were unpaid, there were plenty of others who demanded to be paid large sums of money.

Léon Poliakov gives a detailed description of crossing the demarcation line in autumn 1941:

> There were different ways of crossing the fateful line [...]. You could make your own way to a place near the demarcation line and tell the first café owner you came across that you had a girlfriend you wanted to visit living on the other side; he would point you in the direction of an obliging local, the whole thing would cost you no more than two or three hundred francs, and was very straightforward. Or you could liaise with a smuggler who shuttled back and forth between Paris and the demarcation line; there would be four of five of you who would be given a meeting point at the station and he would drive you to the home of another local person just like the first. Not only would this cost between two and five thousand francs, but a convoy of several people was easier to spot. Some smugglers got in with the Germans by delivering some of their clients directly into their hands. But there was

nothing more dangerous than the most expensive way, in an ambulance, or a food truck, with forged *Ausweis*. Some people were blackmailed on the eve of their departure and only managed to get out by paying a ransom; others endured a rough journey only to be delivered straight into the hands of the Germans…"[132]

For 1,300 francs, Poliakov struck a deal with a train conductor who hid him in the baggage car behind a mountain of parcels, and he arrived in the Free Zone in October 1941. It was not a fortune, but it was a large sum of money for the time.

It was not only a question of greed. Some smugglers were playing a double game, informing on those they were supposed to be helping. Anyone who approached a smuggler without a personal introduction was at risk of being betrayed. Some smugglers, if not guilty of deceit, were guilty of indifference, for example abandoning their "clients" during the journey, as happened to Macha and Szmul Woznica in 1943 as they were trying to cross illegally into Switzerland with their young son Albert, via Douvaine, a market town in the Haute-Savoie not far from the border near Geneva.[133] In April 1944, in the same region, the Dreyfus family crossed the border safely, but it was much easier for them because they had contacts in Switzerland, which the Woznicas did not. When it came down to it, even if it was not a case of active betrayal, even the experienced smuggler was no guarantee against denunciation.

The smuggler and his customers were often traveling through hostile territory and had to make themselves as invisible as possible, though in fact they rarely passed unnoticed by the local population. Rather than informing on them, local inhabitants frequently showed sympathy and offered help. Marthe Hoffnung tells how she was crossing the demarcation line, which cut through the village, when she realized that the villagers were actually praying that she make it.[134] The act of crossing a demarcation line or a border illegally thus takes on a quite different dimension: the help provide by the smuggler, who was paid for his services, tends to be overlooked alongside the unexpected and freely given moral support of the local population. Even these situations were not unattended by economic considerations, however, for the fugitives were an important source of income for local businesses, such as guesthouses and restaurants.

Studying the attitudes of the border population is a useful tool for understanding the role of those who acted as escorts for these clandestine crossings. Most often they were locals, and it was precisely because they knew the terrain—the vicinity of the frontier, which families would accommodate the fugitives—that they were most likely to succeed in getting across. Léon Bouvier, a farmer from Douvaine (Haute-Savoie), was recruited in 1942 by the local curate, Father Rosay, and he made the crossing regularly at night, after a long working day.[135]

The involvement of those who lived near the border in illegal crossings cannot be viewed apart from the history of the region where they operated. Laurent Neury has written one of the only studies on wartime smugglers in the Franco-Genevan border region.[136] Beyond tracing the trajectories of a group of very diverse individuals, the most pertinent aspect of this study is how it takes into consideration the pre-1939 history of the border, as well as how the border was perceived by those who lived in its vicinity.

The local people had no choice but to "live with" the border that had been imposed by political edict, but they were far from unquestioningly accepting of it. The border hindered economic exchange, slowed the circulation of people, and was seen as an obstruction, particularly for those who had family on both sides. The custom of crossing not only via the official border post but also via routes that crossed fields and rivers and were known only to locals had been established long before Vichy. These paths were often used for smuggling goods, but their use was also part of local custom, through which the population showed its contempt by essentially ignoring the border that divided it. The role of the smuggler can thus be seen as an extension of a centuries old local tradition of bypassing the control wielded by the authorities.

In the early months of the war, locals began to come across fugitives who had lost their way as they tried to cross the border into Switzerland. Some turned this into a lucrative business, increasingly from summer 1942 onwards. Others offered their services to different organizations and networks, helping resistance fighters, Jews, and British pilots whose planes had been shot down to cross into Switzerland. These smugglers were undoubtedly particularly exposed; several were arrested and deported, paying for their risk-taking with their lives.

Whether guardian angel, host, forger or smuggler, these rescue-characters were not fixed in their roles. A person might first appear as a guardian angel, and then later become the host of the person whose life he or she had saved. There was a clear fluidity in the sequence of events as well as in the interaction of these key characters. But one thing is certain: these were major roles. Without the involvement of these people, whether fortuitous or solicited, there would have been a much slimmer chance for many Jews of remaining alive at the end of the war.

A Thousand and One Ways of Offering Aid and Protection

Over the course of days and months, many people came to the aid of persecuted Jews. Frequently these characters played only a fleeting role, but their involvement was no less crucial. Sometimes it was only a matter of the briefest of gestures, lasting perhaps no more than a few seconds. At a moment when someone's entire life might be about to change radically, a tiny, often quite humdrum gesture was not in the least insignificant: it might be all that stood between the person concerned and a life-threatening situation. Witnesses often call attention to these fleeting gestures in their testimonies. Historians who base their research only on written archives will miss them; oral histories are far more likely to bring them to light.

It is worth exploring the range of these small gestures of solidarity, which recur frequently in the witnesses' testimonies, to try to understand their significance in a given situation.

The significance of the small gesture

The stranger in the street provides perhaps the most rudimentary example of the small gesture. It might not even be a gesture, but more of a sign—a facial expression, a smile, or merely a glance, as remarked upon by Hélène Berr when she first began wearing the yellow star. Such fleeting demonstrations of sympathy might not offer protection, but they enabled the recipient to take comfort in the basic recognition of their human dignity.

There were more ostentatious gestures, as in the scene in the Paris metro that Annie Becker describes: "I remember when Roger and I were traveling on the metro in the last carriage because I was wearing the yellow star. Roger, wearing the hat that was part of his Polytechnique uniform at a jaunty angle, had his arms around my shoulders. He stood there with such an air of defiance—this young Christian man ardently protecting his even younger, tiny little Jewish fiancée—that the other people in the carriage, far from being shocked, relaxed and smiled. There were passengers who got into the last carriage to show their tacit sympathy for the Jews."[137]

Guy and Simon Benayoun remember the teachers who reprimanded other students who insulted them or tried to get into fights. There were the nuns who tended to the young Adrien Borstein and his sister when they were in hiding with their family in Figeac, who asked no questions and expected nothing in return.

There were also critical situations when just a few words at an opportune moment were all that was needed: "Don't go home," or "be sure to turn right," was all it took for someone to avoid arrest. Arlette Scali remembers such an episode. One day in October 1942, she was out shopping in Toulouse with her children's governess, Mlle Jeanne. They were having lunch in a brasserie. Arlette had just left the dining room to go down to the restroom in the basement. "The door was locked. All of a sudden I heard sounds, cries, chairs being overturned. Someone banged on the door: 'Don't move! Don't open the door!' I could hear a lot of commotion. I didn't move. I stayed in there for half an hour. After a while someone came back and said, 'It's over. They've gone.' There had been a roundup and people had been arrested. They took away everyone they thought was Jewish."[138] Arlette Scali did not go back to Toulouse until the war was over.

Sometimes a person would lie to protect someone from danger. Several testimonies recount instances of an adult spontaneously shielding a child, as when a priest covered for Joseph and Maurice Joffo in the train on which they were traveling to Dax. When German soldiers came aboard to carry out an identity check, he told them that the two children were traveling with him. Afterwards he said to the boys, who thanked him for lying, "I didn't lie [...] You were with me just as all the children of the world are. That's one of the reasons why I am a priest— to be with them."[139]

When Janine Hemmendinger wanted to register for the first part of her baccalaureate, "I went to Romans and asked two people I met in the street if they would come with me and declare in front of the notary that they knew me and that my name was Jacqueline Hamelin. They both agreed without hesitation, which meant that I was able to obtain a birth certificate in my assumed name." This episode, which took place in 1944, is highly revealing about the mood among the general population when it came to obeying the law, and more generally about attitudes towards authority. There are many more examples of these small gestures, which were not as small as all that, perhaps, when one considers their consequences. From the most spontaneous to the most considered, there were a thousand and one ways for a stranger to offer help to someone who was being persecuted for being Jewish.

Of course there are plenty of examples of small gestures performed between people who already knew each other. In such cases, the service rendered seemed more "normal," though that was not necessarily the case when such a gesture entailed a degree of risk. Francine Weiller was on good terms with the local traders in her neighborhood. When Jews were forbidden from going shopping except between the hours of three and four in the afternoon, and after noon at the market (when there was nothing left to buy),[140] certain shopkeepers took to asking her in the afternoon what she was going to need the following day, which they would then put aside for her. Neighbors agreed to look after the possessions of families who were forced to flee, like the Benayouns who hid their furniture in the apartment of their downstairs neighbors to protect it from looting. The Becker family, who left Paris just after the Vel' d'Hiv' roundup, stored their possessions in different neighbors' apartments, and encountered no problems when they came back to reclaim them after the war.[141] However, though many stories ended well, there were also many episodes of spoliation of Jewish property, including the theft of people's belongings from their own homes.[142]

Partial and impartial

The involvement of strangers who offered help to Jews on the run appears to have been entirely at random. These characters made only the briefest appearance in the lives of refugees, turning up and then just as quickly vanishing, usually expecting nothing in return. The fact that they gave their help for no financial recompense is frequently noted in the accounts drawn on here.

When Marthe Hoffnung was organizing her family's escape to the Free Zone, a certain Monsieur Charpentier, a former colleague at the Poitiers city hall, offered to provide her with forged documents. When Marthe tried to offer him money he began to cry. "'Mademoiselle Hoffnung,' he said, his voice tremulous. 'I don't want your money. That's not why I offered to do this for you. [...] I am doing this because it is what I can do. [...] Something has to be done to help people like you. If I can help one family escape from the Germans, then I will. I can't just stand by and watch what's happening. I couldn't live with myself if I didn't at least try."[143]

This idea that people gave their help for entirely altruistic reasons must not, however, be exaggerated, for there were many people, not only smugglers, who insisted on being paid. As has already been seen, shelter often came at a price. People often had to pay—sometimes a great deal—for high quality "genuine" forged identity cards. Even a "guardian angel" might well have been receptive to the question of money. Police and gendarmes might be bribed to slacken their vigilance at a key moment. At the same time, there were others who expressed compunction when the question was raised: when Rachel Zylberberg's mother offered a packet of cigarettes to a train conductor who had allowed her to board a moving train he refused it, saying, "You have already paid. We've profited from your misery enough as it is."

In her memoir, Léa Markscheid points to the case of the mayor of Lacaune, Dr Viguier, accused of corrupt behavior towards Jews placed under house arrest in the town. Sometimes he offered his help for no payment, as he did for example to Tita Engelberg and her mother, while on other occasions he demanded payment or services in kind.[144]

It is clear that those who had the means to pay had a much greater chance of surviving the war. It is easy to understand why Jewish organizations, which gave assistance to the most impoverished Jewish immigrants, with priority given to children, needed funds, if only to be able to pay the costs of their upkeep. Nevertheless, reducing the help and protection that was so crucial to saving the lives of Jews to a question of financial resources diverts attention from the most important issue. Early or late, rich or poor, from the moment they were targeted, if they were to have any hope of surviving, Jews had to rely on the help of other people, be they acquaintances or strangers. The forging of these fragile bonds carved out a space of relative peace of mind in the midst of the turmoil.[145]

The story of Elie and Arlette Scali, as recounted by Arlette in her memoir, offers an excellent illustration of this. The family had solid financial resources and social connections, including in Vichy itself. Nonetheless, as the repression intensified, the couple was forced to separate and from then on they had to depend on the kindness of strangers. At the end of her book, Arlette Scali estimates that between 1940 and 1944 the efforts of a total of thirty-nine people helped save their lives, among them work colleagues and contacts of her husband, friends from before the war, people they met when they moved to Graulhet, domestic staff, particularly their children's nannies, and the inhabitants of the small village of Murat where Arlette took refuge with the children in December 1943. Some of these people worked for the Vichy government, some were resistance fighters, others had no particular political commitment. Arlette does not cite specific people, and did not nominate anyone to be recognized as Righteous. This was simply not how she saw it. She chose to express her gratitude to a disparate group of people who helped her family escape the worst. Her retrospective vision of events could only be plural and her homage collective.

Social reactivity and civil resistance

Because these miniature acts of solidarity, both active and passive, were performed between individuals who so often did not known each other, any personal relationships there may have been between those who were helped and those who came to their aid cannot be used to explain how such acts came about. It is by exploring the evolution of the mood of the entire population that the proliferation of this type of solidarity needs to be understood.

In investigating whether there is a particular personality type that characterizes those who come to the aid of those in need, research suggests that rescuers are characterized by having an altruistic personality, the development of which can be traced back to their early upbringing.[146] Pioneering work on rescuers, and more recently on the Righteous of France, has sought to shed light on their motivation. Most were Christians and Christian humanists.[147] Psychological studies are a first stage in understanding, but their usefulness is arguably limited if one fails to take into consideration the different elements of a given situation, vital for understanding a gesture of solidarity. Clearly a very particular context explains the variety of such gestures performed by people who in other respects have little in common, and a distinct vocabulary is needed to qualify the behavior of individuals that has at the same time a collective dimension. This was a kind of plural and heterogeneous social reactivity, a concept that I explored in my earlier work on the Nazi period.[148] Reactivity, because these individuals did something, spontaneously, without consulting one another, which explains the multiform nature of their small gestures. Social, because the simultaneous development of these different behaviors cannot be interpreted solely through the lens of individual personal histories. Between 1942 and 1944, as the persecution of Jews was stepped up, a significant movement of social reactivity was born, in the sense that many individuals offered aid, unprompted, to people whom they generally did not know, recognizing that they were in need of help. This rather remarkable phenomenon is a distinguishing characteristic of the period.

These gestures, whether small or large, cannot be called acts of resistance, in the generally understood sense of the term, since they were not born of an organized political will to fight, with or without weapons, against the occupying forces and Vichy. It is nonetheless tempting to qualify them as a form of resistance. When, within the same country and during the same period, increasing numbers of farmers began taking in Jewish children, priests and pastors were helping refugees on the run, young women were accompanying children to their new foster families, factory inspectors were closing their eyes to the origins of certain employees, social workers were falsifying documents, school principals were registering students under false names, doctors were employing Jewish assistants, town hall employees were forging French identity cards for foreigners, police and gendarmes were sending warnings to those that they were supposed to be arresting, smugglers were risking their lives to lead small groups to safety on the other side of the border, all these anonymous actors, were, without consulting anyone, in some sense working together towards the same end, as though each and every one was expressing the mood of a civil society in a mode of resistance, a mode of civil resistance.

At the end of the 1980s, I put forward this vision of civil resistance in *Unarmed Against Hitler: Civilian Resistance in Europe, 1939–1943*, in which I sought to qualify different modes of unarmed opposition under dictatorship. However, in the light of more recent historical research on the Resistance, this approach now seems too broad and risks diluting the real meaning of "resistance." It is vital to maintain the intentional and organized dimension of resistance, and to restrict the notion of civil resistance to encompass only organized systems of aid conferred through Jewish and non-Jewish organizations. The more diffuse field of spontaneous help, which was by definition uncoordinated, is better embraced within the parameter of "social reactivity." Of course social reactivity and civil resistance intersect; in general, the former is part of the matrix of the latter. Many people went from offering spontaneous aid to taking part in organized movements. Once established, organized civil resistance could and even had to benefit from occasional spontane- ous "helping hands" to carry out its activities and expand its influence.

The "small gestures" described in this chapter constitute the diverse realm, the living tissue, of this social reactivity. It goes without saying that it was not a response to a centralized command and its scope cannot be evaluated in the way that army troops can be counted. Social reactiv- ity is both spontaneous and fluid. Its gestures of aid towards the perse- cuted were made by very different people, some of whom were involved in collaboration. They were gestures that were both discreet and dis- crete, in other words both inconspicuous and isolated (thus "discrete" as one might say for statistical distributions). But it was a social reactivity, beginning in the summer of 1942, that was sufficiently widespread across France for the doors of private houses and educational establish- ments, both public and private, to be opened to take in people who were being persecuted because they were Jewish. These scattered and multiform responses from individual "helpers" threw a protective and beneficent mantle over a group of people who had become the pariahs of the regime. In occupied France, between 1942 and 1944, this social reactivity, bringing aid to persecuted and hunted Jews, was spread over numberless localities and embodied in countless individuals.

"They Knew We Were Jewish But They Said Nothing"

This remark, often uttered by those who lived through the persecution as a self-evident fact, was heard frequently during the interviews conducted for this book. Is this a generational effect? Is it a way for people as they near the end of their lives to express once again their gratitude towards the people who once gave them protection? That could be partly true. But it also underscores a historical reality that has never really been considered, since it does not draw attention to itself: silence. How should silence be interpreted? There are different types of silence, according to the stages of persecution and the war itself.

Historians of the Holocaust were among the first to emphasize the importance of taking into consideration the silence of public opinion, but in the opposite sense: that of a passive silence, in other words a tacit approval of the persecution. In the early 1950s, Léon Poliakov, by then gaining a reputation as a historian of the period, rightly emphasized how the "tightening of the net" around Jews was directly related to the evolution of public opinion. The method focused on the close observation of the reactions of the German population to increasingly brutal anti-Semitic measures. At each new stage, as the German population appeared unmoved, its passivity constituted a sort of license to keep escalating persecution.[149] Silence was taken to be a form of tacit support for Nazi policies. This approach was also applied to France, at least for the period between autumn 1940 and summer 1942, with historians closely focusing on the silence of the Catholic Church in the wake of the promulgation of the *Statut des Juifs*. However, it is vital to probe the underlying reasons for this apparent widespread indifference on the part of the general population. Was it in fact linked to the specific context of the early part of the Occupation?

Witnesses point out that there was another kind of silence that, conversely, helped to protect them. It consisted of saying nothing when, for example, new faces appeared in the village. Were they foreigners? Refugees? Did they have an accent? And what if they did? It was wartime. Silence created a favorable environment for these new arrivals, about whom little was known, and about whose origins people feigned ignorance or lack of interest.

This silence must not be idealized. Knowing when not to say anything is not necessarily proof of any kind of courage. Remaining silent is sometimes no more than the urge to avoid trouble. This is the silence most common under a dictatorship or occupying forces, which signifies caution; it is in the interests of those who know that they are surrounded by potential informers to remain silent. It is an inglorious silence, often practiced by those who wanted to continue undisturbed with their lives and who simply wanted to avoid any kind of trouble. Their "see nothing, know nothing" attitude might have indirectly helped those who feared being denounced, whether for their political activities or their religious or ethnic origins, but it was a fragile silence that could at any moment be shattered by an informer.

However, there is a third kind of silence, more empathetic towards those who found themselves cast out by the regime: that of complicity. Complicity is often considered to be by definition political. But that is to forget the discreet collusion that was born out of routine work relationships, where an employer might simply have been satisfied with an employee: "What does it matter where he comes from if he's a good worker?" The issue of whether the person was or was not Jewish barely arose. Seen from this perspective, one begins to understand the key role played by important local figures: not only the mayor, but also the parish priest, the local schoolteacher, the doctor, some of whom might have been privy to the secret of the origins of a new arrival—they might indeed have been the only people to know when someone was Jewish. They told no one. Sometimes they helped them procure fake identity cards, if necessary inventing a history that justified a person's presence in the town. Through the various different social ties that these public figures had forged with the townspeople, they were able to find places for the new arrivals to live, adults and children, in this or that family, or such and such institution. No one appeared to be interested in a newcomer's origins. In this way a network founded upon a conspiracy of silence would be established in a village, linking people, families, and places.

Stanley Hoffmann described the lack of communication between the occupiers and the inhabitants of Lamalou-les-Bains (Languedoc) when he and his mother arrived there in December 1943, having fled the Nice area. They found themselves living near a garrison that housed young German soldiers. But "the two groups did not speak to each other. We could not have been safer. No one ever really ever engaged them in conversation. It really was the 'silence of the sea'," he said, referring to the famous novel published under the pseudonym Vercors in February 1942,[150] in which the intentional and prolonged silence of an old man and his niece towards a German officer whom they are forced to billet becomes the deliberate manifestation of a patriotic spirit of resistance.

But the risk of being denounced by a neighbor continued to hang over people like a Damoclean sword right up until the departure of the Germans. It is impossible to overemphasize the difference between the act of informing and the act of protecting. To protect a family from arrest required silence on the part of all the neighbors, quite a remarkable feat in itself. By contrast, when it came to giving up a family to the police, all it took was a single person, driven by hatred or a lust for money, or both.

Neighbors' attitudes might change with time, over the course of the war and the Occupation. Anti-Semites who were ready to denounce Jews in 1941 or 1942 might have grown less disposed to do so by 1943 or 1944 (the opposite might also have been the case). Albert Grunberg, the hairdresser who lived on the rue des Écoles, offers an interesting perspective on this in his diary. He notes that after a while some of his neighbors began to suspect that he and his brother were hiding somewhere in the area. By July 1944, "there was virtually a famine in Paris." Albert's benefactor, Mme Oudard, the concierge, decided to tell the baker and his wife that she was hiding Albert and his brother to justify the quantities of bread she was buying. It was a risky move, considering that back in 1942 the couple had been delighted about the Vel' d'Hiv roundup. But now the baker's wife promised to supply her with bread without a food ticket. And when Marguerite, the hairdresser's wife, begged her not to denounce her husband and brother-in-law, the baker's wife, "who had clearly changed her mind about Jews," responded, "My lips are sealed," and gave her a pound of gingerbread as a gift.[151]

This example makes clear what a difference it made if neighbors supported anti-Semitic persecution or not. Keeping silent was not necessarily synonymous with indifference: it could be one form of "forced adaptation" that was an inherent element of the Occupation. Neighborly help had to be discreet if it were to last any length of time.

In the wake of Raul Hilberg's seminal work on the genocide of the Jews of Europe, the idea of bystander responsibility began to be a focus of study.[152] The bystander was a person who stood by the side of the road, watching events unfold and not intervening. Sometimes bystanders became active participants in mass murder. This was particularly true in Poland, Ukraine, and Belarus, and in other parts of Central and Eastern Europe, which were riven by strong currents of anti-Semitism. However, there has not been a great deal of research into situations where the same person might conversely have hindered the process of persecution, either by protesting openly, or by acting covertly.

The Nazis failed to persuade the French population to sign up to their genocidal anti-Semitic undertaking, in spite of a strong current of anti-Semitism and xenophobia that had existed in France since the end of the nineteenth century. In order to implement the gradual increase of anti-Jewish measures, already tried and tested in the Reich, Berlin was able to rely on the collaboration of the Vichy government forged by Pétain as well as on various other collaborationist movements and groups. These agents of the occupying forces in France caused appalling damage and loss of life, resulting in the deportation and murder of 25 per cent of Jews from France. But it is important to note that, as soon as the mass arrests began, the Nazis ran into the problem of widespread non-acceptance by the general population, who, instead of actively participating in the war on Jews, more often hid them or helped them flee. This is one major reason for the high rate of survival of the Jews in France; it is not, however, the only one.

CONCLUSION

THE SURVIVAL OF THE JEWS IN FRANCE:
A MULTIFACTORIAL APPROACH

This study has focused on the everyday tactics and strategies, often initiated by Jews themselves, to avoid persecution and arrest in France during World War II. It has shown how it was often thanks to the help of individuals that Jews managed to escape getting caught up in a fatal chain of events. However, in order to understand the high rate of survival of Jews in France in this period, it is necessary to go from the how to the why, and to take into account a wide variety of contributing factors. The challenge is to explain these factors, moving from the particular to the general, and towards the respective and decisive significance of both national and international politics.

The Scale of the Territory

The first factor to be taken into account is geographical: France was far larger than Belgium or the Netherlands, and in 1940 many Jews were able to flee from the Occupied to the Free Zone and even beyond, with a small number managing to reach Switzerland or Spain. The vast majority, however, remained in France. While some stayed in or near their homes, many were scattered around often very remote rural areas. The range of intranational migrations that took place between 1940 and 1944 can be seen in the two previously unpublished maps

(Maps 3 and 4) based on material drawn from the Vichy archives, which illustrate this dispersal over the territory of the Southern Zone.

This geographical variable must be considered in conjunction with the attitudes of local inhabitants of the regions where Jews settled. In the countryside it was impossible to hide, for "foreigners" would never have been able to slip unnoticed into the local population. If the French had been as anti-Semitic as one strand of historical thought insists it was, tens of thousands of Jews would have been denounced. But this mass denunciation did not take place.

Anti-Semitism, Social Reactivity, and Self-Interest

The thesis espoused by Marrus and Paxton, that there was a virulent popular anti-Semitism in France, must be put in perspective, not least because three-quarters of the Jews of France survived the war. There is no doubt that anti-Semitism had been a reality in France since at least the nineteenth century. But it is difficult to differentiate it from xenophobia, particularly in the 1930s, when France had the highest level of immigration in the world. After the 1940 defeat, the Vichy regime promulgated a state-sanctioned anti-Semitism at arguably the worst possible moment: under the gaze of the Nazi occupiers. Was this official ideology widely supported by the population? Marrus and Paxton claim that by 1941 a widespread anti-Semitism reigned in France, but the historian Pierre Laborie rejects this vision, arguing that it is exaggerated and biased.

While the extent of anti-Semitism in France can be debated, it is surely of primary importance to acknowledge what people did or did not do in this given historical situation. By the summer of 1942, when the mass roundups began, French non-Jews were already trying to help Jews avoid arrest. Whether they were anti-Semitic or not, whether or not they believed that there was indeed a "Jewish problem," they were outraged by the brutality of a regime that was now arresting women and children. The roundups of July 1942 marked a turning point in public opinion, as is clear from Vichy reports of the time.

This was the context in which the number of "small gestures" of support for the persecuted began to increase. Compassion tended to outweigh stigmatization. Help was not always given for purely altruistic reasons, and those who had money had a significantly greater chance of survival. In the revised edition of their book, Marrus and Paxton acknowledge this in their rewritten conclusion.

Small gestures, including the silence of non-denunciation, cannot be lumped together with acts of resistance. The notion of social reactivity is a way of qualifying the different kinds of spontaneous help that began to be manifested in the critical years between 1942 and 1944. At the exact same time that Jews were being deported and killed, there was a significant movement of social reactivity in France, in the sense that individuals, very often unknown to one another, and without any prior directives, were spontaneously helping people—on the whole strangers—whom they recognized as being in a situation of distress or of great vulnerability. These individuals were helpers, not resistance fighters. Social reactivity is not a totalizing notion: the fact of it does not presume any consensus on the part of the social body, within which there may have been other elements either wholly indifferent to the fate of the Jews, or actively in favor of the persecution, or somewhere in between. There is no evidence to suggest that this behavior can be construed as being typical of the "average" French person during this period. Giving help to Jews coexisted until the end of the war with other modes of behavior towards them that ranged from indifference to self-interest to denunciation.

All over the country, already hugely impoverished by the Occupation, everyone was struggling; accordingly, when refugees—Jewish or not—arrived in a village, they represented a source of both possible tension and potential profit. For many non-Jewish French people who were in a position to offer the refugees food supplies (as attested to by the development of a black market) or services (renting lodgings, looking after children, and so on), the "race" or religion of those seeking asylum was of very little interest as long as they had the means to pay. The central question of money was a far greater determining factor in the way they were treated than whether or not they were Jewish; people were often ignorant of or simply uninterested in the origins of these newcomers. The logic of self-interest was often enough to dissuade people from informing, simply because it was obvious that there was no point in informing on a person who was a source of profit.

Aid and the Question of Risk

There are multiple examples of individuals offering help to Jews, whether or not informed to some degree by self-interest, throughout every country in Nazi Europe. Although it cannot be demonstrated objectively that it was more widespread in France, there are some indications that suggest this might have been the case, as a result of the particular conditions of the Occupation and cultural norms rooted in French society.

Firstly, there is the question of the extent to which people in France who protected Jews put their own lives in danger, as insisted upon by the formal definition of the Righteous. A smuggler certainly took risks when accompanying an individual or a group across the demarcation line or over a border. It must be stressed, however, that helping a Jew in France was not considered a punishable act by the French and German police. This fact has not been widely recognized, even by Marrus and Paxton, who believed that the most courageous risked being killed when they hid a Jew in their house.[1] In this respect, the situation in occupied France was completely different from, for example, the situation in Poland, where a person caught hiding a Jew would be executed on the spot along with their entire family. This was not the case in France and certain other countries of Western Europe, although in Belgium and above all in the Netherlands non-Jews caught helping Jews were severely punished.[2]

On the other hand, the Germans clamped down ruthlessly on anyone who helped save the life of an Allied airman: this was considered to be an act of war, and the rescuer would almost always be deported. In the eyes of the Germans, helping a Jew was not equivalent to rescuing a British or American soldier or someone working for Allied intelligence, and the person who helped a Jew did not receive the same punishment.[3] Although in 1942 Vichy ordained a series of repressive measures against those who came to the aid of Jews, they were not on the whole enforced very seriously.

Thus in France, it was not the case that every non-Jew caught helping a Jew was punished, either by Vichy or the occupying forces. This is not to diminish the worth of the gesture or action on the part of the person who offered help, who often believed that they were doing something forbidden and might well have been afraid of some kind of retaliation. In fact there were no collective reprisals until the very last months of the war when punitive operations were carried out with the specific aim of targeting civilians, including Jews and those who were sheltering them.

A Civil Resistance Rescue Movement

Two figures stand out particularly when evaluating the toll of the Holocaust in France: almost 90 per cent of French Jews and 60 per cent of foreign Jews survived. A quantitative approach offers an interesting new perspective on the period. How to explain this extremely high rate of survival among French Jews who, at the start of the war, did not, as we have seen, consider themselves to be Jews but rather *Israélites*, or French people of the Jewish faith? Some historical perspective is required.

In 1791, during the French Revolution, France became the first European nation to emancipate its Jews. In the course of the nineteenth century Jews were gradually integrated into the nation, with some even rising to become part of the elite. They saw the *Statut des Juifs* brought in on 3 October 1940 as an absolute betrayal.[4] Nevertheless, these French citizens who were now being persecuted for being Jewish had numerous social resources at their disposal which enabled them to circumvent the new discriminatory laws, with many in a position to go for help to relatives in the Free Zone, or at least to send their children to safety there. Friends and colleagues helped them. They were able to draw on a variety of resourceful strategies, facilitated by their century-long integration into French society. In stark contrast, the situation of Jewish citizens in the Netherlands was very different. Bob Moore explains how Dutch Jews were integrated according to a different model, specific to Dutch society, known as the pillar system. Before the war, Dutch Jews had the same rights as any other citizen, which bound them in a vertical manner to the nation. This meant that they tended to live within their community, separate from the rest of society. When the arrests and deportations began, the fact they had few relationships with non-Jews had disastrous consequences.[5]

Foreign Jews who had recently arrived in France spoke little, if any, French. Unlike French Jews, they did not fit into networks of sociability. Those who had managed to escape with some money had a better chance of survival, but it was rarely the case: most lost everything when they escaped their home countries. They tried to find ways to scrape by but were much less likely to. These vulnerable foreign Jews were the first to be targeted by both Vichy and the Germans.

This explains why the main efforts on the part of Jewish and Christian organizations—the Comité Amelot, the OSE, the EIF, the Cimade and *Amitiés chrétiennes* (Christian Fellowship)—were concentrated on protecting foreign Jews and their children. Through their activities, these activists—Jewish, Christian, or completely secular—gradually built up a civil resistance rescue movement, hitherto unknown in France. Their activities began to be stepped up in the summer of 1942. In parallel to resistance movements that were established to fight the occupying forces and Vichy, another form of struggle developed, whose purpose was not to kill Germans or "collabos" but to save lives. By civil resistance, I mean an organized support network working towards three consecutive stages of rescue: the evacuation, transfer, and social integration of individuals in need of protection. If necessary, a fourth element was added: evacuation to another country. This civil resistance was from the start organized largely in conjunction with resistance movements, not least because this facilitated the forging of identity cards for Jews and fugitive opponents of the regime. But it would never had been able to branch out and become more efficient if it had not benefited from the active collusion of the non-Jewish population, particularly when it came to finding shelter for Jewish children in families or educational establishments. Neighboring Belgium saw a similar evolution. The Belgian *Comité de défense des Juifs* (CDJ—Committee for the Protection of Jews), set up in September 1942, was able to partially block some of the schemes proposed by the collaborationist *Association des Juifs de Belgique* (Association of Jewish Belgians), by setting up a highly efficient network of civil resistance, which managed to hide a significant number of Jews, including children in Catholic schools. In a country whose pre-war Jewish population was 90 per cent foreign-born, the final death toll of 45 per cent of foreign Jews could have been a great deal worse.

CONCLUSION

Cultural Factors

The challenge is to understand and explain the strength of a social fabric that was generally sympathetic to protecting Jews, which developed in France in spite of a historical tendency towards anti-Semitism. Historians agree that during the summer of 1942 the triggering factor was the rounding up of children, innocent victims of a brutal authoritarianism. That a government would target children was horrifying. People were so shocked that in some cases they found their anti-Semitic convictions called into question. In May 1943, François Mauriac, writing in his underground diary, expressed the mute horror of a population stunned to see the regime betraying its own children. "At what moment in history did penal colonies become prisons for the innocent? In what other era have children been torn from their mothers and piled into cattle trucks, as I witnessed this morning, this dark morning, at Austerlitz station?"[6] This Catholic writer is surely expressing the dull revolt of public opinion, shocked by a regime going after children. Out of 70,000 children, 11,385 Jewish children were deported from France,[7] and 58,615 children avoided deportation. Serge Klarsfeld makes clear that "France, proportionally speaking, in comparison with other countries, saved more children. Around 14 per cent were killed, while out of a total of 6 million dead [throughout the whole of Europe], a quarter were children."[8]

Should it be assumed that all those who helped Jews were inclined to do so through altruism? Having trained as a psychologist, I have profound reservations about the idea that personality was a determining influence on the behavior of those who came to the aid of Jews. Certainly there will have been some individuals by nature inclined to defy convention and predisposed to behave in a certain way in such circumstances. On the whole, however, those we call "rescuers" were not necessarily people who were intrinsically good or instinctively inclined to help others. In some cases, their motives were unclear; they may even have been collaborating in some way with the regime when they ended up helping someone without ever having planned or intended to do so. The context of a specific situation tends to outweigh personality.[9]

Apart from these psychological factors, it is impossible to understand the variety and breadth of the small gestures of help without looking into the deeper causes, rooted in the history of French society.

I have tried to bring to light the main cultural factors that to a certain extent curbed the extent of the persecution of the Jews in France and helped obstruct it.

Christianity

The first and most obvious factor is religion. We know about the pioneering role of the Protestants in helping Jews, and the early engagement of certain priests, like the Jesuit Pierre Chaillet, who founded the *Cahiers du témoignage chrétien* in Lyon in 1941, or Father Théomir Devaux, head of the Notre-Dame de Sion congregation, who in 1941 began sheltering Jewish children whose parents came to him seeking help. Notwithstanding the silence of Pope Pius XII, many senior Catholic prelates protested openly when foreign Jews first began to be arrested in 1942. Undoubtedly, the pastoral letter sent by the archbishop of Toulouse, Monsignor Saliège, on 23 August 1942, is the letter that had the greatest impact both in France and abroad.

Lower down the Church hierarchy, congregants were also steeped in the culture of Christian charity, a theological virtue taught at catechism in every parish in the country. At the time of the mass arrests, there is no doubt that there were people who were impelled out of a sense of Christian duty to help suffering children and adults, whether or not they were responding to a bishop's statement, as has been noted in several of the nominations for Righteous of France.[10] The importance of religion should not, however, be overestimated: the Catholic Church was equally dominant in neighboring Belgium, but the percentage of Jews deported from there (44 per cent) was much higher. There must therefore be other factors specific to France.

Republican tradition

This factor is deeply linked to French political and cultural heritage. Although the Vichy regime had effectively buried the Third Republic, for most of the population the republican spirit had not been suppressed. Republican values had been disseminated since the nineteenth century, not only in big cities but also in remote villages of rural France. There were schoolteachers committed to secular values in thousands of towns and villages throughout the country who played a vital role in the hospitality afforded to Jewish children. Boarding schools also provided refuge for Jewish students. The widespread acceptance of foreign Jewish children in secular state schools has never been properly acknowledged,[11] though it was hugely significant: in Nazi Europe, only two countries—Denmark and France—continued to enroll Jewish children in school.[12] For foreign Jewish families seeking refuge, being able to sending their children to school was an essential factor in their ability to integrate.

This republican heritage must not be over-idealized: during the 1930s, there were more than a few representatives of the Third Republic who held xenophobic and anti-Semitic opinions. But this political aberration from republican values must not be allowed to obscure the decades-long emancipation of the Jews, which was an integral part of the French Revolution and a major factor in the integration of those who were for decades afterwards called *Israélites*. The intended eradication of Jewish integration into the French nation by the anti-Semitic Vichy regime was only partially successful, since Vichy was unable to sever completely the social bonds that had existed for almost 150 years between these French Jews and their compatriots. This is in contrast with the Dutch Jews who, as has been explained, suffered so much partly because of their social isolation in a country where people of different origins lived in compartmentalized communities. It was the longstanding ties that had bound Jews to the French nation since the end of the eighteenth century that slowed the attacks on French Jews and helped reduce the numbers delivered to the Germans.

Patriotic spirit

The massive impact of the preeminent tragedy of the war for France, the crushing defeat of May–June 1940 followed by the country's occupation by an age-old enemy must, of course, not be ignored. Research on the Holocaust in France over the last thirty years has tended to overlook the fundamental fact that France was militarily occupied by a foreign power. Even the title of Robert Paxton's book, *Vichy France*, erases this strategic reality. It announces the existence of a "France known as Vichy," and ignores the Nazi occupation. Disciples of Paxton have continued to perpetuate this convenient version of reality.[13] Yet research on public opinion has shown that while a majority did have confidence in Pétain, most French were hostile to the German occupiers and broadly Anglophile. This provides another explanation as to why some people helped Jews: not because they "liked" them, but because they wanted to do something to oppose the Germans.

There were other European populations that were no less patriotic, such as the Poles, who were also extremely hostile to a particularly brutal German occupation, where the percentage of Jews who were murdered—nearly 90 per cent—was one of the highest of all. In Belgium, too, another very patriotic country, with the 1914 German occupation still alive in popular memory, the percentage of Jews who were deported and killed was far higher than it was in France. Patriotism alone cannot explain it, but must be considered alongside other factors.

Structural Factors

It is important to distinguish between rescue and survival. If rescue implies intent (the ad hoc establishment of various organizations), structural factors arising from the nature of Nazi oppression played an essential role in determining the survival rates of Jews in different countries. These factors are related above all to the nature of Berlin's objectives for a particular country and its relationship with the various leaderships. From this point of view, France's situation was unique, though in some aspects similar to other Nazi-occupied countries in Europe.

The Free Zone and the statuses of different territories

Some countries were entirely occupied, like Poland, the Netherlands, and Belgium; some were allied to the Reich, like Italy and Slovakia, while others had the status of a satellite country, for example Denmark and Finland. No other defeated country found itself in a hybrid situation like that of France, divided up into different zones: a zone attached to the German military command in Brussels, the Forbidden Zone, the Occupied Zone, and the so-called Free Zone over which the Vichy government retained sovereignty. For the vast majority of French people who remained in mainland France, the Free Zone had an obvious attraction: those who lived there were out of the purview of the occupying forces and in general life was easier. While it had evidently not been planned this way, the existence of the Free Zone was clearly propitious for the survival of Jews (apart from those who were imprisoned in internment camps such as Gurs and Rivesaltes): this could be termed a structural factor with indirect consequences.

More generally, the fate of the Jewish population depended on the political and administrative status of whichever territory they were living in. Specific studies of these places are of particular interest when it comes to bringing to light these different territorial statuses as they evolved during the course of the war.

The development of social welfare policies

We are so used to seeing Vichy from the perspective of its anti-Semitism that we forget the importance of its social welfare program.[14] Jews were, like other refugees, able to benefit from administrative measures taken by the French government as part of its welfare policies. Jews were eligible for the subsistence allowance paid to evacuees and refugees, and their children were eligible to be taken in by the *Assistance Publique* as part of a longstanding tradition of fostering; some Jews were beneficiaries of relief efforts by the *Secours National* aimed at refugees in prisons and camps, while others, in need of shelter, could also receive aid.

This was the paradox that was being played out: on the one hand, Vichy's anti-Semitic laws contributed to the pauperization and marginalization of Jews, while on the other they were partially compensated for this by welfare measures that were available for all those in need, without discrimination.[15]

The continuing existence of the French state

The continuing existence of a national government allowed the Vichy leaders a certain amount of leeway, even while it applied its own *sui generis* anti-Semitic policies. This can be seen by broadening the viewpoint to take in the whole of Europe.[16] Such a comparative analysis highlights two very different political configurations.

Firstly, in countries where the state was completely destroyed, such as Poland and Ukraine, or in those where the national administration was placed directly under the control of the occupying forces (the Netherlands and Belgium), the proportion of Jews who were murdered was very high.

Secondly, in countries which maintained their own governments, whether allied to the Reich (Italy, Bulgaria, Slovakia, and Romania up until 1942, Hungary up until 1944), or in official collaboration with Germany (Denmark, France), Berlin put pressure on their leaders in such a way as to help the local forces of the law to resolve the so-called "Jewish question," while sparing their own personnel. Some governments were "cooperative" while others were not, or not always. In general the number of Holocaust victims in these countries was lower. Timothy Snyder comes to a similar conclusion: "The destruction of states themselves rendered Jews vulnerable as nothing else could. Hitler's aspiration to rid the earth of Jews could only proceed to completion after the states themselves were destroyed. Where any vestige of sovereignty remained, as in Vichy France and Slovakia, Jewish policy could change and deportations could cease, as indeed happened in both places in 1943."[17]

From a structural perspective, Vichy had relative internal autonomy, which it was able to make use of—or not—to protect Jews from deportation. Without in the slightest seeking to exonerate Vichy of its crimes, it is clear that the regime did not behave in a monolithic way throughout the war and that its leadership was riven with contradictions. In terms of the "Jewish question," it was subject to pressure from the Germans, while needing to make concessions to the Church lobby as well as wider French society. The international context also had an influence on its evolution. These factors are of primary importance in explaining the high rate of survival of Jews in France. It is incorrect to claim that 75 per cent of Jews in France were "saved" (in the sense that this high survival rate was due exclusively to intentional factors). It is more correct to say that they survived.

The Evolution of the Relationship Between the Germans and Vichy

The project to annihilate the Jews of Europe was born in the heart of Nazi Germany, not France. In early summer 1942, this horrific enterprise began to spread across Western Europe. The objective of the Vichy leadership was not the extermination of the Jews, and Vichy anti-Semitism was certainly not identical to that of the Nazis. When Vichy began to disseminate the ideas of the 1930s far right, its aim was to "reduce the influence" of the Jews in France, not to kill them. That is why the Nazis had to put pressure on the Vichy leadership to involve them in what was to become the "Final Solution."

During the first two years of the Occupation, Vichy cooperated with the Germans, including organizing the arrest and "delivery" of foreign Jews in the two zones, as made clear by the Bousquet-Oberg agreement of July 1942, which promised to hand over to the Nazis 40,000 stateless Jews, 30,000 from the Occupied Zone, 10,000 from the Free Zone. This Franco-German agreement materialized with the Vel' d'Hiv' roundup in Paris and in the Free Zone with the transfer of internees from the camps at Gurs and Rivesaltes to Drancy.

After the bishops' protest of summer 1942, the French leadership appeared increasingly reluctant to carry out more mass arrests. There are two types of evidence for this. In terms of archival evidence, we have the German report, uncovered by Serge Klarsfeld, of a meeting between Oberg and Laval in which Laval announces that, bearing in mind the problems they were having with the Church, "There will not be a delivery of Jews like some kind of merchandise in Prisunic [supermarket], where you can pick up whatever groceries you want, everything at the same price."[18] Berlin accepted Vichy's change in direction, apparently preferring to back down over the deportation of Jews in order to preserve the strategic role of the government in maintaining order and security for German troops stationed in France.

The decrease in the rate of deportations can be seen in the figures. 1942 was by far the worst, with 42,000 Jews from France killed. In 1943, the figure went down to 17,000, but during the first six months of 1944 it had already risen to 15,000. The number of Jews killed in 1943 and 1944 in total is lower overall than the number killed during the particularly horrific year 1942.

Because of its structural importance as a collaborating government (non-existent in the Netherlands and Belgium), Vichy certainly had the means to hinder the deportations. Pim Griffioen and Ron Zeller have conducted a useful comparative analysis on the subject and come to the same conclusion.[19] At first, the government served as an efficient intermediary for the Nazis. Later it became a sort of passive accessory, less inclined to acquiesce to what was being demanded. Was this a lasting effect of the bishops' protest? Marrus and Paxton contend that it was due to a lack of trains in 1943 available to transport deportees to their deaths. But Wolfgang Seibel argues that it was the weight of the church's "moral power" that put pressure on Vichy and spurred its leaders to exploit their room for maneuver as much as possible in order to limit their participation in the deportation of the Jews.

In fact, the Germans were increasingly obliged to conduct mass arrests on their own, without Vichy's help: they understood that the French police and the gendarmerie were becoming less reliable when it came to carrying out these missions. SS Aloïs Brunner, the commandant of Drancy, went down to Nice in September 1943 to personally organize the roundup of Jews. Vichy had changed course, from a negotiated collaboration to a more reserved position, even a kind of disengagement. Certainly the police continued to arrest both foreign and French Jews, as in Bordeaux in January 1944. But the general direction of Vichy's disengagement when it came to delivering Jews to the occupying forces was decided. In total, the survival rate of foreign Jews in France was around 60 per cent, a high proportion relative to death rates in other countries.

French Jews were rarely arrested. In spite of Nazi pressure, there were two critical occasions when Vichy refused to hand them over for deportation. The first came in June 1942, during the negotiations that led to the signing of the Bousquet-Oberg agreement, when the occupying forces demanded that 40,000 foreign and French Jews be handed over from the Occupied Zone. The initial plan was to deport 15,000 Jews from the Netherlands, 10,000 from Belgium and 100,000 from France. But this last figure was deemed unrealistic and was therefore lowered to around 40,000. As Vichy was unwilling to arrest French Jews, in order to spare them Bousquet and Laval instead offered to hand over 10,000 stateless Jews from the Free Zone.

The second occasion occurred one year later, as Italy was losing the war. While the Bousquet-Oberg agreement did not include the arrest of French Jews, the Nazis were nonetheless trying to find a legal way to deport them as well. They regularly tried to pressure Vichy into revoking all naturalizations of foreign Jews granted since 1927. Several thousand Jews would then have lost their French nationality and become stateless, which would have made them liable to immediate arrest and deportation. In the summer of 1943, the denaturalization law was ready, drawn up by Bousquet and signed by Laval. The strategy was about to be put into action. But on 10 July, the Allied Forces landed in Sicily, and Mussolini was overthrown less than two weeks later. In mid-August, Pierre Laval let it be known that the denaturalization law would not be implemented, which was confirmed by Marshal Pétain in a letter dated 23 August. In it he pointed out the "the French government had enough trouble in this regard to avoid measures that will deeply shock the French and further complicate its task."[20] It is noteworthy that Pétain used the argument of public opinion, probably having in mind the letter received on 21 August from Mgr Chappoulie, in which the Pope's representative warned Pétain that "any further deportations at this point would cause a greater wave of emotion and dismay among Catholics, and bishops would likely believe it their duty to make their voices heard once again."[21] The delegate of the French Episcopate thus openly alluded to the possibility of a protest on the part of the Catholic Church that could be even stronger than the one in 1942. But it is rather the foreseeable likelihood of a German defeat that primarily explains Vichy's turnaround in the summer of 1943, as Laurent Joly also believes.[22] "If those Jews who had been French for several generations were less affected, it is because Vichy performed a last-minute about-face, and in 1943 the rate of deportations decreased," Henry Rousso points out. Of course this also shows "that without the collaboration of the French government, the Nazis would clearly not have been able to deport as many Jews as they did from France."[23]

It is clear that having French citizenship provided considerable protection from deportation, which also explains the black market in "genuine" forged identity cards that so many foreign Jews tried to obtain. This protection was relative, however, since around 10 per cent of French Jews—24,500—were deported and killed. The leaders of Vichy were not alone in wanting to protect "their" Jews. There was a tendency among governments to hand over foreign Jews first in order to save "their" Jews. The Nazis initially accommodated this position, with the intention of taking up the challenge later and insisting that national Jews be included in the deportation convoys. There is no doubt that that was going to happen in France.

"In the last analysis, what governed the scale of the killings was the degree to which the Germans were able to apply their power," write Marrus and Paxton.[24] This is logical: it was the occupying forces who had the upper hand. But there is no doubt that the Nazis also had to contend with the social realities of the countries that they were occupying. This dimension always comes second in the analyses of these historians. From their perspective, what is most relevant is the power wielded by the powerful, rather than the ways in which society reacts to its leadership's actions, because they assume that power wielded—in this case by the Nazis—will always carry the day. In this sense, Marrus and Paxton only give a secondary role to public opinion. In their conclusion, they ignore the bishops' protest of summer 1942, whereas for Serge Klarsfeld, that moment is absolutely key. Their omission is difficult to comprehend, but it is coherent with the general absence of reflection on public opinion in Paxton's work, a shortcoming that Stanley Hoffmann noted in 1973 in his preface to *Vichy France*.[25] My own work on the relationship between dictatorships and the societies they control[26] led me to lean towards a dialectical analysis of these two poles: yes, in principle everything was based on the power that the Nazis wielded, except that the Nazis depended on Vichy to arrest Jews, while Vichy also had to consider the reactions of the Church and the general population, and therefore the way in which popular opinion evolved, which the Nazis therefore also had to consider. As a consequence, there was a chain of interdependence that, to a certain extent, limited the Nazis' power in France. This explains the low rate of deportation of French Jews that was a result of their longstanding integration as French citizens, which operated as a kind of passive dissuasion on the Vichy leadership. In the summer of 1942, even the limited mobilization on the part of civil society and the Church against the arrests of foreign Jews put public pressure Vichy that led its leaders to limit their participation in the deportation. During the critical period when the "Final Solution" was underway, French society acted as a safeguard, holding back Vichy officials from becoming more involved in this criminal enterprise. The journalist Eric Zemmour's provocative assertion that Pétain "saved" the French Jews is completely unfounded,[27] especially

bearing mind that in 1944, as the fascist leanings of the Vichy government became more accentuated, it began to round up French Jews for
deportation as well.

To these internal elements we must add the weight of the international context. The extermination of the Jews in Eastern Europe began
after the German invasion of the USSR in the summer of 1941. After
the United States entered the war the process was stepped up, creating
the conditions for its expansion into Western Europe in 1942. This
period, when Hitler's armies seemed invincible, saw the beginning of
mass arrests in France. Pierre Laval, who returned to power on
18 April, was convinced that Berlin would conquer the whole of
Europe. The strategy of the new head of government was to try to
create a special place for France within this new German Europe. In
the summer of 1942, the delivery to the Nazis of thousands of foreign
Jews, whom Vichy was in any case happy to be rid of, was for Laval a
strategic question of doing what the occupying forces demanded, in the
hope that in return it would mean advantageous German policies
regarding France.

In November 1942, Allied forces landed in Casablanca. In reaction,
the Wehrmacht invaded the Free Zone, which meant that they now
occupied the whole of France, with the exception of the southeastern
part of the country, which it left in Italian hands. From one day to the
next, Jews who had escaped from the Occupied to the Free Zone
found themselves in greater danger. Meanwhile, the Italian authorities
refused to arrest Jews on their territory, and the Italian zone became
for the time being a relative safe haven. This did not last long; a few
months later the international theater of war changed, beginning to
turn against the interests of the Axis powers (Germany, Italy, Japan):
firstly with the battle of Stalingrad, in February 1943, then with the
surrender of Italy, in September 1943. As discussed above, the gradual
reversal on the military front also influenced Vichy's last-minute decision to refuse to ratify the law on denaturalizing the Jews.

Between 1943 and 1944, arresting Jews was not a principal concern
of the Vichy leadership, who had plenty of other things to worry about,
including supplying the work contingents demanded by Berlin as part
of the STO, and fighting the Maquis. Battling the Resistance took up a
huge amount of the resources of both the German and the French

forces. Although protecting Jews was not a specific objective of the Resistance, as it developed it helped divert the attention of the authorities to different priorities. In any case, in Vichy, people were making plans to jump ship.

There were, of course, many who did not forget their plans for the Jews: staunchly committed Nazis as well as French collaborators determined to help the Germans see the destruction of the Jews through to the end. In the final months of the Occupation, Aloïs Brunner enhanced his methods for capturing Jews and the numbers of deportations began to rise. The Allied landings of 6 June 1944 and the subsequent defeat of the Germans were the only events that would eventually put an end to these men's fanatical schemes.

By way of conclusion, I should point out that Marrus and Paxton wrote in 2015, "We find it troubling that some continue to wonder why so many Jews survived in France. Given the opportunities for survival, the question is rather, why did so many die?"[28] I had made the same observation in 1989, like them laying the blame on the French government: "If Vichy had really been determined to defend the Jews, Berlin would probably have had to accept deferring the final solution, either temporarily or permanently, as they did in other European countries. But then, Vichy would not have been Vichy."[29]

It is for this reason that the cause of their astonishment can be turned back at them. Given that the Vichy government was anti-Semitic and xenophobic, and that furthermore, these authors maintain that French public opinion was widely hostile to the Jews, one should instead wonder how it was possible for three-quarters of the Jews to survive in this country. This is the very enigma that is the subject matter of the present book.

It is my hope today that a new historiographical school of thought will develop that takes into account what led to the destruction of the Jews as planned by Hitler and also what curbed, limited and even impeded his endeavor of extermination. In this regard, I have never intended to present the case of France as being exceptional. My work purports to be simply one case study among others that can inspire further research that will take into account both the death and the survival of the Jews. Analyzing the Holocaust involves examining the destruction process as well as its containment.

CONCLUSION

Life, Death, Luck

This dry combination of facts does not evoke another element that I discovered in the course of researching this book. As I dug deeper into the subject, I began to feel increasingly attached to the various witness-participants. As I followed them through their years of suffering, there was one thing that I became aware of, which was that in spite of everything they desperately wanted to survive. In general, when we think about the Holocaust, we tend to think of the Jews as victims of the murderous fervor of the Nazis, forgetting that they were human beings, imbued with vitality and a zest for life. The lives of these men, women and children were not just composed of suffering and isolation. I encountered people who, even at the height of the persecution, built up friendships and embarked on romantic relationships, with Jews and non-Jews. These relationships were formed in wartime and some led to marriage and the birth of children during the Occupation. In the darkest hours of these terrible years, these were people who continued to believe in their own lives and in a future for their families.

There is another fact that we have not yet touched upon, and yet which is present throughout all these stories: luck. What can the historian, searching for rational explanations rather than random causes, do with luck? The theme of luck comes up again and again in the accounts of those who managed to avoid deportation. These people are obviously painfully aware of the fate of those who were sucked into the Nazi extermination machine. They consider their own survival to be almost a miracle. Such an assertion is understandable from a psychological point of view, but from a nuanced historical perspective it needs to be questioned. Yes, these people were lucky, because at any moment in any situation they, too, could have been arrested. But it was not only a matter of chance, just as the high rate of survival of Jews in France cannot only be explained as a being a matter of individual luck. From 1942 to 1944, Jews were able to take advantage of a social fabric woven through with disobedience, a nonconformist refusal to follow rules, and an instinct for resistance, within which, like other social outcasts and enemies of the occupying forces and Vichy, Jews were able to hide and survive. Let us never forget that this situation of apparent safety was always uncertain. No one was safe, whether from a denunciation or a slip-up. Death was always lurking in the shadows, until the very last moment, until the very last soldier from the occupying forces had left France.

NOTES

AUTHOR'S NOTE

1. Serge Klarsfeld, *Mémorial de la Déportation des Juifs de France*, Fils et Filles des Déportés Juifs de France, 2012, p. XVII.
2. The theme of darkness and light ran through Jacques Chirac's speech at the Pantheon in his tribute to the Righteous of France.
3. They are "Quitter la France" [Leaving France] (chap. 1); and "Quelle est ta souffrance?" [What Is Your Suffering?] (chap. 4).

INTRODUCTION: THE ENIGMA OF THE 75 PER CENT

1. US Department of State, "Signing ceremony for the US-France agreement on Holocaust Deportation from France," https://2009–2017.state.gov/p/eur/rls/rm/2014/dec/234917.htm
2. See Jacques Semelin, *Unarmed Against Hitler. Civilian Resistance in Europe, 1939–1943*, translated by Suzan Husserl-Kapit, Westport, CT, Praeger, 1993.
3. In 1941 Bulgaria occupied the territories of former Yugoslavia and Greece, from which 11,341 Jews were deported (98 per cent of them from Macedonia).
4. Pim Griffioen and Ron Zeller, "Comparing the persecution of the Jews in the Netherlands, France and Belgium, 1940–1945: similarities, differences, causes," in *The Persecution of the Jews in the Netherlands, 1940–1945*, New perspectives, Amsterdam, Vossiuspers UvA, Amsterdam University Press, 2012, pp. 55–92.
5. Marie-Anne Matard-Bonucci, *L'Italie fasciste et la persécution des Juifs*, Paris, Perrin, 2007.
6. Michael R. Marrus and Robert O. Paxton, *Vichy France and the Jews*, with a new foreword by Stanley Hoffmann, Stanford, CA, Stanford University Press, 1995, pp. 371–372.

7. The original edition of the book came out in French in 1981. In 2015, a revised and augmented version came out with the same publisher. It is worth noting that the forty lines devoted to the 75 per cent in the original edition were deleted. Michael R. Marrus and Robert O. Paxton, *Vichy et les Juifs*, Paris, Calman-Levy, 2015.

8. Susan Zuccotti, *The Holocaust, the French, and the Jews*, New York, Basic Books, 1993, p. 284.

9. Wolfgang Seibel, *Persecution and Rescue. The Politics of the "Final Solution" in France, 1940–1944*, Ann Arbor, MI, University of Michigan Press, 2016, [*Macht und Moral. Die Endlösung der Judenfrage in Frankreich, 1940– 1944*, Konstanz University Press, 2010].

10. Lucien Lazare, *La Résistance juive en France*, Paris, Stock, 1987; and Renée Poznanski, *Jews in France During World War II*, trans. Nathan Bracher, Hanover, NH, Brandeis University Press, 2001.

11. Bob Moore, *Survivors. Jewish Self-Help and Rescue in Nazi-Occupied Western Europe*, Oxford, Oxford University Press, 2010.

12. Laurent Joly, *Dénoncer les juifs sous l'Occupation. Paris, 1940–1944*, Paris, CNRS Éditions, 2017.

13. See my introduction to Jacques Semelin, Claire Andrieu, Sarah Gensburger (eds), *Resisting Genocide. The Multiple Forms of Rescue*, translated by Emma Bentley and Cynthia Schoch, London, Hurst, 2011.

14. Annie Kriegel, "De la résistance juive," *Pardès*, February 1985, p. 202.

15. A new edition of René Poznanski, *Les Juifs en France pendant la Seconde Guerre mondiale* was published in French in January 2018 with a new afterword: Paris, CNRS Éditions/"Biblis."

16. Ibid., p. 609.

17. See Serge Klarsfeld's figures in this book, chapter 1, pp. 10–11 and his interview concerning children with François-Guillaume Lorrain, *Le Point*, supplement to the 21 June 2012 edition. URL: http://www.lepoint.fr/culture/chaque-fois-que-j-ouvre-une-lettre-que-je-recois-une-photo-c-est-comme-si-la-vie-revenait-02-07-2012-1479961_3.php

18. Daniel Lee, *Pétain's Jewish Children: French Jewish Youth and the Vichy Regime, 1940–1942*, Oxford, Oxford University Press, 2014.

19. *L'Express*, 27 February 2008 (interview with Anne Vidalie).

1. IN SEARCH OF SAFETY

1. Doris Bensimon and Sergio Della Pergola, *La Population juive de France: socio-démographie et identité*, Jerusalem, The Institute of Contemporary Jewry, Hebrew University of Jerusalem, Paris, CNRS Éditions, 1984, pp. 25–35.

2. See Anne Grynberg, *Les Camps de la honte. Les internés juifs des camps*

français, 1939–1945, Paris, La Découverte, 1991 and Denis Peschanski, *La France des camps. L'internement, 1938–1946*, Paris, Gallimard, 2002.

3. Jean-Luc Leleu, "Les déplacements de population," in Jean-Luc Leleu, François Passera, Jean Quellien and Michel Daeffler (eds), *La France pendant la Seconde Guerre mondiale. Atlas historique*, Paris, Fayard/ Ministère de la Défense, 2010, p. 135.

4. Based on an estimate made in May 1944 by Maurice Brenner, a Jewish official living in France and working for the American Jewish Joint Distribution Committee, known as the JDC or Joint.

5. Serge Klarsfeld, *Vichy-Auschwitz. La "solution finale" de la question juive en France*, Paris, Fayard, 1983, new ed. published under the title *La Shoah en France*, vol. 1, Paris, Fayard, 2001, pp. 359–360.

6. See Chapters 2 and 3.

7. See David H. Weinberg, *Les Juifs à Paris de 1933 à 1939*, Paris, Calmann-Lévy, 1974, p. 15. "Sepharad" in medieval Hebrew refers to Spain, but the term took on a broader meaning to signify Spanish and Portuguese Jews who had fled the Inquisition to Italy and the Ottoman Empire; Jews from Avignon, Bordeaux, Bayonne; and from Palestine and North Africa.

8. The Ashkenazim are Jews with ties to the Germanic world: from Russia, Poland, and Alsace. Yiddish was the language of Eastern European Jews, while in Alsace and Germany, the Jews spoke Judeo-Alsatian or Judeo-German.

9. Doris Bensimon and Sergio Della Pergola, *La Population juive de France*, op. cit., pp. 25–35.

10. In Part One, I introduce a range of French and foreign Jews, individuals and families, whose experiences before and during the German occupation of France will be traced throughout the book.

11. Annie Kriegel, *Ce que j'ai cru comprendre*, Paris, Robert Laffont, 1991 and Jean-Jacques Becker, *Un soir de l'été 1942. Souvenirs d'un historien*, Paris, Larousse, 2009.

12. This is drawn from the testimony of Gérard Dreyfus written up by his son Jean-Marc in 2008 and sent to the author.

13. Michael R. Marrus, *Les Juifs de France à l'époque de l'affaire Dreyfus*, Paris, Calmann-Lévy, 1972.

14. See Marc Bloch, *Strange Defeat. A Statement of Evidence Written in 1940*, New York, W. W. Norton & Co., 1968, reissued 1999, pp. 3–4.

15. See Renée Poznanski, *Jews in France*, op. cit., p. 4.

16. Anne Grynberg and Catherine Nicault, "Le culte israélite pendant la Seconde Guerre mondiale, droits et réalités d'exercice," *Archives Juives*, no. 28, 1995, pp. 72–88.

17. Nancy L. Green, *The Pltezl of Paris. Jewish Immigrant Workers in the Belle Époque*, New York, Holmes and Meier, 1986, p. 206.

18. Albert Grunberg, *Journal d'un coiffeur juif à Paris sous l'Occupation*, Paris, l'Atelier, 2001.

19. Michel Boivin, "Les populations étrangères," in Jean-Luc Leleu, François Passera, Jean Quellien and Michel Daeffler (eds), *La France pendant la Seconde Guerre mondiale. Atlas historique*, op. cit., p. 20.

20. Yves Lequin (ed.), *Histoire des étrangers et de l'immigration en France*, Paris, Larousse, 2006, p. 281.

21. See André Kaspi, *Les Juifs pendant l'Occupation*, Paris, Le Seuil, 1991, p. 29.

22. Bundists subscribed to the doctrine upheld by the *Bund* (the Yiddish acronym for the General Jewish Labor Alliance of Russia, Lithuania and Poland, a political and labor organization founded in Vilnius in 1897), which promoted Yiddish cultural identity while advocating non-Bolshevik revolutionary socialism. See Henri Minczeles, *Histoire générale du Bund*, Paris, Denoël, 1999.

23. See Renée Poznanski, *Jews in France*, op. cit., pp. 2 and 11.

24. Michel Roblin, *Les Juifs de Paris*, edited by A. et J. Picard, Paris, 1952, p. 73.

25. Joseph Minc, *L'Extraordinaire Histoire de ma vie ordinaire*, Paris, Le Seuil, 2006.

26. This is recounted by Stanley Hoffmann in Linda B. Miller and M. J. Smith, (eds) "To Be or Not to Be French," in *Ideas and Ideals. Essays on Politics in Honor of Stanley Hoffmann*, Boulder, CO, Westview Press, 1993, pp. 19–46; and in *Decline or Renewal? France since the 1930s*, New York, Viking Press, 1974; and in an interview with the author on 28 January 2009.

27. According to an interview conducted on 30 March 2006 by Jean-Baptiste Péretié for the "Mémoires de la Shoah" series available on the INA website.

28. Edgar Morin, *Vidal and his Family: From Salonica to Paris: the Story of a Sephardic Family in the Twentieth Century*, translated by Deborah Cowell, Brighton/Portland, Sussex Academic Press, 2009.

29. See Elkbir Atouf, "Une communauté prolétaire: les Juifs marocains de Saint-Fons, 1919–1946," *Archives Juives*, 2003/2, Vol. 36, pp. 121–130.

30. See André Kaspi, *Les Juifs pendant l'Occupation*, op. cit., pp. 179–180.

31. Jean Laloum, "Des Juifs d'Afrique du Nord au Pletzl? Une présence méconnue et des épreuves oubliées (1920–1945)," *Archives juives* 2005/2, no. 382, pp. 47–83.

32. According to the account of Edith Bloch-Hanau, recorded by her daughter Évelyne Bloch-Dano in 1991–1992 and provided to the author.

33. Alfred Grosser, *Une vie de Français. Mémoires*, Paris, Flammarion, 1997, pp. 17–27. The agreement signed by Hitler, Daladier, Chamberlain,

and Mussolini at the Munich Conference gave approval for Hitler's annexation of mainly German-speaking regions of Czechoslovakia, in particular the area called the Sudetenland.

34. Saul Friedländer, *When Memory Comes*, New York, Farrar, Straus and Giroux, 1979, pp. 24–31, 37–40, 44.

35. Mia Amalia Kanner, (with Eve Rosenzweig Kugler), *Shattered Crystals*, Lakewood, New Jersey, Cis Communications, 1997.

36. Among them, see Gérard Noiriel's important study, *Les Origines républicaines de Vichy*, Paris, Hachette, 1999.

37. Vicki Caron, *Uneasy Asylum. France and the Jewish Refugee Crisis, 1933–1942*, Palo Alto, CA, Stanford University Press, 1999.

38. Emmanuel Debono, *Aux origines de l'antiracisme. La LICA, 1927–1940*, Paris, CNRS Éditions, 2012, pp. 296–309.

39. Cited by Vicki Caron, ibid., p. 448.

40. See Rita Thalmann and Emmanuel Feinermann, *La Nuit de Cristal*, Paris, Robert Laffont, 1972.

41. Ralph Schor, *L'Antisémitisme en France dans l'entre-deux-guerres*, Complexe, 1991, pp. 9–10.

42. *Action française*, 28 April 1933, cited by Vicki Caron, *Uneasy Asylum*, p. 66.

43. Louis-Ferdinand Céline, *L'Ecole des cadavres*, Paris, Denoël, 1938, p. 161. Editor's translation.

44. See Vicki Caron, *Uneasy Asylum*, op. cit., pp. 23–24.

45. Maurice Rajsfus, *Des Juifs dans la collaboration. L'UGIF 1941–1944*, Paris, EDI, 1980.

46. See for example what Jean-Jacques Becker says about his father's feelings at the time, described in *Un soir de l'été 1942… Souvenirs d'un historien*, op. cit., p. 34.

47. See Michel Laffitte, *Les Juifs dans la France allemande*, Paris, Tallandier, 2006.

48. For greater detail on these various organizations, their activities, and the criticisms leveled at them, see the original French edition of the present book, *Persécutions et entraide*, Paris, Le Seuil/Les Arènes, 2013, pp. 55–56.

49. Catherine Nicault, "L'accueil des Juifs d'Europe centrale par la communauté juive française" in Karel A. Bartosek, René Gallissot and Denis Peschanski (eds), *De l'exil à la résistance. Réfugiés et immigrés d'Europe centrale en France, 1933–1945*, Saint-Denis/Paris, Presses Universitaires de Vincennes, Arcantère, 1989, p. 57.

50. It is important not to be misled by these figures. It was a conscript army whose actual strength was essentially limited to its fighting units. See Jean-Luc Leleu, "La défense nationale," *La France pendant la Seconde Guerre mondiale*, op. cit, p. 33.

51. See for example Eric Alary, *L'Exode, un drame oublié*, Paris, Perrin, 2010, p. 36.

52. Hanna Diamond, *Fleeing Hitler. France 1940*, Oxford, Oxford University Press, 2007, p. vii.

53. Marc Bloch, *Strange Defeat*, op. cit.

54. Irène Némirovsky, *Suite Française*, translated by Sandra Smith, New York, Random House/Vintage, 2006, p. 50.

55. Ibid., p. 46.

56. Robert Paxton, *Vichy France. Old Guard and New Order, 1940–1944*, New York, Columbia University Press, 2001.

57. Claire Zalc, *Dénaturaliser, les retraits de nationalités sous Vichy*, Paris, Le Seuil, 2016.

58. Léon Strauss, *Réfugiés, expulsés, évadés d'Alsace et de Moselle*, Colmar, Jérôme do Bentzinger Editeur, 2010, p. 13.

59. René Mayer, "Une tragédie frontalière," in *Saisons d'Alsace* no. 105, 1989, republished in 2009 as *Alsace, la grande encyclopédie des années de guerre, 1939–1945*, Strasbourg, Éditions La Nuée Bleue, pp. 45–46.

60. Regarding this period, see for example the account of Madame Edith Bloch, née Hanau, recorded by her daughter Evelyne Bloch-Dano, in January/February 1991 and October 1992, and given to the author.

61. Léon Strauss, *Réfugiés, expulsés, évadés d'Alsace et de Moselle*, op. cit., p. 113.

62. Serge Klarsfeld, *Le Calendrier...*, op. cit.

63. See Daniel Fuchs, "Enquête sur les victimes d'Alsace-Moselle: le cas du Haut-Rhin. Spécificité des départements concordataires," in Patrick Cabanel and Jacques Fijalkow (eds), *Histoire régionale de la Shoah en France*, Paris, Les Éditions de Paris, 2001, pp. 447–448.

64. Frederick Raymes and Menachem Mayer, *Are the Trees in Bloom Over There?* Jerusalem, Yad Vashem, 2002.

65. Éric Alary, *L'Exode, un drame oublié*, op. cit., pp. 41–42.

66. Interview with Simon and Guy Benayoun, 4 November 2011.

67. Interview with Serge Klarsfeld, 17 May 2009. This regiment put up fierce resistance to the Germans in the Battle of the Somme and lost two-thirds of its men.

68. Stanley Hoffmann, "To Be or Not to Be French," op. cit., pp. 20–21.

69. Interview with Joseph Minc, 23 April 2010.

70. Arlette Scali, *Les Justes de Graulhet*, Paris, Editions Scali, 2007, p. 77.

71. Ibid., p. 81.

72. Interview with Denis Lindon, 24 February 2010.

73. Jean-Jacques Becker, *Un soir de l'été 1942*, op. cit, pp. 42–45.

74. Interview with Francine Wolff, née Weiller, 17 June 2010.

75. Nicolas Mariot and Claire Zalc, *Face à la persécution. 991 Juifs dans la guerre*, Paris, Odile Jacob, 2010, p. 75.

76. Léa Markscheid, *Le Passé au présent*, Nages, Centre de Recherches du Patrimoine de Rieumontagné, 2009, pp. 23, 73 and 75.

77. Figure given by Éric Alary on the basis of estimations by the Vichy administration. See *L'Exode, un drame oublié*, op. cit, p. 342.

78. Léon Werth, *33 jours*, Paris, Viviane Hamy, 1992; new ed. Paris, Magnard, 2002, pp. 17, 23–24, 33, 69–70, 171, 177, 179–180, 181.

79. Mia Amalia Kanner, *Shattered Crystals*, op. cit., pp. 66–91.

80. Jean-Jacques Becker, *Un soir de l'été 1942*, op. cit., pp. 46–50

81. Annie Kriegel, *Ce que j'ai cru comprendre*, op. cit., p. 118.

82. Stanley Hoffmann, "A Retrospective on World Politics," in *Ideas and Ideals. Essays on Politics in Honor of Stanley Hoffmann*, op.cit., p. 4.

83. Philippe Burrin, *La France à l'heure allemande. 1940–1944*, Paris, Le Seuil, 1995, pp. 183–192.

84. Eric Alary, *L'Exode, un drame oublié*, op. cit., p. 354.

85. Archives de la Délégation française auprès de la commission allemande d'armistice (DFCCA), IV, cited by Léon Strauss, *Réfugiés, expulsés, évadés d'Alsace et de Moselle*, op. cit., p. 98.

86. Edgar Morin, *Vidal and his Family*, op. cit., pp. 158–165.

87. Léon Poliakov, *L'Auberge des musiciens*, Paris, Mazarine, 1981, pp. 71–77.

88. Jean-Jacques Becker, *Un soir de l'été 1944*, op. cit., pp. 53–54.

89. Mia Amalia Kanner, *Shattered Crystals*, op. cit., pp. 123–125. Sal was able to get out of Gurs because he had been interned as a foreigner without papers. It was not until later, as of 3 October 1940, that a Vichy law authorized prefects to intern foreigners merely for being Jewish.

90. See Jean-Marie Guillon, "La Provence refuge et piège. Autour de Varian Fry et de la filière américaine," in Max Lagarrigue (ed.) *L'Europe de la défaite, 1940, la France du repli*, Toulouse, Editions Privat, 2001, p. 284. See also Varian Fry, *Assignment Rescue. An Autobiography*, New York, Scholastic (reprint), 1993.

91. The subsection entitled "Quitter la France" in the original French edition of this book was deleted due to space requirements for the English edition.

92. See Olivier Philipponnat and Patrick Lienhardt, *The Life of Irène Némirovsky*, translated by Euan Cameron, New York, Knopf, 2010.

93. See Laurent Joly, *Vichy et la solution finale. Histoire du Commissariat général aux questions juives.1941–1944*, Paris, Grasset, 2006, pp. 53 ff.

94. Tal Bruttmann, "Les camps d'internement," in *La France pendant la Seconde Guerre mondiale. Atlas historique*, op. cit., pp. 202–203.

95. Ibid.

96. Éric Alary, "Les Juifs et la ligne de démarcation, 1940–1943," *Les Cahiers de la Shoah*, 5, 2001, p. 33.

97. See Jacques Biélinky, *Un journaliste juif à Paris sous l'Occupation. Journal 1940–1942*, Paris, Editions du Cerf, 1992, p. 176.

98. Edgar Morin, *Vidal and his Family*, op. cit., pp. 167–169.

99. Serge Klarsfeld, *Le Calendrier...*, op. cit., pp. 69, 123, 168.

100. Laurent Joly, "La persécution des Juifs," in *La France pendant la Seconde Guerre mondiale. Atlas historique*, op. cit., pp. 190–191.

101. In the Occupied Zone, these figures refer only to those over age 15.

102. Laurent Joly, "La persécution des Juifs," in *La France pendant la Seconde Guerre mondiale. Atlas historique*, op. cit., p. 191.

103. On 16 and 17 July 1942 over 13,000 people, mostly foreign Jews, were arrested in Paris. A total of 8,160 of them—4,115 children, 2,916 women, and 1,129 men—were imprisoned in the Vélodrome d'Hiver, known as the "Vel' d'Hiv,'" an indoor cycle racetrack located in the 15th arrondissement of Paris, for five days, without food, in stifling heat. Sanitary provisions were minimal. From there they were taken to the camps at Drancy, Beaune-la-Rolande and Pithiviers, and then deported to Auschwitz. Fewer than 100 survived the war.

104. Figures sent by *SS-Oberstrurmführer* Rothke to the Reich Main Security Office on 18 July 1942, in a letter reproduced by Serge Klarsfeld in *Le Calendrier...*, op. cit., p. 531.

105. Annie Kriegel, *Ce que j'ai cru comprendre*, op. cit., pp. 156–157.

106. Jean-Jacques Becker, *Un soir de l'été 1942*, op. cit., pp. 77–81.

107. Éric Alary, "Les Juifs et la ligne de démarcation, 1940–1943," op. cit., p. 37.

108. Laurent Joly, "Rafles et déportations des Juifs," *La France dans la Seconde Guerre mondiale*, op. cit., pp. 208–209.

109. Daniel Carpi, *Between Mussolini and Hitler. The Jews and the Italian Authorities in France and Tunisia*, Hanover, NY, Brandeis University Press/University Press of New England, 1994, p. 142.

110. Léon Poliakov, *La Condition des Juifs en France sous l'Occupation italienne*, Paris, Editions Du Centre, 1946.

111. See Serge Klarsfeld, *Vichy-Auschwitz*, op. cit., chapter 7, pp. 209–258.

112. David Rodogno, "La politique des occupants italiens à l'égard des Juifs en France métropolitaine. Humanisme ou pragmatisme?" *Vingtième Siècle*, no. 93, 2007.

113. Paola Bartilotti et al., "L'occupation italienne," in *La France pendant la Seconde Guerre mondiale*, op. cit., pp. 68–69.

114. Serge Klarsfeld, *Vichy-Auschwitz*, op. cit., p. 211. A study of the area suggests that there were around 20,000 Jews in the Alpes-Maritimes department in March 1943: see Jean-Louis Panicacci, "Les persécutions antisémites dans les Alpes-Maritimes—été 1940–été 1944," in Robert Mencherini (ed.), *Provence-Auschwitz. De l'internement des étrangers à la déportation des Juifs (1939–1944)*, Aix-en-Provence, PUP, 2007,

and Jean Kleinmann, *La Vie des Juifs à Nice Durant la Seconde Guerre mondiale et leur déportation*, PhD thesis, University of Nice, 2003.

115. Liliane Klein-Lieber, "Témoignage sur les opérations de sauvetage," *Annales ESC*, May–June 1993, no. 3, p. 674. On 3 June 1941, a warrant for expulsion was issued against Jews living in the Vichy-Cusset-Bellerive zone. See Renée Poznanski, *Jews in France*, op. cit., p. 72.

116. Jean-Jacques Becker, *Un soir de l'été 1942*, op. cit., p. 89.

117. Léon Poliakov, *L'Auberge des musiciens*, op. cit., pp. 113 ff.

118. Edgar Morin, *Vidal and his Family*, op. cit., p. 171.

119. Jean-Jacques Becker, *Un soir de l'été 1942*, op. cit., pp. 93–95.

120. Oser Warszawski, *On ne peut pas se plaindre*, French translation by Marie Warszawski, Paris, Liana Levi, 1997, pp. 93 and 99.

121. Express letter from the Interior Ministry—National Police to Regional Prefects, 6 December 1942, ADC-976 W 104, *Instructions* file.

122. ADC-976 W104.

123. Renée Poznanski, *Jews in France*, op. cit., p. 394.

124. See AIU, CC-17, "Albert Lévy's trip to Nimes, Toulouse, Pau, Montauban, Agen from June 22 to July 3, 1943." cited by Renée Poznanski, *Jews in France*, op. cit., p. 394.

125. Ibid.

126. See the report "l'État actuel du problème juif en France" by Röthke, 21 July 1943, cited by Serge Klarsfeld, *La Shoah en France*, vol. III, *Le Calendrier...*, op. cit., p. 1583.

127. Report by the Section d'Enquête et de Contrôle du CGQJ (AN, AJ, 38–243).

128. Renée Poznanski, *Jews in France*, op. cit., p. 390.

129. See for example Jean-William Dereymez (ed.), *Le Refuge et le piège. Les Juifs dans les Alpes, 1938–1945*, Paris, L'Harmattan, 2008.

130. Tal Bruttmann, "The 'Brunner Aktion': A Struggle against Rescue (September 1943–March 1944)," in Jacques Semelin, Claire Andrieu, Sarah Gensburger (eds), *Resisting Genocide*, op. cit., p. 290.

131. Stanley Hoffmann, "To Be or Not to Be French," op. cit., pp. 24–25.

132. Léon Poliakov, *L'Auberge des musiciens*, op. cit., pp. 113–153.

133. Léon Werth, *Déposition*, Paris, Viviane Hamy, 1946, new ed. Paris, Le Seuil, coll. "Points," 2007, pp. 246 and 248.

134. Hans-Ulrich Jost, "Menace et repliement," *Nouvelle Histoire de la Suisse et des Suisses*, Lausanne, Payot, 1998 [2nd ed.], p. 689.

135. Ruth Fivaz-Silbermann, "The Swiss Reaction to the Nazi Genocide: Active Refusal, Passive Help," in Jacques Semelin, Claire Andrieu, Sarah Gensburger (eds), *Resisting Genocide*, op. cit., pp. 231–258.

136. Confidential memo of 1 September 1942 sent to the district of Geneva, State, Justice and Police Archives of Geneva, Eb. A7.17.1.67,

cited in Catherine Santschi (ed.), *Les Réfugiés civils et la frontière gene-voise durant la Deuxième Guerre mondiale*, Geneva, Geneva State Archives, 2000, p. 7.

137. The orders were subsequently modified and while unaccompanied children under 16 continued to be admitted, only families with a child under age 6 were allowed to enter the country.

138. Claude Klein, "Un témoignage des années d'Occupation: de Grenoble à la Suisse," *Esprit*, Nov. 2008, no. 349, p. 191. Cécile Klein-Hechel writes in her testimony that Berthe was sixteen when they crossed the Swiss border; her son Claude, who published his mother's account, pointed out that it was a mistake, and that his sister, who was born in 1928, was fourteen at the time.

139. See ibid., pp. 192–193.

140. Ibid., pp. 195–195.

141. See Ruth Fivaz-Silbermann, *Le Refoulement de réfugiés civils juifs à la frontière franco-genevoise durant la Seconde Guerre mondiale*, Paris, Beate Klarsfeld Foundation, 2000, 140 p. This study is based on archives from the territorial arrondissement of Geneva (the military author-ity in charge of reception or *refoulement*), which have been preserved nearly in their entirety. It also draws on the departmental archives of Haute-Savoie.

142. See the Final Report of the Independent Commission of Experts Switzerland-Second World War [Bergier report], *Switzerland, National Socialism and the Second World War*, Zurich, Pendo, 2002, p. 117.

143. Ruth Fivaz-Silbermann, in Jacques Semelin, Claire Andrieu and Sarah Gensburger (eds), *Resisting Genocide*, op. cit., p. 258.

144. Regarding the ambiguities and contradictions of Switzerland's poli-cies, see the final report by Cicad, *La Suisse, le national-socialisme et la Seconde Guerre mondiale*, Berne, 2002, available at https://www.uek. ch/fr/schlussbericht/synthese/uekf.pdf (accessed 28 January 2018).

145. Danièle Rozenberg, *L'Espagne contemporaine et la question juive. Les fils renoués de la mémoire et de l'histoire*, Toulouse, Presses universitaires du Mirail, 2006, p. 174.

146. Saul Friedländer, *When Memory Comes*, op. cit., pp. 88–90.

147. Laurent Joly, "La persécution des Juifs," dans *La France pendant la Seconde guerre mondiale*, op. cit., pp. 190–191.

148. Maurice Brenner's report for the Joint, on file at the Ghetto Fighters' House, Israel.

149. Jacob Kaplan, "French Jewry under the Occupation," *The American Jewish Year Book 5706, 1945–1946*, Philadelphia (PA), The Jewish Publication Society of America, vol. 47, 1945–1946, pp. 71–118.

150. Michel Laffitte, *Les Juifs dans la France allemande*, 2006, op. cit., p. 223.

151. Report on file at the Ghetto Fighters' House Museum, Israel.

152. "Legitimation cards" were identification cards brought into circulation as of July 1942. They theoretically protected UGIF employees and volunteers, as well as their family, from internment and deportation. They had to be renewed quarterly. See Michel Laffitte, "L'UGIF face aux mesures antisémites de 1942," *Les Cahiers de la Shoah*, 2007/1, no. 9, pp. 123–180.

153. The term "synthesized" was sometimes used to describe Jews who had "real-fake" identification, endowing them with an apparently legal, "Aryan" identity.

154. Interview with Madeleine Scherman, née Grunfeld, 15 June 2010.

155. Joseph Minc, *L'Extraordinaire Histoire de ma vie ordinaire*, op. cit.

156. Alfred Grunberg, *Journal d'un coiffeur juif à Paris sous l'Occupation*, op. cit.

157. Anne Frank, *The Diary of a Young Girl*, New York, Random House/ Doubleday, 1967.

2. IN THE FACE OF PERSECUTION: STRATEGIES FOR SURVIVAL

1. Annette Wieviorka, *Déportation et génocide. Entre la mémoire et l'oubli*, Paris, Plon, 1992, p. 161.

2. See for example Jacqueline Mesnil-Amar, *Maman, What Are We Called Now?* translated by Francine Yorke, London, Persephone Books, 2015.

3. See the now classic work by the sociologist Helen Fein, *Accounting for Genocide. National Responses and Jewish Victimization during the Holocaust*, New York, Macmillan, 1979.

4. Saul Friedländer, *When Memory Comes*, op. cit., pp. 36, 40, 50.

5. See Vivette Samuel, *Rescuing the Children. A Holocaust Memoir*, translated by Charles B. Paul, Madison, University of Wisconsin Press, 2002.

6. Nicolas Mariot and Claire Zalc, *Face à la persécution. 991 Juifs dans la guerre*, op. cit., p. 127. The quantitative approach taken by these sociologists on the factors of persecution in Lens (a city in northern France located in the "forbidden zone") is particularly rich (cf. chapter 2, pp. 91–92). Applying similar methodology, Marnix Croes studied the factors of survival in an area of the Netherlands. Marnix Croes, "Facteurs de survie face à la Shoah: le cas de la province néerlandaise d'Overijssel," in Claire Zalc, Tal Bruttmann, Ivan Ermakoff et al., *Pour une microhistoire de la Shoah*, Paris, Le Seuil, 2012.

7. Laurent Joly, *L'Antisémitisme de bureau. Enquête au cœur de la préfecture de Police de Paris et du Commissariat général aux questions juives, 1940–1944*, Paris, Grasset, 2011, pp. 34, 42, 112 and 134.

8. Jean-Jacques Becker, *Un soir de l'été 1942*, op. cit., p. 57.

9. A law dated 7 October 1940 revoked the Crémieux decree for Algerian Jews (art. 1). Their status was henceforth assimilated to that of "indigenous Muslims" (art. 2). Only war veterans, recipients of the Legion of Honor for military feats, the Military Medal and the Croix de Guerre were exempt (art. 4), as well as those who had given their service to France (art. 5).

10. See Edgar Morin, *Vidal and his Family*, op. cit., p. 174.

11. See Robert Badinter, "Mort d'un israélite français. Hommage à maître Pierre Masse," *Le Débat*, no. 158, 2010/1.

12. Renée Poznanski, *Jews in France During World War II*, op. cit., pp. 88–89.

13. Article 8 of the second *Statut des Juifs*, dated 2 June 1941, specified that Jews who could prove five generations of French ancestry could request an exemption.

14. See Pierre Vidal-Naquet, *Mémoires 1. La brisure et l'attente 1930–1955*, Paris, Le Seuil/La Découverte, 1995, pp. 107–111.

15. "Honorary Aryan" was a term used in German anti-Semitic legislation to designate "useful Jews."

16. See Maurice Martin du Gard, *La Chronique de Vichy*, Paris, Flammarion, 1948, p. 152.

17. Léon Werth, *Déposition*, op. cit., pp. 225–226.

18. Léa Markscheid, *Le Passé au présent*, op. cit., p. 89.

19. Mia Amalia Kanner, *Shattered Crystals*, op. cit., p. 68.

20. Léon Poliakov, *L'Auberge des musiciens*, op. cit., pp. 78–79.

21. Edgar Morin, *Vidal and his Family*, op. cit., p. 167.

22. Albert Grunberg, *Journal d'un coiffeur juif à Paris sous l'Occupation*, op. cit., pp. 46–47.

23. David Diamant, *Le Billet Vert*, Paris, Éditions Renouveau, 1977, p. 26.

24. Renée Poznanski, *Jews in France*, op. cit., p. 61.

25. Nicolas Mariot and Claire Zalc, *Face à la persécution*, op. cit., p. 49.

26. Ibid., p. 61.

27. Jacques Biélinky, *Un journaliste juif à Paris sous l'Occupation*, op. cit, p. 44.

28. Léon Poliakov, *L'Auberge des musiciens*, op. cit., p. 82.

29. Danielle Rozenberg, *L'Espagne et les Juifs pendant la Seconde Guerre mondiale*, op. cit., p. 169.

30. Serge Klarsfeld, "Le calendrier de la persécution des Juifs de France," in *La Shoah en France*, Paris, Fayard, 2001, p. 655.

31. In addition to Spanish and Italian, there were a few other protected nationalities, including Jews of Turkish and Argentine citizenship. But this diplomatic protection remained relative and was subject to the evolution of Berlin's relations with these countries.

32. Annie Kriegel, *Ce que j'ai cru comprendre*, op. cit., p. 127.

33. Robert Debré, *L'Honneur de vivre*, Stock/Hermann, Paris, 1974.

34. See Nadine Satiat, *Gertrude Stein*, Paris, Flammarion, 2010, pp. 849–966.

35. Jean-Marc Dreyfus and Sarah Gensburger, *Des camps dans Paris. Austerlitz, Lévitan, Bassano, juillet 1943–août 1944*, Paris, Fayard, 2003, p. 78.

36. Liora Israel, *Robes noires, années sombres. Avocats et magistrats en résistance pendant la Seconde Guerre mondiale*, Paris, Fayard, 2005.

37. See Philippe Fabre, "L'identité légale des Juifs sous Vichy. La contribution des juges," *Labyrinthe*, 2000, no. 7, *La Fabrique de l'identité*, pp. 23–41.

38. See Philippe Fabre, *Le Conseil d'État et Vichy. Le contentieux de l'antisémitisme*, Publication de la Sorbonne, Paris, 2002, p. 363.

39. André Kaspi, *Les Juifs pendant l'Occupation*, op. cit., pp. 274–275.

40. Serge, Klarsfeld, *Le Calendrier…*, op. cit., p. 835.

41. See Jean-Marc Dreyfus and Sarah Gensburger, *Des camps dans Paris. Austerlitz, Lévitan, Bassano, juillet 1943–août 1944*, op. cit., p. 78.

42. See especially Jean-Marc Dreyfus and Sarah Gensburger, *Des camps dans Paris*, op. cit., p. 248.

43. Joseph Billig, *Le Commissariat général aux questions juives (1941–1944)*, Paris, Editions du Centre, 3 vol., 1955–1960.

44. Jean Mattéoli and Claire Andrieu, *La Spoliation financière, mission d'étude sur la spoliation des Juifs en France*, Paris, La Documentation française, 2000, vol. 2, p. 10.

45. Jean Mattéoli and Claire Andrieu, *La Spoliation financière*, vol. 1, p. 10.

46. Jean-Marc Dreyfus, *Pillage sur ordonnances. Aryanisation et restitution des banques en France. 1940–1943*, Paris, Fayard, 2003.

47. Jean-Jacques Becker, *Un soir de l'été 1942*, op. cit., pp. 69–70.

48. Interview with Annette Krajcer-Janin, 12 March 2010.

49. Jean Mattéoli and Claire Andrieu, *La Spoliation financière*, op. cit., vol. 2, p. 15.

50. Cited by Jean-Marc Dreyfus, *Pillages sur ordonnances*, op. cit., p. 86.

51. See Pierre Assouline, *Le Dernier des Camondo*, Paris, Gallimard, 1997, pp. 251–275.

52. Tal Bruttmann, *Aryanisation économique et spoliations en Isère (1940–1944)*, Grenoble, Presses Universitaires de Grenoble, 2010.

53. Antoine Prost (ed.), *Aryanisation économique et restitutions*, Paris, La Documentation française, 2000, p. 41.

54. "Situation in Paris," archives of the Prefecture de Police, cited by Renée Poznanski, *The Jews in France*, op. cit., p. 40.

55. See as an example the leather trade, Florent le Bot, *La Fabrique réactionnaire. Antisémitisme, spoliations et corporatisme dans le cuir, 1930–1950*, Paris, Presses de Sciences Po, 2007. For real estate, see the figures in Antoine Prost's report (ed.), *Aryanisation économique et spoliations*, op. cit., p. 41.

56. See Françoise Job, *Gustave Nordon (1877–1944)*, Nancy, Presses Universitaires de Nancy, 1992.

57. Albert Grunberg, *Journal d'un coiffeur juif à Paris sous l'Occupation*, op. cit., pp. 207–302.

58. See Renée Poznanski, *Jews in France*, op. cit., p. 41.

59. Jean-Jacques Becker, *Un soir de l'été 1942*, op. cit., p. 69.

60. Jean-Marc Dreyfus, *Pillages sur ordonnance*, op. cit., pp. 185–186.

61. Ibid., pp. 113–114.

62. Arlette Scali, *Les Justes de Graulhet*, op. cit., pp. 77–90.

63. Ibid., p. 114.

64. Philippe Erlanger, *La France sans étoile*, Plon, 1974, p. 170.

65. See AJ 40548, dossier 6, 2 April 1942.

66. Such was the case of Dean Dottin in Toulouse, who cancelled all the courses given by prestigious Jewish and Freemason professors in his institution, including Jankelevitch and Meyerson.

67. Tristan Lecoq, "Gustave Monod, l'inspecteur qui a dit non," *L'Histoire*, no. 357, Oct. 2010. See the report Gustave Monod sent to the rector in Claude Singer, *Vichy, l'université et les Juifs*, Paris, Les Belles Lettres, 1992, pp. 373–374.

68. Claude Singer, *Vichy, l'université et les Juifs*, op. cit., pp. 170–177.

69. See Samuel Abrahamovitsch's testimony filed with the Commission d'Histoire de la Deuxième Guerre Mondiale, 1957 session, A.D. Valence. It was made available to me by Bernard Delpale, to whom I address my thanks.

70. Claude Singer, *Vichy, l'université et les Juifs*, op. cit., pp. 165–167.

71. Bruno Halioua, *Blouses blanches, étoiles jaunes*, Paris, Liana Lévi, 2000, pp. 112–114.

72. Léo Hamon, "Étude sur la situation des Juifs en zone occupée," *Cahiers de l'IHTP*, no. 22, 1992.

73. Ibid., pp. 94–95.

74. CDJC/CXVII-116; René Leriche, *Souvenir de ma vie morte*, Paris, Le Seuil, 1956. See also Joseph Billig, *Le Commissariat général aux questions juives*, op. cit., pp. 29–31.

75. See the book of recollections written by his daughter, Pierrette Epsztein, *L'Homme sans larmes. Roman*, Paris, Petite Capitale, 2009.

76. Joseph Minc, *L'Histoire extraordinaire de ma vie ordinaire*, Paris, Le Seuil, 2006.

77. See for example the experience of Serge Lapidus as a young man. Serge Lapidus, *Étoile jaune dans la France des années noires. Onze récits parallèles de jeunes rescapés*, Paris, L'Harmattan, 2000, pp. 15–98.

78. Marie-Juliette Vielcazat-Petitcol, *Lot-et-Garonne, Terre d'exil terre d'asile. Les réfugiés Juifs pendant la Seconde Guerre mondiale*, Editions d'Albret, 2006, p. 191–194.

79. See also Peter Gaida, *Camps de travail sous Vichy. Les "Groupes de Travailleurs Étrangers" (GTE) en France et en Afrique du Nord 1940–1944*, 2008.

80. Anne Grynberg and Catherine Nicault, "Le culte israélite pendant la Seconde Guerre mondiale, droits et réalités d'exercice," *Archives juives*, no. 28, 1995, p. 74.

81. According to the biography of Julien Weill by Yvette Rachel Kaufman published in the *Almanach du KKL*, Strasbourg, 1982.

82. Alain-René Michel, *Les Éclaireurs israélites de France pendant la Seconde Guerre mondiale*, Paris, Éditions des EIF, 1984, p. 85.

83. Ibid., p. 93.

84. See Daniel Lee, *Pétain's Jewish Children. French Jewish Youth and the Vichy Regime, 1940–1942*, Oxford, Oxford University Press, 2014.

85. Katy Hazan and Georges Weill, "The OSE and the Resue of Jewish Children, from the Prewar to the Postwar Period," in Jacques Semelin, Claire Andrieu, Sarah Gensburger, *Resisting Genocide*, op. cit., p. 269.

86. Mia Amalia Kanner, *Shattered Crystals*, op. cit.

87. Ibid.

88. The complete list can be found in Michel Laffitte, *Juif dans la France allemande*, 2006, op. cit., pp. 398–403.

89. Maurice Rajsfus, *Des Juifs dans la collaboration. L'UGIF, 1941–1944*, Paris, EDI, 1980 and Jacques Adler, *Face à la persécution. Les organisations juives à Paris de 1940 à 1944*, Paris, Calmann-Lévy, 1985.

90. Interview with Serge Klarsfeld in *Combat pour la Diaspora*, nos. 23–24, 3rd quarter 1988, p. 89.

91. Michel Laffitte, *Un engrenage fatal. L'UGIF face aux réalités de la Shoah, 1941–1944*, preface by Pierre Vidal-Naquet, Paris, Liana Levi, 2003.

92. See the passages Michel Laffitte devoted to Jewish furriers in his book *Un engrenage fatal*, op. cit., pp. 117–120.

93. See Boris Schreiber, *Un silence d'environ une demi-heure*, Paris, Le Cherche-Midi, 1996, p. 624.

94. Mia Amalia Kanner, *Shattered Crystals*, op. cit., pp. 158–159.

95. Peter Gaida. "Les camps de travail de l'Organisation Todt en France 1940–1944," in Christian Chevandier and Jean-Claude Daumas (eds), *Travailler dans les entreprises sous l'Occupation*, Besançon, Presses universitaires de Franche-Comté, 2007, p. 253.

96. *Revue d'histoire de la Shoah*, "Les Éclaireurs israélites de France dans la guerre," Sept.-Dec. 1997, no. 161, p. 90.

97. See Asher Cohen, *Persécutions et sauvetages, Juifs et Français sous l'Occupation et sous Vichy*, Paris, Editions du Cerf, 1993, p. 183.

98. Martin de La Soudière, *Jours de guerre au village. 1939–1950. Années noires, années vertes en Auvergne et Margeride*, Polignac, Editions du Roure, 2011, pp. 94–95.

99. Jean Samuel and Jean-Marc Dreyfus, *Il m'appelait Pikolo. Un compagnon de Primo Levi raconte*, Paris, Robert Laffont, 2007.

100. Interview with Jacqueline Feldman, 4 November 2009.

101. Martin de La Soudière, *Jours de guerre au village*, op. cit., p. 96.

102. For a discussion of the criteria distinguishing internment from house arrest, see Sandra Marc, *Les Juifs de Lacaune sous Vichy (1942–1944). Assignation à résidence et persécution sous Vichy*, Paris, L'Harmattan, 2001, p. 38.

103. Testimony of Maurice Friedländer, cited in ibid., p. 55.

104. Interview with Jacques Fogelman, cited in ibid., p. 84.

105. Léa Markscheid, *Le Passé au présent*, op. cit., pp. 99–100, 108 and 114–115.

106. Léon Poliakov, *L'Auberge des musiciens*, op. cit., p. 114.

107. Alfred Grosser, *Une vie de Français. Mémoires*, Paris, Flammarion, 1997.

108. Michel Laffitte, *Juif dans la France allemande*, 2006, op. cit., p. 253.

109. See chapter 4.

110. Philippe-Jean Hesse and Jean-Pierre Le Crom (eds), *La Protection sociale sous le régime de Vichy*, Rennes, Presses Universitaires de Rennes, 2001.

111. Ibid., p. 163.

112. Regarding the notion of "state of need" justifying payment of this allowance, see the decree of 13 September 1940, *JO*, 14 September 1940, p. 4990.

113. Refugees from evacuated regions of Alsace and Moselle were granted preferential treatment. See Léon Strauss, *Réfugiés, expulsés, évadés d'Alsace et de Lorraine, 1940–1945*, Colmar, Bentzinger éditeur, 2010, p. 92.

114. See Renée Poznanski's interesting analysis in this regard in *Jews in France*, op. cit., p. 469.

115. Philippe-Jean Hesse and Jean-Pierre Le Crom (eds), *La Protection sociale sous le régime de Vichy*, op. cit., p. 168.

116. See Christophe Capuano's dissertation, *Le "familial" en France sous le régime de Vichy: territoires, réseaux, trajectoires. Les exemples de la Bourgogne et de la Franche-Comté*, Université de Bourgogne, 2008, pp. 543–550.

117. Fred Raymes and Menachem Mayer, *Are the Trees in Bloom Over There?* op. cit., pp. 72–76.

118. Bernard Reviriego, "Les étrangers dans la région de Limoges, entre "accueil" et détention," *Histoires et Mémoires*, no. 2, 2010, pp. 39–40.

119. Mia Amalia Kanner, *Shattered Crystals*, op. cit., p. 169.

120. Ibid., p. 190; see also Bernard Reviriego, "Les étrangers dans la région de Limoges…," op. cit., pp. 39–40.

121. Denis Peschanski, *La France des camps. L'internement 1938–1946*, Paris,

Gallimard, 2002, p. 146; Frederick Raymes and Menachem Mayer, *Are the Trees in Bloom Over There?* op. cit., p. 130.

122. Cited by Renée Poznanski, *Jews in France*, op. cit., p. 189.

123. Frederick Raymes and Menachem Mayer, *Are the Trees in Bloom Over There?* op. cit., p. 115.

124. Mia Amalia Kanner, *Shattered Crystals*, op. cit., pp. 135–137.

125. Frederick Raymes and Menachem Mayer, *Are the Trees in Bloom Over There?* op. cit., pp. 112–114.

126. Denis Peschanski, *La France des camps. L'internement, 1938–1946*, op. cit., p. 411.

127. See David Cesarani, *Final Solution: The Fate of the Jews 1933–1949*, Macmillan, 2016, and Christian Gerlach, *The Extermination of the European Jews*, Cambridge, Cambridge University Press, 2016.

3. BLENDING IN TO AVOID ARREST

1. Regarding the various phases of these negotiations, see Serge Klarsfeld, *Vichy-Auschwitz*, op. cit.

2. Simone Veil, *A Life* (trans. T. Black), London, Haus Publishing, 2009, p. 25.

3. This measure was not enforced in all western kingdoms. See Jean Chélini, *Histoire religieuse de l'Occident médiéval*, Paris, Hachette, 1991.

4. Serge Klarsfeld, *La Shoah en France…*, op. cit., vol. 2, p. 380, letter to General Oberg in Brinon dated 29 May 1942 which outlines which countries' citizens were obliged to wear the yellow star.

5. Michel Laffitte gives the following figures: of the 100,455 registered, 92,600 Jews received the badge, 78,655 sof whom answered the summons on time. See Michel Laffitte, *Juif dans la France allemande*, op. cit., pp. 129–130.

6. *La Lettre des résistants et déportés juifs*, no. 40, Sept./Oct. 1998, p. 6.

7. Jacques Biélinky, *Journal, 1940–1942*, op. cit., pp. 213–214.

8. Interview with Guy and Simon Benayoun by Philippe Landau (no. 191).

9. René Poznanski, *Jews in France…*, op. cit., p. 240.

10. Hélène Berr, *Journal*, translated by David Bellos, London, MacLehose Press, 2008, pp. 53–54.

11. Ibid., p. 56.

12. On the theme of the gaze, see also Henri Szwarc, "Souvenirs: l'étoile jaune," *Annales. Économies, Sociétés, Civilisations*, 1993, vol. 48, no. 3, p. 630.

13. Lieven Saerens, *Rachel, Jacob, Paul et les autres. Une histoire des Juifs à Bruxelles*, Wavre (Belgium), Mardaga, 2014, p. 184.

14. Hélène Berr, *Journal*, op. cit., p. 54, p. 100.

15. Interview with Madeleine Schermann, née Grunfeld, 15 June 2010.

16. Annie Kriegel, *Ce que j'ai cru comprendre*, op. cit., pp. 151–152.

17. Interview with Francine Wolff, née Weiller, 17 June 2010.

18. Jean-Jacques Becker, *Un soir de l'été 1942*, op. cit., pp. 72–74.

19. See Jacques Biélinky, *Journal 1940–1942*, op. cit., p. 221.

20. See Simone Rubin Gerber, "Témoignage sur le port de l'étoile juive à Paris," *Diasporas*, no. 16, pp. 113–120.

21. Joseph Joffo, *A Bag of Marbles*, translated by Martin Sokolinsky, Chicago, IL, University of Chicago Press, 2001, p. 20.

22. Robert Debré, *L'Honneur de vivre*, op. cit., p. 231.

23. Joseph Minc, *L'Extraordinaire Histoire de ma vie ordinaire*, op. cit., p. 113.

24. Annie Kriegel, *Ce que j'ai cru comprendre*, op. cit., p. 155.

25. See Hélène Berr, *Journal*, op. cit, p. 93.

26. Annie Kriegel, *Ce que j'ai cru comprendre*, op. cit., p. 156.

27. Claude Lévy and Paul Tillard collected several accounts of Jews who managed to escape. See *Ce jour-là, 16 July 1942. La grande rafle du Vel' d'Hiv'*, Paris, Robert Laffont, 1967, new ed. 1992, especially pp. 53–54.

28. Interview with Lili Garel née Tager (24 February 2011).

29. Bob Moore, *Survivors*, op. cit., p. 262.

30. "Le travail clandestin de l'OSE," testimony by Georges Garel before the Centre de documentation sur la persécution nazie, Nice, 1946 (CDJC, CC XVIII-104); Georges Garel, *Le sauvetage des enfants juifs par l'OSE*, Le manuscrit—FMS; Paris, 2012).

31. Simone Veil, "Réflexions d'un témoin," *Annales. Économies, Sociétés, Civilisations*, 1993, vol. 48, no. 3, pp. 696 and 697.

32. Saul Friedländer, *When Memory Comes*, pp. 49–51, 64, 70–74, 76–79, 81, 88–90. Saul Friedländer later learned that "Mme M. de L. was Jewish by birth herself" (p. 115).

33. Frederick Raymes and Menachem Mayer, *Are the Trees in Bloom Over There?* op. cit., p. 79.

34. Joseph Minc, *L'Extraordinaire Histoire de ma vie ordinaire*, op. cit., pp. 121–122, 124–125, 133–134.

35. Mia Amalia Kanner, *Shattered Crystals*, op. cit., pp. 128–30.

36. Claude Lanzmann, *The Patagonian Hare*, translated by Frank Wynne, London, Atlantic Books, 2012, pp. 60–61.

37. Interview with Serge Klarsfeld by Jean-Baptiste Péretié, 30 March 2006 for the Mémoire de la Shoah series, FMS/INA.

38. Albert Grumberg, *Journal d'un coiffeur juif à Paris sous l'occupation*, op. cit. Foreword by Roger Grimberg, pp. 17–18.

39. Ibid., p. 286.

40. Ibid., pp. 347 ff.

41. Interview with Francine Wolff, née Weiller, 17 June 2010.
42. Hélène Berr, *Journal*, op. cit., p. 252.
43. Ibid., p. 271.
44. Mia Amalia Kanner, *Shattered Crystals*, op. cit., pp. 165–67.
45. Simone Veil, "Réflexions d'un témoin," op. cit., p. 697.
46. Interview with Boris Cyrulnik by Catherine Bernstein on 25 April 2006 for the "Mémoire de la Shoah" series, FMS/INA. See also Boris Cyrulnik, *Sauve-toi, la vie t'appelle*, Paris, Odile Jacob, 2012.
47. Renée Poznanski, *Jews in France*, op. cit., p. 282.
48. David Diamant, *Le Billet vert*, p. 176.
49. Mia Amalia Kanner, *Shattered Crystals*, op. cit., pp. 198–200.
50. See Anna Traube, *Evadée du Vel'd'Hiv'*, Paris, Éditions Le Manuscrit, 2005, pp. 28–34. This episode was used in Rose Bosch's film *La Rafle* [*The Round Up*], released in cinemas on 10 March 2010.
51. See Janet Thorpe, *Nous n'irons pas à Pitchipoï. Le tunnel du camp de Drancy*, Paris, De Fallois, 2004.
52. Jacques Ravine, *La Résistance organisée des Juifs en France*, Paris, Julliard, 1973, p. 85; Jacques Adler, *Face à la persécution. Les organisations juives à Paris de 1940 à 1944*, Paris, Calmann-Lévy, 1985, pp. 172–174; David Diamant, *Les Juifs dans la Résistance française*, 1940–1944, Paris, Le Pavillon, 1971, pp. 76–83.
53. See Simone Veil, "Réflexions d'un témoin," op. cit., p. 696.
54. For a detailed and exhaustive list, see Ahlrich Meyer, *Täter im Verhör. Die "Endlosung der Judenfrage" in Frankreich 1940–1944*, Darmstadt, Wissenschaftliche Buchgesellschaft, 2005. One can also refer to Serge Klarsfeld, "Le Calendrier de la persécution des Juifs en France, 1940–1944," in *La Shoah en France*, vol. 2 and 3, op. cit.
55. Ahlrich Meyer, *Täter im Verhör…*, op. cit., p. 263.
56. Léon Poliakov, *L'Auberge des musiciens*, op. cit., p. 126.
57. Ibid., p. 97.
58. Ibid., p. 98.
59. Ibid., p. 101.
60. Joseph Minc, *L'Extraordinaire Histoire de ma vie ordinaire*, op. cit., pp. 129–130.
61. See Sarah Kaminsky, *Adolfo Kaminsky. A Forger's Life*, translated by Mike Mitchell, Los Angeles, DoppelHouse Press, 2016.
62. Arlette Scali, *Les Justes de Graulhet*, Paris, Scali, p. 125.
63. See Annie Kriegel, *Ce que j'ai cru comprendre*, op. cit., p. 192. The MOI (Main-d'oeuvre immigrée) was a trade union organization founded in the 1920s that grouped together in immigrant workers affiliated to the Confédération générale du travail unitaire. During the Occupation it developed an armed section called the FTP-MOI.

64. Emmanuel Lemieux, *Edgar Morin. L'indiscipliné*, Paris, Le Seuil, 2009, p. 158.

65. Renée Poznanski, *Jews in France*, op. cit., p. 341.

66. See the story of Madame J. recounted by Jean Estèbe in *Les Juifs à Toulouse*, op. cit., p. 252.

67. See Nina Gourfinkel, *Aux prises avec mon temps*, vol. 2, Le Seuil, 1953, pp. 284–285. Nina Gourfinkel (1900–1984) was a Russian-born Jewish activist who came to in France in 1925. During the Occupation she worked for the Direction des centres d'accueil (DCA—Management of Reception Centers), which looked after prisoners whom the OSE had managed to get out of the internment camps.

68. Robert Debré, *L'Honneur de vivre*, op. cit., p. 247.

69. Martin de La Soudière, *Jours de guerre au village*, op. cit., p. 102.

70. Ibid.

71. The situation was different in Algeria, where the law of 21 June 1941 established a quota of 14 per cent of Jewish schoolchildren in state primary and secondary schools. The quota was reduced to 7 per cent on 19 October 1942, leading to the exclusion of 19,484 pupils from state schools. See Michel Ansky, *Les Juifs d'Algérie, du décret Crémieux à la Libération*, Paris, CDJC, 1950.

72. Saul Friedländer, *When Memory Comes*, op. cit., p. 90.

73. Martin de La Soudière, *Jours de guerre au village*, op. cit., p. 97.

74. Ibid., p. 98. See also François Stupp, *Réfugié au pays des Justes. Araules, 1942–1944*, Polignac, Editions du Roure, 1997, pp. 64–66.

75. Danielle Bailly, in *Traqués, cachés, vivants. Des enfants juifs en France 1940–1945*, Paris, L'Harmattan, 2004, quoted in Martin de La Soudière, *Jours de guerre au village*, op. cit., p. 99.

76. Albert's testimony, quoted by Martin de La Soudière, *Jours de guerre au village*, op. cit., p. 107.

77. The Finaly Affair broke in the early 1950s. Antoinette Brun, the head of a municipal crèche in Grenoble, took in the two sons of a Jewish couple killed at Auschwitz in 1944. Having had the boys baptized, when she became their guardian she refused to allow them to return to live with their aunt who had emigrated to Israel. After a trial, a compromise was negotiated by Chief Rabbi Kaplan and the Catholic authorities, and the children were eventually sent back to live with their relatives.

78. Saul Friedländer, *When Memory Comes*, op. cit., p. 79.

79. For more accounts of conversion during this period, see Marcel David, *Croire ou espérer*, Paris, Éditions ouvrières, 1981 and Renée David, *Traces indélébiles. Mémoires incertaines*, Paris, L'Harmattan, 2000.

80. Martin de La Soudière, *Jours de guerre au village*, op. cit., p. 108.

81. Ibid.

82. Jewish children were excluded from public schools in Vichy Algeria; see Georges Bensoussan, *Juifs en pays arabes, le grand déracinement (1850–1975)*, Paris, Tallandier, 2012.

83. This was someone appointed by the Germans to manage logistics and make up lists of prisoners to be deported.

84. Annette Janin, née Krajcer, recounted the conditions of her internment at Pithiviers and Drancy to Eric Conan, author of *Sans oublier les enfants*, Grasset, 1991. She published her own testimony (with Philippe Barbeau) in *Le Dernier Eté des enfants à l'Étoile. 1942, une rescapée se souvient*, Oskar Editions, 2010. She spoke to the author, on 12 March 2010, in detail about the period after her imprisonment in Drancy up to the Liberation.

85. Jean-Jacques Becker, *Un soir de l'été 1942...*, op. cit., p. 54.

86. Ibid., pp. 87–88.

87. Alfred Grosser, *Une vie de Français*, op. cit., p. 30.

88. Emmanuel Lemieux, *Edgar Morin. L'indiscipliné*, op. cit., pp. 89, 18, 19 and 53.

89. See for example the case of Kanovitch brothers in "Enfants cachés, enfants retrouvés," by Kathy Hazan, *Cahiers de la Shoah*, no. 9, 2007, pp. 187–188.

90. The *Nouvelle revue française* (NRF) is a prestigious literary journal founded in 1909.

91. Edgar Morin, *Vidal and His Family*, op. cit., p. 261.

92. Dominique Missika, *La guerre sépare ceux qui s'aiment. 1939–1945*, Paris, Grasset, 2001.

93. Jean Estèbe, *Les Juifs à Toulouse et en Midi toulousain sous Vichy*, op. cit., p. 262.

94. Arlette Scali, *Les Justes de Graulhet*, op. cit., pp. 79, 85, 98 and 113–114.

95. Vivette Samuel, *Rescuing the Children*, op. cit., p. 75.

96. Ibid., p. 92.

97. See Jacqueline Mesnil-Amar, *Maman, What Are We Called Now?* op. cit.

98. See *Revue de la Shoah. Le Consistoire durant la Seconde Guerre mondiale*, no. 169, May–August 2000, in particular the article by Philippe Landau, "Vivre la Torah en France sous l'Occupation."

99. Philippe Landau, "Vivre la Torah en France sous l'Occupation," op. cit., p. 114.

100. Renée Poznanski, *Jews in France*, op. cit., pp. 47–48.

101. Philippe Landau, "Vivre la Torah en France sous l'Occupation," op. cit., p. 116.

102. Hélène Berr, *Journal*, op. cit., p. 129.

103. See Renée Poznanski, *Jews in France*, op. cit., p. 424.

104. See Jean Estèbe, *Les Juifs à Toulouse et en Midi toulousain au temps de Vichy*, op. cit, p. 261.

105. Serge Klarsfeld, *Vichy-Auschwitz*, op. cit., pp. 168–169.

106. Philippe Landau, "Vivre la Torah en France sous l'occupation," op. cit., p. 122.

107. Renée Poznanski, *Jews in France*, op. cit., p. 427.

108. Léa Markscheid (with Jacques Fijalkow), "La vie religieuse des Juifs à Lacaune (août 1943–septembre 1944)," *Revue du Tarn*, 2009, no. 231, pp. 79–118.

109. See Alain Michel, "Qu'est-ce qu'un scout juif? L'éducation juive chez les Éclaireurs israélites de France, de 1923 au début des années 1950," *Archives juives*, 2002/2, p. 85.

110. Saul Friedländer, *When Memory Comes*, op. cit., p. 94.

111. See Denise Siekierski, *MiDor LeDor. De génération en génération*, L'Harmattan, Paris, 2004.

112. Jean-Paul Sartre, *Anti-Semite and Jew. An Exploration of the Etiology of Hate* [1946], translated by George J. Becker, New York, Schocken Books, 1995, p. 49.

113. Ibid., p. 103.

114. Jacqueline Mesnil-Amar, *Maman, What Are We Called Now?*, op. cit, pp. 55–56.

115. Adolfo Kaminsky, *A Forger's Life*, op. cit, pp. 38–39

116. Annie Kriegel, *Réflexion sur les questions juives*, Hachette, 1984, p. 51.

117. Stanley Hoffmann, *Decline or Renewal? France since the 1930s*, op. cit., 1974, p. 59.

118. Stanley Hoffmann, "To Be or Not to Be French," op. cit., p. 21.

119. Jean-Jacques Becker, *Un soir de l'été 1942*, op. cit., p. 139.

120. Nicole Lapierre, *Changer de nom*, Stock, Paris, 1995, new ed. Gallimard, "Folio," 2006, p. 142.

121. Ibid., p. 136. Figures taken from Doris Bensimon and Sergio Della Pergola, *La Population juive de France. Socio-démographie et identité*, Hebrew University of Jerusalem/CNRS, Jerusalem, 1984.

122. Nicole Lapierre, "Les changements de nom," in Jean-Jacques Becker and Annette Wieviorka (eds), *Les Juifs de France de la Révolution française à nos jours*, Paris, Liana Levi, 1998, p. 266.

123. Nicole Lapierre, *Changer de nom*, op. cit., p. 168.

4. RANDOM ACTS OF SOLIDARITY TOWARDS THE PERSECUTED

1. Stanley Hoffmann, "To Be or Not to Be French," op. cit., and interview on 28 January 2009 with the author.

2. *Les armes de l'esprit*, USA/France, 1989, 90 minutes.

3. Jean Estèbe, *Les Juifs à Toulouse et en Midi toulousain au temps de Vichy*, op. cit., p. 259.

4. The author undertook some brief research on the subject. The results were startling: most articles revealed an astounding lack of knowledge as well as marked biases on the part of British journalists about the situation of Jews in France during the war. One of the most disturbing articles, published in *The Independent*, lumped together French anti-Semitism with the anti-Semitism of Nazi Germany: ("The French as well as the Germans were strongly anti-Semitic," 19 March 2010). *The Guardian* claimed that the film deals with a subject that remains taboo in France: their role in the collaboration (9 March 2010). These articles are based on biased presumptions and completely ignore recent historical research.

5. Pierre Laborie, *L'Opinion française sous Vichy*, Paris, Le Seuil, 1990.

6. See Henry Rousso, *The Vichy Syndrome. History and Memory in France since 1944*, translated by Arthur Goldhammer, foreword by Stanley Hoffmann, Cambridge, MA, Harvard University Press, 1994.

7. For further reading on the subject, see articles in *Hermès*, edited by Dominique Wolton.

8. Elisabeth Noelle-Neumann, "The Spiral of Silence: A Theory of Public Opinion," *Journal of Communication*, Spring 1974, p. 44.

9. Mia Amalia Kanner, *Shattered Crystals*, op. cit., pp. 31 and 35–39.

10. Frederick Raymes and Menachem Mayer, *Are the Trees in Bloom Over There?* op. cit., 2002, p. 26.

11. See Jan T. Gross, *Neighbors. The Destruction of the Jewish Community in Jedwabne, Poland*, Princeton, NJ, Princeton University Press, 2001.

12. Léo Hamon, "Étude sur la situation des Juifs en zone occupée," op. cit.

13. Claude Lanzmann, *The Patagonian Hare*, op. cit., pp. 89–92.

14. Paul Thibaud, "La longue mémoire du 'délaissement' des Juifs de France," *Esprit*, May 2007, p. 117.

15. Michael R. Marrus and Robert O. Paxton, *Vichy France and the Jews*, op. cit., pp. 181–2.

16. Ibid., p. 181.

17. Asher Cohen, *Persécutions et sauvetages. Juifs et Français sous l'Occupation et sous Vichy*, op. cit., p. 192.

18. The "Renseignements Généraux" domestic intelligence services had offices in each prefecture and provided the government with periodic reports on the state of public opinion.

19. Departmental Archives of the Rhône, office of the prefecture (unclassified), report dated 23 November 1940, cited by Asher Cohen, *Persécutions et sauvetages*, op. cit., pp. 195–196.

20. Ibid., p. 237.

21. René Poznanski, *Jews in France*, op. cit. p. 76. See also Raymond-Raoul Lambert, *Carnet d'un témoin, 1940–1943*, Paris, Fayard, 1984, "le 22 juin 1941," pp. 107–112.

22. Hélène Berr, *Journal*, op. cit., p. 160.

23. Paul Thibaud, "La longue mémoire du 'délaissement' des Juifs de France," op. cit., p. 116.

24. Pierre Laborie, "Juifs et non-Juifs, 1940–1944, histoire et représentation," in Jacques Fijalkow (ed.), *Vichy, les Juifs et les Justes. L'exemple du Tarn*, Toulouse, Privat, 2003, p. 23.

25. Pierre Laborie, *Le Chagrin et le Venin*, Montrouge, Bayard, 2011, pp. 253–255.

26. Jacques Biélinky, *Journal, 1940–42*, op. cit., p. 77.

27. Jean-Louis Crémieux-Brilhac, "La France Libre et le 'problème juif,'" *Le Débat*, no. 162, Nov.-Dec. 2010.

28. The second part of the book by Ralph Schor, *L'Antisémitisme en France dans l'entre-deux-guerres*, op. cit., focuses on the "protection of Jews, or the progression of reason," while one of the most original aspects of Vicki Caron's *Uneasy Asylum. France and the Jewish Refugee Crisis*, op. cit., is the analysis of how different elements of French society were mobilized to welcome the arrival of Jewish immigrants during the 1930s.

29. Michèle Cointet, *L'Eglise sous Vichy: 1940–1945. La repentance en question*, Perrin, coll. "Vérités et légendes," Paris, 1998, pp. 197–203.

30. Laurent Joly, *Vichy dans la "solution finale." Histoire du Commissariat Général aux Questions juives 1941–1944*, Paris, Grasset, 2006, pp. 546–550.

31. "Ménardais, abbé Henri," in Israel Gutman (ed.), *Dictionnaire des Justes de France*, op. cit., pp. 408–409.

32. See for example Hélène Berr, *Journal*, op. cit., pp. 54–58.

33. Jacques Biélinky, *Journal 1940–42*, op. cit., entries dated 6 June 1942 (p. 215), 8 June 1942 (p. 216), 11 June 1942 (p. 220), 16 June 1942 (p. 223).

34. Georges Wellers, *L'Etoile jaune à l'heure de Vichy*, Paris, Fayard, 1973, p. 262.

35. Cédric Gruat and Cécile Leblanc, *Amis des Juifs: les résistants aux étoiles*, Paris, Tirésias, 2005, pp. 175–176.

36. Léa Markscheid, *Le Passé au présent*, op. cit., pp. 117–118.

37. It was customary for Church officials to use the first few words of a text as its title. Saliège chose to begin his letter with a brief quote in Latin from the book of Jeremiah 14:2, describing strife in the land of Judah, the capital of which was Jerusalem. There was a drought at the time. It is translated in the *King James Bible* as "and the cry of Jerusalem is gone up."

38. Cited by Jean-Louis Clément, *Monseigneur Saliège, Archevêque de Toulouse, 1929–1956*, Paris, Beauchesne, 1994, p. 215.
39. "French Rift Grows on Deporting Jews," *New York Times*, G. H. Archambault, 9 September 1942. See Yves-Marie PÉRÉON, *L'image de la France dans la presse américaine, 1936–1947*, P.I.E. Peter Lang, Bruxelles, 2011, p. 286.
40. Pierre Laborie, "1942 et le sort des Juifs. Quel tournant dans l'opinion?" *Annales, Economies, Sociétés, Civilisations*, no. 3, May–June 1993.
41. Asher Cohen, "'Pour les Juifs,' des attitudes philosémites sous Vichy," *Pardès*, no. 1, 1985.
42. French National Archive, AN AJ 38–6 (see Bibliography).
43. Renée Pozanski, "Anti-Semitism and Rescue of Jews in France," in Jacques Semelin, Claire Andrieu, Sarah Gensburger, *Resisting Genocide*, op. cit., p. 95.
44. Marthe Cohn (with Wendy Holden), *Behind Enemy Lines. The True Story of a French Jewish Spy in Nazi Germany*, Harmony, 2002, p. 76.
45. See Nechama Tec, *When Light Pierced the Darkness. Christian Rescue of Jews in Nazi-Occupied Poland*, Oxford, Oxford University Press, 1986, 262 p.
46. See Léon Poliakov, *L'Auberge des musiciens*, op. cit., p. 135.
47. Laurent Joly (ed.), *La Délation dans la France des années noires*, Paris, Perrin, 2012.
48. See Grégoire Kauffmann, *Edouard Drumont*, Paris, Perrin, 2008.
49. Laurent Joly, *Dénoncer les Juifs sous l'Occupation*, Paris, CNRS Éditions, 2016.
50. André Halimi, *La Délation sous l'Occupation*, Paris, Alain Moreau, 1983.
51. See Barbara Engelking's study on letters of denunciation sent during 1940 and 1941, in a paper given at the French-Polish conference in Lublin, "History and memory of Jewish communities in France and Poland after 1945," January 2004.
52. See Serge Klarsfeld, *Vichy-Auschwitz*, op. cit., p. 311 (AN-FI CIII 1137).
53. Shannon L. Fogg, *The Politics of Everyday Life in Vichy France. Foreigners, Undesirables, and Strangers*, Cambridge, Cambridge University Press, 2009.
54. See Simon Ostermann, "La clandestinité des Juifs dans les villes de province sous Vichy. L'exemple de Châteauroux (1940–1944)," in Sylvie Aprile (ed.), *Les Clandestinités urbaines en Occident de l'époque moderne à nos jours*, Rennes, Presses Universitaires de Rennes, November 2008, pp. 255–275.
55. Philippe Erlanger, *La France sans étoile*, op. cit., pp. 183–184.
56. See Oser Warszawski, *On ne peut pas se plaindre*, op. cit., p. 103.

57. Léa Markscheid, *Le passé au présent*, op. cit., p. 77.

58. See the "registre des sœurs de Notre-Dame de Sion" held in the archives of the CDJC (unclassified).

59. Testimony of Nelly Scharapan in Danielle Bailly (ed.), *Traqués, cachés, vivants. Des enfants juifs en France (1940–1944)*, op. cit., p. 146.

60. Sarah Kofman, *Rue Ordener, rue Labat*, op. cit.

61. Jeannine Levana Frenk, "Righteous Among the Nations in France and Belgium: A Silent Resistance," *Search and Research—Lectures and Papers*, no. 12, Jerusalem, Yad Vashem Publications, 2008.

62. See for example Marc Dupont and Françoise Salaün Ramalho, *L'Assistance publique-Hôpitaux de Paris*, Presses Universitaires de France, "QSJ," 2010, p. 19.

63. Ivan Jablonka, *Ni père ni mère. Histoire des enfants de l'Assistance publique (1874–1939)*, Paris, Le Seuil, 2006.

64. Ibid., p. 84.

65. Ariela Palacz, *I Love You My Child, I'm Abandoning You*, Tel Aviv, Contento De Semrik, 2013.

66. Yad Vashem, Maurice file (no. 10737). See also the Roy file (no. 10613) and the Allibert file (no. 10095).

67. Ivan Jablonka, *Histoire des grand-parents que je n'ai pas eus. Une enquête*, Paris, Le Seuil, 2012, p. 302.

68. Jean-Pierre Le Crom, "Lutter contre la faim: le rôle du Secours National" in Isabelle von Bueltzingsloewen (ed.), *"Morts d'inanition." Famines et exclusions en France sous l'Occupation*, Rennes, Presses Universitaires de Rennes, 2005, pp. 251–252.

69. Ibid., pp. 254–255.

70. Cyril Le Tallec, *Les Assistantes sociales dans la tourmente. 1939–1946*, Paris, L'Harmattan, 2004, p. 47.

71. From January 1942, *Secours National* huts began to appear in internment camps where food was distributed (interview with Jean-Pierre Le Crom, 11 November 2011).

72. Liliane Klein-Lieber "Témoignage sur les opérations de sauvetage," op. cit., pp. 673–678.

73. Jeannine Levana Frenk, "Righteous Among the Nations in France and Belgium: A Silent Resistance," op. cit.

74. See Yad Vashem, Louis Collet file (no. 9536). See also the examples of Aristide Gasnier (no. 10489) and Marie-Thérèse Goumy (no. 10521).

75. See Céline Marrot-Fellag Ariouet, *Les Enfants cachés pendant la Seconde Guerre mondiale*, thesis for a Master's degree in history, University of Versailles-Saint-Quentin-en-Yvelines, 1998 (available online) and Jean-Pierre Le Crom, "De la Révolution prolétarienne à la Révolution nationale? Roger et Yvonne Hagnauer dans la tourmente de la Seconde

Guerre mondiale," in David Hamelin and Vincent Chambarlhac (eds), *Histoire du syndicalisme révolutionnaire*, Dijon, Éditions universitaires de Dijon (forthcoming). See also the website dedicated to the memory of the Sèvres children's home: http://lamaisondesevres.org/

76. Frederick Raymes and Menachem Mayer, *Are the Trees in Bloom Over There?* op. cit., pp. 77–84 and 144.

77. Lucienne Chibrac, *Les Pionnières du travail social auprès des étrangers. Le Service social d'aide aux émigrants des origines à la Libération*, Rennes, Éditions de l'École Nationale de la Santé Publique, 2005.

78. Ibid., p. 170.

79. Ibid., pp. 81, 121 and 125–126.

80. See ibid., pp. 232–237.

81. See *supra*, chap. 1; see also Claude Klein, "Un témoignage des années d'Occupation: de Grenoble à la Suisse," op. cit.

82. Albert Grunberg, *Journal d'un coiffeur juif…*, op. cit., p. 22.

83. Stanley Hoffmann, *Decline or Renewal? France since the 1930s*, op. cit., pp. 86–87.

84. Saul Friedländer, *When Memory Comes*, op. cit., pp. 71–72.

85. Stanley Hoffmann, *Decline or Renewal? France since the 1930s*, op. cit., p. 87.

86. *Mishnah Sanhedrin*, 4.4.

87. Sarah Gensburger, *National Policy, Global Memory. The Commemoration of the "Righteous" from Jerusalem to Paris, 1942–2007*. Translated by Katharine Throssell, New York and Oxford, Berghahn Books, 2016.

88. Yad Vashem, file no. 57.

89. See Patrick Cabanel's book on Alice Ferrières, drawing on multiple sources including her private diaries and correspondence from 1941 to 1944: *Chère Mademoiselle. Alice Ferrières et les enfants de Murat, 1941–1944*, Paris, Calmann-Lévy/Mémorial de la Shoah, 2010.

90. Yad Vashem, file no. 8783.

91. Yad Vashem, file no. 3830.

92. Yad Vashem, file no. 9792.

93. Yad Vashem, file no. 579.

94. Sarah Gensburger, "Les figures du Juste et du Résistant et l'évolution de la mémoire historique française de l'Occupation," *Revue française de science politique*, September 2002, no. 2, pp. 291–322.

95. Israel Gutman (ed.), Jerusalem, Yad Vashem/Paris, Fayard, 2003. See also Lucien Lazare's essay, *Le Livre des Justes. Histoire du sauvetage des Juifs par les non-Juifs en France, 1940–1944*, Paris, Lattès, 1993.

96. The story of Oskar Schindler, made famous by Steven Spielberg's 1993 film *Schindler's List*, was first popularized by Thomas Keneally, in his novel *Schindler's Ark*, London, Hodder and Stoughton, 1982. See also David Crowe, *Oskar Schindler. The Untold Account of His Life, Wartime*

Activities, and the True Story Behind the List, New York, Basic Books, 2004.

97. See Gabriel Nicime, *Le Jardin des Justes. De la liste de Schindler au tribunal du Bien*, Paris, Payot, 2007.

98. Bob Moore, *Survivors*, op. cit., p. 14.

99. Patrick Cabanel, *Histoire des Justes en Frances*, Paris, Armand Colin, 2012.

100. See Jeannine Levena Frenk, "Righteous Among The Nations in France and Belgium: A Silent Resistance," op. cit., p. 10. Jeanine Levana Frenk also analyzed 214 Belgian Righteous files. Her work on France follows on from that of Hubert Hannoun on the files of French Righteous recognized between 1963 and 2000: Hubert Hannoun, *L'Epopée des Justes de France (1939–1945)*, Paris, Connaissance et savoir, 2005. Since the 1960s Yad Vashem's methods of inquiry have been professionalized; Jeannine Levana Frenk considers therefore that her analysis is among the most reliable.

101. Jeannine Levena Frenk, "Righteous Among The Nations in France and Belgium: A Silent Resistance," op. cit., p. 14.

102. Ibid., p. 8.

103. Ibid., p. 28.

104. Ibid., p. 43.

105. Ibid., p. 41.

106. Cindy Banse-Biesse, *Les Justes parmi les Nations de la région Rhône-Alpes. Étude prosopographique*, doctoral dissertation, Université Lyon 3–Jean-Moulin, 2015. p. 215 ff.

107. Léon Poliakov, *L'Auberge des musiciens*, op. cit., p. 114.

108. See Joseph Minc, *L'Extraordinaire Histoire de ma vie ordinaire*, op. cit., p. 114.

109. See Olivier Philipponnat and Patrick Lienhardt, *The Life of Irène Némirovsky*, op. cit., pp 309–10.

110. See Odette Meyers, *Doors to Madame Marie*, Seattle and London, McLellan, 1997, pp. 88–93.

111. Bob Moore has demonstrated the importance of prewar relationships in making it more likely that Jews would find help during the war, as has Ben Braber in *This Cannot Happen Here. Integration and Jewish Resistance in the Netherlands, 1940–1945*, Amsterdam, Amsterdam University Press, 2013.

112. Alfred Grosser, *Une vie de Français*, op. cit., pp. 32–33.

113. Jean-Jacques Becker, *Un soir de l'été 1942…*, op. cit., p. 72.

114. Ibid., pp. 77–78.

115. Edgar Morin, *Vidal and his Family*, op. cit., p. 182.

116. Arlette Scali, *Les Justes de Graulhet*, op. cit., p. 89.

117. Ibid., pp. 123–124.
118. Interview with Pierre Nora by the author, 23 June 2010. See François Dosse, *Pierre Nora. Homo historicus*, Paris, Perrin, 2011, pp. 15–35. See also *Le Procès de Xavier Vallat, présenté par ses amis*, preface by Marie-Madeleine Martin, Paris, Éditions du Conquistador, 1948, pp. 246–248.
119. Bob Moore, *Survivors*, op. cit., p. 113.
120. Françoise Frenkel, *No Place to Lay One's Head*, translated by Stephanie Smee, Pushkin Press, 2018, p. 124. First published in 1945 in Geneva, this extraordinary book describing Frenkel's life as a refugee was completely forgotten until a copy was discovered in an attic in Nice. The new edition, published in French in 2010, includes a preface by Patrick Modiano.
121. Joseph Minc, *L'Extraordinaire Histoire de ma vie ordinaire*, op. cit., p. 122.
122. Yad Vashem, file no. 8913.
123. Mia Amalia Kanner, *Shattered Crystals*, op. cit., pp. 139–140.
124. Yad Vashem, file no. 5825.
125. Testimony of Henri Steiner, included in the Yad Vashem file of Jeanne Bagarades, no. 9934.
126. Sarah Kofman, *Rue Ordener, rue Labat*, op. cit., pp. 70–71.
127. Lucie Aubrac, *Outwitting the Gestapo*, translated by Konrad Bieber and Betsy Wing, Lincoln, NE, University of Nebraska Press, 1994, p. 47.
128. Rod Kedward, *In Search of the Maquis. Rural Resistance in Southern France, 1942–1944*, Oxford, Clarendon Press of Oxford University Press, 1993 p. 340.
129. Marthe Cohn, *Behind Enemy Lines*, op. cit., p. 71.
130. Claude Lanzmann, *The Patagonian Hare*, op. cit., p. 23.
131. Jean-Jacques Becker, *Un soir de l'été 1942.*, op. cit., pp. 79–80.
132. Léon Poliakov, *L'Auberge des musiciens*, op. cit., pp. 82–83.
133. See Serge Lapidus, *Étoiles jaunes dans la France des années noires*, op. cit., pp. 108–109.
134. Marthe Cohn, *Behind Enemy Lines*, op. cit., p. 83.
135. Laurent Neury, *Entre les mailles du filet? Vivre et survivre sur le versant français de la frontière franco-genevoise de 1933 à 1947*, Genève, IHEID (international relations), 2008, p. 629; from an interview between Laurent Neury and Léon Bouvier, 16 October 2002.
136. Neury's research was conducted between 1999 and 2006 for his doctoral thesis in international relations. It is based on the accounts of 39 smugglers, 24 relatives of former smugglers, and 17 officials. See Laurent Neury, *Entre les mailles du filet?* op. cit.
137. Annie Kriegel, *Ce que j'ai cru comprendre*, op. cit., p. 50.

138. Arlette Scali, *Les Justes de Graulhet*, op. cit., p. 115.

139. Joseph Joffo, *A Bag of Marbles*, op. cit., p. 50.

140. German ordinance dated 8 July 1942.

141. Jean-Jacques Becker, *Un soir de l'été 1942*, op. cit., p. 78.

142. See Shannon L. Fogg, *Stealing Home: Looting, Restitution, and Reconstructing Jewish Lives in France, 1942–1947*, Oxford, Oxford University Press, 2017.

143. Marthe Cohn, *Behind Enemy Lines*, op. cit., p. 72.

144. See Léa Markscheid, *Le passé au présent*, op. cit., p. 99.

145. Research focusing on the Jews of Brussels has also brought to light the significance of these "small gestures": Lieven Saerens, *Rachel, Jacob, Paul et les autres. Une histoire des Juifs à Bruxelles*, op. cit.; pp. 189 ff.

146. See Samuel P. and Pearl M. Oliner, *The Altruistic Personality. Rescuers of Jews in Nazi-Europe*, New York, The Free Press, 1988.

147. Nechama Tec, *When Light Pierced the Darkness*, op. cit.; Hubert Hannoun, *L'Epopée des Justes de France, 1939–1945*, op. cit.

148. See "Laws of Reactivity," in Jacques Semelin, *Unarmed Against Hitler. Civilian Resistance in Europe, 1939–1943*, op. cit., pp. 84–88.

149. Léon Poliakov, *Harvest of Hate: The Nazi Program for the Destruction of the Jews of Europe*, London, Elek Books, 1956.

150. See Anne Simonin, *Les Éditions de Minuit, 1942–1955. Le devoir d'insoumission*, Paris, IMEC, 1994, pp. 65–74. After the war, Éditions de Minuit, the underground publishing house that first published *Le Silence de la Mer* in 1942, was headed by Jérôme Lindon, brother of Denis Lindon, one of the witnesses whose testimony is central to this book.

151. Albert Grunberg, *Journal d'un coiffeur juif...*, op. cit., pp. 321 and 323.

152. Raul Hilberg, *Perpetrators Victims Bystanders. Jewish Catastrophe, 1933–1945*, New York, Aaron Asher Books, 1992.

CONCLUSION: THE SURVIVAL OF THE JEWS IN FRANCE

1. Michael. R. Marrus and Robert. O. Paxton, *Vichy France and the Jews*, op. cit., p. 334.

2. See Lieven Saerens, *Rachel, Jacob, Paul et les autres. Une histoire des Juifs à Bruxelles*, op. cit., p. 188; and Bob Moore, *Survivors*, op. cit., p. 366.

3. See Claire Andrieu, "Assistance to Jews and to Allied Soldiers and Airmen in France: A Comparative Approach," in Jacques Semelin, Claire Andrieu, Sarah Gensburger (eds), *Resisting Genocide*, op. cit., pp. 51–63.

4. Pierre Birnbaum *The Jews of the Republic. A Political History of State Jews in France from Gambetta to Vichy*. Translated by Jane Marie Todd, Stanford, CA, Stanford University Press, 1996.

5. Bob Moore, *Survivors*, op. cit., p. 357.

6. François Mauriac, *Cahier noir*, Paris, Éditions de Minuit, 1943, new edition, Desclée de Brouwer, 1994.

7. Interview with Serge Klarsfeld, *Le Point*, supplement to the edition dated 21 June 2012.

8. Ibid.

9. See Michael L. Gross, "Jewish Rescue in Holland and France during the Second World War: Moral Cognition and Collective Action," *Social Forces*, 1994, vol. 73, no. 2, pp. 463–496.

10. See Étienne Fouilloux, *Les Chrétiens français entre crise et libération, 1937– 1947*, Paris, Le Seuil, 1997; and Sylvie Bernay, *L'Église de France face à la persécution des Juifs, 1940–1944*, Paris, CNRS Éditions, 2012, for further discussion of the deep-rooted spirit of bringing help to the suffering in the Christian tradition of charity.

11. See Maurice Rajsfus, *Opération Étoile jaune*, and *Jeudi noir*, Paris, Le Cherche midi, 2002.

12. Jewish children were, however, excluded from public schools in Vichy Algeria. See Georges Bensoussan, *Juifs en pays arabes, le grand déracine-ment (1850–1975)*, Paris, Tallandier, 2012.

13. See Sarah Fishman and Leonard V. Smith, in Sarah Fishman, Robert Zaretsky, Ioannis Sinanoglou, Leonard V. Smith, Laura Lee Downs (eds), *France at War. Vichy and the Historians*, London, Bloomsbury 2000.

14. Philippe-Jean Hesse and Jean-Pierre Le Crom (eds), *La Protection soci-ale sous le régime de Vichy*, Rennes, Presses universitaires de Rennes, 2001.

15. See the letter from Louis Darquier de Pellepoix dated 14 January 1944, AN, AJ38–281, cited by Asher Cohen, in *Persécutions et sauvetages*, op. cit., p. 480.

16. See Jacques Semelin, *Unarmed against Hitler. Civilian Resistance in Europe, 1939–1943*, op. cit.

17. Timothy Snyder, "In the Cage, Trying to Get Out," *The New York Review of Books*, 24 October–6 November 2013, vol. LX, no. 16, pp. 60–62. This thesis forms the basis of Snyder's *Black Earth: The Holocaust as History and Warning*, New York, Tim Duggan Books, 2015.

18. Serge Klarsfeld, *Vichy-Auschwitz*, op. cit., pp. 179–180.

19. Pim Griffioen and Ron Zeller, "Comparing the persecution of the Jews in the Netherlands, France and Belgium, 1940–1945: similarities, differences, causes," in *The Persecution of the Jews in the Netherlands, 1940–1945. New Perspectives*, op. cit., pp 77.

20. Cited by Serge Klarsfeld, *Vichy-Auschwitz*, op. cit., pp. 179–180.

21. Cited by Serge Klarsfeld, *Vichy-Auschwitz*, op. cit., pp. 293–295 and "Le Calendrier de la persécution des Juifs de France, septembre 1942– août 1944," in *La Shoah en France*, vol. 3, op. cit., p. 1635.

22. Laurent Joly, *L'Etat contre les Juifs*, Paris, Grasset, 2018.

23. Henry Rousso, *Le Régime de Vichy*, Paris, Presses Universitaires de France, 2007, p. 92.

24. Michael R. Marrus and Robert O. Paxton, *Vichy France and the Jews*, op. cit., p. 357.

25. Stanley Hoffmann, preface to ibid. p. xi.

26. Jacques Semelin (ed.), *Quand les dictatures se fissurent...*, Paris, Desclée de Brouwer, 1995.

27. Eric Zemmour, *Vichy et la Shoah. Enquête sur le paradoxe français*, Paris, Editions CLD, 2012.

28. M. Marrus and R. O. Paxton, *Vichy et les Juifs*, 2015, op. cit. p. 13.

29. Jacques Semelin, *Unarmed against Hitler. Civilian Resistance in Europe, 1939–1943*, op. cit., p. 148.

SELECTED BIBLIOGRAPHY

Adler, Jacques, *Face à la persécution. Les organisations juives à Paris de 1940 à 1944*, Paris, Calmann-Lévy, coll. "Diaspora," 1985.

Alary, Eric, "Les Juifs et la ligne de démarcation, 1940–1943," *Les Cahiers de la Shoah*, 5, 2001.

————, *L'Exode, un drame oublié*, Paris, Perrin, 2010.

Andrieu, Claire, *La Spoliation financière*, report of the study mission on the spoliation of Jews in France, Paris, La Documentation Française, 2000, 2 vol.

Azéma, Jean-Pierre, *La France des années noires. De la défaite à Vichy*, Paris, Point Seuil, 2000.

Bailly, Danielle (ed.), *Traqués, cachés vivants. Des enfants juifs en France 1940–1945*, Paris, L'Harmattan, 2004.

Banse-Biesse, Cindy, *Les Justes parmi les Nations de la région Rhône-Alpes. Étude prosopographique*, doctoral dissertation, Université Lyon 3—Jean-Moulin, 2015.

Baruch, Marc-Olivier, *Servir l'État français. L'administration en France de 1940 à 1944*, Paris, Fayard, 1997.

Beauvoir (de) Simone, *La Force de l'âge*, Paris, Folio, 1986.

Bédarida, Renée, *"Témoignage chrétien", 1941–1944*, Paris, Editions Ouvrières, 1977.

Benz, Wolfgang and Wetzel, Juliane (eds), *Solidarität und Hilfe für Juden während der NS-Zeit*, vol. 2, Berlin, Metropol, 1998, pp. 193–280.

Bensoussan, Georges, *Juifs en pays arabes, le grand déracinement (1850–1975)*, Paris, Tallandier, 2012.

Berlière, Jean-Marc, *Policiers français sous l'Occupation*, Paris, Perrin 2001, new edition, 2009.

————, "Mémoires en souffrance: rafles et répressions antisémites par la police parisienne (1942–1944)," in Jean-Marc Berlière and René Lévy,

Le Témoin, le sociologue et l'historien, Paris, Le Nouveau Monde éditions, 2010, pp. 88–118.

Bernay, Sylvie, *L'Église de France face à la persécution des Juifs 1940–1944*, Paris, CNRS Édition, 2012.

Billig, Joseph, *Le Commissariat général aux questions juives (1941–1944)*, Paris, Éditions du Centre, 3 vol., 1955–1960.

Birnbaum, Pierre, *The Jews of the Republic. A Political History of State Jews in France from Gambetta to Vichy*. Translated by Jane Marie Todd, Stanford, CA, Stanford University Press.

Blom Johannes, Cornelis Hendrik, "The Persecution of the Jews in the Netherlands: A Comparative Western European Perspective," *European History Quarterly*, Volume 19, 1989, pp. 335–351.

Bolle, Pierre (ed.), *Le Plateau Vivarais-Lignon. Accueil et résistance, 1939–1944*, Proceedings of the Chambon-sur-Lignon colloquium, Le Chambon-sur-Lignon, Société d'Histoire de la Montagne, 1992.

Borzeix, Jean-Marie, *Jeudi Saint*, Paris, Stock, 2008.

Boulet, François, *Les Montagnes françaises, 1940–1944. Des montagnes-refuges aux montagnes-maquis*, 2 volumes, Villeneuve-d'Ascq, Presses universitaires du Septentrion, 1999.

Braber, Ben, *This Cannot Happen Here. Integration and Jewish Resistance in the Netherlands*, 1940–1945, Amsterdam, Amsterdam University Press, 2013.

Bruttmann, Tal, *La Logique des bourreaux (1939–1944)*, Paris, Hachette, 2003.

————, *Aryanisation économique et spoliations en Isère (1940–1944)*, Grenoble, Presses universitaires de Grenoble, 2010.

————, Joly, Laurent; and Wieviorka, Annette (eds), *Qu'est-ce qu'un déporté? Histoire et mémoires des déportations de la Seconde Guerre mondiale*, Paris, CNRS Éditions, 2009.

Burrin, Philippe, *La France à l'heure allemande. 1940–1944*, Paris, Le Seuil, 1995.

Cabanel, Patrick, *Histoire des Justes en France*, Paris, Armand Colin, 2012.

Cabanel, Patrick; Joutard, Philippe; Semelin, Jacques; and Wieviorka, Annette (eds), *La Montagne Refuge. Accueil et sauvetage des Juifs autour du Chambon-sur-Lignon*, Paris, Albin Michel, 2013.

Caron, Vicki, *Uneasy Asylum. France and the Jewish Refugee Crisis, 1933–1942*, Stanford, CA, Stanford University Press, 1999.

———— (guest editor), "The Rescue of Jews in France and its Empire During World War II: History and Memory," *French Politics, Culture & Society*, vol. 30, no. 2, June 2012.

Cesarani, David, *Final Solution. The Fate of the Jews 1933–1949*, London and New York, Macmillan, 2016.

Chibrac, Lucienne, *Les Pionnières du travail social auprès des étrangers. Le Service social d'aide aux émigrants, des origines à la Libération*, Paris, Éditions de l'École nationale de la santé publique, 2005.

SELECTED BIBLIOGRAPHY

Cholvy, Gérard, *Marie-Benoît de Bourg d'Iré (1895–1990). Un fils de saint François "Juste des nations,"* Paris, Éditions du Cerf, coll. "Cerf Histoire, Biographies," 2010.

Cohen, Asher, *Persécutions et sauvetages. Juifs et Français sous l'Occupation et sous Vichy,* Paris, Editions du Cerf, 1993.

Comte, Madeleine, *Sauvetages et baptêmes. Les religieuses de Notre-Dame de Sion face à la persécution des Juifs en France (1941–1944),* Paris, L'Harmattan, 2001.

Conan, Eric and Rousso, Henry, *Vichy, un passé qui ne passe pas,* Paris, Fayard, 1994.

Costagliola, Bernard, *Darlan. La collaboration à tout prix,* Paris, CNRS Éditions, 2015.

Croes, Marnix, "The Holocaust in the Netherlands and the Rate of Jewish Survival," *Holocaust and Genocide Studies,* 11/2006, Volume 20, No. 3, pp. 474–499.

———, "Facteurs de survie face à la Shoah: le cas de la province néerlandaise d'Overijssel," in Claire Zalc, Tal Bruttmann, Ivan Ermakoff et al., *Pour une microhistoire de la Shoah,* Paris, Le Seuil, 2012.

———, "Holocaust Survival Differentials in the Netherlands, 1942–1945: The Role of Wealth and Nationality," *Journal of Interdisciplinary History,* 05/2014, Volume 45, No. 1, pp. 1–24.

——— and Peter Tammes, "De lokale percentages overlevenden van de jodenvervolging in Nederland," *Historisch tijdschrift Groniek,* 2005, no. 168, pp. 437–457.

———, Tammes, Peter; et al., "Organized resistance and the persecution of Jews in the Dutch province of Overijssel," *The Netherlands Journal of Social Sciences,* 2002, Volume 38, no. 1, pp. 3–23.

Crowe, David, *Oskar Schindler. The Untold Account of His Life, Wartime Activities, and the True Story Behind the List,* New York, Basic Books, 2004.

Delanoë, Nelcya, *D'une petite rafle provençale…,* Paris, Le Seuil, 2013.

Delpal, Bernard, *A Dieulefit, nul n'est étranger. Désobéir et résister pour protéger et sauver pendant les années difficiles de la guerre 1939–1945,* Saint-Jean-en-Royans (Drôme), Un comptoir d'Edition, 2014.

——— (ed.), *Résistances juives. Solidarités, Réseaux, Parcours,* Lyon, Editions Libel, 2018.

Doorslaer, Rudi (ed.), *Les Juifs de Belgique. De l'Immigration au Génocide, 1925–1945,* Brussels, Centre de Recherches et d'Etudes Historiques de la Seconde Guerre Mondiale, 1994.

Doulut, Alexandre, *La Spoliation des biens juifs en Lot-et-Garonne, 1941–1944,* Narrosse, Editions d'Albret, 2005.

Douzou, Laurent, *La Résistance. Une morale en action,* Paris, Gallimard, 2010.

Dray-Bensousan, Renée, *Les Juifs à Marseille,* Paris, Les Belles Lettres, 2005.

SELECTED BIBLIOGRAPHY

Dreyfus, Jean-Marc, *Pillage sur ordonnances. Aryanisation et restitution des banques en France. 1940–1943*, Paris, Fayard, 2003.

————, "Le pillage des biens juifs dans l'Europe occidentale occupée: Belgique, France, Pays-Bas", in C. Goschler, P. Ther, C. Andrieu, *Spoliations et restitutions des biens juifs. Europe XXe siècle*, Paris, Autrement, 2007, pp. 75–97.

———— and Gensburger, Sarah, *Des camps dans Paris. Austerlitz, Lévitan, Bassano. Juillet 1943–août 1944*, Paris, Fayard, 2003.

Diamond, Hanna, *Fleeing Hitler. France, 1940*, Oxford, Oxford University Press, 2007.

Eismann, Gaël, *Hôtel Majestic. Ordre et sécurité en France occupée, 1940–1944*, Paris, Tallandier, 2010.

Fahl, Sylvie, *Être juif à Lyon de l'avant-guerre à la Libération*, history thesis, Université Lumière Lyon 2, October 2016.

Fein, Helen, *Accounting for Genocide. National Responses and Jewish Victimization during the Holocaust*, New York, Macmillan, 1979.

Finkiel, Evgeny, *Ordinary Jews: Choice and Survival during the Holocaust*, Princeton, Princeton University Press, 2017.

Fishman, Sarah; Lee Downs, Laura; Sinanoglou, Ioannis et al. (eds), *France at War. Vichy and the Historians*, London, Bloomsbury, 2000.

Fogg, Shannon L., *The Politics of Everyday Life in Vichy France Foreigners, Undesirables, and Strangers*, Cambridge, Cambridge University Press, 2009.

————, *Stealing Home. Looting, Restitution, and Reconstructing Jewish Lives in France, 1942–1947*, Oxford, Oxford University Press, 2017.

Frenk, Jeannine (Levana), "Righteous Among the Nations in France and Belgium: A Silent Resistance," *Search and Research—Lectures and Papers*, no. 12, Jerusalem, Yad Vashem Publications, 2008.

————, "Hiding in Plain View: The Jewish Children in the Homes of La Creuse", in Dan Michman, ed., *Hiding, Sheltering, and Borrowing Identities. Avenues of Rescue during the Holocaust*, Yad Vashem, The International Institute for Holocaust Research, Jerusalem, 2017, pp. 207–229.

Friedländer, Saul, *Nazi Germany and the Jews. Vol. 1. The Years of Persecution, 1933–1939; Vol. 2. The Years of Extermination, 1939–1945*, London, Weidenfeld & Nicholson, 1997, and New York, Harper Collins, 2007.

Gaida, Peter, "Les camps de travail de l'Organisation Todt en France 1940–1944," in Christian Chevandier and Jean-Claude Daumas (eds), *Travailler dans les entreprises sous l'Occupation*, Besançon, Presses universitaires de Franche-Comté, 2007.

————, *Camps de travail sous Vichy. Les "Groupes de Travailleurs Étrangers" (GTE) en France et en Afrique du Nord 1940–1944*, thesis under the direction of Denis Peschanski and Helga Bories at Paris 1 and Universität Bremen, 2008.

Gardet, Mathias; Hazan, Katy; Hobson Faure, Laura; and Nicault, Catherine,

SELECTED BIBLIOGRAPHY

Prévenir et guérir dans un siècle de violences. L'OSE et les populations juives au 20e siècle, Paris, Armand Colin, 2014.

Garel, Georges, *Le sauvetage des enfants juifs par l'OSE*, Le manuscrit—FMS; Paris, 2012.

Gensburger, Sarah, *National Policy, Global Memory. The Commemoration of the "Righteous" from Jerusalem to Paris, 1942–2007*. Translated by Katharine Throssell, New York and Oxford, Berghahn Books, 2016.

Gerlach, Christian, *The Extermination of the European Jews*, Cambridge, Cambridge University Press, 2016.

Gildea, Robert, *Fighters in the Shadows. A New History of the French Resistance*, Cambridge, MA, The Belknap Press of Harvard University Press, 2017.

Grenard, Fabrice, *La France du marché noir (1940–1949)*, Paris, Payot, 2008.

Griffioen, Pim and Zeller, Ron, "Anti-Jewish Policy and Organization of the Deportations in France and the Netherlands, 1940–1944: A Comparative Study," *Holocaust and Genocide Studies*, vol. 20, no. 3 (Winter 2006), pp. 437–473.

———— and Zeller, Ron, *Jodenvervolging in Nederland, Frankrijk en België, 1940–1945. Overeenkomsten, verschillen, oorzaken*, Amsterdam, Boom Publishers, 2011.

———— and Zeller, Ron, "Comparing the persecution of the Jews in the Netherlands, France and Belgium, 1940–1945: similarities, differences, causes" in *The Persecution of the Jews in the Netherlands, 1940–1945, New perspectives*, Amsterdam, Vossiuspers UvA, Amsterdam University Press, 2012.

Gross, Jan T., *Neighbors. The Destruction of the Jewish Community in Jedwabne*, New York, Penguin Books, 2002.

Gruat, Cédric and Leblanc, Cécile, *Amis des Juifs. Les résistants aux étoiles*, Paris, Tirésias, 2005.

Grynberg, Anne, *Les Camps de la honte. Les internés juifs des camps français, 1939–1945*, Paris, La Découverte, 1991.

Gutman, Israël (ed.), *Dictionnaire des Justes de France*, Jerusalem, Yad Vashem/Paris, Fayard, 2003.

Haan (de), Ido, "The Paradoxes of Dutch History-Historiography of the Holocaust in the Netherlands," in Bankier, D. and Michman, D., *Holocaust Historiography in Context. Emergence, Challenges, Polemics and Achievements*, Jerusalem, Yad Vashem and New York, Berghahn Books, 2008.

Hannoun, Hubert, *L'Épopée des Justes de France (1939–1945)*, Paris, Connaissance et savoir, 2005.

Hazan, Katy, *Le Sauvetage des enfants juifs pendant l'Occupation dans les maisons de l'OSE 1938–1945*, Paris, OSE, Somogy, 2008.

Hesse, Philippe-Jean and Le Crom Jean-Pierre (eds), *La Protection sociale sous le régime de Vichy*, Rennes, Presses Universitaires de Rennes, 2001.

Hilberg, Raul, *The Destruction of the European Jews*, New York, Holmes and Meier, 1985, 2 vols.

————, *Perpetrators Victims Bystanders. The Jewish Catastrophe, 1933–1945*, New York, Harper Collins, 1992.

Hobson Faure, Laura, "'Guide and Motivator' or 'Central Treasury'? The 'Joint' in France, 1942–1944," in Jacques Semelin, Claire Andrieu and Sarah Gensburger (eds), *Resisting Genocide. The Multiple Forms of Rescue*, translated by Emma Bentley and Cynthia Schoch, London, Hurst, 2011, pp. 293–312.

Israël, Liora, *Robes noires, années sombres. Avocats et magistrats en résistance pendant la Seconde Guerre mondiale*, Paris, Fayard, 2005.

Jackson, Julian, *France. The Dark Years, 1940–1944*, Oxford, Oxford University Press, 2001.

————, *La France sous l'Occupation, 1940–1944*, Paris, Flammarion, 2004.

Joly, Laurent, *Vichy et la solution finale. Histoire du Commissariat général aux questions juives. 1941–1944*, Paris, Grasset, 2006.

———— (ed.), *La Délation dans la France des années noires*, Paris, Perrin, 2012.

————, *Dénoncer les Juifs sous l'Occupation (1940–1944)*, Paris, CNRS Éditions, 2017.

————, *L'Etat contre les Juifs*, Paris, Grasset, 2018.

Joutard, Philippe and Cabanel Patrick, *Cévennes. Terre de refuge, 1940–1944*, Montpellier, Presse du Languedoc, 1987, reissued by Club Cévenol/ Nouvelles Presses du Languedoc, 2012.

Kaminker, Jean-Pierre, *La Persécution contrariée. Les Kaminker à Valréas, 1943–1944, entre antisémitisme d'État et bienveillance d'une population*, Limoges, Lambert-Lucas, 2007.

Kaspi, André, *Les Juifs pendant l'Occupation*, Paris, Le Seuil, 1991, reissued in "Points Histoire," 1997.

Kauffmann, Grégoire, *Edouard Drumont*, Paris, Perrin, 2008.

Keneally, Thomas, *Schindler's Ark*, London, Hodder and Stoughton Ltd., 1982.

Klarsfeld, Serge, *Le Mémorial de la déportation des Juifs de France*, Paris, B. and S. Klarsfeld, 1978.

————, *Le Calendrier de la persécution des Juifs en France, 1940–1944*, Paris, Les fils et filles des déportés juifs de France, 1993, reissued in 2001 as vol. 2 and 3 of the series *La Shoah en France*, Paris, Fayard.

————(ed.), *Les Enfants d'Izieu. Une tragédie juive*, Paris, Les fils et filles des déportés juifs de France, 2000.

————, *Vichy-Auschwitz. La "solution finale" de la question juive en France*, Paris, Fayard, 1983, reissued in 2001 as vol. 1 of the series *La Shoah en France*, Paris, Fayard.

Laborie, Pierre, *L'Opinion française sous Vichy*, Paris, Le Seuil, 1990.

————, *Le Chagrin et le Venin. La France sous l'Occupation, mémoire et idées reçues*, 2011, Gallimard, coll. "Folio," 2015.

Laffitte, Michel, *Un engrenage fatal. L'UGIF face aux réalités de la Shoah, 1941–1944*, Paris, Liana Levi, 2003.

Lagrou, Pieter, *The Legacy of Nazi Occupation. Patriotic Memory and National Recovery in Western Europe, 1945–1965*, Cambridge, Cambridge University Press, 2000.

———, *Mémoires patriotiques de l'occupation nazie*, Brussels, Complexe, 2003.

Laloum, Jean, "Des Juifs d'Afrique du Nord au Pletzl? Une présence méconnue et des épreuves oubliées (1920–1945)," *Archives juives* 2005/2, no. 382, pp. 47–83.

Lammers, Cor, "Introduction: Persecution in Perspective," *The Netherlands' Journal of Social Sciences*, Volume 34, No. 2, 1998, pp. 111–125.

Latour, Anny, *La Résistance juive en France*, Paris, Stock, 1970.

Lazare, Lucien, *La Résistance juive en France*, Paris, Stock, 1987.

Lee, Daniel, *Pétain's Jewish Children. French Jewish Youth and the Vichy Regime, 1940–1942*, Oxford, Oxford University Press, 2014.

Leleu, Jean-Luc; Passera, Françoise; Quellien, Jean and Daeffler Michel (eds), *La France pendant la Seconde Guerre mondiale. Atlas historique*, Paris, Fayard/Ministère de la Défense, 2010, p. 135.

Levendel, Isaac and Weisz, Bernard, *Hunting Down the Jews. Vichy, the Nazis and their Mafia Collaborators in Provence 1942–1944*, New York, Enigma Books, 2012.

Lévy, Claude and Tillard, Paul, *La grande rafle du Vel' d'Hiv', Ce jour-là, 16 juillet 1942*, Paris, Robert Laffont, 1967, reprint 1992.

Loinger, Georges, *Les Résistances juives pendant l'Occupation*, Paris, Albin Michel, 2010.

Lustiger, Arno, *Rettungswiderstand. Über die Judenretter in Europa während der NS-Zeit*, Göttingen, Wallstein, 2011.

Marc, Sandra, *Les Juifs de Lacaune sous Vichy (1942–1944). Assignation à résidence et persécution sous Vichy*, Paris, L'Harmattan, 2001.

Mariot, Nicolas and Zalc, Claire, *Face à la persécution. 991 Juifs dans la guerre*, Paris, Odile Jacob, 2010.

Marrus, Michael R. and Paxton, Robert O., "The Nazis and the Jews in Occupied Western Europe, 1940–1944," *The Journal of Modern History*, vol. 54, no. 4 (Dec. 1982), pp. 687–714.

——— and Paxton, Robert O., *Vichy France and the Jews*, New York, Basic Books, 1981, reissued by Stanford University Press, 1995.

——— and Paxton, Robert O., *Vichy et les Juifs*, Paris, Calman-Levy, 2015.

Matard-Bonucci, Marie-Anne, *L'Italie fasciste et la persécution des Juifs*, Paris, Perrin, 2007.

Mencherini, Robert (ed.), *Provence-Auschwitz. De l'internement des étrangers à la déportation des Juifs (1939–1944)*, Aix-en-Provence, Presses Universitaires de Provence, 2007.

Meyer, Ahlrich, *Täter im Verhör. Die "Endlösung der Judenfrage" in Frankreich 1940–1944*, Darmstadt, 2005.

Michel, Alain-René, *Les Éclaireurs israélites de France pendant la Seconde Guerre mondiale*, Paris, Éditions des EIF, 1984.

————, *Vichy et la Shoah: enquête sur le paradoxe français*, Tours, CLD Éditions, 2012.

Michman, Dan, ed., *Belgium and the Holocaust. Jews, Belgians, Germans*, Jerusalem, Yad Vashem, 1998.

————, ed., *Hiding, Sheltering, and Borrowing Identities. Avenues of Rescue during the Holocaust*, Yad Vashem, The International Institute for Holocaust Research, Jerusalem, 2017.

Moore, Bob, *Victims and Survivors. The Nazi Persecution of the Jews in Netherlands 1940–1945*, London, Hodder, 1997.

————, *Survivors. Jewish Self-Help and Rescue in Nazi-Occupied Western Europe*, Oxford, Oxford University Press, 2010, reissued 2016.

Neury, Laurent, *Entre les mailles du filet? Vivre et survivre sur le versant français de la frontière franco-genevoise de 1933 à 1947*, Genève, IHEID (relations internationales), 2008.

Noiriel Gérard, *Les Origines républicaines de Vichy*, Paris, Hachette, 1999.

Oliner, Samuel P. and Oliner, Pearl M., *The Altruistic Personality. Rescuers of Jews in Nazi Europe*, foreword by Rabbi Harold M. Schulweis, New York, The Free Press, 1988.

Organisation Juive de Combat, *Résistance, sauvetage. France, 1940–1945*, Paris, Autrement, 2002, reissued 2006.

Ostermann, Simon, "La clandestinité des Juifs dans les villes de province sous Vichy. L'exemple de Châteauroux (1940–1944)," in Aprile Sylvie (ed.), *Les Clandestinités urbaines en Occident de l'époque moderne à nos jours*, Rennes, Presses universitaires de Rennes, November 2008, pp. 255–275.

Paldiel, Mordecai, *Saving the Jews, Amazing Stories of Men and Women who Defied the "Final Solution,"* Rockville, MD, Schreiber Publishing, 2000.

Paxton, Robert, *Vichy France. Old Guard and New Order, 1940–1944*, New York, Knopf, 1972; reprint 2001.

Peschanski, Denis, *La France des camps. L'internement, 1938–1946*, Paris, Gallimard, 2002.

———— and Poznanski, Renée, *Drancy. Un camp en France*, Paris, Fayard, 2015.

Philipponnat, Olivier and Lienhardt, Patrick, *The Life of Irène Némirovsky*, translated by Euan Cameron, New York, Knopf, 2010.

Poliakov, Léon, *Harvest of Hate. The Nazi Program for the Destruction of the Jews of Europe*, London, Elek Books, 1956.

———— and Sabille, Jacques, *Jews under the Italian Occupation*, Paris, Éditions du Centre, 1955.

Poznanski, Renée, *Jews in France during World War II*, translated by Nathan Bracher, Hanover, NY, Brandeis University Press, 2001.

————, *Propagandes et persécutions. La Résistance et le "problème juif," 1940–1944*, Paris, Fayard, 2008.

SELECTED BIBLIOGRAPHY

Rajsfus, Maurice, *Des Juifs dans la collaboration. L'UGIF, 1941–1944*, Paris, EDI, 1980.

Rayski, Adam, *Le Choix des Juifs sous Vichy. Entre soumission et résistance*, Paris, La Découverte, 1992.

Reviriego, Bernard, *Les Juifs en Dordogne 1939–1944. De l'accueil à la persécution*, Périgueux, Archives départementales de la Dordogne, 2003.

Roberts, Sophie B., *Citizenship and Antisemitism in French Colonial Algeria, 1870–1962*, Cambridge and New York, Cambridge University Press, 2018.

Roseman, Mark, *Rescued from Memory. The "Bund," Resistance, and Rescue in Nazi Germany*, Oxford, Oxford University Press, 2017.

Rousso, Henry, *The Vichy Syndrome. History and Memory in France Since 1944*, translated by Arthur Goldhammer, foreword by Stanley Hoffmann, Cambridge, MA, Harvard University Press, 1994.

———, *Le Régime de Vichy*, Paris, PUF, 2007.

Saerens, Lieven, *Rachel, Jacob, Paul et les autres. Une histoire des Juifs à Bruxelles*, Wavre Belgium, Mardaga, 2014.

——— and Dirk Martin, *Anvers sous l'Occupation: 1940–1945*, Brussels, La Renaissance du livre, 2010.

Sartre, Jean-Paul, *Anti-Semite and Jew. An Exploration of the Etiology of Hate* [1946], translated by George J. Becker, New York, Schocken Books, 1995.

Schnapper, Dominique, *Juifs et Israélites*, Paris, Gallimard, 1980.

Seibel, Wolfgang, *Macht und Moral. Die Endlösung der Judenfrage in Frankreich, 1940–1944*, Konstanz University Press, 2010.

———, *Persecution and Rescue. The Politics of the "Final Solution" in France, 1940–1944*, translated by Ciaran Cronin, Ann Arbor, MI, University of Michigan Press, 2016.

Semelin, Jacques, *Unarmed Against Hitler. Civilian Resistance in Europe, 1939–1943*, translated by Suzan Husserl-Kapit, Westport, CT, Praeger, 1994.

———, *Purify and Destroy. Political uses of Massacre and Genocide*, New York, Columbia University Press and London, Hurst, 2007.

———, *Persécutions et entraides dans la France occupée*, Paris, Seuil-Les Arènes, 2013.

———, Andrieu, Claire, and Gensburger, Sarah (eds), *Resisting Genocide. The Multiple Forms of Rescue*, translated by Emma Bentley and Cynthia Schoch, London, Hurst, 2011.

Singer, Claude, *Vichy, l'université et les Juifs*, Paris, Les Belles Lettres, 1992.

Snyder, Timothy, *Black Earth. The Holocaust as History and Warning*, New York, Tim Duggan Books, 2015.

Soudière (de la), Martin, *Jours de guerre au village. Années noires, années vertes en Auvergne et Margeride, 1939–1950*, Polignac, Éditions du Roure, 2012.

Steinberg, Maxime, "Le paradoxe français dans la solution finale à l'Ouest," *Annales*, 1993, vol. 48, no. 3, pp. 583–594.

————, *La persécution des Juifs en Belgique (1940–1945)*, Brussels, Editions Complexe, 2004.

Suleiman, Susan Rubin, *The Némirovsky Question: The Life, Death, and Legacy of a Jewish Writer in Twentieth-Century France*, New Haven, CT, Yale University Press, 2017.

Tammes, Peter, "Le 'paradoxe néerlandais': nouvelles approches," in Claire Zalc, Tal Bruttmann, Ivan Ermakoff et al., *Pour une microhistoire de la Shoah*, Paris, Le Seuil, 2012.

Tammes, Peter, "Jewish Immigrants in the Netherlands during the Nazi Occupation," *Journal of Interdisciplinary History*, 04/2007, Volume XXXVII, no. 4, pp. 543–562.

————, "Survival of Jews during the Holocaust: The Importance of Different Types of Social Resources," *International Journal of Epidemiology*, 04/2007, Volume 36, No. 2, pp. 330–335.

————, "Residential Segregation of Jews in Amsterdam on the Eve of the Shoah," *Continuity and Change*, 08/2011, Volume 26, No. 2, pp. 243–270.

————, "'Hack, Pack, Sack': Occupational Structure, Status, and Mobility of Jews in Amsterdam 1851–1941," *Journal of Interdisciplinary History*, 05/2012, Volume 43, No. 1, pp. 1–26.

————, "Surviving the Holocaust: Socio-demographic Differences Among Amsterdam Jews," *European Journal of Population*, 01/2017.

Tec, Nechama, *When Light Pierced the Darkness. Christian Rescue of Jews in Nazi-Occupied Poland*, Oxford, Oxford University Press, 1986.

Vielcazat-Petitcol, Marie-Juliette, *Lot-et-Garonne, Terre d'exil terre d'asile. Les réfugiés juifs pendant la Seconde Guerre mondiale*, Editions d'Albret, 2006.

Wieviorka, Annette, *Déportation et génocide. Entre la mémoire et l'oubli*, Paris, Plon, 1992.

———— and Laffitte, Michel, *À l'intérieur du camp de Drancy*, Paris, Perrin, 2012.

Wieviorka, Olivier, *Histoire de la Résistance, 1940–1945*, Paris, Perrin, 2012.

Zalc, Claire, *Dénaturalisés. Les retraits de nationalité sous Vichy*, Paris, Le Seuil, 2016.

————, Bruttmann, Tal; Ermakoff, Ivan and Mariot, Nicolas (eds), *Pour une microhistoire de la Shoah*, Paris, Seuil, 2012.

Zeitoun, Sabine, *L'Œuvre de secours aux enfants, OSE, sous l'Occupation en France. Du légalisme à la Résistance, 1940–1944*, Paris, L'Harmattan, 1990.

Zuccotti, Susan, *The Holocaust, the French, and the Jews*, New York, Basic Books, 1993.

SOURCES AND DOCUMENTS

1. Archives of the Centre de documentation juive contemporaine (CDJC)

CDJC Registre des sœurs de Notre-Dame de Sion (non classé) CDJC
219–68
CDJC XXXVIII CDJC CX-4 CDJC CXV-100 CDJC CXVIII-16
CDJC CXVIII-104 CDJC CMIII, 1–55
CDJC CMIII, 1–57
CDJC UGIF 23–756

2. French National Archives (AN)

AN AGIII-460
AN AJ 40 548 dossier 6
AN AJ 38–243
AN AJ 38–281
AN AJ 38–3803
AN AJ 38–61
AN AJ 38–6 AN F7–14895 AN F21–5169
AN FI CIII 1 137
AN Z6–1387 scellé 41

3. Departmental Archives

Archives départementales du Cher, 976 W 104.
Archives départementales du Rhône, cabinet du préfet (non classé), rapport
du 23 novembre 1940.
Archives départementales de Seine-Saint-Denis, fonds David Diamant
335J1–191.
Archives départementales du Tarn, cont. 18. Archives départementales du
Tarn, 506W38.

SOURCES AND DOCUMENTS

4. Other archives

Archives of religious institutions:

Archives of the Central Consistory during World War II deposited at the Alliance israélite universelle, fonds Maurice Moch, AIU CC 17.

Archives historiques de l'évêché de Paris, fonds Suhard, 1D XIV-24. Archives historiques de la maison diocésaine de Paris, 3 B 614.

Archives de la police d'État de Genève, Justice et police Eb. A17.17.1.67. Yad Vashem Archives M31/264.

5. Testimonies and Documents of the Period

Journal de Louis Aron, directeur de la Maison israélite de refuge pour l'enfance: Neuilly-sur-Seine, 1939, Crocq (Creuse), 1939–1942, Chaumont (Creuse), 1942–1944, Paris, Les Fils et Filles de déportés juifs de France, 1998.

Berr, Hélène, *Journal*, translated by David Bellos, London, MacLehose Press, 2009.

Biélinky Jacques, *Un journaliste juif à Paris sous l'Occupation. Journal 1940–1942*, Paris, Editions du Cerf, 1992.

Bloch, Marc, *Strange Defeat. A Statement of Evidence Written in 1940*, New York, W. W. Norton & Co., 1968, reissued 1999.

Cabanel, Patrick, *Chère Mademoiselle*, Paris, Calmann-Lévy/Mémorial de la Shoah, 2010.

Dreyfus, Lucien, Journal, *20 décembre 1940–24 septembre 1943. Une époque terrible et terriblement intéressante*, introduced and annotated by Jean-Marc Dreyfus and Alexandra Garbarini, Editions Le Manuscrit, Collection Témoignages de la Shoah, Paris, 2018.

Feuchtwanger, Lion, *The Devil in France: My Encounter with Him in the Summer of 1940*, Los Angeles, USC Libraries, Figueroa Press, 2010.

Frenkel, Françoise, *No Place to Lay One's Head*, translated by Stephanie Smee, London, Pushkin Press, 2018.

Fry, Varian, *Assignment Rescue. An Autobiography*, New York, Scholastic (reprint), 1993 (first edition New York, Random House, 1945).

Garel, Georges, testimony before the Centre de documentation sur la persécution nazie, Nice, 1946 (CDJC, CC XVIII–104).

Grunberg, Albert, *Journal d'un coiffeur juif à Paris pendant l'Occupation*, Paris, Les Éditions de l'Atelier, 2001.

Hamon, Léo, "Étude sur la situation des Juifs en zone occupée," *Cahiers de l'IHTP*, no. 22, 1992.

Kaplan, Jacob, "French Jewry under the Occupation," in *The American Jewish Year Book 5706*, 1945–1946, Philadelphia (PA), *The Jewish Publication Society of America*, vol. 47, 1945–1946.

Lambert, Raymond-Raoul, *Diary of a Witness: 1940–1943*, edited with an introduction by Roger I. Cohen, Chicago, Ivan R. Dee, 2007.

Laval, Pierre, *Laval parle... Notes et mémoires rédigés à Fresnes d'août à octobre 1945*, preface by his daughter, Mme Josée Laval de Chambrun, Paris, À l'enseigne du Cheval ailé, 1948.

Limagne, Pierre, *Éphémérides de quatre années tragiques, 1940–1944*, vol. 2, Lavilledieu, Éditions de Candide, 1987.

Mauriac, François, *Cahier noir*, Paris, Éditions de Minuit, 1943, réédition Desclée de Brouwer, 1994.

Mesnil-Amar, Jacqueline, *Maman, What Are We Called Now?* Translated by Francine Yorke, London, Persephone Books, 2015.

Werth, Léon, *33 jours*, Paris, Viviane Hamy, 1992, reissued Paris, Magnard, 2002.

————, *Déposition*, Paris, Viviane Hamy, 2000, reissued Paris, Le Seuil, 2007.

6. *Memoirs and Postwar Testimonies*

Writings

CDJC, collection 967—Latour collection.

CDJC, hidden children collection, testimony of Rachel Jeanmaire-Wolf. Files in support of Righteous among the Nations medal deposited at Yad Vashem.

Anciens de la Résistance juive en France, *Organisation juive de combat: Résistance-sauvetage, France 1940–1945*, Paris, Autrement, 2002.

Abramovitsch, Samuel, testimony deposited at the Commission d'histoire de la Deuxième Guerre mondiale, session of 1957, A.D. Valence.

Badinter, Robert, "Mort d'un israélite français. Hommage à maître Pierre Masse," *Le Débat*, 2010/1, no. 158.

Becker, Jean-Jacques, *Un soir de l'été 1942. Souvenirs d'un historien*, Paris, Larousse, 2009.

Belbéoch, Roger, *Je n'ai fait que mon devoir. 1940–1944, un Juste dans les rangs de la police*, Paris, Robert Laffont, 2007.

Berri, Claude, *Le Vieil Homme et l'enfant*, Paris, Jérôme Martineau, 1967.

Bily, Henry, *Destin à part*, Paris, L'Harmattan, 1995.

Cahen, Pierre, *Le Médecin malgré eux*, Paris, Librairie Arnette, 1972.

Clément, Jean-Louis, *Monseigneur Saliège, Archevêque de Toulouse, 1929–1956*, Paris, Beauchesne, 1994.

Cohn, Marthe (with Wendy Holden), *Behind Enemy Lines. The True Story of a French Jewish Spy in Nazi Germany*, Harmony, 2002.

Cyrulnik, Boris, *Sauve-toi, la vie t'appelle*, Paris, Odile Jacob, 2012.

Debré, Robert, *L'Honneur de vivre*, Paris, Stock, 1974.

Denis, Jean-Pierre, *Nos enfants de la guerre*, Paris, Le Seuil, 2002.

Diamant David, *Le Billet vert*, Paris, Éditions Renouveau, 1977.

Dreyfus, Gérard, testimony edited by his son Jean-Marc, 2008, and given to the author.

SOURCES AND DOCUMENTS

Erlanger, Philippe, *La France sans étoile*, Paris, Plon, 1977.

Friedländer, Saul, *When Memory Comes*, translated by Helen R. Lane, New York, Farrar, Straus and Giroux, LLC, 1979.

Gourfinkel, Nina, *Aux prises avec mon temps*, Paris, Le Seuil, 1953.

Grosser, Alfred, *Une vie de Français. Mémoires*, Paris, Flammarion, 1997.

Gruat, Cédric and Leblanc, Cécile, *Amis des Juifs. Les résistants aux étoiles*, Paris, Éditions Tirésias, 2005.

Hoffmann, Stanley, "To Be or Not To Be French," in *Ideas and Ideals: Essays on Politics in Honor of Stanley Hoffmann*, ed. Linda B. Miller and M. J. Smith Boulder, CO, Westview Press, 1993 and "Le chagrin et la pitié," *Decline or Renewal? France since the 1930s*, New York, Viking Press, 1974.

——, "Le chagrin et la pitié", in *Essai sur la France. Déclin ou renouveau?*, Paris, Le Seuil, 1974.

Jacoubovitch, Yehuda (Jules), *Rue Amelot*, first published in Yiddish in 1948, translated by Gabrielle Jacoubovitch-Bouhana in 1992, available at http://lamaisondesevres.org/ame/ame1.html

Joffo, Joseph, *A Bag of Marbles*, translated by Martin Sokolinsky, Chicago, University of Chicago Press, 2001.

Kaminsky, Sarah, *Adolfo Kaminsky. A Forger's Life*, translated by Mike Mitchell, Los Angeles, DoppelHouse Press, 2016.

Kanner, Mia Amalia, (with Eve Rosenzweig Kugler), *Shattered Crystals*, Lakewood, NJ, Cis Communications, 1997.

Klein, Claude, "Un témoignage des années d'Occupation: de Grenoble à la Suisse," *Esprit*, November 2008, no. 349.

Klein-Lieber, Liliane, "Témoignage sur les opérations de sauvetage," *Annales ESC*, May–June 1993, no. 3.

Kofman, Sarah, *Rue Ordener, rue Labat*, Paris, Galilée, 1994.

Krajcer-Janin, Annette and Conan Éric, *Le Dernier Été des enfants à l'Étoile. 1942, une rescapée se souvient*, Oskar Éditions, 2010.

Kriegel, Annie, *Ce que j'ai cru comprendre*, Paris, Robert Laffont, 1991.

Lanzmann, Claude, *The Patagonian Hare. A Memoir*, translated by Frank Wynne, New York, Farrar, Strauss and Giroux, 2012.

Lapidus, Serge, *Étoile jaune dans la France des années noires. Onze récits parallèles de jeunes rescapés*, Paris, L'Harmattan, 2000.

Lazare, Lucien, *Le Livre des Justes. Histoire du sauvetage des Juifs par des non-Juifs en France, 1940–1944*, Paris, Hachette, 1996.

Lowrie, Donald, *The Hunted Children*, New York, W. W. Norton & Co., 1963.

Markscheid, Léa, *Le Passé au présent*, Nages, Centre de recherches du patrimoine de Rieumontagné, 2009, reissued with the title *Le Passé au présent. Des Juifs d'Europe dans la tourmente du XXe siècle*, Paris, L'Harmattan, 2012.

Meyers, Odette, *Doors to Madame Marie*, Seattle and London, McLellan, 1997.

Minc, Joseph, *L'Extraordinaire Histoire de ma vie ordinaire*, Paris, Le Seuil, 2006.

Morin, Edgar, *Vidal and His Family. From Salonica to Paris: The Story of a Sephardic*

Family in the Twentieth Century, translated by Deborah Cowell, Eastbourne, Sussex Academic Press, 2009.

Palacz, Ariela, *I Love You My Child, I'm Abandoning You*, Tel Aviv, Contento De Semrik, 2013.

Poliakov, Léon, *L'Auberge des musiciens*, Paris, Mazarine, 1981.

Raymes, Frederick and Mayer, Menachem, *Are the Trees in Bloom Over There?* Jerusalem, Yad Vashem, 2002.

Rayski, Adam, *Nos illusions perdues*, Paris, Balland, 1985.

Rubin, Gerber Simone, "Témoignage sur le port de l'étoile juive à Paris," *Diasporas*, no. 16, 2011.

Samuel, Vivette, *Rescuing the Children. A Holocaust Memoir*, translated by Charles B. Paul, Madison, WI, The University of Wisconsin Press, 2002.

Samuel, Jean and Dreyfus, Jean-Marc, *Il m'appelait Pikolo. Un compagnon de Primo Levi raconte*, Paris, Robert Laffont, 2007.

Scali, Arlette, *Les Justes de Graulhet*, Paris, Éditions Scali, 2007.

Schreiber, Boris, *Un silence d'environ une demi-heure*, Paris, Le cherche midi, 1996.

Schwartz, Laurent, *Un mathématicien aux prises avec le siècle*, Paris, Odile Jacob, 2007.

Siekierski, Denise, *MiDor LeDor. De génération en génération*, Paris, L'Harmattan, 2004.

Soubeyran, Marguerite, testimony dated 1974, published par Sandrine Suchon-Fouquet, *Résistance et Liberté. Dieulefit, 1940–1944*, Die, A Die, 1994, reissued by Grenoble, Presses Universitaires de Grenoble, 2010.

Steinberg, Paul, *Chroniques d'ailleurs*, Paris, Ramsay, 1996.

Stora, Benjamin, *Les Trois Exils. Juifs d'Algérie*, Paris, Stock, 2006.

Stupp, François, *Réfugié au pays des Justes. Araules, 1942–1944*, Polignac, Éditions du Roure, 1997.

Szwarc, Henri, "Souvenirs: l'étoile jaune," *Annales* ESCI, 1993, volume 48, no. 3.

Traube, Anna, *Évadée du Vél' d'Hiv*, Paris, Éditions Le Manuscrit, 2005.

Trauner, Alexandre, *Décors de cinéma* (interviews with Jean-Pierre Berthomé), Flammarion, Paris, 1988.

Vallat, Xavier, *Le Nez de Cléopâtre. Souvenirs d'un homme de droite 1919–1944*, preface by Charles Maurras, Paris, Éditions Les Quatre fils Aymon, 1957.

Vidal-Naquet, Pierre, *Mémoires 1. La Brisure et l'attente 1930–1955*, Paris, Le Seuil / La Découverte, 1995.

Veil, Simone, "Réflexions d'un témoin," *Annales ESC*, no. 3, May–June 1993.

———, *A Life*, trans. T. Black, London, Haus Publishing, 2009.

Warszawski, Oser, *On ne peut pas se plaindre*, Paris, Liana Levi, 1997.

Weill, Joseph, *Le Combat d'un juste. Essai autobiographique*, Le Coudray-Macouard, Cheminements, 2002.

SOURCES AND DOCUMENTS

Audiovisual testimonies

Collection of interviews in the "Mémoire de la Shoah" series, FMS/INA, in particular:

Badinter, Robert, interviewed by Jean-Baptiste Péretié, 4 January 2006.

Cohen, Gabby, née Wolff, interviewed by Catherine Bernstein, 21 February 2006.

Cyrulnik, Boris, interviewed by Catherine Bernstein, 25 April 2006.

Oral history interview by Rachel Jeanmaire-Wolff née Zylberberg, given on 17 December 1997 to Betty Saville, (Hidden Children Archives, no. 101), filed with the CDJC.

Klarsfeld, Serge, interviewed by Jean-Baptiste Péretié, 30 March 2006.

Lustiger, Jean-Marie, interviewed by Jean-Baptiste Péretié, 24 January 2006.

The Fortunoff Video Archive for Holocaust Testimonies, Yale University Library.

Interviews conducted by the author for the present book

Benayoun, Simon and Guy, interview, 4 November 2011.

Feldman, Jacqueline, interview, 4 November 2009.

Hoffmann, Stanley, interview, 28 January 2009.

Klarsfeld, Serge, interview, 17 May 2009.

Klein-Lieber, Liliane, interview, 25 February 2009.

Krajcer-Janin, Annette, interview, 12 March 2010.

Lazare, Janine, née Hemmendinger, interview, 23 October 2010.

Lazare, Lucien, interview, 20 July 2010.

Lindon, Denis, interview, 24 February 2010.

Lyon-Caen, Pierre, interview, 8 July 2010.

Minc, Joseph, interview, 23 April 2010.

Nora, Pierre, interview, 23 June 2010.

Weill, Denise, née Lefschetz, interview, 9 April 2009.

Wolff, Francine, née Weiller, interview, 17 June 2010.

Other witness accounts

Abadi, Moussa, talk given at the colloquium on hidden children, 21 May 1995.

Bloch-Hanau, Édith, account recorded by her daughter Évelyne Bloch-Dano in 1991–1992 and provided to the author.

Wormser, Pierre, interviewed by Daniel Fuks, 27 April 2010.

INDEX

INDEX

INDEX

INDEX

INDEX

INDEX